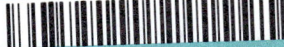

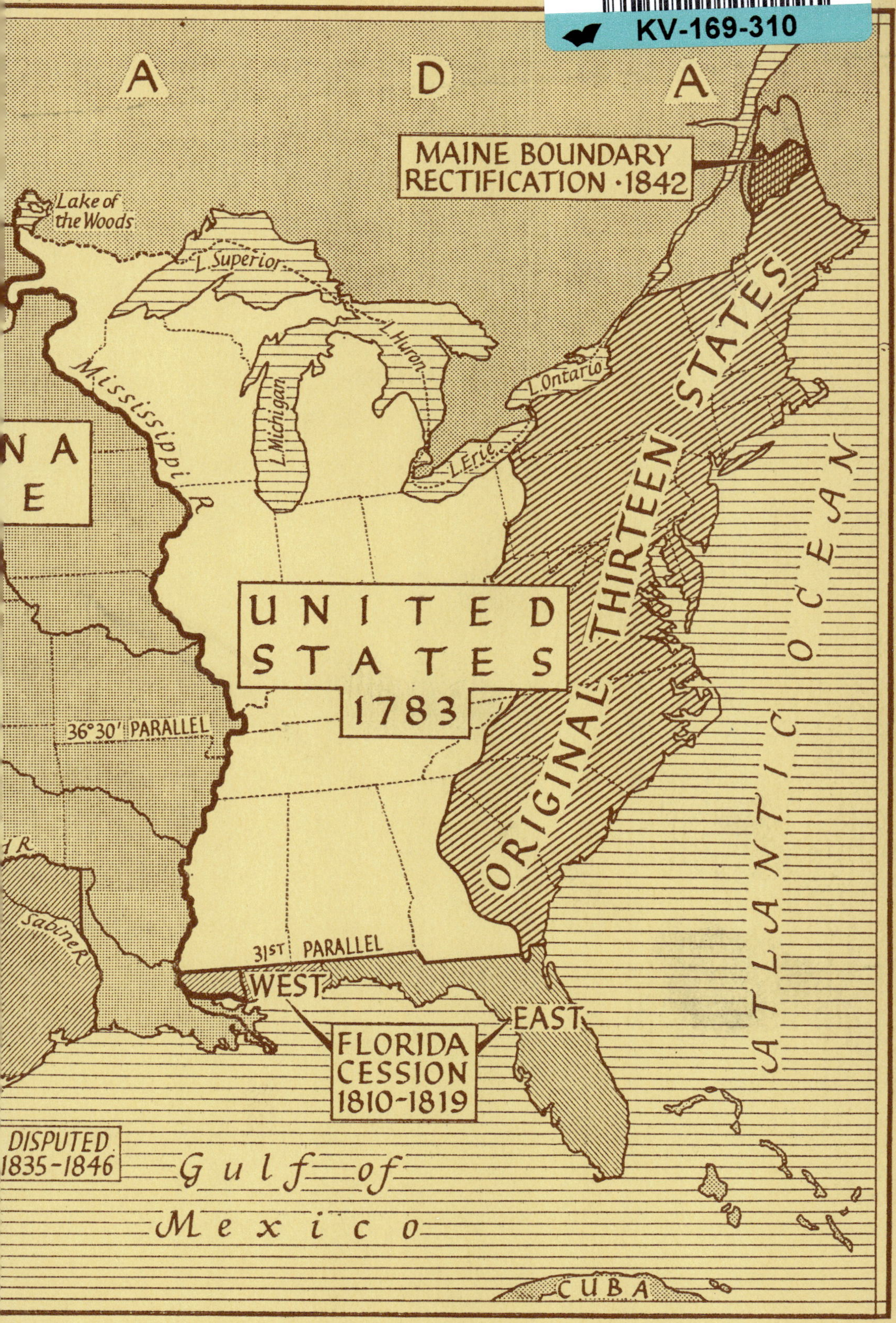
A D A
MAINE BOUNDARY
RECTIFICATION ·1842
Lake of the Woods
L. Superior
L. Huron
L. Michigan
L. Ontario
L. Erie
Mississippi R
N A
E
UNITED
STATES
1783
ORIGINAL THIRTEEN STATES
ATLANTIC OCEAN
36°30′ PARALLEL
Sabine R
31ST PARALLEL
WEST
EAST
FLORIDA
CESSION
1810-1819
DISPUTED
1835-1846
Gulf of
Mexico
CUBA

THE AMERICAN WEST

The American West

JOHN A. HAWGOOD
Professor of American History
University of Birmingham

FRONTIER LIBRARY
EYRE AND SPOTTISWOODE · LONDON

TO

RALPH H. GABRIEL

who also said

"Go West, Young Man"

First published in Great Britain 1967

Simultaneously published in U.S.A. as
'America's Western Frontiers'
Printed in Great Britain by
Richard Clay (The Chaucer Press), Ltd.,
Bungay, Suffolk

Contents

Plates

ACKNOWLEDGEMENTS

Special acknowledgements and thanks are due to the Northern Natural Gas Company Collection, Joslyn Art Museum, Omaha, Nebraska for pictures listed above (and two drawings on pages 102 and 394) by Karl Bodmer and Alfred Jacob Miller; to Alfred A. Knopf Inc. for the photographs by F. Jay Haynes from *Following the Frontier with F. Jay Haynes* by Freeman Tilder; to the Manuscripts Library, University of Oklahoma for plates 25a, 27–9, 30a; and to the Whitney Gallery of Western Art, Cody, for plate 23b, the Finger-bone necklace.

Drawings

NOTE

Special acknowledgements and thanks are due to The Henry E. Huntington Library and Art Gallery, for 'River Mining', and 'Chestnut Street, Leadville'; to *Harper's Magazine*, Centennial Issue, October 1950, for 'Virginia City, Nevada', 'Indian Attack on the Overland Express', 'America on the Move', 'Visiting a Colorado Sheep Ranch', and 'Cowboy Riding the Fence Line'; to the Trustees of the British Museum, for 'Fargo, Dakota'; and to The Historical Society of Montana, for Cowboy's Best Friend', 'Centerfire Man on a Bronc', and 'Steer Rider', from the catalogue of *The Works of Charles Marion Russell, 1864–1926*, in the Permanent Collection.

Maps

Drawn by W. H. Bromage

Preface

The edition of this work to be published in the United Kingdom has been planned from the first as a companion and complement to the *Frontier Library* of Messrs Eyre & Spottiswoode, for which its author acts as Editorial Advisor. It was felt that British readers would find a comprehensive, systematic, and detailed History of the American West – and particularly of the trans-Mississippi West – to be of interest and value to them, especially if they possessed or had read other volumes in the *Frontier Library* or other books on the West dealing with special aspects only – such as the Mormons, or the Indian Wars, or the fur trade – of this very large theme.

No similar work has previously been published, it is believed, designed for the adult British public, although the popularity of the American West as a theme is exhibited daily in moving-picture theatres and on the television screen as well as in books, magazines, and newspapers.

While the treatment aims to be comprehensive it does not aim or claim to be exhaustive, and if the reader's favourite hero, or villain, or expedition, or battle, is not dealt with as fully as he would desire, he will usually find references in footnotes or in the Bibliographical Note to places where he can find out more about any particular aspect or personality in Western History than has been considered worthy of mention in the text.

An attempt has been made to keep the history of the West in proper perspective. Bad Men and Bad Women tended to be the scum on the surface and the dregs at the bottom of the American West, and they are treated as such. Certain 'frontier types' who have perhaps received exaggerated or distorted notice elsewhere are here deliberately cut down to proper size; others who, in the opinion of this author, have received too little attention have been given what he considers their due. This is an individual choice with which all his readers will not agree, but it is really a fruitless exercise to set up Wyatt Earp against Old Bill Williams, Kit Carson against James Glidden, Sitting Bull against Collis P. Huntington, or Davy Crockett against Frederick Jackson Turner. Their contributions were all important – and all different. Some (like Crockett and General Custer) galloped across the Western stage in a flash and were gone like Davy's own greased lightning; others (like Jim Bridger and Ezra Meeker) grew up with the West and grew old with it as well. Who can really judge whether the man who 'cleaned up' an unruly cow town or mining camp, or the man (or, more probably, woman) who caused its first school to be opened, contributed more to the history of the West? The anonymous Chinese cook or Negro roustabout was often as important as the more spectacular character who roped steers, broke mustangs, and 'painted the town red'. The most important person in any new frontier community tended (if only for a short time) to be the sign-writer – or the undertaker – rather than the Marshal or the Saloon Keeper, the Minister, or the Madam. Without the one you often wouldn't know where to look for the others.

The pageant of the West was a rich mosaic made up of many parts, not all of them essential to its well-being and progress, but all of them interesting and some of them absorbingly so. Not all frontier types were glamorous – even the cowboy had his 'off' moments, riding the fences in the depths of winter or choking with dust and flies on a long cattle drive. That 'dirty little coward who shot Mr Howard'[1] possibly contributed more to the well-being and peace of mind of the trans-Mississippi West than did many a Judge, Governor, Congressman, Marshal, Sheriff, or Deputy. Judge Roy Bean took the law into his own hands 'West of the Pecos', and so did Billy the Kid. So also did the Cattle Kings, the Railroad Tycoons, the Oil Magnates, the Lumber Barons, and the Union Bosses. Let he who is without sin among those who made the West cast the first stone!

The writer of this book is indebted to everybody else who ever wrote, or thought, or talked about the West, and in many cases his debt is an unconscious one. But he is very conscious of the help and inspiration given him by such distinguished contemporary historians of the West whom he has the privilege to number among his friends and mentors as Ray Billington, Oscar Winther, Tom Clark, and Ralph Gabriel. He has also sat at the feet of Frederick Logan Paxson, Joseph Schafer, Frank Dobie, Pablo Martinez del Rio, Walter Prescott Webb, and Robert Glass Cleland, now, alas, no longer around to receive his thanks. Those with whom he has explored the West and attempted to recapture its true atmosphere include Sam and Betty Arnold, John Bloom, Olwen Brogan, Jack Carroll, Merrill Burlingame, Lee Harlan, Robin Humphreys, Al Larson, Edgeley Todd, and Robert Utley. Many of his other excursions into and across the West have been as lone as those of Old Bill Williams, but in 1956 he took his son John, in 1963 his daughter Anne, and in 1965 his son David with him, and hopes that he has made

[1] Robert Ford, who assassinated Jesse James, as described in a popular ballad.

them Western *aficionados*, too – or at least moderately tolerant of his enthusiasms.

Librarians and Curators of manuscript collections in every part of the United States and also in Canada and Mexico have given the author advice and assistance. He cannot list them all, though he wishes to thank them collectively. He owes a very special and long-standing debt of gratitude to Leslie Bliss, Haidée Noya, Edwin Carpenter, and their colleagues at the Huntington Library, George P. Hammond and his whole staff at the Bancroft Library, Agnes Wright Spring at the Colorado Historical Society in Denver, and Margaret Haford and her colleagues at the American Library in London.

The complete manuscript of this book was read through by Brian Hutton of Birmingham, greatly to its benefit, though the author remains fully responsible for any legal, technical, stylistic, or other errors which it may still contain. John Bright-Holmes has passed his publisher's and editor's tooth-comb through the typescript several times, and any remaining blemishes have been retained by a stubborn author (as are all authors to all publishers) over his dead body. Valerie Hawgood has typed the manuscript – a task which must have been almost as hard in places as Winning the West – correcting spelling and other mistakes as she went along, with skill, patience, and celerity.

The illustrations were assembled by the author and publisher from a wide field and a special tour of Western art galleries and museums was made by the author in the autumn of 1965 to complete the selection from which those printed in the book were taken. The use of these is acknowledged in the Lists of Illustrations, but the author and publisher also wish to thank the officials of the Joslyn Art Museum in Omaha, Nebraska, the Gilcrease Institute in Tulsa, Oklahoma, the Whitney Art Gallery in Cody, Wyoming, the South West Museum, Los Angeles and the Smithsonian Institution in Washington, D.C., for having given them special facilities.

Last, and by no means least, the author's students in Universities and Colleges both in Britain and in America have had portions of this book inflicted upon them in lectures and seminars from time to time over the last two or three years. These they may still recognize in the printed version, though many changes have been made on the basis of how students have reacted in class, asked questions, written essays, and answered examination papers. He thanks them one and all for having been such cheerful and friendly guinea pigs.

June, 1966 JOHN A. HAWGOOD

THE AMERICAN WEST

THE UNITED STATES OF AMERICA
Present-day Political Boundaries
1 VERMONT 2 NEW HAMPSHIRE 3 MASSACHUSETTS
4 CONNECTICUT 5 RHODE ISLAND 6 NEW JERSEY
7 DELAWARE 8 MARYLAND
CANADA
MEXICO
PACIFIC OCEAN
ATLANTIC OCEAN
Gulf of Mexico
WASHINGTON
OREGON
CALIFORNIA
NEVADA
IDAHO
MONTANA
WYOMING
UTAH
ARIZONA
COLORADO
NEW MEXICO
NORTH DAKOTA
SOUTH DAKOTA
NEBRASKA
KANSAS
OKLAHOMA
TEXAS
MINNESOTA
IOWA
MISSOURI
ARKANSAS
LOUISIANA
WISCONSIN
MICHIGAN
ILLINOIS
INDIANA
OHIO
KENTUCKY
TENNESSEE
MISSISSIPPI
ALABAMA
GEORGIA
FLORIDA
SOUTH CAROLINA
NORTH CAROLINA
VIRGINIA
WEST VIRGINIA
PENNSYLVANIA
NEW YORK
MAINE
WASHINGTON D.C.
ROCKY MOUNTAINS
Appalachian Mts
Cascade Range
Sierra Nevada
Seattle
Portland
San Francisco
Reno
Los Angeles
Gt. Salt Lake
Death Valley
Grand Canyon
Denver
Santa Fé
Dallas
Houston
New Orleans
St Louis
Chicago
Detroit
Philadelphia
New York
Boston
Charleston
Miami
Lake Superior
Lake Michigan
L. Huron
L. Erie
L. Ontario
Milk R
Missouri R
Yellowstone R
Columbia R
Salmon R
Snake R
Humboldt R
Colorado R
Gila R
Niobrara R
Platte R
Kansas R
Arkansas R
Cimarron R
Canadian R
Red R
Trinity R
Brazos R
Colorado R
Pecos R
Rio Grande
Sabine R
Mississippi R
Wabash R
Ohio R
Cumberland R
Tennessee R
Savannah R
Miles 0 500
W. Bromage

Introduction

What is this American West which the cinema and television have brought so close up to us that perhaps we cannot see it in a proper perspective? We have had a broad view of 'How the West was Won', and know only too well the shape of a flatboat, a stage coach, and a covered waggon. For us Destry has ridden again; the guns have gone off at High Noon and in the O.K. Corral; the Sioux, the Comanche, and the Apache have come yelling over the skyline, and the buffalo have thundered over the Great Plains, pursued to destruction by the Iron Horse. It is a stimulating – and a confusing – picture.

The 'Western' is as popular today in Japan and the Philippines as in London, Paris, and New York. People even read and view 'Westerns' in places like Laramie (Wyoming), Helena (Montana), and Tombstone (Arizona) with relics of the old West all around them. Californians take what they call 'a Western holiday', meaning that they spend two weeks on an air-conditioned dude-ranch in Nevada, riding nicely broken-in 'mustangs', and being held up at all hours by 'One-Armed Bandits'.

If the American West has such a powerful and compelling magnetic field, even today, when much of the old West is gone, it must be worthy of careful and systematic study. The movies and the television serials, and even some of the 'documentaries', provide much atmosphere but little enlightenment. Why were stage coaches still so important in the American West as late as the 1870s and 1880s, half a century after they had ceased to run in western Europe or in the American East? Why should a cowboy be any more glamorous than an ostler? How did a 'Mountain Man' differ from a 'Hill Billy'? Was a squaw-man necessarily a reprehensible character, and were half-breeds always mean and slinky? What did the frontier farmer fear most: Indians, Cattlemen – or Grasshoppers? Why were Collis Huntington, Leland Stanford, Charles Crocker, John Mackay, and Benjamin Holladay so much more important in the making of Western America than Wild Bill Hickok, George Armstrong Custer, Billy the Kid, Jesse James, the Earp Brothers, and even Buffalo Bill? Why does every serious history of the American West give more space to Frederick Jackson Turner (who was *he*, anyway?) than to Temple Houston, Davy Crockett, Pat Garratt, or

Calamity Jane? Who on earth was Jedediah Smith? Narcissa Prentiss Whitman? Josiah Gregg? John Augustus Sutter? Adolph Sutro? Helen Hunt Jackson?

To be described the American West must first be defined. In its broadest sense it is (or was) every part of the great North American continent lying west of Roanoke Island, Plymouth Rock, and St Augustine, Florida. When the Spaniard Ponce de León landed on the Florida coast in search of the Fountain of Perpetual Youth in 1513 he was exploring 'The American West' as it then was; so was Cortez when he landed at Vera Cruz in 1519 and pushed inland over the mountains of Mexico to capture the Aztec capital; so were Raleigh's colonists in Virginia, the Pilgrim Fathers in New England, the French on the St Lawrence River, the Swedes on the Delaware, and the Dutch on the Hudson.

The colonial experiences of Spain and Portugal, England and France, Holland and Sweden in the Americas were high adventures and necessary preliminaries to the eventual settlement of the whole American West in the nineteenth century, but it is on this last that it is intended to concentrate here. The earlier explorers and colonists played their essential part, and in the opening chapters this is discussed as a prologue to the nineteenth-century opening up of the West; but the curtain really rises in 1803 when Thomas Jefferson more than doubled the size of the United States – which only extended to the Mississippi's eastern bank before – by the Louisiana Purchase, and sent out Captains Meriwether Lewis and William Clark to find a practicable overland route to the Pacific. In the footsteps of Lewis and Clark came fur traders and trappers, prospectors for precious metals, missionaries, ranchers, sheepmen, farmers, bankers, saloon keepers, 'road agents' (a polite Western name for highwaymen), and innumerable others, ending with the town-planners, real-estate developers, and exploiters of natural resources for industry, tourism, and 'show business'. The historian has to follow up all of these, plot their courses, and assess their significance. The history of the American West appeared 'all confusion'[1] until, in 1893, a young scholar, Frederick Jackson Turner, provided a key to its systematic study and to its understanding. His seminal essay, *The Significance of the Frontier in American History*, made it possible to look at the opening up of America's Western frontier regions

[1] Compare Theodore Roosevelt's untidy and melodramatic *Winning of the West* (1890–2) with Turner's own *Rise of the New West* (1906).

as a *process* rather than as a series of disconnected episodes. He provided a key to the understanding of the West. He stimulated the writing of the first scholarly *History of the American Frontier* by F. L. Paxson (1924), and such classics as Walter Prescott Webb's *The Great Plains* (1931) and *The Great Frontier* (1952). He even inspired the politicians. Both Theodore Roosevelt and Franklin Delano Roosevelt admired his work and used his ideas, and John Fitzgerald Kennedy made 'The New Frontier' the theme and catch-phrase of his presidential campaign in 1960.

It is perhaps necessary to explain to British and European readers, to whom the word 'frontier' can conjure up pictures of vexatious waiting at customs barriers and national boundaries, that Americans do not use the word in that sense with regard to their own West. They speak of the 'border' with Canada or with Mexico, but to them 'the frontier' is the outermost edge of civilization, the last settled communities before the Western wilderness is reached, or perhaps even the beginning of the wilderness itself. It is an area technically defined as possessing fewer than six but at least two persons per square mile. Such a definition of a frontier would have satisfied that great frontiersman Daniel Boone (1734–1820), who thought it was time to move on as soon as you could hear a neighbour's dog bark. It was this moving line between settled and unoccupied land that was the American 'Frontier' of the nineteenth century and with which this book is principally concerned. Lewis and Clark started off from St Louis on the Mississippi in 1803 and went up the Missouri and down the Columbia. The American West described and chronicled in this book, therefore, is the great area west of the Mississippi all the way to the Pacific Ocean. In 1803 it was virtually empty; by 1903 it contained nearly one-third of the population of the United States, which in a century had risen from under five millions to over one hundred millions.

The history of the American West has a number of unique features; others it shares with formerly unexplored and undeveloped parts of the world in which similar conditions existed – in South America, Australia, Siberia, and Africa in modern times; in eastern and south-eastern Europe in medieval times; in the Mediterranean basin and in northern and north-western Europe in ancient times. The great Chinese Empire, growing eventually to eighteen provinces and spilling over even from these into areas such as Manchuria and Mongolia, Turkestan and Tibet, must have seen, during its long period of expansion, the creation of many sets of 'frontier conditions' that resembled phases in the history of the

American West.[1] Some of these were described, with wide-eyed wonder, by the European traveller Marco Polo in the thirteenth century A.D.[2] Pending the twentieth-century filling-in of the vast undeveloped plains and rain-forests of Brazil the closest parallels to the conditions of the American West may be said to have existed in Australia and Siberia: vast empty lands, large areas of them within the temperate zones, uninhabited but by a scattering of nomads apart from a relatively few sedentary agricultural settlements in the richer river valleys, or colonies of fishermen around the coasts; great mineral wealth only belatedly discovered and that mostly in the remoter and more inaccessible regions; poor or non-existent communications; remoteness from the existing centres of world population. Both the Americas and Australia required long sea voyages before they could be reached; Siberia, though approachable by land (but over high mountain chains from Europe and southern Asia) was almost equally inaccessible. Neither the Americas nor Siberia could expect to be heavily populated until railroads had traversed them, and this did not come until towards the end of the nineteenth century. In the year 1800 the United States had only five million inhabitants and Siberia under one million.[3] Today the United States has nearly 200 million; Siberia over forty million; Brazil over eighty million; but Australia (saddled with a virtually uninhabitable central desert) eleven million.

Africa and Central America tend to fall outside these patterns of frontier development. In both areas large indigenous populations existed, in places, before the white man came, and in a few regions a high (though very different) cultural standard had been reached. The Ashanti kings did not consider themselves inferior to the Portuguese when they first came into contact, nor did the Aztecs and the Incas to the Spaniards. An indigenous population far larger than the number of white settlers in an area presents problems which are quite different from those existing in most parts of North America or in Australia, and if this imbalance persists (as it has done in most of Africa, and in all parts of it south of the equator) the problems become more dissimilar

[1] *The Seven Samurai*, a romance of medieval Japan, was recognized in its moving picture version as a 'Western' in the oriental idiom and remade as an American 'Western', *The Magnificent Seven.*

[2] The western world still awaits a full exposition of Chinese history in terms of this great expansion, relatively over-much attention having been paid to the process of contraction and decay of the last century and a half.

[3] Of these, 363,362 were 'Siberian Natives' and 575,800 were 'Russians and Foreigners' according to A. Schulz, *Siberien: eine Landeskunde* (Breslau, 1923), p. 167.

as time goes on. In Siberia the numbers of immigrants from European Russia have grown since the late nineteenth century, greatly to outnumber the indigenous population,[1] except in a few areas; in South Africa this has not been the case, and the 'Great Trek' of the Boers, now over a century ago, remains their one striking parallel with the frontier experiences of North and South America and of Australia where the settlers very early came to outnumber the indigenes.[2]

In North America the red man tended to disappear as the white man increased and multiplied. According to the census of 1850, the first taken by the United States government in the American South-west, the Indian population of New Mexico – which then also included Arizona – numbered 92,130 or nearly one quarter of the 388,229 Indians enumerated in the whole of the United States. According to H. R. Schoolcraft the rest (apart from 32,231 in California and 22,733 in the Oregon Territory) were very widely scattered and many of them were still nomadic. The sedentary Indians of the South-west were, numerically as well as culturally, by far the most important (though by no means the most troublesome) tribes encountered by the Spaniards in the sixteenth and seventeenth centuries, by the British and French in the seventeenth and eighteenth, and by the Americans in the nineteenth century, in their exploration and settlement of the West. Such nomadic tribes as the Apache, the Comanche, and the Sioux, though more primitive and far less numerous, were much more troublesome, and continued to be so until well into the latter half of the nineteenth century. Before that the 'Woodland Indians' of the eastern parts of North America, many of them already settled agriculturalists, had to be subdued or destroyed by the early European colonists in Virginia, in the middle Atlantic region, in New England, and in the St Lawrence basin and the Great Lakes area. But the story of the American West really *begins* on the other side of the continent – in Alaska, in the Columbia River basin, in California, and in Mexico.

[1] *See* D. Treadgold, *The Great Siberian Migration* (Princeton, 1957, *passim*). By the year 1897 it was nearly ten times as great (*ibid.*, p. 32).

[2] It would require a further volume to make a proper comparison of these different 'Westward' movements and of the frontier experiences which accompanied them; the literature of the subject, although still patchy, is already extensive (see Bibliographical Note). For similar reasons the 'frontier experiences' of the ancient world cannot here be brought into detailed comparison with the history of the American West, but there is no reason why it should not be done. An attempt is being made in *The Frontiers of Rome and America* by Donald R. Dudley (a Professor of Classics) and the present writer, to be published as a *Mentor Book* by the New American Library.

CHAPTER I

The Pre-Columbian West

The earliest man in the American continent appears to have been *homo sapiens*. No remains of ape-men or near-men or 'missing links' have been found in America, North or South, and, indeed, very few of any man who lived more than three thousand years ago. But artifacts such as only man could have made or used, associated with the bones of animals that were extinct fifteen to twenty thousand years ago, exist in profusion, and one human remain, that of 'Tepexpan Man', discovered near Mexico City in 1947, appears to date back at least eleven thousand years. Authenticated older human remains may still be found, and a number of claims, as yet not generally accepted by the experts, would, if true, push man's tenure of the American continents back another five or ten thousand years, or in the case concerning 'Puebla Man' to thirty-thousand years ago. But *homo sapiens* is believed to have existed on earth as long as a hundred thousand years, so only within the last third, or quarter, or fifth of this existence does he appear to have inhabited the Americas. For long ages after he had established himself in Europe, in Asia, and in Africa, the two Americas remained unknown to, and all their rich flora and fauna unexploited by man.

Into these vast empty continents man first appears to have made his way by the Bering Straits from Siberia to Alaska. Some early European settlers in North America, observing the Mongoloid features of the tribes they encountered there, imagined that they were getting near to China. It would have been more true to conclude that China had come half-way to meet them. The first 'westward movement' was indeed a south-easterly one and it only took two or three thousand years for man to spread all the way from Alaska to Tierra del Fuego and the stormy shores of Cape Horn. He remained at the hunting stage, and a food gatherer rather than a food grower, for upwards of another ten thousand years (in many places he never did proceed beyond the hunting stage) and the earliest traces of agriculture found are not more than about seven thousand years old.[1]

[1] Very recent excavations in the Tehuacan area of central Mexico would seem to indicate that primitive 'agriculturists' harvested wild corn even earlier, but had

At about the same time metals first appear to have been worked in Wisconsin, but their use was not developed on anything like the scale of the Old World. Those early copper workings were not succeeded by an American Bronze or Iron Age. Stone tools were in general use right up to, and indeed long after, the arrival of Columbus. Evidence of farming activities (for which the discovery of early milling stones, which may have been used to pound the wild grain, is not conclusive, but for which the finding of caches of primitive cultivated corn *is* conclusive) is followed some four thousand years ago by the traces of permanent village communities, growing corn and cotton, notably in the Valley of Mexico. Pottery does not appear to have come until a full millennium later, and the earliest receptacles and cooking pots of these farmers (they could not, of course, have been placed directly over a fire) seem to have been closely woven watertight baskets. Charles Lummis (in *Mesa, Canyon and Pueblo*) claims to have invented the name 'Basketmakers' for these people, but this has been disputed. Still, the name has stuck.

At this point it is perhaps necessary to refer, if only in passing, to the Diffusionist school of thought, which presupposes that all New World cultures derive their essence from Old World origins, and that the Mayan pyramids in Mexico must derive somehow from the Egyptian. These theorists have claimed that the trunk-like nose of the water god, carved all over the façades of some Mayan buildings (such as the Palace of the Warriors at Chichén Itza in Yucatan) is in reality an elephant's trunk, derived from either Africa or Asia, for the elephant is unknown to the Americas. Others have sought to demonstrate that American cotton was not indigenous but must have been imported from southern Asia.[1] The Diffusionists, however, despite the immense popularity of the writings of Thor Heyerdahl, have not been able to convince more than a small minority of scholars that their case is proved, and the consensus of learned opinion is that man, coming late into the New World, already *homo sapiens* but still in a savage state – without agriculture, without the ability to form permanent settlements, without any but the crudest tools, none of them metal – developed all his pre-Columbian cultures

---

not 'domesticated' the maize plant until about 5000 B.C. See P. C. Mangelsdorf, R. S. MacNeish, and W. C. Galinat, 'The Domestication of Corn', in *Science*, Vol. 143 (February 1964), pp. 538–45.

[1] Nobody, though, has been able to prove that maize, unknown to the Old World before the time of Columbus, is anything else than the Americas' greatest and most significant gift to agriculture, though the potato, the tomato or the cacao and the tobacco plants would, according to some tastes, be claimants to the same honour.

and civilizations without any but the most fitful and accidental contacts with the Old World. He did not use the wheel, either for transportation or for shaping pottery (though wheeled toys have been found) and did not domesticate animals other than the dog and (in the Andean region of South America only) certain of the cameloids. The domestic cattle, the horse, and the fowl of the Old World, were unknown. On the other hand, certain fruits, grains, and vegetable drugs entirely unknown to the Old World were widespread in the New by the time of Columbus. Alphabetized writing does not seem to have been used, but an elaborate system of glyphs was developed, to facilitate dating and the keeping of records, by the Olmecs and the Maya; a most expressive style of picture-writing by the Aztecs and Mixtecs; and the conveying of messages by a system of 'shorthand' on knotted cords, or *quipus*, by the Incas of Peru. Numerals were used and elaborate mathematical calculations could be made. A sign for zero was hit upon and a highly accurate calendar worked out. This calendar was one of the finest achievements of the human, and not merely of the Mezo-American, mind, for it calculated the solar year a fraction more accurately even than that of the Gregorian calendar which we use today and which in Britain and her American and other colonies was so reluctantly adopted in the year 1753.

However, the most rapid and far-reaching advances from primitive origins through 'archaic' beginnings to truly 'high' cultures, comparable to those of the Old World, appear to have been concentrated in the two general areas of Mezo America, and in the high Andes and the coastal strip between them and the Pacific Ocean in western South America. These areas now include parts of Mexico, Guatemala, the two Honduras, and Costa Rica in North America, and parts of Peru, Bolivia, and Ecuador plus smaller areas of southern Colombia, northern Chile, and extreme western Brazil in the southern continent. North of the border between Mexico and the United States (as finally established in 1853) the cultural situation was not too inaccurately described by H. R. Schoolcraft, even in 1851, as 'The antiquities of the United States are the antiquities of barbarism and not of ancient civilization . . . whatever judgment may be formed respecting the ruins of Palenque, Cuzco, Yucatan and the Valley of Mexico.'[1] Little

[1] H. R. Schoolcraft, *The Indian Tribes of the United States of America*, illustrated by Seth Eastman (Lippincott, New York, 1851, Vol. 1, Preface, p. v). Understandably dazzled by the recent writing of such men as John Lloyd Stephens and William H. Prescott, and influenced also, no doubt, by the almost simultaneous publication of an

was at that time known about the pre-Columbian cultures of the American South-west (which had only recently become part of the United States), though reports emanating from Army expeditions were beginning to fill this gap. The great cliff-dwelling complex of Mesa Verde still remained to be rediscovered. The 'Horse-Indians' who attracted perhaps the most admiring attention of mid-nineteenth-century anthropologists and artists were of course a post-Columbian phenomenon and their cultural importance had been greatly increased by their use and mastery of the lower half of the Spanish Centaur and their adoption of some of the habits and devices – both good and bad – of the upper half.

The added perspective of a further hundred years of research and observation has placed the pre-Columbian Indians of the South-west (and particularly of New Mexico and Arizona) on a slight eminence in the cultural scale compared with the other tribes and groups of the United States and Canada, but on nothing approaching the towering heights of the Maya or the Inca.

Significant cultural development may be said to have begun in North America when, between ten and twelve thousand years ago, men fashioned rude weapons of stone and used them in hunting at places such as Folsom in north-eastern New Mexico. Little is known of these ancient inhabitants except that they used their 'Folsom points' to some effect on the primitive bison and other animals of the time. Few human remains from this period have been found and even the direct relationship of Folsom man to later Indian tribes is conjectural. The early Indian farmers of the 'four corners' area of New Mexico, Arizona, Colorado, and Utah were already Basketmakers two thousand years ago. When they began to shelter in the caves of the area they left more and more remnants behind for the archaeologist. They grew corn and squash, and used the *metate* or milling stone. They employed the throwing stick or *atlatl*, but not the bow and arrow. They used corn husks and reeds, strips of fur and animal skins, and the hair of the dog (the only animal they appear to have domesticated) for weaving into baskets,

---

eighth edition of the less scholarly but more vivid and popular *opus* of the showman-artist George Catlin, Schoolcraft perhaps tended to paint too unrelieved a picture of barbarism north of the Border. See J. L. Stephens, *Incidents of Travel in Central America, Chiapas and Yucatan* (2 vols, New York, 1843, illustrated by R. Catherwood); W. H. Prescott, *The Conquest of Mexico* (Boston, 1843), and *The Conquest of Peru* (Boston, 1847); G. Catlin, *Illustrations of the Manners, Customs and Conditions of the North American Indians* (2 vols, eighth edition, London, 1851).

1*a*. Ruins of Cliff Palace, Mesa Verde National Park, Colorado.

1*b*. Spruce Tree House, the third largest cliff dwelling in the Mesa Verde – this reconstruction shows Indian life as it might have appeared, *c*. 1200 A.D.

2*a*. De Batz's rendering of an Acolapissa Temple on the Mississippi, 1732.

2*b*. California Indians at Mission San José de Gaudelupe 1806 (painted by a member of the Russian exploring expedition).

bags, sashes, and sandals. They stored their goods (and sometimes buried their dead) in stone-lined pits in the cave floors. Sea-shells (obtained from afar by trade) and turquoises were used as adornment. They probably did not build houses of any sort before about A.D. 450, the very time that the Maya were constructing their great temple-pyramids and ceremonial plazas.

From A.D. 450 to about 750 the more progressive of these Basket-makers of the 'four corners', while sticking to their caves for shelter and protection, began to construct pithouses inside them, of wood and dried mud, with stone foundations, and hearths. These were small and mean, and much of their life – preparing food, cooking, curing hides, and so on – must still have been lived *al fresco*. These 'modified Basket-makers' had pottery, in which they could cook, and used the bow and arrow, both undoubtedly borrowed from other peoples. Beans were grown and must have rapidly become a staple article of diet, as they have ever since remained in this area. Turkeys were domesticated, and the population seems to have increased considerably with the expanding means of subsistence.

By the end of the seventh century these people had spilled out of their cave-dwellings and were living – at least during the warmer months and until the crops were harvested each year – in pithouse villages near their fields in the valleys and on the mesa-tops. This also indicates that it was probably a period of peaceful development relatively free from intertribal warfare or raids by nomads. By about A.D. 850 the farmer basketmakers had become true villagers and what is called 'the Developmental Pueblo Period' had begun. They joined their houses together in terraces (thus exploiting the architectural economy of the 'party wall') and made extensive use of adobe bricks, though still using a wooden framework. These long curving terraces – the foundations of which still exist in a number of places – were still only one storey high in this region, though the flat roofs, reached by wooden ladders, could have been used for drying, storage, sunbathing, or sleeping out. Pithouses were still built, but these were used less for living in than for ceremonial and recreational purposes and were to evolve into the *Kivas* – sometimes likened to primitive Men's Clubs – which are still a feature of the pueblos of the South-west. In the course of time more and more stone was used in construction, and by about A.D. 1100 complete stone houses, mortised with adobe, were in common use. Pottery became more elaborate and decorated, but basketmaking appears to have been going out. Cotton cloth was imported, for cotton could not be grown in the four corners area and there is no evidence that it could as yet have been woven locally.

The culminating phase of this society, what is collectively called the 'Anasazi[1] Culture', began around the middle of the eleventh century and the period from A.D. 1100 to 1273 is therefore known as the 'Great Pueblo' era. Larger and larger communities inhabited great communal structures, some containing hundreds of rooms and rising to five storeys high. Some were in river valleys, like Pueblo Bonito,[2] others in canyons, like Chaco, yet others on mesa-tops or in caves in the cliff-side, as at Mesa Verde, in the south-west corner of present-day Colorado. Their small *Kivas* were supplemented by great *Kivas*, or sunken, roofed ceremonial halls or auditoriums, some capable of holding hundreds of people, such as that near the town of Aztec, New Mexico. Defensive needs, by about A.D. 1300 were driving the villagers off the mesa-tops, back into the caves, where these existed, and such remarkable structures as 'The Cliff Palace' with room for up to five hundred inhabitants or 'Spruce Tree House' holding up to two hundred, both at Mesa Verde, were constructed of timber and stone and dried mud during the thirteenth century. Then suddenly these were abandoned, at the beginning of the great drought which lasted from 1276 to 1299; and their inhabitants, no doubt also beset by the increasing raids of the nomadic Navajo and Apache invaders, moved south and east to become the ancestors of the modern Pueblo Indians of the Rio Grande valley. Meanwhile all their arts and crafts had developed to a cultural peak, and standards of comfort in these great caves were infinitely higher than those of the primitive Basketmakers thirteen centuries before.[3]

The pueblos that the Spaniards in 1540 first discovered and conquered (and found so disappointing) were nearly all founded in or after the fourteenth century, like Zuñi and the great pueblo of Pecos. These belong to the 'Regressive Pueblo' epoch following the great drought of 1276–99. The Hopi villages, though older, had not experienced the

[1] *Anasazi* is a Navajo word meaning 'the ancient ones'.

[2] Pueblo Bonito 'could have sheltered 1,200 inhabitants and it was the largest "apartment house" in the world until a larger one was erected in New York in 1882'. H. M. Wormington, *Prehistoric Indians of the Southwest* (Denver, 1959), p. 86.

[3] The Mesa Verde cultural area remained unknown to the Spaniards, and throughout the Mexican and early American periods, until it was accidentally rediscovered by cowboys in search of straying stock in 1874, almost five hundred years after it had been evacuated. It is now one of the most impressive of all the United States' National Monuments, though still in a remote and sparsely settled area, far from any transcontinental highway.

florescence of the 'Great Pueblo' expansion. The evacuation of Mesa Verde and similar 'Great Pueblo' sites is in some ways comparable (though their previous cultural achievement had been far less), to the remarkable migration of the Maya from their 'Classical Period' (which used to be called 'Old Empire') sites in Chiapas, Honduras, and Guatemala, into hitherto much more thinly settled Yucatan, where they were to experience a renaissance and a new florescence. It has been said of the Pueblo Indians of the American South-west that, 'The latter part of the thirteenth and the beginning of the fourteenth century was a period of great instability, migrations occurred, and centres of population shifted. Once the shift had been made, however, important new communities developed in the drainage of the Little Colorado and the Rio Grande, and a renaissance began. It seems entirely possible that the Pueblo people might have achieved another remarkable high cultural stage had it not been for the arrival of the Spaniards. Even when other Europeans arrived in the Southwest, the native culture was far from being completely submerged, and while aboriginal progress was retarded, it was not entirely stopped.'[1]

Beside the Anasazi, the Hohokam[2] culture of the Gila and Salt river valleys of south central Arizona, although equally ancient and perhaps descended from the even more ancient Cochise people, is relatively unimportant. Irrigation by an extensive network of canals, built between A.D. 600 and 1400 was its most significant achievement, for the multi-storeyed ruin known as Casa Grande (situated in their culture area near present-day Coolidge, Arizona) and similar structures, since completely destroyed, seem to have been the work of Pueblo (Anasazi) people moving into Hohokam territory around A.D. 1300. The Hohokam may have been the ancestors of the Pima and Papago encountered in this area by the Spaniards in the sixteenth and seventeenth centuries and still inhabiting the region. The so-called 'Mogollan' culture of the Upper Gila and the Mimbres valleys of south-west New Mexico (even if truly distinct from the Anasazi and the Hohokam) produced nothing comparable to the giant pueblos of the one or the canal complex of the other, and had in any case passed away by the middle of the twelfth century. The 'Sinagua' people of northern Arizona, associated primarily with the Sunset crater area (where a major volcanic eruption occurred about A.D. 1066) also seem to have melted into the Hohokam and the Pueblo cultures and to have produced nothing distinctive. Even less is

[1] H. M. Wormington, *op. cit.*, p. 107.

[2] *Hohokam* in the Pima language means 'those who have vanished'.

known as yet of the 'Patayan' (or Yuman) culture of the lower Colorado valley on the borders of Arizona and the two Californias. In the year 1700, when these people were visited by Father Kino,[1] they were still primitive agriculturalists, food gatherers, and hunters, barely higher in the cultural scale than the wretched Californian Indians encountered near San Francisco bay in 1579 by Sir Francis Drake.

In 1540 when the Indian tribes of the South-west were first encountered by the white men of Coronado's expedition – in the seven Zuñi pueblos, on the three Hopi mesas, at Acoma and up and down the Rio Grande valley – they had perhaps reached a stage comparable to that of the Aztecs just before they began to raise Tenochtitlán out of the swamps of Lake Texcoco or of the Incas just before their empire began to expand out of the valleys immediately surrounding Cuzco. The South-western tribes did not federate or unite, no great conqueror arose among them, they practised a subsistence agriculture with little trading outside their immediate culture area, they had little knowledge of metals, they did not pursue the buffalo into the plains beyond their own mountains (though something was known to them of the buffalo or Plains Indians), and their villages were of dried mud at the best. They did not create the fabled cities of gold, paved with silver and studded with diamonds of the Spanish imagination, enflamed by the loot of Montezuma and Atahualpa. Yet they were people of no mean achievement and 'barbarism' is too extreme a description for them. They extracted all that they could to make life bearable, and even at times good, from an inhospitable environment. The white man had something to learn from them, and their indigenous culture had eventually come to blossom rather than to fade, under the impact of the *Anglo*,[2] almost uniquely among the Indian tribes of North America.

Wherever else one looks among the tribes of the trans-Mississippi West (or even of the Cis-Mississippi East with which we are less directly concerned), it is impossible to match the cultural achievement of these South-western tribes. Only they, by the time of Columbus, had approached the half-way point from barbarism to a truly florescent culture. Whether if left alone by the white man, if unharassed by the Indian horse-nomads the white man was to create on their borders, if favoured

[1] See Chapter III, p. 62ff.

[2] *Anglo* is the South-western Indian's name for a white American. *Gringo* is the Mexican term for him, of uncertain etymology but somewhat less polite. So is the American 'Greaser' as applied to a Mexican!

by more extensive cultural interchange with Middle America (so that they too might have shared something of the Toltec heritage), they could ever have built the topless towers of a Tenochtitlán or a Chichén-Itza, could have plotted the stars in their course with almost Palomar-like accuracy, could have invented a sign for zero, could have created an empire and a road system stretching from Oregon to Texas or from the Great Lakes to the Sea of California – all this remains an unanswerable question. They were never given the chance.

In the little mesa-top village of Old Oraibi, probably the longest continuously occupied settlement in the present United States, the Hopi have, for upwards of a thousand years, tended to mark time rather than to be marked by it. They still conduct their pre-Columbian tribal ceremonies and speak their pre-Columbian tongue; they still hate the Spanish conquistadors and their handmaiden the Roman Catholic Church (which has never been allowed, since its destruction in the seventeenth century, to rebuild a Mission Chapel on the mesa); they still whittle colourful *Kachinas* for their children from the roots of the cottonwood tree in the images of their many gods;[1] they still defang or mesmerize (they won't tell) rattlesnakes for the snake-dance, which the *Anglo* is permitted to witness in his thousands but not to photograph; they still catch eagles (whether legally or not) on the black mesa over towards the distant Grand Canyon. They send their children often to high school and sometimes to the University and some of these even come back. They have trucks and electricity and the radio, their schoolmaster is a gifted artist, their hotel keeper (until recently) an author and musician who stayed away twenty years and married an *Anglo* from Chicago. The Boeing jets and the DC8s fly over them higher far than the eagle, but Old Oraibi remains Old Oraibi. Its people can make their way in the great world outside, but if they return to the pueblo on the mesa-top they are subject to tribal law and must relearn the tribal ritual. White Bear, who had once played with Fred Waring's Pennsylvanians, once back was expected to don his *Kachina* costume with the rest and engage in an endless chant and shuffle until the rains came, or to wear the striped regalia of a delight-maker and provide amusement to the assembled crowd. Back on the mesa he must shed his camera and his tape recorder, his hi-fi, and his city suit. He must become once again, for an hour, a day, or a week, a pre-Columbian Indian. Then back (if he wishes) to the fleshpots of Phoenix, Paris, or Pekin.

[1] Down in the valley below a veritable Santa's workshop mass-produces inferior *Kachinas* for the tourist trade.

The Hopi were never really reconquered by the Spaniards after the Great Pueblo revolt of 1680, and under the United States government they have been fortunate in that the reservation allotted to them was the region of their ancestral mesas, and not some distant place of exile. Most of the other tribes have migrated or been shifted so far and so often that continuity with the pre-Columbian existence has been lost. Even where, like the Zuñi, they still remain where the Spaniards first found them, some of their most important pre-Columbian pueblos, like Hawikuh, have been abandoned and allowed to fall into ruins. A similar fate to that of Hawikuh has befallen Pecos, one of the greatest of the Rio Grande region's pueblos. Both Acoma and Taos have had to be rebuilt several times since the sixteenth century and both suffered badly when taken by storm by the white men. Only therefore on the three Hopi mesas – though even here a number of the villages are post-Columbian foundations – can the spirit of pre-Columbian Indian life in the American South-west be said to have persisted without major dilution.

Elsewhere the achievements of the pre-Columbian culture of the United States, and how their peoples lived and thought, must be judged from archaeological evidence alone. This, unfortunately, is meagre, but the low humidity of the American South-west (like that of the Peruvian deserts) has helped to preserve many things (including textiles, basketwork and even wood used in construction) which in more destructive climates would have disappeared completely, leaving only bones, metal and stone articles, and pottery, for the archaeologist. Even of these the metal articles (mostly jewellery and very rarely implements) were naturally most rare in communities which were still living in the Stone Age as they were still at the time when Columbus came to the New World and the Spaniards, coming up from Mexico in 1540, arrived in the South-west.

CHAPTER II

Overland Exploration of North America (to 1800)

Although Columbus may be claimed to have discovered the mainland of Central America (on his fourth and last voyage in 1502) his colonization and exploitation was entirely, and even then not very successfully, confined to the islands of the Caribbean. Although he vaguely realized that he had stumbled against a New World of colossal dimensions,[1] he did not know, and could not imagine, that the Pacific Ocean existed. It was the swashbuckling absconding debtor Bilbao who (in 1513) 'first gazed on the Pacific'. Cortez himself was not to see the Pacific until his expedition to the Gulf of California – 'the Sea of Cortez' – in 1535. Meanwhile, not only had his own spectacular conquest of Mexico taken place (1519–21) but Ponce de León had sailed twice to Florida (1513 and 1521) in his fruitless search for the fountain of perpetual youth, and Pánfilo de Narváez, Cortez' old rival, with a grant from the King of Spain of all the Gulf coast from Mexico to Florida, had led his six hundred into the jaws of death in 1528. The four survivors of this ill-fated expedition (the worst disaster in all Spain's exploration and colonization in North America until the Pueblo revolt of 1680 was to lose her, temporarily, the whole of New Mexico) walked and begged their way, suffering unimaginable hardships, right across from the final shipwreck off the Texas coast, to western Mexico, via the inhospitable lower Rio Grande and Pecos river valleys, to return to Mexico City in 1536 and tell a wondrous tale. The leader of these four wanderers, Cabeza de Vaca, said that, after eight years of wilderness living 'I could not wear any clothing for some time, nor could we sleep anywhere else but on the ground'.[2]

[1] 'Of this half part (of the world) Ptolemy had no knowledge . . . Your highnesses have here another world [*otro mundo*].' R. H. Major, *Select Letters of Columbus* (second edition, 1890), pp. 147 and 148.

[2] F. W. Hodge and T. H. Lewis (eds), *Spanish Explorers in the Southern United States 1528–1543*, New York, 1907, reprinted 1959 ('The Narrative of Alvar Nuñez Cabeça de Vaca', translated by T. Buckingham Smith), p. 120.

The travels of Cabeza de Vaca and his three companions, though one of the most remarkable human odysseys in history, were without plan or objective other than simply to survive and to return to civilization. Until their final rescue they only very vaguely knew where they were. 'We resolved to go in search of the maize. We did not wish to follow the path where the cattle [buffalo] are, because it is towards the north and for us very circuitous, since we ever held it certain that going towards the sunset we must find what we desire. Thus we took our way, and traversed all the country until coming out at the South Sea [the

Pacific Ocean]',[1] is a typical passage in Cabeza de Vaca's narrative.[2] In the exploration of North America the journey and the narrative of Cabeza are mainly important for having inspired the organization and influenced the routes of the two great expeditions led by Coronado and De Soto which set out in 1540.

Cabeza de Vaca's assessment of the riches of the lands he had traversed and the unvisited regions to the north about which he had heard was not very enthusiastic. 'There is no blatant announcement of great mineral wealth – a mountain with scoria of iron, some small bags of mica, a quantity of galena with which the Indians painted their faces, a little turquoise a few emeralds and a small silver bell was all.'[2] Everybody seemed to think that Cabeza de Vaca was withholding vital information either to use on a new expedition led by himself or for the ear of the King and Emperor Charles I and V alone. He refused to serve under the Viceroy Mendoza and Coronado in Mexico or under De Soto, after his return to Spain. Says the Gentleman of Elvas, a Portuguese who accompanied De Soto to Florida in 1539 and who wrote the

[1] Hodge and Lewis, *op. cit.*, p. 105. [2] *Ibid.*, p. 8.

fullest and best account of his expedition, 'Cabeza de Vaca . . . brought with him a written relation of adventures, which said in places: Here I have seen this; and the rest which I saw I leave to confer of with his Majesty . . . he and another [his companion Dorantes] had sworn not to divulge certain things which they had seen, lest someone might beg the government in advance of them, for which he had come to Spain; nevertheless he gave them to understand that it was the richest country in the world.'[1] Whether he did so or not, that people were *prepared* to believe it richer than both Mexico and Peru was sufficient incentive. Grandees and gentlemen flocked to De Soto's banner, even including some of Cabeza de Vaca's own relatives. 'He went for Governor to Rio de la Plata, but his kinsmen followed Soto' noted the Gentleman of Elvas, with some satisfaction, and said that one of these, Baltasar de Gallegos, received the appointment of castellan, and took his wife with him. 'He sold houses, vineyards, a rent of wheat and ninety ajeiras of olive-field in the Xarafe by Seville.'[2] The gold fever had assuredly seized upon the adventurous –though uxorious – Baltasar.

Although De Soto's expedition, after landing at Tampa Bay in Florida, discovered no great treasure of silver or gold, for which its members hungrily inquired everywhere that they went, and although its leader himself was not to return from it, the expedition resulted in 'our first geographical knowledge of the interior of the states of Florida, Georgia, North and South Carolina, Tennessee, Alabama, Mississippi, Arkansas, Texas, and the Indian Territory [Oklahoma]',[3] and possibly also of Missouri and Louisiana. De Soto's were the first white men to see and traverse the Mississippi, which they named the River of the Holy Spirit and where De Soto himself found a watery grave, and the first to encounter the Cherokees, the Choctaws, the Chickasaws, and other important Indian tribes. The future cotton kingdom (to be the last stronghold of the 'peculiar institution' of Negro slavery) was their discovery.

The Narváez expedition had been all but wiped out, but better organization, wiser leadership, and greater luck brought over three hundred of De Soto's men safely if precariously back to Panuco in north-east Mexico in 1543, to be greeted and received by the Viceroy

[1] Hodge and Lewis, *op. cit.*, p. 136. 'The Narrative of the Expedition of Hernando de Soto, by the Gentleman of Elvas,' Chapter II, translated by T. Buckingham Smith. (First published in Portuguese, 1557. First English translation by Hakluyt, 1609.)

[2] *Ibid.*, p. 138.

[3] *Ibid.*, p. 129.

Mendoza, when they finally reached Mexico City, much more warmly than the leaders of the Coronado expedition, which Mendoza himself had sent out. At the time it was obviously thought that 'the conquerors of Florida' had achieved more for Spain than had Coronado in Arizona, up and down the Rio Grande valley, in the Buffalo plains and on the

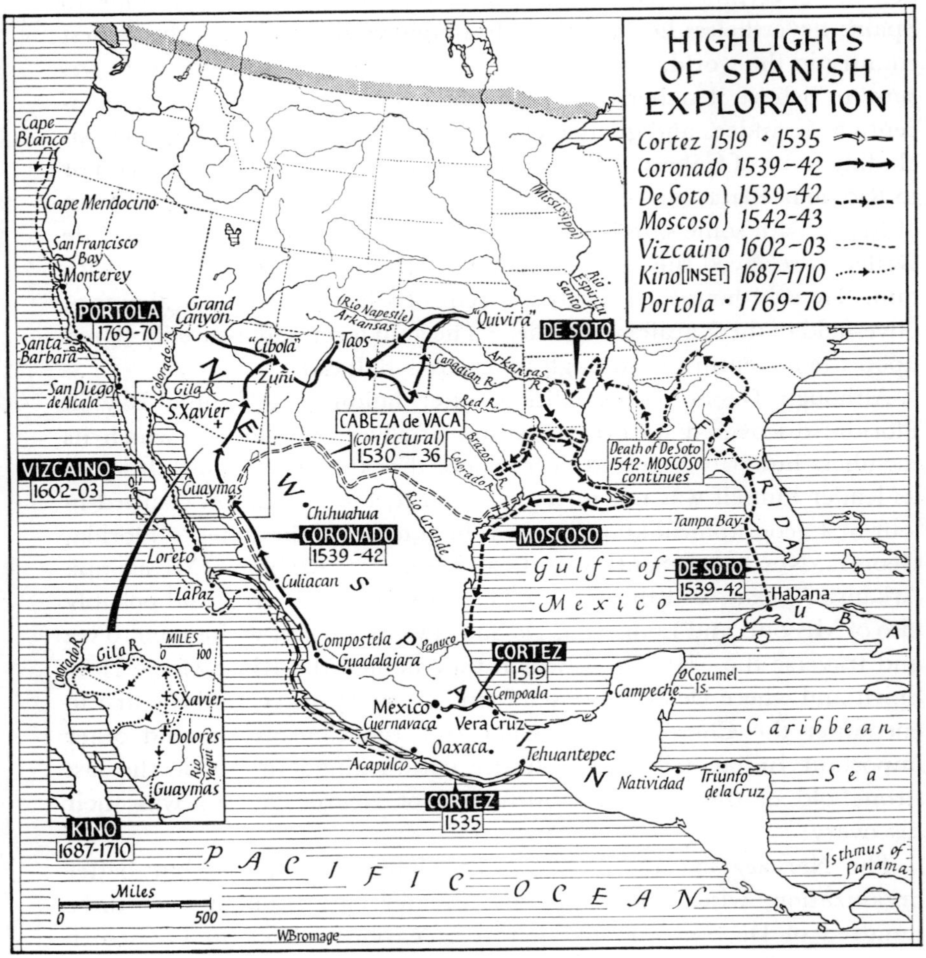

Arkansas. Later appraisals would perhaps rank the two expeditions as equally important – and equally remarkable. Neither of them established new European colonies in North America or permanently subdued any Indian tribes. Neither discovered or blazed a viable route right across the mainland of North America, though they came very near to an accidental juncture on the Brazos river of Texas, the upper reaches of which were most probably explored by Coronado and the lower reaches by De Soto's second (and successor) in command, Luys de Moscoso. But in the annals of geographical discovery both are of great significance.

Coronado started off from Compostela, in west-central Mexico, and travelled north over a thousand miles across mountains and deserts to southern Arizona, then eastward nearly another thousand miles across what are now New Mexico and the Panhandles of Texas and Oklahoma, most probably as far as eastern Kansas and just possibly into Nebraska or Missouri. His were the first white men to see and live with the Pueblo Indians in their multi-storeyed apartment-house villages of adobe or dried mud, the first to see and describe the wonders of the Grand Canyon of Arizona, and the first to hunt the buffalo.

We know a great deal about the Coronado expedition, not only from letters and reports that Coronado himself sent back and from the records of the official inquiry into his conduct and leadership but also because several other members of the party wrote diaries and reminiscences. The most famous of these is that of Pedro de Castañeda, a private soldier born in Castile and one of the earliest Spanish colonists in northern Mexico.

The Mexican border country and that part of southern Arizona through which Coronado and his three hundred Spanish gentlemen passed with their retainers and upwards of a thousand Indian allies, driving large numbers of cattle and sheep before them to provide fresh meat for the expedition, was to remain virtually uninhabited except by the fierce nomadic Apache Indians, until after the middle of the nineteenth century, when the Gadsden Purchase[1] and the discovery of silver and other precious metals brought in the Americans and caused such tough towns as Tombstone to flourish briefly and violently and then to wither away to insignificance. Northward from the vicinity of Tombstone Coronado's men journeyed on to their primary objective, the fabled Seven Cities of Cíbola, around which travellers' tales had woven such a web of fantasy. These Seven Cities of gold and silver and turquoise turned out to be merely the seven Zuñi Indian pueblos, one of which, Hawikuh, they had to take by storm before the Indians would submit. The ruins of Hawikuh, destroyed and

[1] James Gadsden negotiated the purchase by the United States of what is now the southern part of the State of Arizona from the government of the Mexican dictator, Antonio López de Santa Anna, in 1853.

abandoned some years later, can still be inspected today, but the centre of Zuñi life and ceremonial, including the famous Shalaka dances, with their giant human effigies, not unlike those of the carnival at Nice, has moved today some dozen miles eastward.

Oddly enough it was a native of Nice, on the Riviera in far-off Europe, who had led Coronado and his men to the so-called Seven Cities of Gold. He was a Franciscan friar called Marcos, a veteran of the conquest and conversion of Peru, who had been sent out by Mendoza in 1539 on a pilot expedition, together with the Negro slave, Estevan, one

of the four survivors with Cabeza de Vaca of the Narváez expedition. Estevan, proud of his reputation among the Indians as a medicine-man, went ahead of the more prudent Friar Marcos, to be captured and killed by the Zuñi Indians at Hawikuh when his medicine at last failed and his demands for turquoises and women became too outrageous. Marcos, on hearing this, had simply gazed on Hawikuh from a distant hill, and then turned back to tell the tale of its riches, which he was able to imagine from seeing the fierce Arizona sun gilding the mud walls of the pueblo, and possibly a mirage paving its plaza with silver. When Coronado, taking a shame-faced Friar Marcos with him, discovered nothing but 'a little crowded village looking as if it had been crumpled up all together . . . a village of about two hundred warriors . . . three or four storeys high' Castañeda says that 'Such were the curses that some hurled at Friar Marcos that I pray God may protect him from them'.[1] The friar

[1] Hodge and Lewis, *op. cit.*, p. 300.

was packed off back to Mexico in disgrace, but at least his life was spared, unlike that of another imparter of misinformation to the expedition.

This second 'villain' was a Plains Indian, found by Coronado captive in the pueblo of Pecos east of the Rio Grande. The captive undertook to guide Coronado across the plains beyond the mountains which lay to the east of the Rio Grande to another great river in which there were, he claimed, 'fishes as big as horses . . .' He also said that 'the lord of that country took his afternoon nap under a great tree on which were hung a large number of little gold bells, which put him to sleep as they swung in the air. . . . Everyone had their ordinary dishes made of wrought silver plate and their jugs and bowls of gold.'[1] He called this eldorado the province of Quivira.

'The Turk', as the Spaniards called him 'because he looked like one' – he was probably a Pawnee Indian – was obviously an accomplished liar, and he may perhaps be designated as the inventor, though apparently not the patentee, of the Texas tall tale. Anyway, his tall tale took Coronado and his men, after wintering somewhat uneasily among the Pueblo Indians of the upper Grande valley, off on another wild-goose chase even more spectacular and much more disappointing than their search for the Seven Cities of Gold.

'The Turk' was later to confess that the Pueblo Indians had induced him to lead Coronado into the Great Plains in order that the expedition might get lost and perish. He almost succeeded.

After Coronado became convinced that 'the Turk' was a scoundrel, he sent the bulk of his force back to what is now New Mexico and with thirty horsemen and half a dozen foot soldiers the General himself turned northward 'by the needle' (as Castañeda says) from the neighbourhood of Lubbock in Texas on the upper reaches of the Brazos river and finally reached the Great Bend of the Arkansas river. But the province of Quivira contained only the straw-hutted villages of the primitive Wichita Indians and the only metal, precious or otherwise, that they saw was a copper plate around the neck of a chief. In disgust Coronado had 'the Turk' strangled, and after a few days turned back for the long forty-day trek to join his main force on the Rio Grande.[2]

[1] Hodge and Lewis, *op. cit.*, p. 314.

[2] I have followed the route of Coronado to Quivira, crossing the Arkansas river at the point where he is supposed to have done so. The town of Great Bend I found to be hustling and modern, with ugly grain elevators and an aggressively new drive-in theatre advertising a film about teenage gang warfare in New York. The countryside here is dreary in the extreme, the great treeless plain stretching to the horizon and all the towns just like each other. Driving at sixty miles an hour it is tedious.

Of the buffalo plains as a whole Castañeda, in a striking phrase, complained that they consisted of 'nothing but cows and sky'. The whole life of the Plains Indians was dominated by the buffalo and based upon a buffalo economy. Another member of the expedition put it this way: 'The Indians live or sustain themselves entirely from the buffalo, for they neither grow nor harvest corn. With the skins they build their houses; with the skins they clothe and shoe themselves; from the skins

they make rope and also obtain wool. With the sinews they make thread, with which they sew their clothes and also their tents. From the bones they shape awls. The dung they use for firewood, since there is no other fuel in that land. The bladders they use as jugs and drinking containers. They sustain themselves on their meat, eating it slightly roasted and heated over the dung. Some they eat raw.'[1]

Coronado sent out small parties of his men on a number of side ex-

Coronado's men, who sometimes didn't exceed six miles a day, must have found it unbearably dull. No wonder they went back and reported it to be incapable of settlement!

[1] G. P. Winship, *The Journey of Coronado* (New York, 1922), p. 214.

peditions and several of these made discoveries at least as remarkable as those of the main party. One under Tovar visited the Hopi Indians on their Mesas in central Arizona. Yet another side expedition led by Cardenas pushed on north-westward from Cíbola, past the Hopi Mesas to the mighty canyon of the Colorado river. Gazing down the vistas of fantastically eroded and gorgeously coloured pinnacles and stratified cliffs of the canyon, from the southern rim of a cleft in the earth's surface in places more than ten miles to the north rim and over a mile deep, the Spaniards judged that the river below was 'only six feet across, although the Indians said it was half a league wide'. Three of them climbed down about a third of the way into the canyon – taking most of the day to do so – and, on returning, said that the river seemed very large from the place which they reached, while rocks which from the top had 'seemed to be about as tall as a man' were found to be 'bigger than the great tower of Seville', which is 275 feet high.

Coronado and his fellow Spaniards were the first Europeans and the first white men to see all these things, now visited every year by many thousands of tourists. The buffalo are gone from the plains, but the great mountains and the great canyon of the Colorado remain just as the Spaniards first found them. The villages of the Pueblo Indians are still almost exactly as they described them. Taos, perhaps the most celebrated pueblo of all, seven thousand feet up in the mountains of northern New Mexico, near the source of the Rio Grande, was described by Coronado and Castañeda very much as D. H. Lawrence was to describe it when he went to live nearby nearly four centuries later. It has obviously changed very little in external appearance.[1] Castañeda describes it as 'a large and powerful village . . . the river flowed through the

[1] But beneath the surface perhaps the changes are much greater. I was there once for the fiesta and fair of San Geronimo (29 and 30 September) when the Indians of Taos perform their autumn sunset dance (waving branches of the quaking aspen, the leaves of which have already by then turned to gold) and their dawn races, as they have for hundreds of years. One of the elders of the Pueblo, hearing me speak, asked if I was English, and when I said I was he requested me to wait a minute while he went away and brought back another younger man, who told me haltingly – for the normal speech of the Pueblo is still Spanish – that he had been in England during the war as a 'G.I.' 'I was in hospital at Huntingdon,' he said. 'Do you know Huntingdon?' I admitted that I had been there. 'Then perhaps you know a girl-friend I had there?' he asked. 'Her name was Elsie Brown.' Had I been a Spaniard perhaps I should have been told, 'Another Spaniard was here some time ago. His name was Captain Hernando de Alvarado. He was sent up from Pecos pueblo by his General, Don Francisco Vázques de Coronado. Perhaps you know them?'

middle of it. The natives crossed it by wooden bridges . . . at this village they saw the largest and finest hot rooms or estufas that there were in the whole country . . . Hernando de Alvarado visited this village when he discovered Cicuye [Pecos]. The country is very high and very cold.'[1]

After 1542 there was a lull in Spanish exploration. The sons and grandsons of the conquistadors were less adventurous and less impecunious than their fathers, and had much to consolidate. The disappointments of the Coronado and De Soto expeditions had seemed to indicate that there was more wealth to be extracted from the mines and haciendas of the Mexico that Cortez had won than from fresh colonizing endeavours to the north. Though remaining ever vigilant in the face of intruders, French, British, and Dutch, Spain in America went on the defensive after the middle of the sixteenth century.

Yet, although the conquistadors may be said to have over-reached themselves at last, the original impetus died but slowly. Men still talked wistfully about Quivira well into the seventeenth century and dreamed about the 'Straits of Anian' providing a short cut to China, for even longer. Many expeditions went out, but they were smaller, less confident and often without government sponsorship. They helped to redraw and correct the map of North America (though at times adding fresh misconceptions, like the great supposed island of Upper and Lower California invented by Father Antonio de la Ascensión in 1620 when he chronicled Vizcaino's seaborne expedition).

By the end of the sixteenth century the Spaniards appear to have acquired their second wind and a new expedition on the grand scale was assembled by Juan de Oñate in 1598, with a contract to colonize what Coronado had seen but failed to conquer. The result was the subjection and settlement of the upper Rio Grande valley, the country of the Pueblo Indians, and the most important achievement of the seventeenth century for Spain in North America.[2]

Juan de Oñate, the *Adelantado*, or colonization-contractor, for New Mexico was not a conquistador, adventuring out of Spain with a band of gold-hungry adventurers, though the blood of the conquistadors as well as of the Aztec rulers flowed in the veins of his family, for he married a descendant both of Cortez and of Montezuma. This creole empire-builder, born in Mexico and brought up in Zacatecas, prepared his expedition with great care, and after two years of delays caused by

[1] Hodge and Lewis, *op. cit.*, pp. 340–1.

[2] Vividly described in Paul Horgan's *Great River* (New York, 1954), Vol. 1.

official red-tape and by the machinations of his rivals, started off for the Rio Grande early in 1598 with four hundred men, a hundred and thirty families and over seven thousand head of animals. They passed the 'Great River' at the Pass of the North on 4 May, reached the pueblo of Santo Domingo on 7 July and he was joined by the slower units of his caravan at his headquarters near there, which he had named San Juan, in August. Santa Fé was not to be founded until several years later. A church was built and the submission of the various pueblo communities peaceably secured. The colony of New Mexico was in being. It was to prosper, with only minor setbacks for over three-quarters of a century.[1] By that time, despite the magnitude and the triumphs of the Pueblo Revolt of 1680, Christian civilization had been too firmly established in the province to be permanently eradicated. New Mexico was firmly in Spanish hands again in 1693, though it remained a turbulent province even under Mexican and United States sovereignty, as late as the nineteenth century.

With justifiable pride and pardonable exaggerations Oñate reported his success in a long letter to the Count of Monterey, the Viceroy of New Spain, on 2 March 1599. Its tone contrasts vividly with the melancholy confessions of frustration and failure sent by Coronado (who had sought only gold and other portable treasures) to the Viceroy Mendoza sixty years before, from that same region. 'Greatly to His [God's] advantage and that of his royal Majesty, they have acquired a possession so good that none other of his Majesty in these Indies excels it,'[2] claimed the ebullient Oñate. He continued:

> There must be in this province and in the others above mentioned, to make a conservative estimate, seventy thousand Indians, settled after our custom, house adjoining house with square plazas. They have no streets, and in the pueblos which contain many plazas or wards one goes from one plaza to the other through alleys. They are of two and three storeys, of an *estado* [the height of a man] and a half, or an *estado* and a third each, which latter is not so common; and some houses are of four, five, six, and seven storeys. Even whole pueblos dress in very highly coloured cotton *mantas*, white or black, and some of thread – very good clothes. Others wear buffalo hides, of which

[1] Like the trouble at Acoma at the end of 1598 when the massacre of a Spanish party was avenged by the storming and sacking of the mesa-top pueblo.

[2] Translation in H. E. Bolton (ed.) *Spanish Exploration in the Southwest, 1542–1706* (New York, 1908; reprinted, 1959), pp. 212–22; original Spanish version printed in Pacheco and Cardenas, *Coleccion de Documentos Ineditos*, XVI, 302–15.

there is a great abundance. They have most excellent wool, of whose value I am sending a small example.

It is a land abounding in flesh of buffalo, goats with hideous horns, and turkeys; and in Mohoce there is game of all kinds. There are many wild and ferocious beasts, lions, bears, wolves, tigers, *penicas*, ferrets, porcupines, and other animals, whose hides they tan and use. Towards the west there are bees and very white honey, of which I am sending a sample. Besides, there are vegetables, a great abundance of the best and greatest salines in the world, and a very great many kinds of very rich ores, as I stated above. Some discovered near here do not appear so, although we have hardly begun to see anything of the much there is to be seen. There are very fine grape vines, rivers, forests of many oaks, and some cork trees, fruits, melons, grapes, watermelons, Castilian plums, *capuli*, pine-nuts, acorns, ground-nuts, and *coralejo*, which is a delicious fruit, and other wild fruits. There are many and very good fish in this Rio de Norte, and in others. From the ores here are made all the colors which we use, and they are very fine.

The people are in general very comely; their color is like those of that land, and they are much like them in manner and dress, in their grinding, in their food, dancing, singing, and many other things, except in their languages, which are many, and different from those there. Their religion consists in worshipping idols, of which they have many; and in their temples, after their own manner, they worship them with fire, painted reeds, feathers, and universal offering of almost everything they get, such as small animals, birds, vegetables, etc. In their government they are free, for although they have some petty captains, they obey them badly and in very few things.

We have seen other nations such as the Querechos, or herdsmen, who live in tents of tanned hides, among the buffalo. The Apaches, of whom we have also seen some, are innumerable.

The further expeditions which Oñate proposed to send out from New Mexico would, he thought, make him more famous even than Cortez: 'I should never cease were I to recount all of the many things that occur to me. I can only say that, with God's help, I shall see them all, and give new worlds, new, peaceful and grand, to his Majesty, greater than the good Marquis gave to him, although he did so much.'

We do not today think of Juan de Oñate, Governor, *Adelantado* and Captain-General of the Province of New Mexico, in the same breath as Hernando Cortez, Marquis of the Valley of Oaxaca, Captain-General of New Spain and of the Coasts to the South, but in the short time remaining to him (until 1608) he saw a great deal more of the

American West and South-west than the actual Rio Grande valley area that he colonized. In person he led an expedition towards the east in 1601, across the buffalo plains as far as the vicinity of Wichita, Kansas, and another in 1604, even more enterprising, to Lower California by land, forcing his way along the Gila and down the Colorado river to the head of the Gulf of California, and he sent his Captain of the Guard, Marcos Farfan, out from Zuñi in 1599 to rediscover the silver mines on or near the Big Sandy river in Arizona, which Espejo's expedition had found in 1583. Apart from these mines (which he did not exploit) and the pearls of the South Sea, or Pacific Ocean (which he talked about a great deal but did not amass), Oñate, unlike the early conquistadors, was primarily interested in the lands he visited as possible agricultural and ranching settlements. Instead of dismissing the buffalo plains and the Kansas prairies as 'nothing but cows and sky' he depicts them as a land flowing with milk and honey:

> We remained here for one day in this pleasant spot surrounded on all sides by fields of maize and crops of the Indians. The stalks of the maize were as high as that of New Spain and in many places even higher. The land was so rich that, having harvested the maize, a new growth of a span in height had sprung up over a large portion of the same ground, without any cultivation or labour other than the removal of the weeds and the making of holes where they planted the maize. There were many beans, some gourds, and, between the fields, some plum trees. The crops were not irrigated, but dependent on the rains, which, as we noted, must be very regular in that land, because in the month of October it rained as it does in August in New Spain. It was thought certain that it had a warm climate, for the people we saw went about naked, although they wore skins. Like the other settled Indians they utilize cattle in large numbers. It is incredible how many there are in that land.

He speaks of 'the fertility of the soil, of its many people, of the wealth of the innumerable cattle, so much beyond number that they alone would suffice to enrich thousands of men with suet, tallow and hides; of the suitableness of the land for founding many important settlements, fortunately possessing all materials necessary for the purpose'.[1] A Kansas–Pacific Railroad land agent could hardly have done better!

Oñate also vividly describes the villages and mode of life of the Plains Indians little realizing that these tribes were on the eve of a great revolution, which would make them infinitely more mobile, resourceful,

[1] Bolton, *op. cit.*, pp. 261–3.

and formidable than the relatively peaceful people he, and before him Coronado, had encountered. In the year 1600, as Oñate noted, the Plains Indians followed the buffalo on foot and their only means of transportation was the dog *travois*. By 1700 they had the horse. They proved infinitely harder to subdue and displace from their hunting grounds in the nineteenth century than would have been the case in the seventeenth. But Oñate and his men only came and saw and rode away.

The Spaniards, after a false start (1540) and one enforced retreat (1680) finally established a flourishing colony in New Mexico, but comparable efforts in Texas met with almost complete failure. It was left to immigrants from the United States and from Europe to establish the first prosperous colonies there, as late as the 1820s, 1830s, and 1840s. Yet Texas, first seen by Cabeza de Vaca and his fellow castaways, and first partially explored by De Soto and Coronado, was of the utmost strategic importance to Spain in America, and was recognized as such from the sixteenth century onwards.

Farther east a French attempt to colonize Florida with a party of Huguenots sent out by Admiral Coligny had led promptly to the first permanent Spanish settlement being established there (at St Augustine) in 1565, after Admiral Pedro Menéndez de Avilés had sacked the French fort at the mouth of the St John's river and slaughtered its garrison. It was also the threat of French rivalry in Texas, rather than any independent desire to colonize that region, which first caused the Spaniards to establish outposts there. During the sixty years after the 'Memorial' in which Father Benavides had in 1630 first pointed to the possible ambitions in Texas and Louisiana of the English and the Flemings, a number of Spanish expeditions had crossed the Pecos eastwards and the Rio Grande northwards, but they all returned without leaving settlers or missionaries behind. The country, though fertile, was rendered highly inhospitable by unfriendly Indians. Captain Juan Domínguez de Mendoza, who reached the Nueces river in 1684 found the Apaches hostile all the way. A significant passage in his report reads 'The hostile Apaches stole nine animals, seven from the Jumana Indians, and the others, a horse and a mule, from the chief and Ensign Diego de Luna, respectively. Because of carelessness these animals joined those of the Indians. It was not possible to follow them because of the great advantage which they had.'[1] But it was not troublesome

[1] Bolton, *op. cit.*, p. 335.

Indians or the cure of souls that led Alonzo de León on five separate expeditions into Texas, each one probing more deeply than the last, between 1686 and 1690. It was the ominous news of a landing by a French party in 1684 which really brought the Spaniards into Texas. La Salle, whose tragic story has been told so unforgettably by Francis Parkman,[1] had travelled down the Mississippi from New France all the way to its mouth, in 1682, had claimed for his King Louis XIV 'possession of this Country of Louisiana . . . from the mouth of the great River St Louis on the eastern side otherwise called Ohio . . . as also along the River Colbert or Mississippi, and rivers which discharge themselves therein, from its source . . . as far as the mouth at the sea or Gulf of Mexico'.[2] To consolidate and exploit this claim La Salle had returned to France and outfitted a new expedition, which sailed for the Gulf of Mexico in 1684, but missed the mouth of the Mississippi where he had intended to establish a colony and finally landed at Matagorda Bay in Texas. The colonists he left behind in Texas when he departed on his ill-fated attempt to return to New France by land were all massacred or captured by the Indians. The few survivors were located by De León whose fifth expedition, in 1690, established two missions under Father Massanet on or near the Nueces river. Though abandoned in 1793 these were the first Spanish settlements in what is now the state of Texas. The Spaniards continued intermittently to patrol the Texas coasts from the sea, but not until another quarter-century had passed did they make a fresh attempt to colonize it by land.

Once again French colonial ambition and enterprise provided the spur. The French had finally established themselves and the colony of Louisiana in 1699, at the mouth of the Mississippi river, and in 1714 the French trader St Denis journeyed, greatly daring, right across Texas from the Red river at Natchitoches to the Spanish post of San Juan Bautista on the Rio Grande. His reception was mixed, but his arrival stirred the Spanish authorities to establish six missions along the route that St Denis (who obligingly guided them back along it) had followed, and in 1718 to found the settlement of San Antonio, which was to remain the most considerable Spanish establishment in Texas for the

[1] F. Parkman, *Discovery of the Great West* (Boston, 1869) retitled *La Salle and The Discovery of the Great West* in its eleventh and extensively revised edition (Boston, 1879). Reprinted in the *Frontier Library*, with introductory essay by John A. Hawgood (London, 1962).

[2] B. F. French (ed.), *Historical Collections of Louisiana and Florida*, translated from the *Narrative of the expedition of M. de La Salle*, by Jacques de la Metairie, pp. 18–19 (New York, 1875).

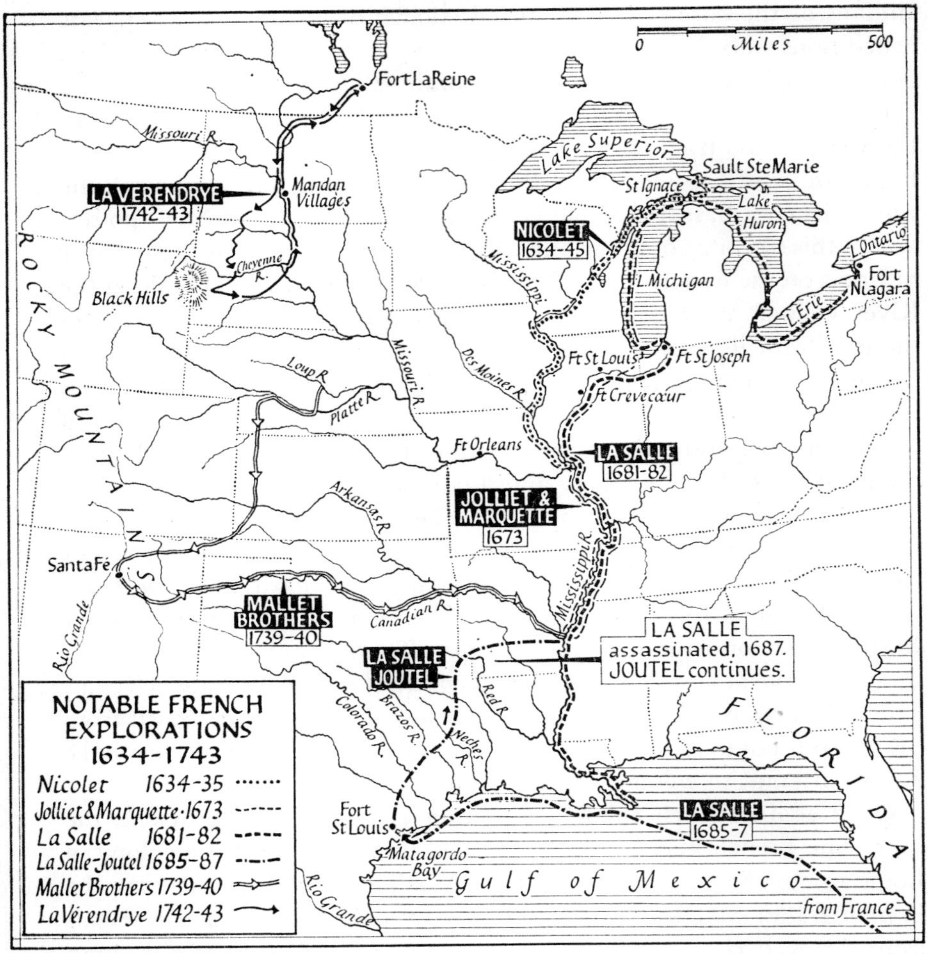

whole century that still remained to Spain in America. Spain and France were at last face to face on their North American frontiers. South-eastern Texas could now be firmly settled, and by 1770 the province of Neuva Santander established there had six thousand inhabitants. Farther north and east the French continued to challenge Spanish power until, in 1762, Louisiana was transferred to the Spanish crown. The wild nomadic Indians of the plains, now completely masters of the horse, turned out to be more durable and more formidable. A mission and presidio on the San Saba river, requested by the Apaches, was liquidated by the Comanches in 1759. This seems to have taken the heart out of the Spaniards and in 1772 the Texan frontier was officially withdrawn, as a result of the Rubi Report, advocating this course, of 1767.[1] Everything northward of a line of fifteen new presidios was to be given back 'to nature and the Indians' with the exception of one or two strong outposts, and the Apaches were, as far as possible, to be exterminated. The mission period in Texas ended almost before it had properly begun. The only good Indian was now a dead and not a converted one. But the Apaches were not exterminated and their resistance to the white man was to continue until long after Spanish power was to disappear from Texas in 1821. It may indeed be said to have survived, with Geronimo, almost into the twentieth century.

[1] See H. E. Bolton, *Texas in the Middle Eighteenth Century* (Berkeley, 1915), pp. 89–91, and W. P. Webb, *The Great Plains* (New York, 1931; paperbound reprint, New York, 1962), p. 129ff, and S. B. Brinckerhoff and O. B. Faulk, *Lancers of the King* (Phoenix Arizona, 1965), *passim,* which discusses Spain's military failure in northern Mexico and prints a translation of the royal *Reglamento* of 1772.

CHAPTER III

Imperialism on the Pacific

If Texas was Spain's worst rebuff in her northward advance out of Mexico, California was her most remarkable success, all the more so because this success was belated and almost unexpected. Apart from the most tenuous of landfalls up and down her coasts, the Spaniards left Upper California severely alone for nearly two and a half centuries after Cortez' first tentative probing, in 1535, in the direction of that 'island' where a fabled 'monstrous regiment of women' rivalled the realm of the Amazons of ancient times.

In May of that year Cortez actually believed he had reached the 'island', when he landed at what is now Puerta de la Paz on the west shore of the sea which had been called after him; and he gave California its name, out of the romance published in 1510 by García Ordoñez de Montalva, which had claimed that 'on the right hand of the Indies is an island called California, very close to the Terrestrial Paradise, and it was peopled by Black Women without any man among them, for they lived in the fashion of Amazonia. They were of strong and hardy bodies, of ardent courage and of great strength. Their island was the mightiest in the world, with its steep cliffs and rocky shores. Their arms were all of gold and so was the harness of the wild beasts which they tamed and rode. For in the whole island there was no metal but gold . . .'[1]

What Cortez met were not Black Amazons but Stone Age savages. It is not known very precisely how large was the Indian population of California before the coming of the white man, but estimates run as high

[1] That Hernando Cortez had long known this romantic story is proved from his instruction issued to his kinsman Francisco Cortez, in 1524, urging him to further exploration of the Pacific's shores 'because I am informed that down the coast . . . there are many provinces thickly inhabited by people and containing, it is believed, great riches, and that in these parts of it there is one which is inhabited by women, with no men, who procreate in the way in which the ancient histories ascribe to the Amazons and because, by learning the truth regarding this and whatever else there is on the said coast, God our lord and their Majesties will be greatly served'. (Pachcco and Cardenas, *op. cit.*, XXVI, p. 153, translated by H. E. Bolton, *Spanish Exploration in the Southwest*, p. 3, n.l.)

as a hundred to a hundred and fifty thousand. These Indians, of many different tribes and speaking many different languages, were very low in the cultural scale. They lived by hunting and food gathering, and did not practise agriculture. Acorns and shellfish were among the principal items of their meagre diet. They painted their faces and their bodies, and when they wore clothes at all they dressed themselves in animal skins. The climate was kind to them and nature abundant if only they had known better how to use her bounty.

Ulloa, sent out by Cortez in 1539, sailed all round the shores of the Gulf of California and up the Pacific shore of Lower California, thereby demonstrating (though few men at first accepted this fact) that it was a peninsula and not part of an island; and Alarçón, in 1540, had explored enough of the lower Colorado river to prove that it was not the opening of the mythical Straits of Anian. In 1542 Cabrillo's mixed Spanish and Portuguese expedition, still in search of the Straits of Anian, coasted all the way up the Pacific shores of the two Californias – taking formal possession of the territory and discovering San Diego Bay, Santa Monica Bay,[1] and Point Conception (but missing Monterey Bay, Half Moon Bay, and the Golden Gate by standing out too far from the shore) – as far as latitude 42° N, approximately at the mouth of the Rogue river in southern Oregon, where it turned back. This was a remarkable achievement for two tiny vessels, poorly built and badly outfitted, underprovisioned and manned by conscripts and natives.[2] Cabrillo died in the course of the voyage on the island of Juan Rodriguez (now San Miguel Island) in the Santa Barbara Channel group. His lieutenant, Ferello, completed the expedition, which lasted nine months.

The diary of the Cabrillo expedition was not available to Francis Drake when he took the *Golden Hind* up the coast of California nearly three decades later, nor indeed was he aware that Upper California had ever been formally taken possession of by Spain. He was therefore able to claim in all sincerity (and Hakluyt to repeat) that 'the Spaniards hitherto had never been in this part of the country, neither did ever

[1] Prophetically christened 'Bahia de los Fumes' on account of the smog caused by the many camp and signal fires of the Indians on its shores.

[2] See further G. Davidson in Geographical Society of the Pacific, *Transactions and Proceedings*, Second Series, IV (1907), and in *Report of the Superintendant of the U.S. Coast* and Geodetic Survey for 1880 (Washington, D.C.), pp. 160–241: 'An Examination of some of the Early Voyages of Discovery and Exploration on the Northwest Coast of America, from 1539 to 1603.' Davidson was able to identify 'with practical certainty' (says Bolton) some seventy of the points mentioned by the diary of the expedition, which was not published in Spanish until 1857 or in English until 1879.

discover the land by many degrees, to the southwards of this place'.[1] There is this to be said for his claim: that Cabrillo's ships made no landfall north of Point Conception, and that Cabrillo's formal taking of California into the possession of Spain was as far south as the site of the modern city of Ventura. If his expedition did find what was afterwards named Drake's Bay it certainly did not land there or at any point nearer than three hundred miles to the south. In 1579, therefore, it was

literally *terra incognita* on which Drake landed, when 'on the 5. day of June, being in 43. degrees towards the pole Arctic we found the air so cold, that our men, being grievously pinched with the same, complained of the extremity thereof . . . we thought it best for that time to seek the land, and did so, finding it not mountainous, but low plain, till we came within 38. degrees towards the line. In which height it pleased God to send us into a fair and good bay, with a good wind to enter the same.'[2]

[1] Richard Hakluyt, 'The Famous Voyage of Sir Francis Drake into the South Sea, and therehence about the Whole Globe of the earth, begun in the yeere of our Lord, 1577' (in *Divers Voyages,* London, 1582; many subsequent editions).

[2] *Ibid.*

Although 'to the student of ethnology the diary of the Cabrillo expedition is of great interest as the record of the first contact of white men with the Indians of California above latitude 30°'[1] Drake's observation of the Indians he encountered north of San Francisco Bay in the summer of 1579, as recorded in Hakluyt and later amplified in Fletcher's *The World Encompassed*, was more detailed by far. Unlike the Spaniards and Portuguese of Cabrillo's fleet, he did not content himself with merely claiming for his sovereign the land he had reached, but persuaded himself that this land had been freely offered to him by the chieftains of the tribes who welcomed him to its shores. Neither knowing nor probably caring whether this was California or not, or whether it was part of the mainland or an island (though Hakluyt in his 1582 map showed it as the latter), Drake conveniently interpreted the sign-language and the gifts of the friendly and subservient Indian leaders as acts of submission to the English Crown and, naming the land he graciously accepted on behalf of his Sovereign Lady *Nova Albion*, 'set up a monument of our being there, as also of Her Majesty's right and title to the same, upon a fair great post'.[2]

The naming of Nova Albion[3] and the setting up of Drake's plate of brass[4] in the year 1579 came on the eve of England's era of overseas

[1] Bolton, *Spanish Exploration in the Southwest*, p. 12.

[2] Hakluyt, *op. cit.*

[3] 'Our general called this country Nova Albion, and that for two causes; the one in respect of the white banks and cliffs, which lie toward the sea; and the other because it might have some affinity with our country in name, which sometime was so called.' (Hakluyt, *op. cit.*) The name long remained a close rival to Cortez' choice of 'California' to describe this region, and very soon appeared upon maps, sometimes alongside the other (as in Hondius' *Vera totius expeditionis nauticae Description D. Franci* of 1595 – where Upper California is 'Nova Albion' and Lower California is 'California') and sometimes to its exclusion (as in Van Sype's *Le Voyage curieux faict autour du monde par Francais Draek, Admiral D'Engleterre* of 1581 where 'Nova Albio' appears directly to the north of, and in larger letters than 'Nova Hispanie' and in much larger ones than 'Nova France'). The name Nova or New Albion, indeed, continued to be used occasionally on British and French maps right up to the nineteenth century, though Father Kino on his celebrated map of 1705 did not use it, nor, for obvious reasons, did other mapmakers in the service of Spain. Richard Hakluyt, in his revised Latin edition (1587) of Peter Martyr's *De Orbe Novo* (of 1534) had neatly solved the problem by inserting 'NOVA ALBION' in large capitals on the mainland and simply putting 'Puncta California' thus against the extreme southern tip of the peninsula, making it appear a geographical description rather than a territorial claim, though he knew all about Cabrillo's voyage by that date.

[4] In the year 1937, three hundred and forty-eight years later, Dr Herbert E. Bolton announced the rediscovery of the original plate of brass by a young man called Beryle Shinn, while picnicking with his girl-friend on a hill near Greenbrae in Main County, just north of San Francisco Bay. The eminent Director of the Bancroft Library satisfied himself and many (though not all) other authorities concerning

settlement. Six years later the Roanoake experiment in colonization began off the coast of 'Virginia' (actually North Carolina). Had Drake been an empire-builder rather than an empire-looter or had the journey to Nova Albion by sea been shorter and less hazardous, who knows but that Britain's first plantation in the New World might have been on the west rather than on the east coast of North America. The friendly natives, the rich soil and the abundant game of Nova Albion would have made a 'starving time' less likely than in either Virginia or in New England, and much of the subsequent course of North America's history would have been different. What the Spanish response to such a challenge would have been is not hard to imagine, but whether it could have been effective is doubtful. Though thoroughly alarmed by the appearance of Drake in the Pacific and quickly hearing about his journey up the coast of California, Spain did nothing serious about effecting even a token occupation of that coast. Indeed, it was rather the need for a safe port of call for the Manila galleon than the desire to save California from the English that produced, over half a century after Cabrillo, Spain's next serious coastal survey of that area by Vizcaino in 1602.

In 1595 a single vessel expedition, set across the Pacific under Cermeño, had rediscovered Drake's Bay only to be shipwrecked there. At that time Sebastian Vizcaino, a veteran of the Manila trade (Cavendish had plundered his galleon, the *Santa Ana*, in 1588) was unsuccessfully attempting to plant a colony on the inner side of Lower California, but in 1599 the Council of the Indies commissioned him to re-explore the Pacific or outer side of the peninsula and to continue northward as far as he could. By contrast with Cabrillo's little cockle-shells this was a well-equipped expedition of three ships; the chief pilot had been wrecked with Cermeño at Drake's Bay, so he presumably knew what to avoid; a trained cosmographer, Father Ascensión (who also had once been a pilot), was also taken along. Visiting San Diego Bay and going through the Santa Barbara Channel (to each of which they gave their modern names), Vizcaino's fleet sailed into Monterey Bay on

the plate's authenticity, after exhaustive tests. If it is not genuine then it is one of the finest historical fakes of all time, worthy of the genius of a Van Megeren. A photograph of a replica of the plate which now reposes in the Bancroft Library at Berkeley, is reproduced as plate 3a, by courtesy of the Drake Navigators' Guild. An Elizabeth I sixpenny piece has been placed in the jagged hole in the plate. See H. E. Bolton (ed.), *Drake's Plate of Brass: Evidence of his visit to California in 1579* (San Francisco, 1937, California Historical Society Special Publication No. 13), and Colin G. Fink and E. P. Polushkin, *Drake's Plate of Brass Vindicated* (*ibid.*, No. 14, 1938).

15 December 1602, thus discovering not only a good harbour for the Manila galleon but the future capital (under both Spain and Mexico) of the two Californias. Christmas was spent ashore at this lovely if not oversafe bay. 'We found ourselves to be in the best port that could be desired, for, besides being sheltered from all the winds,[1] it has many pines for masts and yards, and live oaks and white oaks, and water in great quantity all near the shore. The climate is fertile, with a climate and soil like that of Castile; there is much wild game . . . and many game birds . . . The land is thickly populated with numberless Indians . . . They appeared to be a gentle and peaceable people.'[2]

From Monterey two of the ships sailed to about 42° and 43° respectively, their crews imagining for a time that buffeting storms were carrying them right into the Straits of Anian; but they turned back past Cape Mendocino (40° 27′ N) and returned separately, in sore distress, to Mexico. They had not either of them made any landfall north of Monterey. Once again the Golden Gate was not observed. Although no settlers were left behind in California Father Ascensión subsequently drew up a report[3] in which its suitability for settlement was stressed and the way in which this should be done described in detail. Somewhat deluded by his conviction (reached some years after the expedition returned) that the Californias constituted a great island separated by a 'Mediterranean Sea' from the mainland of North America, Father Ascensión nevertheless made recommendations which were in effect to be followed over a century and a half later in the actual colonization of Upper California by Spain. 'If it should seem lost to his Majesty he can command that his Spaniards go by land to settle, some at the port of San Diego . . . and others at the Port of Monterey . . . for to endeavour to go by sea to settle there will be a very great and diffi-

[1] It is, in fact, little protected from north-westerly storms, and that coast has been the scene of many shipwrecks since Vizcaino's day, as when the *Star of the West*, out of Liverpool with iron bedsteads and bales of cloth, piled herself upon Point Pinos in 1845, and provided a rich harvest to the beachcombers of the tiny village of Carmel.

[2] Bolton, *Spanish Exploration in the South West* (The Diary of Sebastian Vizcaino, set down by Diego de Santander, Chief Scrivener, Mexico, 8 December, 1603, Chap. XIV), pp. 91–2. This bay must have appeared to the Spaniards, who went on to explore the Carmel river as well, to be very near indeed to the Terrestrial Paradise. All they could find to complain of was the cold, for on New Year's Day of 1603 it snowed and 'the hole from which we were taking water was frozen over more than a palm in thickness'. *Ibid.* (Chap. XV), p. 93.

[3] Dated Mexico, 12 October 1620. *Ibid.*, pp. 104–34.

cult task, on account of the head winds that prevail along the coast, because of the great difficulty of sailing there, as I have seen and experienced.'[1]

The persistent delusion that California was an island was finally demolished only at the beginning of the eighteenth century, by the explorations and writings of one of the most remarkable men ever to have worked and dwelt near that 'rim of Christendom'. This was Father Eusebio Kino (originally 'Kuehn') born near Trent in the South Tirol, and educated at Freiburg and Ingolstadt Universities, a frustrated missionary to the Far East who was sent instead to Mexico by the Order of Jesus. After a brief spell in Lower California he went to the land of the Pima Indians on the mainland of north-west Mexico in 1687 and spent the rest of a most fruitful life there, dying at one of the missions he had founded in what is now Sonora, in the year 1711. His biographer and the rediscoverer, editor, and translator of his principal work,[2] Herbert E. Bolton, says of Kino's achievements, 'In his day Father Kino was the principal personage in his field. It was he who created Pimería Alta as a Spanish province and inspired the occupation of Lower California. Had life and strength been spared him to push with his wonted zeal and skill his projects for conversion and conquest in Alta California, six decades would not have elapsed, perhaps, before his dreams were realized, and then by the Franciscans, after his own order had been expelled from Spanish America. He not only created Pimería Alta, but he first made known its geography. His map is the earliest extant showing the Gila, the Colorado, and southern Arizona, on the basis of actual exploration. His letters, diaries, and map, and his recently rediscovered *History* are indispensable sources for knowledge of the development of geographical ideas concerning California and for the early history of the region south of the Gila on both sides of the Gulf.'[3]

The title of Kino's famous map, *Passage par Terre à la Californie* (first published in Paris in 1705), itself contains a flat denial of Father Ascen-

[1] Dated Mexico, 12 October 1620. *Ibid.*, p. 132.

[2] 'Favores Celestiales de Jesus y de Maria SS^{ma} del Gloriosissimo Apostol de las Yndias,' edited and translated by H. E. Bolton as *Kino's Historical Memoir of Pimería Alta* (2 vols, Cleveland, 1919). Bolton's scholarly biography of Kino, *Rim of Christendom* (1936) (according to John Caughey this 'deserves consideration as his most impressive work' – which is saying something), supplemented Bolton's shorter and more popular *The Padre on Horseback* (1932; paperbound reprint, Chicago, 1963), an absorbing biographical sketch.

[3] Bolton, *Spanish Explorations*, pp. 429–30.

sión's theories. This map[1] had been produced at the pressing request of the Rector of the College of Vera Cruz, who had written 'My Father Eusevio Kino, from Spain persons to whom I cannot excuse myself, asking an exact account of the provinces which your Reverence has discovered, to what degrees of latitude and longitude they extend, the disposition of the nations, what rivers and land they comprise, especially those which slope to California from South and North, and whether California is an island or a peninsula . . . for they write me that upon this matter there is now much controversy in Madrid, with a variety of opinions. If everything can be shown on a map, so much the better.'[2]

The charm and vigour of *Favores Celestiales* cannot be conveyed by summaries and short quotations. 'The thing to do is to read the records of Kino's dozens of itinerant missions, along the map he made of the dry broken mountain masses and the little fertile, irrigated valleys between the Altar and the Gila rivers (Pimería Alta)', as J. B. Brebner says. 'They recapture the inimitable enthusiasm and courage of the man.'[3] This exceedingly muscular Christian, who saw no visions and has never been claimed to have performed a miracle,[4] said, 'In these twenty-one years up to the present time, I have made . . . more than forty expeditions to the north, west, north-west and south-west, of fifty, eighty, one hundred, two hundred and more leagues, sometimes accompanied by other fathers, but most of the time with only my servant and with the [Indian] governors . . . of different rancherias or incipient pueblos from here and from the interior. To the north and north-east I have travelled on different occasions more than one hundred and thirty leagues to Casa Grande, which is a building of the ancients of Montesuma who set out from those lands when they went to found the City of Mexico.'[5] Some of these journeys were thus in the country of the dreaded Apaches, for whom Father Kino had very

[1] Reproduced as plate 3b. A later Kino map (dated 1710) has recently been discovered and published by Ernest J. Burrus, S.J., in *Kino and the Cartography of Northwestern New Spain* (Tucson, 1965).

[2] Bolton, *Spanish Explorations*, p. 436.

[3] J. B. Brebner, *The Explorers of North America 1492–1806* (London, 1933; reprinted in paperbound edition, New York, 1955), pp. 340–1.

[4] 'Kino will never make Saint' was the way in which a very modern western Jesuit, Professor at a college as much renowned for its football team as for its learning, put it to me. And he did not seem to mind.

[5] *Favores Celestiales*, Part V, Book 2, as translated in Bolton, *Spanish Explorations*, p. 443. For Casa Grande (near Coolidge, Arizona), see *supra*, p. 35.

little use. Unless caught very young and promptly removed from Apacheria, they neither could be nor would stay converted. He thought it would be 'very advantageous . . . to restrain the enemies of this province of Sonora, the Hocomes and Apaches' and on one occasion reports with very obvious approval that he 'found Captain Coro [a Christianized Pima Indian Chief] with his people . . . dancing over the scalps of some hostile Hocomes whom he had killed a little while before'.[1] Kino was always very careful to defend his faithful Pimas to the Spanish authorities against accusations of horse-stealing. It was those Apaches again, he would explain.

Father Kino was also careful, wherever possible, to secure independent witnesses to his discoveries. On one occasion (in 1706 when he was sixty-two years old) he lugged an unfortunate Franciscan, Father Manuel de la Oxela who had 'come from Guadalaxara to these provinces of Sonora . . . to ask alms' all the way across to the head of the Gulf of California 'far enough to plainly sight the land route to [Lower] California from the very high hill of Santa Clara' – which he forced Father Manuel to climb – 'traversing in going and returning more than two hundred and fifty leagues'.[2] To the observed fact that 'California has a continental connection with the mainland of New Spain', Kino then made the Franciscan give him a 'sworn certificate', and only then let him return foot- and saddle-sore to Guadalajara, perhaps resolved never again to poach on the preserves of this doughty Jesuit.

Kino's geographical understanding, though at times exuberant (especially where the possibilities of exploiting his own discoveries were concerned) was very advanced for his day. 'And here,' he writes,[3] 'I answer the question asked me in the letter of the Father Rector Juan Hurtasum [of the College of Vera Cruz] as to whether some rivers run into the North Sea or all empty into the Sea of California by saying that this Colorado river, which is the Rio de Norte of the Ancients, carries so much water, it must be that it comes from a high and remote land . . . therefore the other rivers of the land of fifty-two degrees latitude [the Colorado actually rises at about 43° 20′ N] probably have their slope toward the Sea of the North, where Husson [Hudson] wintered.' Kino thus deduced the existence of an Arctic Ocean drainage system in North America. His twenty-five-page treatise 'A Cosmographical Proof that California is not an Island but a Peninsula' has been lost and

[1] *Favores Celestiales*, *op. cit.*, Bolton, *Spanish Explorations*, p. 446.
[2] *Ibid.*, Part V, Book 1, Bolton, p. 435.
[3] *Ibid.*, Part V, Book 2, Bolton, p. 450.

3*a*. Drake's plate of brass, 1579, with an Elizabeth I sixpence inset.

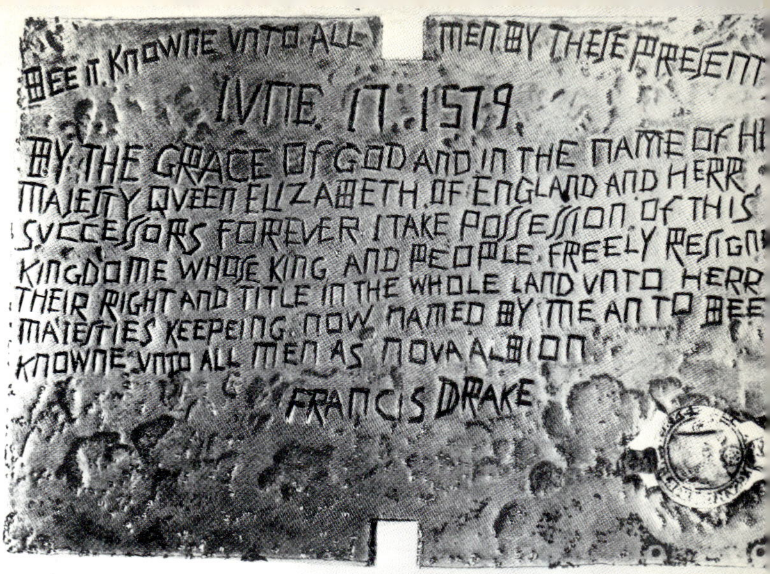

3*b*. Father Kino's map 'A Passage by Land to California', 1705, as published in 1721 in the *Philosophical Transactions of the Royal Society of London*.

4*a*. Acoma, New Mexico, where the Spaniards stormed the mesa top in 1598, and where the Mission San Esteban Rey was begun in 1629.

4*b*. Mission San Xavier del Bac, Papago Reservation, Tucson, Arizona.

was never printed, nor was *Favores Celestiales* published in his own day, but his map ran through many editions and turned up in 1721 in the *Philosophical Transactions* of the Royal Society of London. Nevertheless, British cartographers like Moll continued (as in his map of 1727) to show Lower California as an island, as well, of course, Upper California as 'Nova Albion'.

Kino, who was normally a tolerant and a broad-minded man could not abide that heretic Francis Drake mainly because – according to Kino – he was unsound on the subject of California as an island and on the location of the Straits of Anian: 'Although Drake, in order to carry his point that California was an island, would feign another strait of Anian with another much-talked-of sea of the North over here above California and that he had turned back from his navigation, yet it is all false.'[1] In another place Kino says, 'Drake is very much in error in his fabulous demarcation, in which he very wrongly depicts California as an island'.[2] Nothing is said about the error of Father Ascensión, no heretic, but a Carmelite monk.

If Father Kino had no visions, he dreamed dreams, and his dream of the future (contained in Book 3 of Part V of *Favores Celestiales* written in 1710, the year before his death) is a remarkable declaration of faith, giving a cosmic view of western North America's position and importance such as few men in his day could have achieved:

> By promoting the new conversions of this extensive Pimería, with the favour of Heaven we shall be able shortly to enter upon the reduction and conversion of the neighbouring Apachería, which lies to the north and northeast of us, and extends northwest to the very large Colorado river, or Rio del Norte, above the thirty-fifth, thirty-sixth, and thirty-seventh degrees of latitude and beyond, for we know that it flows from northeast to southwest and issues about ten leagues west of the province of Moqui; for, we having sent messages to those natives up the Colorado river, already they invite us to enter to see them, and already they give us certain reports that soon, in imitation of the rest over here, they will become reduced to our friendship and to the desire of receiving our holy Catholic faith.
>
> By way of the same Apachería, which is in thirty-two degrees latitude, we shall be able, with the divine grace, to enter to trade with New Mexico and with its nearest provinces, Moqui and Zuñi . . . and as far as thirty-seven degrees, in which is found the Villa of Santa Fé

[1] *Favores Celestiales, op. cit.*, Part V, Book 3, Bolton, pp. 454–5.
[2] *Ibid.*, Part V, Book 2, Bolton, pp. 444–5.

of New Mexico; for we have also certain reports that before the revolt of New Mexico the Spaniards of those provinces used to come by way of Apachería to these our most remote Pimas Sobaiporis to barter hatchets, cloth, sackcloth, blankets, *chomite*, knives, etc., for maize.

With the promotion of these new conversions not only will the Christian settlements already formed, new and old, have more protection, and be defended by them, as has been suggested, but at the same time a way will be opened to many other new conquests and new conversions, in many other more remote new lands and nations of this still somewhat unknown North America: as for example, to the northward, to the Gran Teguayo; to the northwest, to the Gran Quibira; and to the west, to California Alta, of this our same latitude of thirty-four, thirty-five, thirty-six degrees, and farther, and to its opposite coast and the South Sea; and to its great Bay of the Eleven Thousand Virgins, to the famous port of Monte Rey, which is in neighboring and fertile lands (and a royal *cédula* came to Sebastian Biscaino that he should go to colonize it), and to the very renowned Cape Mendozino.

At the same time, after having entered to Moqui and New Mexico, to the northwest and the east, it will be possible to have communication with New France, and with the new conquests, conversions, and missions which at present they are making with their glorious and apostolic journeys from east to west. And if we enter to the north and northeast, and afterwards turn to the east, it will be possible to open a way to Europe from these new conquests and conversions of this North America where we are, only half as long as the road which we now have and are accustomed to travel, by way of the City of Mexico and the Port of Vera Cruz; for if the one road is much more than two thousand leagues, the other will be little more than a thousand.

Just as to the northeast and east of this North America we shall be able to have a shorter road to Europe, in the same way we shall be able to have by the northwest and the west a convenient land route to Asia . . . and the land nearest to Japan; and afterward the narrow Strait of Anian, which is no more than ten or twelve leagues across, and has the convenience of an island in the middle by which to pass to Great Tartary, and from there to Great China.

The realistic Kino concludes Book 3 with a valedictory protest against the myth-makers. 'If we continue with the promotion and advancement of these new conversions we shall be able to continue to make correct maps of this North America, the greater part of which has hitherto been unknown, or practically unknown, for some ancients blot the map with so many such errors and with such unreal grandeurs and feigned riches as a crowned king whom they carry on chairs of gold, with walled cities, lakes of quicksilver, of gold, of amber and of corals.' How can all this nonsense be compared with Kino's own actual achievements (which he goes on to describe in Book 4)? Besides 'The salvation of so many souls in the very fertile and pleasant lands and valleys of these new conquests and conversions', there are already 'very rich and abundant fields, plantings and crops of wheat, maize, frijoles, chick-peas, beans, lentils . . . vineyards . . . reed brakes of sweet cane . . . many Castilian fruit-trees, all sorts of garden stuff . . . Castilian roses, white lilies . . . very good timber for all kinds of building . . . plentiful ranches', and – as a sop to the old Adam – 'many good veins of mineral lands bearing gold and silver; and in the neighbourhood and even in sight of these new missions and new conversions some very good mining camps' – so that God and Mammon could continue to co-exist.

By the year 1711 Kino and his fellow-workers had advanced the frontier of Spain and of Christendom significantly, but not very extensively, up through north-western Mexico into what is now southern Arizona. He was in every sense, therefore, one of the true founders of the civilization of the American West. The traveller who today circles for a landing at the Municipal Airport of Tucson, Arizona, catches a slanting view of the mission of San Xavier del Bac, founded by Father Kino in the year 1692, though the mission church which exists today was rebuilt in 1783 on the ruins of the original one destroyed in the Pima rising of 1750. The Papago Indians, long since converted to Christianity, live on their reservation around the mission and attend its school, now run by the Franciscan fathers who succeeded the Jesuits there when the Order to which Kino had belonged was dissolved.

The direction in which Father Ascensión in 1620, and Father Kino in 1710 (reinforced by much more reliable geographical knowledge) had pointed, was not to be followed by Spanish colonists and empire-builders until 1769.

Lower California, the conversion of which had also been Kino's ardent desire, though he never worked there himself in his later days, proved extremely hard to settle, even in the eighteenth century. By 1768 the Jesuits had established fourteen scattered missions there, as far up as 20° N. These, too, were inherited by the Franciscans, and later handed over to the Dominicans. It was a barren and inhospitable peninsula and nearly two hundred years later is sparse of population, lacking a proper transportation network and still mainly of interest only to fishermen. But it served as a base for the final settlement of Upper California, a much more promising – if not indeed *the* promised – land, and but for the Jesuits' endeavours there, and the publicity they gave to them,[1] the securing of a foothold in the more northerly colony might have been considerably more delayed, for after the Pima rebellion of 1751 and a series of subsequent Indian troubles in Pimería Alta the approach by land towards San Diego had to be from Lower California.

The Spanish colonization of Upper California is one of the best-documented and most frequently retold stories in the whole history of Western America. Only its most salient features need here be repeated. The stimulus once more, as in Texas, was the fear of the foreigner getting there first. The Russians were already trading in Alaska; the English had returned to Pacific waters and had captured the Manila galleon in 1742; it was thought that both powers had designs on California. The man who blue-printed their circumvention was José de Galvez, appointed *Visitador General* of New Spain in 1765 by that exceptionally energetic Spanish Bourbon Carlos III. In 1769 he sent out expeditions by land and sea, to rendezvous at San Diego Bay. Starting out from Velicitá in Lower California the first overland expedition (under Fernando de Rivera and Father Crespí) reached San Diego without undue difficulty on 14 May, and the second (under Gaspar de Portolá and Father Serra) after greater hardships, for the dry season had commenced, on 1 July. Portolá, a really tough character, was off again on 14 July in search of Monterey Bay. Following approximately the course of the still tortuous California State Highway 1, it took him until 18 October to find Monterey, and then he did not recognize it from the landward side as the same harbour that Vizcaino and Father Ascensión had described and the Manila galleons had occasionally visited. So he pushed on northward and stumbled upon a much greater discovery – San Francisco Bay – first seeing it from its southern, shallow end, near the site of the present city of San José. Only in May 1770 was Monterey first properly identified and settled. 'I proceeded to erect a fort to occupy and defend the port from the atrocities of the Russians,' reported Portolá somewhat melodramatically.[2]

[1] Father A. M. Burriel's *Noticia de la California* (Madrid, 1757) was immediately translated into English as *A Natural and Civil History of California* (London, 1759). It dealt only with the peninsula.

[2] See H. E. Bolton (ed.), *Historical Memoirs of New California by Fray Francisco Palóu, O.F.M.* (4 vols, Berkeley, 1926), for the Portolá diary and other accounts of this expedition.

Meanwhile a presidio and a Franciscan mission had been founded at San Diego, and Father Serra established the mission of San Carlos Borromeo at the mouth of the Carmel river near Monterey, making it the headquarters of the missions of Upper California, during the summer of 1770. Here he remained until he died in 1784, establishing new missions and bringing Christianity and some civilization to thousands of Indians along the five hundred miles of coast, and in some of the inland valleys, all the way from San Diego to San Francisco Bay. By the

time of Serra's death[1] the colonization of Upper California with the Franciscan mission as its main instrument was an accomplished fact and a resounding success.

The overland route was rendered safer, quicker and more comfortable before the mid-seventies of the eighteenth century, by the pioneering work of Juan Bautista de Anza and Father Francisco Garcés, who in 1774 set out from San Xavier del Bac in Pimería Alta (now at last repacified), past the other Kino missions of northern Sonora to Sonóita, to the Gila river and the lower Colorado, finally to burst through the Sierras into the Santa Ana river valley and emerge, to everybody's surprise, at the recently founded mission of San Gabriel, some twenty miles east of the centre of the present city of Los Angeles. The next year

[1] Father Junipera Serra, unlike Kino, is now well on his way to sainthood. Copies of the supporting documentation, assiduously collected at the Santa Barbara mission by Father Maynard Geiger, O.F.M., are now being examined in Rome. The year 1969 is an obvious target for the beatification, at least, of Father Serra.

Anza led a larger expedition, complete with civilian colonists, to San Francisco Bay.[1] The mission of San Francis of Assisi (or Dolores) was built in what is now mid-town San Francisco in 1776. It still stands, having survived the many fires of the 1850s and the great earthquake and fire of 1906 which destroyed many more modern buildings.

By the late eighteenth century Spain was short of manpower as well as wealth. Her resources in the Indies as well as in Europe were stretched to the utmost. Luckily for her the way in which she colonized Upper California, her empire's last successful fling in the New World, was the most economical possible. A few able officers and administrators, a few devoted Franciscan fathers, a few companies of soldiers and several hundred colonists were all that she needed. She could not have provided more. The three institutions of presidio, mission, and pueblo were used to pacify and convert the Indians and to set them to work. There was nothing spectacular about this technique of colonization; it made nobody rich quickly; the settlements grew but slowly; but it worked. Two years after Father Serra's death, and after Anza had departed to govern New Mexico, a French exploring and scientific expedition, led by the Comte de la Pérouse, visited several of the Spanish establishments in Upper California, and described the colony in its report. Said La Pérouse,[2] 'A lieutenant-colonel who resides at Monterey is governor of the two Californias. His domain is more than eight hundred leagues in extent, but his true subordinates are 282 cavalrymen who must form the garrison of five little forts and furnish squads of four or five men at each of the twenty-five missions or parishes established in Old and New California. So small a force controls about fifty thousand Indians roving over this vast part of America, of whom about ten thousand have embraced Christianity . . . New California, in spite of its great distance from Mexico, seems to me to possess infinitely more advantages . . . But not until 1770 [*sic*] did the Franciscans establish the first mission here. There are now ten of them, in which they count 5,143 Indian converts . . . New California, in spite of its fertility, does not yet have a single agricultural settler [*Habitant*]. A few soldiers married to Indian women living in the forts or scattered

[1] See H. E. Bolton (ed.), *Anza's California Expeditions* (5 vols, Berkeley, 1930).

[2] *Voyage de La Pérouse autour du monde* (Paris, 1797). The translation used is that made by Professor John W. Caughey for his contribution to *Problems in American History* (eds R. W. Leopold and A. S. Link, New York, 1952), pp. 6–16, and in his *California Heritage* (with Laree Caughey, San Francisco, 1962), pp. 77–82, and is here reprinted with permission.

out as squads of guards at the different missions are the only representatives of Spain in this part of America. California is no less attractive than Virginia on the other side of the continent, except that it is farther from Europe. Proximity to Asia should make up for that . . .'

La Pérouse's description of life at the Carmel mission as it was in 1786 could have applied to most of the other nine missions established at that time, except perhaps the newly founded one at Santa Barbara, only opened, as he noted, on 3 September of that year:

> The fathers from Mission San Carlos, two leagues from Monterey, came to the presidio. They were as obliging to us as were the officers of the fort and the two frigates. They invited us to go and dine with them and promised to help us know in detail the régime of their missions, the mode of life of the Indians, their arts, their new customs, and in general all that could interest the curiosity of travellers. . . .
>
> Before entering the church we had crossed a plaza where Indians of both sexes were ranged in line. Their expressions revealed no astonishment and left us no doubt that we were the subject of their conversation during the rest of the day. The church is a regular fort, although covered with thatch. It is dedicated to St Charles and ornamented with reasonably good pictures, copies of Italian originals. . . . On leaving the church we passed the same file of Indians; they had not left their post during the *Te Deum*. The children were a little apart and formed in groups before the house of the missionaries, which faces the church, together with the storerooms. On the right is the Indian village, consisting of about fifty huts which lodge the 740 persons of both sexes, children included, who make up Mission San Carlos, or of Monterey.
>
> These huts are the most miserable that one could find anywhere. They are round, six feet in diameter by four in height. Sticks of the size of an arm, fixed in the ground and coming together in an arch at the top, are the framework. Eight or ten bundles of straw badly arranged on these sticks more or less protect the occupants from the wind or rain. When the weather is fair, these huts are left half uncovered. The only precaution is to have two or three bundles of straw in reserve.
>
> The exhortations of the missionaries have never been able to change the general architecture of the two Californias. The Indians say that they like the open air, that it is better to set fire to your house whenever you are eaten up by too many fleas, and to be able to build another in less than two hours. The wild Indians, who change camp frequently, like the hunting Indians, have another good reason. . . .
>
> The monks, by their answers to our questions, left us ignorant of

nothing about the régime, which is a sort of religious community, for no other name can be given to the rules that they have established. They are the temporal as well as the spiritual rulers; the products of the land are entrusted to their control.

There are seven hours' work a day, two hours of prayer, and four or five on Sundays and feast days which are consecrated entirely to repose and divine worship. Corporal punishment is inflicted on Indians of both sexes who neglect the exercises of piety, and several sins which in Europe are punished only by divine justice are here punished with irons or the stocks. To revert to the comparison with the religious communities, the moment that a neophyte has been baptized it is as though he had pronounced eternal vows. If he runs away to return to the home of his relatives in the rancherías [the wild villages], he is asked three times to return and if he refuses the missionaries call on the authority to send soldiers to take him from the bosom of his family and bring him back to the mission where he is condemned to receive a certain number of lashes. These people have so little courage that they never offer any resistance to three or four soldiers who in this fashion violate so obviously their rights, and the custom against which reason protests so strongly is maintained because the theologians have decided that they cannot conscienciously administer baptism lightly, and the government serves as a sort of godfather, aiding their perseverance. . . .

We wished to witness the distribution that is made at each meal, and as all the days are the same in this religious order, in tracing the history of one of these days, the reader will have that of the entire year.

The Indians, as also the missionaries, rise with the sun. They go to prayers and mass, which lasts an hour. During that time there is being prepared in the middle of the plaza, in three great kettles, out of barley which has been roasted before being ground, that kind of gruel which the Indians call *atole*, of which they are most fond, although it is not seasoned with butter or salt and would be for us a most insipid meal.

Each hut sends to get the ration for all its people in a bark vase [an urn-shaped basket]. There is no confusion or disorder, and when the caldrons are empty, they distribute the scrapings to the children who have best learned the catechism lessons. The meal lasts three quarters of an hour, after which they all go to their work. Some go to till the land with oxen, others work in the garden, each according to the needs of the community and always under the supervision of one or two of the religious.

The women are only charged with the care of their households and of their children and to roast and grind the grains. This operation is most laborious and tedious, because they have no other means but to crush the grain on a stone with a pestle. M. de Langle, observing this operation, presented his mill to the missionaries. It would be difficult to render them a greater service. With it four women can do the work of a hundred. It will release time for spinning wool and for weaving rough cloth. But thus far the padres, more occupied with heavenly than worldly interests, have neglected to introduce even the most useful arts. They are so ascetic themselves, that they have not a single chamber with heat, although the winter here is sometimes rigorous. The greatest anchorites never practised a more edifying life.

At noon the bells announce dinner. The Indians leave their work and send for their ration in the same basket as for breakfast. This second stew is thicker than the first, having wheat, corn, peas, and beans added to it. The Indians call it *pozole*. They go back to work from two o'clock to four or five. They then go to evening prayers, which last about an hour, and then follows another ration of *atole* like that at breakfast. These three distributions subsist a large number of Indians. Perhaps we should adopt this most economical soup in our years of famine. Some seasoning could be added to it. The whole science of this cuisine is in roasting the grain before grinding it. As the Indian women have no pottery or metal vessels for this operation, they do it with basketry trays over glowing coals. They turn the trays with such dexterity and quickness that they manage to puff and crack the grains without singeing the tray, though it is most combustible. The best roasted coffee does not approach the perfection of toasting that the Indians know how to give their grain. It is distributed [for roasting] every morning, and the least irregularity with the issue is punished with the lash, but it is rare that anyone exposes herself to such punishment.

These punishments are administered by Indian magistrates called *caciques*. In each mission there are three, chosen by the people from those whom the missionaries have not excluded. To give a fair idea of the office we should say that these caciques, like the heads of the quarters, are passive instruments carrying out the wishes of their superiors, and their principal functions are to serve as beadles in the church and to maintain order and rectitude there. The women are never whipped in public but in a closed room far enough removed so that their cries will not by any chance rouse a compassion which might lead the men to revolt. The latter, on the contrary, are exposed to the view of all their fellows so that their punishment may serve as an example. They usually beg for mercy; the executor then reduces the force of the blows, but the number is always irrevocably fixed.

The rewards are small distributions of grain, which they make into small biscuits cooked on the coals. On great feast days the ration is beef. Many eat it raw, especially the fat, which to them is as delicious as excellent butter or the best cheese. They skin the animals with dispatch, and if they are fat, they are like crows croaking their pleasure and devouring immediately the parts of which they are most fond.

They are often allowed to hunt and fish, and on their return they customarily give the missionaries a present of fish or game, proportioning the amount to what is necessary, increasing it if they know that guests are visiting their superiors At their huts the women raise some chickens, giving the eggs to their children. These chickens belong to the Indians, as do their clothes and the other small things of the household and the chase. No instances of thievery have ever occurred among them, although their doors consist only of a bundle of straw placed across the entrance when all the occupants are away.

These customs may seem patriarchal to some of our readers. They will not consider that any of these dwellings had any object to tempt the cupidity of the neighbors. The Indians' nourishment is assured; they have no other need but to give birth to other beings who must be as stupid as they.

The men at the missions have made a greater sacrifice to Christianity than the women, because polygamy was permitted and it was the usage to marry all the sisters of a family. The women, on the contrary, have acquired the advantage of receiving exclusively the favors of one man. . . .

The missionaries have constituted themselves as guardians of female virtue. An hour after supper, they lock up all those whose husbands are absent and all the girls over nine years of age, and until morning keep them under the surveillance of matrons. Even these precautions are not always sufficient. We saw men in the stocks and women in irons for having eluded the vigilance of these female arguses for whom two eyes were not enough.

The converted Indians have kept all the old usages that their new religion does not prohibit: the same huts, the same games, the same costumes. The richest consists of a cloak of otter skins which covers the loins and reaches to the knees. The lazier have only a scrap of cloth which the mission has furnished to cover their nakedness and a small mantle of rabbitskin covering their shoulders and reaching only to the waist. The rest of the body is absolutely bare, even the head, although some have straw hats, very neatly plaited.

The women's garb is a cloak of poorly tanned deerskin. Those at the mission are in the habit of making a corselet with sleeves. It is their only garment except a small apron of rushes and a deerskin skirt which covers the loins and reaches to the knee. The young girls under nine wear only a simple girdle and the boys go naked.

When Captain Vancouver came to Monterey in the 1790s and a Russian scientific expedition to San Francisco Bay a decade later their descriptions of these places were very similar to that of La Pérouse. The missions of Alta California, which grew in number to twenty-one, continued to thrive until the 1830s, when their secularization by the Mexican government soon brought this first, pastoral and (for the Spaniards living there at least) almost idyllic phase of the country's history to an end.

No other new colony was founded by Spain in the eighteenth century, for Louisiana came to her ready-made in 1762 and she was to lose it again in 1801, though she regained Florida in 1783. New Mexico she retained but did not extend (despite the heroic explorations of Fathers Garcéz and Escalante in the seventies). Texas she almost lost. In the newly opening territory west of the Missouri she proved less enterprising than the British, the French or the Americans.[1] Her star of empire had almost set.

[1] See Chapter IV.

CHAPTER IV

Exploring the Louisiana Purchase: Lewis and Clark, Pike and Long

The Americans, who were to be the ultimate inheritors of the whole of that great region, still did not have sovereignty over one inch of the trans-Mississippi West in the year 1800; nor by that date had they played any significant part in its exploration. This had been the work of Frenchmen, Spaniards, and British and French Canadians. In 1792, nine years after the Independence of the U.S.A. was recognized by Britain, the little ship *Columbia* of the American Captain Gray had carried the Stars and Stripes of the new nation into the mouth of that great river of the West, which now bears his ship's name, ahead of the flag of any other country; yet it had been the Spaniard Ulloa who first had found the mouth of the Colorado and circumnavigated the Gulf of California or 'Sea of Cortez'. Another Spaniard, De Soto, had been the first white man to find that 'River of the Holy Spirit' which is now the Mississippi; and a Frenchman, La Salle, was the first to traverse it from its upper reaches, west of the Great Lakes, to its delta on the Gulf of Mexico (and to rename it the Colbert). De Soto and Coronado respectively had explored the lower and the upper Arkansas river valley and had come within about three hundred miles of each other – and of spanning the continent.

As early as 1739 two intrepid Frenchmen, the Mallet brothers, had pioneered the route up the Platte river, far west of the mountains, which later became the well-beaten Santa Fé Trail. They had returned to French Louisiana by way of the Canadian river, the name which it has borne ever since to commemorate their exploit. Though it flows from its source in New Mexico, through the Panhandle of Texas, and Oklahoma, to its confluence with the Arkansas, it is still 'the river of the Canadians' Pierre and Paul Mallet.[1]

Nor was the 'Wide Missouri' – the only river which had ever shown

[1] J. B. Thorburn, in *Chronicles of Oklahoma*, Vol. VI, No. 2, June 1922, pp. 181–5, expounds the argument against the validity of other explanations of the name of the Canadian River of the South. See Brebner, *op. cit.*, p. 287.

real promise of leading to a practicable route, by water and easy portages (as it was believed) to the far Pacific Ocean or 'South Sea or to the fabulous North-west Passage to Asia' – first seen and traversed by the Americans. Frenchmen again had been there first. Jolliet and Marquette had crossed its mouth where it empties into the Mississippi one day in 1673 and had been told by local Indians that, up its broad valley, California was not so very far away; in addition to their explorations in Canada as far west as Manitoba, La Vérendrye and his sons had struck overland across the prairies of what are now Minnesota and the Dakotas to the Upper Missouri and traded with the Mandan Indian villages, where for so long men were to believe that the 'Welsh Indians' of Prince Madoc's 'migration' dwelt. In 1743 they had even reached the Badlands of South Dakota and seen (but not traversed) the Black Hills. Some would even claim that what they saw were the most easterly peaks of the Rockies.[1]

Last but by no means least, the first man to travel overland from the Middle-Western settlements all the way to the Pacific Ocean was Alexander Mackenzie, a Scots Canadian. Mackenzie (later Sir Alexander Mackenzie) led several important expeditions in the service of the North-west Company, travelling mostly by canoe and accompanied only by Indian guides. Part of the way to the Pacific having been blazed for him by such men as Hendaye, Hearne, and Peter Pond, Mackenzie reached Puget Sound on the Pacific shore of North America via the Fraser river 'from Canada, by land, the 22nd July, 1793' (as he commemorated his achievement in a carving on a rock on the Sound); he had not discovered a route that could be followed by any of the mass migrations of the nineteenth century, but he had beaten Lewis and Clark – the first Americans, as far as is known, to reach the Pacific overland – by more than a decade.

It was, indeed, the publication of Alexander Mackenzie's book *Voyages from Montreal through the Continent of North America* (London, 1801) which inspired Thomas Jefferson, then President of the United States, to organize the Lewis and Clark expedition. This was by no means the earliest attempt of this first American imperialist to put his countrymen to the forefront of the opening up of the trans-Mississippi West, and within a decade he had so far succeeded that American explorers had taken their place on at least an equal footing with the

[1] L. J. Burpee (ed. and trans.), *Journals and Letters of La Vérendrye and his Sons*, Champlain Society, Toronto, 1927, and A. S. Norton in *Canadian Hist. Review*, Vol. IV, pt 4, December 1928. See Brebner, *op. cit.* p. 300 ff.

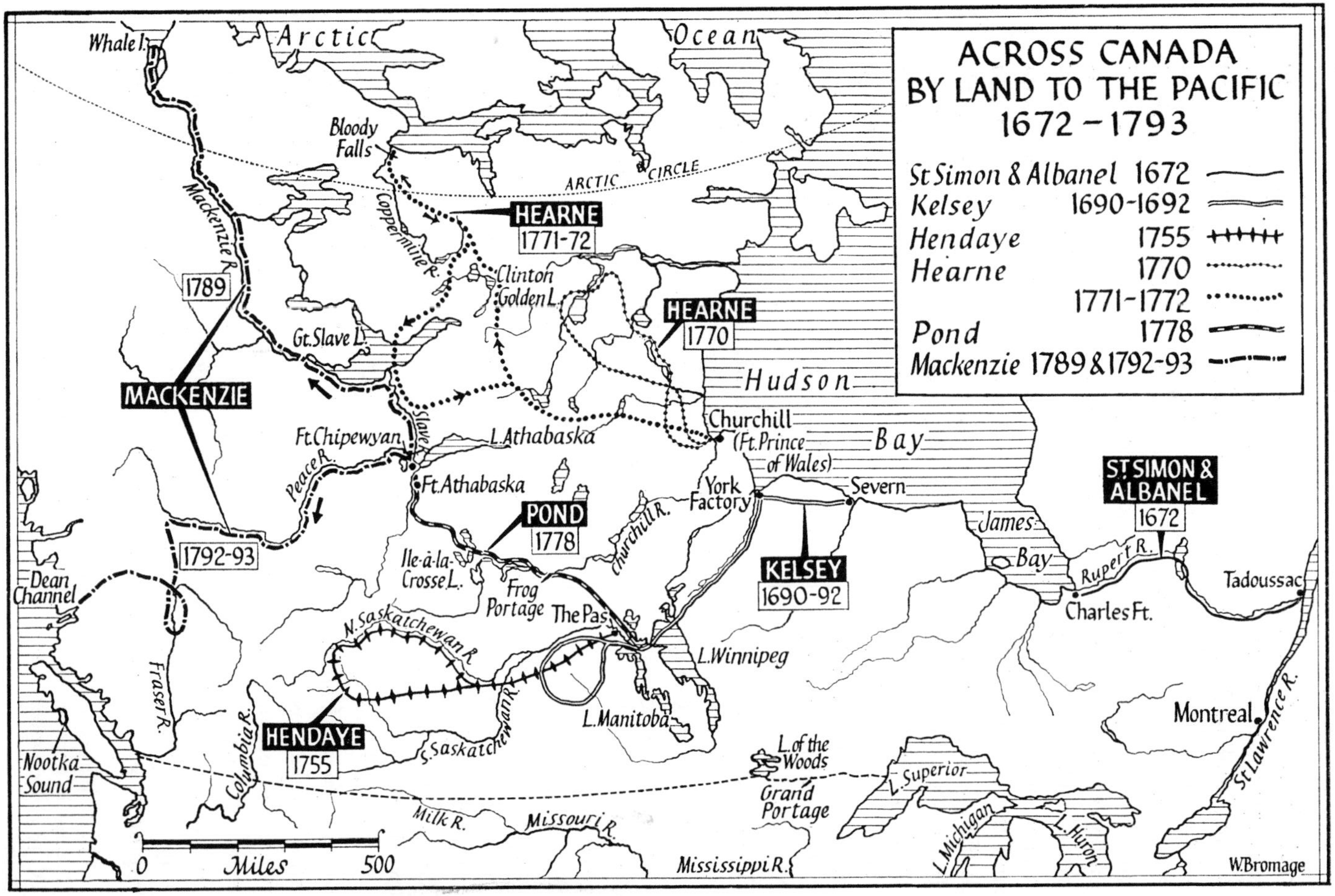

ACROSS CANADA
BY LAND TO THE PACIFIC
1672 – 1793
St Simon & Albanel 1672
Kelsey 1690-1692
Hendaye 1755
Hearne 1770
1771-1772
Pond 1778
Mackenzie 1789 & 1792-93
Arctic
Ocean
Whale I.
Bloody Falls
ARCTIC CIRCLE
HEARNE 1771-72
Coppermine R.
Clinton Golden L.
HEARNE 1770
Mackenzie R.
1789
Gt. Slave L.
Hudson
MACKENZIE
Churchill (Ft. Prince of Wales)
Bay
Ft. Chipewyan
Slave R.
L. Athabaska
Peace R.
Ft. Athabaska
York Factory
Severn
ST. SIMON & ALBANEL
1672
POND
1778
Churchill R.
James
Bay
Rupert R.
1792-93
KELSEY
1690-92
Tadoussac
Dean Channel
Ile-à-la-Crosse L.
Frog Portage
The Pas
Charles Ft.
N. Saskatchewan R.
L. Winnipeg
Fraser R.
S. Saskatchewan R.
L. Manitoba
Montreal
Columbia R.
HENDAYE
1755
L. of the Woods
Grand Portage
L. Superior
St. Lawrence R.
Nootka Sound
Milk R.
Missouri R.
L. Michigan
L. Huron
0
Miles
500
Mississippi R.
W. Bromage

others. They were to dominate the nineteenth century exploration and exploitation of the trans-Mississippi West.

Earlier, in the eighteenth century, Bishop Berkeley had used the word 'Empire' quite innocuously in 'Westward the Course of Empire takes its way', and Jedediah Morse, in his *American Geography* (1789), spoke more purposefully of 'the American Empire which will eventually comprehend millions of souls west of the Mississippi'. Jefferson, and even more so his disciple John Quincy Adams, believed in the expansion of the American people (though not necessarily of the sovereignty of the United States under the Constitution of 1787) over all the American continent, and so were among the first to strike a note which was to be banged very hard indeed in the age of 'Manifest Destiny',[1] during the 1840s.

From a very early date Thomas Jefferson had been interested in American expansion westward beyond the limits of the thirteen colonies. He was a boy of seven when Dr Walker, 'an English chap', became in 1750 'the first white man through the Cumberland Gap' (not so very far from Jefferson's birthplace at Shadwell in upstate Virginia); he was a man of thirty-two when in 1775 Daniel Boone led his party of emigrants through it into Kentucky in defiance of the British Royal Proclamation of 1763; and, at thirty-three, partially inspired by such events, he drafted the Declaration of Independence, which contains a protest against the hated Proclamation line, a barrier that was equally vehemently attacked, both for its injustice and for its impracticability, by Edmund Burke in Parliament at Westminster. In 1785, when American Minister to France, Jefferson sent John Paul Jones to spy out the plans of the Comte de la Pérouse, then preparing his circumnavigation of the globe,[2] and soon afterwards he dispatched John Ledyard (a corporal of Marines under Captain Cook but now a loyal American) across Siberia to nose out a land route from the Pacific to the Atlantic. 'Wrong-Way Ledyard' almost reached Kamchatka before Catherine the Great sent him packing back under escort to the Polish border. 'Thus failed the first attempt to explore the western part of our northern continent,' wrote Jefferson[3] many years later. He meant the first American attempt.

[1] See below, Chapter VII.

[2] J. P. Boyd (ed.), *The Jefferson Papers*, Vol. VIII, p. 373 ff.

[3] In his 'Memoir of Meriwether Lewis' in *The History of the Lewis and Clark Expedition* (4 vols, ed. E. Coues, New York, 1893), Vol. I, pp. xviii–xix. See also Boyd, *Jefferson Papers*, Vol. X, pp. 220–2, 315–16, 548–9, and Vol XI, pp. 216–18 and 637–9; and R. Van Alstyne, *The Rising American Empire* (Oxford, 1960), pp. 79–80, whose citation of the above references is here acknowledged.

Jefferson went on trying. In the early 1790s, when Secretary of State, he was encouraging George Rogers Clark to explore beyond the Mississippi border of the U.S.A., and the French scientist Michaux (who was to be assisted by a young protégé of Jefferson's, Lieutenant Meriwether Lewis) to make an expedition up the Missouri and over the continental divide to the Pacific ostensibly under the patronage of the American Philosophical Society of Philadelphia. Michaux was to find 'the shortest and most convenient route of communication between the United States and the Pacific Ocean, within the temperate latitudes'; unknown to Jefferson and to Michaux when these instructions were issued in April 1793, Captain Grey had already discovered the mouth of the Columbia river from the sea and Mackenzie was well on his way to Puget Sound overland. Jefferson, Michaux, and the unfortunate George Rogers Clark (no longer supported by his French backers, who had made him a General of the Republic one and indivisible) were left at the post, and neither projected expedition even crossed the Mississippi.

Early in 1801 Jefferson learned through his agents the momentous news that France had regained sovereignty over Louisiana. This huge territory, comprising upwards of a third of the area of what is now the continental United States (excluding Alaska) had been handed over to Spain in 1762 by its French founders. Spain had, in her years of decline, done little to develop it, even under the relatively enterprising King Carlos III and the more energetic governors he appointed, but she did cling tenaciously to the strategic settlement of New Orleans – a city which, nevertheless, retained much of its French character – at the mouth of the Mississippi. While Spain failed to keep the Americans from establishing their boundary on that river down to the 31st degree of latitude in 1783 she did bottle them off from the Gulf of Mexico by regaining Florida from Great Britain in that same year. But as the Americans pushed westward into Kentucky and Tennessee, down the Ohio river on their flatboats, to colonize the Ohio, Indiana, and Illinois territories north and west of the river, and along the Natchez Trace[1] to open up new cotton and trading country beyond the Carolinas and Georgia, they found the Mississippi river, as an artery of trade and commerce, becoming even more important to them. Spain's various attempts to keep the Americans from trading down the Mississippi to the Gulf had never been very effective, and were brought

[1] The road from Nashville, Tennessee, to Natchez on the Mississippi, made with the aid of federal funds. See J. Daniels, *The Devil's Backbone* (New York, 1962)

to a temporary end by the terms of Pinckney's Treaty of 1794 which settled the U.S.–Spanish boundary. Now, less than a decade later, Jefferson found that New Orleans and the river's mouth, in addition to its huge hinterland, had been transferred back from the effete hands of Spain into the ruthlessly ambitious control of the young general Bonaparte, just returned from his misadventures on the Nile in search of newer worlds to conquer, and recently established, under the thin disguise of 'First Consul', as absolute dictator of a reinvigorated France, more powerful than she had been since the middle years of Louis XIV. The prospect for the infant United States was alarming. Bonaparte was known to have the intention of sending an army to the Mississippi valley, and the expedition to the island of Santo Domingo – which could act as a stepping stone – was already in being. He might easily reconquer Canada and then push his empire to the Rocky Mountains and even beyond. Had not La Pérouse surveyed the shores of the Pacific and the posthumous report of his voyage been published by the Convention? The expansion of the United States might thus easily be strangled in infancy.

Despite his great love for France, which had not been materially shaken by the plots of Citizen Genet and the cooling of the alliance with that country in the 1790s, Jefferson fully recognized the menace which faced the future of the United States. France was now her rival and her potential enemy on her home ground and from end to end of the Father of the Waters. If necessary a close if unwelcome alliance with the Great Britain of George III itself must be sought in order to counteract this menace. Jefferson resorted at first to psychological warfare. That he might be forced to seek a close alliance with Great Britain was 'leaked' through the Franco-American gunpowder manufacturer Dupont de Nemours to government circles in Paris. When the First Consul read Jefferson's 'confidential' opinion – 'the day that France takes possession of New Orleans . . . seals the union of two nations who in conjunction can maintain exclusive possession of the ocean. From that moment we must marry ourselves to the British fleet and nation' – he must have been strengthened in his already half-formed resolve to cut his losses in the New World, as he had already done in the Levant, and concentrate on the sufficiently formidable task of becoming the Master of Europe. His lightning *volte-face*, when he offered all Louisiana to the American plenipotentiaries Livingston and Monroe, through his ministers Talleyrand and Marbois, resulted in the transfer of the great territory to the United States for a mere consideration of $15 million.

When asked to define the limits of this cession Talleyrand simply said, 'You have a noble bargain, make the most that you can of it.'[1] Jefferson did exactly that.

On 8 Frimaire of the Year XII of the Republic (30 November 1803) the city of New Orleans was formally handed over by France to her 'loyal and faithful ally' (so ran the proclamation), the United States of America. News travelled more slowly to the Upper Mississippi and it was not until 9 March 1804 that St Louis was transferred. By then Meriwether Lewis and William Clark had reached that frontier outpost and witnessed the ceremony; for they were the men through whom Jefferson was to realize his dream of reaching the Pacific Ocean, although to his way of thinking, the Lewis and Clark expedition (as it came to be called) was 'twenty years behind its schedule'.[2]

'The object of your mission,' ran Jefferson's instructions to Lewis and Clark, 'is to explore the Missouri river, and such principal stream of it, as, by its course and communication with the waters of the Pacific, may offer the most direct and practicable water communication across this continent for the purposes of commerce.' The Louisiana Purchase now meant, of course, that the first year of exploration would be on American soil instead of the whole of it outside United States' sovereignty.

On 14 May 1804 Lewis and Clark set off from St Louis up the Missouri valley. By 3 August they reached and named Council Bluffs, because there they went into council with the dangerous and incalculable Sioux Indians, whose hunting grounds they would have to traverse. They reached the villages of the more friendly and settled Mandans in time to go into winter quarters among them. Setting out again in April 1805 it took them until November of that year to reach their goal, the shore of the Pacific Ocean.

One day during the summer of 1955, while I was driving from Chicago to California, I halted about noon at an historic spot a few miles west of Bozeman in the State of Montana, known as Three Forks. Almost exactly a hundred and fifty years earlier, Meriwether Lewis and William Clark reached this same place. The scene they observed on that summer day in the year 1805 could have been little different from the one I saw a century and a half later. A wide plain surrounded by

[1] See B. Hermann, *The Louisiana Purchase* (U.S. Government Printing Office, Washington, D.C., 1898), for details, documentation and maps of the Purchase.

[2] Van Alstyne, *The Rising American Empire*, p. 80.

rolling and lightly wooded hills stretched to the horizon, with not a human habitation in sight. Where the three moderate-sized streams came together to make the one big Missouri river, there were sand-bars; and below their point of confluence stood low bluffs of bare rock. On the narrow V-shaped spit of land between the Madison and the Gallatin rivers I found the inscriptions on the three historical markers put up by the State of Montana. On the centre one I read:

WHERE THE MISSOURI BEGINS

> The Lewis and Clark Expedition, leaving St Louis . . .
> May 14, 1804, traveling by boats up the
> Missouri River into unexplored country,
> reached here July 27, 1805. They had arrived at their
> first objective, fulfilling a vital function of their
> mission. . . .
> Caution is taken to preserve this part of the area just
> as nature carved it, the way it must have been when
> Lewis and Clark first saw it . . .

LET NO MAN DESTROY IT

I sat down on the bank and searched in my copy of the *Journals of Lewis and Clark* to find the words in which they themselves had described the scene. William Clark had written: 'A fine morning. We proceeded on a few miles to the three forks of the Missouri. Those three forks are nearly of a size; the North fork appears to have the most water and must be considered as the one best calculated for us to ascend.' And Meriwether Lewis commented: 'Both Captain Clark and myself correspond in opinion with respect to the impropriety of calling either of these streams the Missouri, and accordingly agreed to name them after the President of the United States and the Secretaries of the Treasury and State, having previously named one river in honour of the Secretaries of War and Navy. In pursuance of this resolution we called the South West fork Jefferson's River, in honor of that illustrious personage Thomas Jefferson (*the author of our enterprise*). The Middle fork we called Madison's River in honor of James Madison, and the South East fork we called Gallatin's River in honor of Albert Gallatin. The two first are 90 yards wide and the last is 70 yards.'

Every American schoolgirl has heard of the young Shoshone Indian Squaw Sacajawea – meaning the 'bird woman' – who accompanied the Lewis and Clark expedition from April 1805 until its return to comparative civilization nearly eighteen months later; and of her husband, the French-Canadian interpreter Charbonneau, and baby boy Baptiste, who was born a little before the expedition started off from its winter quarters among the Mandans. More monuments to Sacajawea have been raised in the United States than to any other woman, American or foreign. She has become an American folk-heroine of major importance, rivalling, if not outshining, such figures as Virginia Dare, Pocahontas, Barbara Frietchie, and Calamity Jane. It has even been claimed that if Sacajawea had not accompanied the expedition it could not have succeeded. Yet at the time she was only a

Minatarees Village with earth covered Wigwams

girl of eighteen, bought out of slavery by Charbonneau from the Minnetarees who had captured her some five years earlier in an attack on a party of her own people in the vicinity of these same Three Forks of the Missouri. Meriwether Lewis refers briefly to her capture in his *Journal* dated Sunday, 28 July 1805: 'Our present camp is precisely on the spot that the Snake Indians were encamped, at the time the Minnetarees of the Knife River first came into sight of them five years since. From hence they retreated about three miles up Jefferson's river and concealed themselves in the woods. The Minnetarees pursued. attacked them, killed 4 men, 4 women, a number of boys, and made prisoners of all the females and four boys. Sah-cah-jar-we-ah, our Indian woman, was one of the female prisoners taken at that time; tho' I cannot discover that she shews any emotion of sorrow in recollecting this event, or of joy in being restored to her native country; if she has enough to eat and a few trinkets to wear I believe she would be perfectly content anywhere.'

Sacajawea seems to have returned with her husband to the Upper Missouri valley and to have died of a fever at Fort Manuel Lisa on the Yellowstone river at the age of twenty-five in the year 1812. Desperate attempts (including the promotion of a bill before Congress) have been made to identify Sacajawea with an Indian woman who lived to the great age of ninety-seven, and who was buried in 1884 on the Shoshone Indian Reservation in the Wind river valley of Wyoming (I was shown her alleged grave when I camped near by). Even more zealous romancers have manufactured a love affair between her and William Clark, but there is not a shred of evidence for this. Nevertheless, the story dies hard and improves with retelling. Bernard DeVoto[1] speaks scornfully of how the Lewis and Clark expedition has been promoted into 'the Sacajawea expedition' in which they and their command 'were privileged to assist', but if we go back to the facts, Lewis and Clark and their men were interesting enough in themselves to make embroidery quite unnecessary.

William Clark, born in Virginia and brought up in Kentucky, was the more experienced frontiersman. At the age of thirty-three he was a striking figure, with his head of flaming red hair, and everywhere he went he was accompanied by his faithful Negro slave York and his Labrador retriever Scammon. York became a legend on the Upper Missouri and many a kinky-haired papoose appeared in due course up and down the river in testimony to his extraordinary popularity among the squaws. After the expedition returned Clark settled down in St Louis first as Superintendent of Indian Affairs and then as Territorial Governor of Missouri. He died in 1838.

Meriwether Lewis, also a gentleman of Virginia, had attended the College of William and Mary. His family were neighbours of Thomas Jefferson in Albemarle County, and in the year 1801 President Jefferson invited his young friend and protégé (who was then a captain in the Army, serving on the Michigan frontier at Detroit) to come to Washington and be his Private Secretary. It was while he was filling that office and residing at the recently completed White House that Lewis was entrusted by the President with the leadership of the expedition to the West. Lewis's claim to fame rests almost entirely upon the success and the achievements of that expedition, for he did not long survive its

[1] Bernard DeVoto (ed.), *The Journals of Lewis and Clark*, New York, 1953, and London, 1954, from which these extracts are taken.

return to civilization. Appointed Governor of the Louisiana Territory by Jefferson in 1807, he died in October 1809 in somewhat mysterious circumstances, either having been murdered by thieves, or (as Jefferson always believed) having killed himself in a fit of depression.[1]

Lewis was only thirty-five years old when he died, and his early death lends special interest and poignancy to the somewhat optimistic entry that he made in his *Journal* on 18 August 1805, his birthday, when the expedition was crossing the Continental Divide from the Salmon river into the Bitterroot valley. That evening, in a rather more philosophical mood than usual, he wrote: 'This day I completed my thirty-first year, and conceived that I had in all human probability now existed about half the period which I am to remain in this Sublunary world. I reflected that I had done but little, very little, indeed, to further the happiness of the human race or to advance the information of the succeeding generation. I viewed with regret the many hours I have spent in indolence, and now sorely feel the want of that information which those hours would have given me had they been judiciously expended. But since they are past and cannot be recalled, I dash from me the gloomy thought, and resolved in future to redouble my exertions and at least endeavour to promote those two primary objects of human existence, by giving them the aid of that portion of talents which nature and fortune have bestowed on me; or in future, to live for *mankind*, as I have heretofore lived for myself.'

The expedition had spent a long, cold and relatively inactive winter (1804–5) in log cabins surrounded by a stockade at the Mandan Indian villages near the present site of the city of Bismarck in North Dakota, and Lewis and Clark had no intention of spending yet another winter on the long journey to the shores of the Pacific. Unfortunately, when they reached the Three Forks of the Missouri in July 1805 – more than a year after they first set out west from St Louis, and with nearly a thousand miles still to go – they made a decision which jeopardized the whole success of their venture. Having to choose which of the three rivers they should follow to its source on the Continental Divide, they selected the most westerly of them, which they had named the Jefferson because it appeared to be the most important. This led them into some of the most difficult country of the whole of their journey, a jungle of towering peaks, rushing torrents and deep forests, interspersed with bare uplands devoid of pasture for the horses which they had purchased from the Snake Indians for use when they were forced to abandon their

[1] See Jefferson's Memorial to Meriwether Lewis in Coues (ed.), *op. cit.*, Vol. I.

boats and to strike overland. Meriwether Lewis, not unmindful of the dramatic significance of passing the watershed from the Atlantic to the Pacific river systems (they were the first white men to cross the fabulous Continental Divide in this part of North America) wrote in his diary on 12 August 1805: 'At the distance of 4 miles further the road took us to the more distant fountain of the waters of the Mighty Missouri in search of which we have spent so many toilsome days and restless nights.

Village of Mandan Indians with earth Covered Wigwams

This far I had accomplished one of those great objects on which my mind has been unalterably fixed for many years. Judge, then, of the pleasure I felt in allaying my thirst with this pure and ice-cold water which issues from the base of a low mountain or hill of a gentle ascent for half a mile. The mountains are high on either hand and leave this gap at the head of this rivulet through which the road passes. Here I halted a few minutes and rested myself. Two miles below, McNeal had exultingly stood with a foot on each side of this little rivulet and thanked his God that he had lived to bestride the mighty and heretofore-deemed-endless Missouri. After refreshing ourselves we proceeded on to the top of the dividing ridge from which I discovered immense ranges of high mountains still to the west of us with their tops partially covered with snow. I now descended the mountain about three-quarters of a mile which I found much steeper than on the opposite side, to a handsome bold running creek of cold clear water. Here I first tasted the water of the great Columbia river.'

Misled by inaccurate maps and by even more inaccurate Indian tales, the party spent over fifty days getting through this terrible stretch of the headwaters of the Jefferson river and the upper reaches of the westward-flowing Salmon river – aptly named by the fur traders of the following generation 'the river of no return'. When they finally came down the long Bitterroot valley out of this mountain wilderness into the small plain of Missoula, that they thankfully called 'Travellers' Rest', it was already September. The ability of Sacajawea to interpret for them and the skill of new and friendlier Snake Indian guides now took them much more rapidly over the Lolo Pass, and – water-borne once again – down the Clearwater river valley to its junction with the Snake river. Here, at a point which is now appropriately called Lewiston, they were within a few days' travel of the mighty Columbia river, which was to lead them directly down to the Pacific. William Clark described his first sight of this spot, on 10 October 1805: 'The country about the forks is an open plain on either side. I can observe at a distance on the lower larboard side a high ridge of thinly timbered country. The water of the South fork is a greenish blue, the North as clear as crystal. Immediately in the point is an Indian cabin and in the South fork a small island we came to on the starboard side below with a view to make some lunar observations; the night proved cloudy and we were disappointed. The Indians came down all the courses of this river on each side on horses to view us as we were descending. Worthy of remark that not one stick of timber on the river near the forks and but a few trees for a great distance up the River we descended. I think Lewis's River is about 250 yards wide, the Koos Koos Ke River about 150 yards wide and the river below the forks about 300 yards wide.' Lewiston, Idaho, today is a flourishing city of some fifteen thousand inhabitants, the centre of a prosperous lumbering and agricultural region. Two great modern bridges span the Clearwater (Lewis's) river and the Snake river (the Koos Koos Ke), leading across to the much smaller city of Clarkston in Washington, both of them links in a projected Lewis–Clark Highway.[1]

Despite a heartbreaking series of rapids and portages to be negotiated in the fresh canoes they had been forced to construct when they

[1] The memory of the explorers is indeed kept green in every possible way in these twin-cities that bear their names. You can sleep at a Lewis and Clark motel, fill up with gas at the Lewis and Clark garage and eat at the Lewis and Clark Cafeteria.

handed over their horses for safe-keeping to the Indians of Idaho, Lewis and Clark did manage to reach what they called 'Cape Disappointment at the Entrance of the Columbia River into the Great South Sea or Pacific Ocean' on 19 November 1805, and their mission seemed to be accomplished. So wide was the Columbia river in its final stretches, so high were the waves and so strong the tides on its shores, that the explorers had imagined they were already in sight of the ocean almost a fortnight before they actually reached the river's mouth. On 7 November 1805 Clark had written in his diary: 'Ocean in view! O! The joy!' And described it already as 'This great Pacific Ocean which we have been so long anxious to see.' It was the end – or nearly the end – of the long journey about which Meriwether Lewis had philosophized in characteristic fashion seven months earlier, on the day they had left their first winter's quarters at Fort Mandan. 'Our vessels consisted of six small canoes, and two large perogues. This little fleet, altho' not quite so respectable as those of Columbus or Captain Cook, were still viewed by us with as much pleasure as those deservedly famed adventurers ever beheld theirs; and I dare say with quite as much anxiety for their safety and preservation. We were now about to penetrate a country at least two thousand miles in width, on which the foot of civilized man had never trodden; the good or evil it had in store for us was for experiment yet to determine, and these little vessels contained every article by which we were to expect to subsist or defend ourselves. However, as the state of mind in which we are generally gives the colouring to events, when the imagination is suffered to wander into futurity, the picture which now presented itself to me was a most pleasing one. Entertaining, as I do, the most confident hope of succeeding in a voyage which had formed a darling project of mine for the last ten years, I could not but esteem this moment of my departure as among the most happy of my life.'

They had chosen a bad season to sample the weather of the Pacific-North-west for the first time. On 15 November Clark complained: 'The rainy weather continued without a longer intermission than two hours at a time: from the 5th in the morning until the 16th is *eleven* days rain, and the most disagreeable time I have experienced . . . where I can neither get out to hunt, return to a better situation, or proceed on: in this situation have we been for six days past.' But, drenched to the skin as they were every day, with their tents leaking and all their bedding and equipment soaked, Lewis and Clark soon set their party to work, and themselves carefully reconnoitred the country around for a suitable place to go again into winter quarters. By 7 December they had found a reasonably sheltered site a little way back from the coast. Clark was relieved to withdraw from the stormy shore where 'the sea which is immediately in front roars like a repeated rolling thunder and has roared in that way ever since our arrival in its borders, which is now 24 days since we arrived in sight of the great Western Ocean'. And he adds plaintively: 'I can't call it Pacific, as since I have seen it it has been the reverse.' Many a voyager, both before and since his time, must have felt the same about it.

The month being December it was now too late in the season to turn back up the Columbia river on the beginnings of their return journey. In addition, they still had hopes that the relief-ship half promised them by Thomas Jefferson might one fine – or more likely wet – day come sailing round via Cape Horn. They inquired searchingly of the local Indians concerning any white men who might be in the habit of visiting the mouth of the Columbia river, and were given a garbled list of names of ships' captains and descriptions of their vessels. On 9 January 1806 Lewis recorded: 'The persons who usually visit the entrance of this river for the purpose of traffic or hunting I believe are either English or Americans. The Indians inform us that they speak the same language with ourselves and give us proofs of their veracity by repeating many words of English, as musket, powder, shot, knife, file, damned rascal, son of a bitch . . .', and equally tangible evidence was provided by the name 'J. Bowman' tattooed on the arm of one of the Chinook squaws who visited their camp.

At the mouth of the Columbia river Meriwether Lewis and William Clark and their little party of twenty-nine white men, one black man, one red-skinned woman, one half-breed baby and a dog, set up their second winter's quarters, Fort Clatsop. They had achieved the main objective of their mission, but it was to be nearly another year before they were back on the Mississippi at St Louis. The journey back east to St Louis and to Washington, D.C., was to be as hazardous as the way west, if not so tedious. They had already learned much that was new and they had reinforced a claim that was eventually to give a great north-western Empire to the United States.

Poring over their maps and notes in their quarters at Fort Clatsop on the Pacific coast during the winter of 1805, Meriwether Lewis and William Clark decided even before they started off again, early in 1806, to divide their party when they reached Travellers' Rest into two groups. One (under Lewis) would travel overland by what is now known as the Great Blackfoot valley by a short cut to the Falls of the Missouri; and the other (under Clark) would return to the Jefferson river and Three Forks, but then portage across what is now the Bozeman Pass to the upper Yellowstone valley and use that river as a return route to the Missouri. The rendezvous was to be the mouth of the Yellowstone.[1]

But before they were to traverse this better way back, before even they were to start out on their return journey, Lewis and Clark ahd much to do and even more to think about. As defined by Thomas Jefferson, theirs was to be a scientific, fact-finding, and specimen-gathering expedition as well as a voyage of exploration. They had already sent back by water from their first winter's quarters at Fort Mandan on the middle Missouri a mass of notes and trophies, including such items as 'The tail of a mule deer, a weasel and three squirrels from the Rocky Mountains . . . the skin of a yellow bear . . . one tin box containing insects, mice, etc. . . . one buffalo robe painted by a Mandan man representing a battle fought 8 years since by the Sioux and the Recaras [Arikaras] against the Mandans' and even three cages containing respectively 'a living burrowing squirrel of the prairies' . . . 'living magpies', and 'a living hen of the prairie'. Even before Lewis and Clark could return to civilization the indefatigable Jefferson had issued a sort of interim report on their expedition in the shape of a message to Congress entitled *A Statistical View of the Indian Nations inhabiting the Territory of Louisiana*, drawing extensively on this material. But the fruits of the winter's labours at Fort Clatsop had to be brought back with them, and the number of specimens and artifacts they could carry over the snows of the Continental Divide, even in the interests of science (and for Thomas Jefferson and the American Philosophical Society of Philadelphia) was strictly limited by logistic considerations. They did not do so badly,[2] but such things as 'male and female antelope,

[1] I have travelled over most of the return routes of Lewis and of Clark in one direction or the other – up the Blackfoot river, over the Bozeman Pass, down the Yellowstone – and I have visited most of the landmarks the explorers described. Sometimes, of course, the country is almost unrecognizable from their descriptions: at and below the Great Falls of the Missouri, for instance, where the scars of industry and the backing-up to the waters of the river caused by the building of the Fort Peck Dam have imposed a new pattern on the landscape. But elsewhere, as at the spot where Lewis camped on a little hill above the Clearwater stream near its confluence with the Blackfoot at Greenough, Montana, almost everything remains exactly as it must have been in July 1806.

[2] *Pace* Walter Prescott Webb, who, in *The Great Plains* (Boston, 1931; paperbound edition, New York, 1962), pp. 145–6, is at his grouchiest in his none-too-generous

with their skeletons . . . horns of the mountain ram, or *big horn*' could not be included. Nor could another miniature zoo.

Jefferson had enjoined the two captains to acquire what knowledge they could of 'the state of morality, religion, and information' among the Red Indian tribes they encountered. They did their best, but their ethnological researches were sometimes a cause of embarrassment to them. On their way west they had been forced to put up with the avariciousness, and bad manners mixed with menaces, of the Teton Sioux: on the way back Lewis and three of his men nearly came to grief trying to make friends with a Blackfoot war party, and while in winter quarters at Fort Clatsop they were plagued by the unwelcome presence of a very persistent and importunate band of Chinooks, a people for whom they both had the profoundest contempt. They tell the story of these Chinooks in their *Journals*, in several instalments, in a tone of mounting exasperation, though at times they saw the funny side of it all. On 21 November 1805 Clark, in his direct way, reports: 'An old woman and wife to a Chief of the Chinooks came and made a camp near ours. She brought with her 6 young squaws (her *daughters and nieces*) I believe for the purpose of gratifying the passions of the men of our party and receiving for those indulgences such small presents as she (the old woman) thought proper to accept of. . . . The women of the Chinook nation have handsome faces, low and badly made, with large legs and thighs which are generally swelled by a stoppage of the circulation in the feet (which are small) by many strands of beads or curious strings which are drawn tight around the leg above the ankle.' But despite this somewhat unfavourable picture of the Chinook squaws, the prudent captains took no chances with human nature: 'We gave to the men, each a piece of ribbon to bestow on their favorite lasses, this plan to save valuable articles.'

On 15 March 1806 the same group of Indians reappeared. Lewis reported their second advent with some asperity. 'We were visited this afternoon by Delashshelwilt, a Chinook Chief, his wife, and six women of his nation which the old bawd his wife had brought for market. This was the same party that had communicated the venereal to so many of our party in November last, and of which they have finally recovered.

---

tribute to Lewis and Clark: 'Why a man of Jefferson's philosophical and scientific turn of mind should have been unable to select more capable men for the enterprise, keen observers with trained minds, it is hard to understand . . . of course, the fact remains that the expedition succeeded in its main objective. It went to its destination and returned, and this success tends to obscure the imperfections of the reports.'

I therefore gave the men a particular charge with respect to them which they promised me to observe.' Two days later Lewis was able to comment, with obvious satisfaction: 'Notwithstanding every effort of their winning graces the men have preserved their constancy to the vow of celibacy which they made on this occasion to Captain Clark and myself.' Even when the members of the expedition finally departed from Fort Clatsop on 23 March 1806, this persistent group of Indians pursued them up the Columbia river in canoes. 'Soon after we set out from Fort Clatsop,' wrote Clark, 'we were met by Delashshelwilt and his old bawd and his six girls. They had a canoe, a sea-otter skin, dried fish and hats for sale. We purchased a sea-otter skin and proceeded on.' No other articles of commerce were apparently offered or accepted on this occasion before this singular floating emporium of millinery and vice disappeared from their ken and from history.

The solicitude for the moral and physical well-being of their men that Meriwether Lewis and William Clark showed on this occasion is typical of them, and it helps to account for the fact that all of their party of thirty men, one woman and a baby, and a dog, who left the Mandan villages on their way west in 1805 returned safely to civilization in 1806. The only death on the whole expedition had occurred during the summer of 1804, when Sergeant Floyd died of what has since been diagnosed as a ruptured appendix. Of the thirty men who constituted the permanent party, all came through their various ills and mishaps safely, if somewhat precariously. When Private Whitehouse had a fever Lewis bled him with a penknife. 'I had no other instrument with which to perform this operation,' he wrote 'however it answered very well.' When Sacajawea's baby son was ill, Meriwether Lewis was equal to the occasion. On 24 May 1806 he wrote: 'The child was very restless last night; its jaw and the back of its neck are much more swollen than they were yesterday though its fever has abated considerably. We gave it a dose of cream of tartar and applied a fresh poultice of onions.' The child survived.[1]

Soon after starting on their return journey by boat up the Columbia river the party explored the entrance to a large tributary which they had missed on the way down because it was masked by an island. This they called the Multnomah river, and though the Indian name is still used locally today and has been given to one of the leading hotels

[1] See Chapter V. Baptiste Charbonneau was, in his thirties and forties, often at Bent's Fort. He was taken to Europe by one of his noble patrons, Prince Paul of Württemberg. Everybody seems to have liked and respected him.

of Portland, Oregon, the river is now known as the Willamette. William Clark and his seven men who paddled into its waters on 2 April 1806 were the first Americans at the site of Fort Vancouver and of Portland, and the first precursors of the countless thousands of their countrymen and of immigrants who have since come over the Oregon trail to the Great North-west through the gorges of the Columbia river known as the Dalles. Clark described the scene at the mouth of the Multnomah: 'Multnomah discharges itself in the Columbia on the south-east and may justly be said to be a quarter the size of that noble river . . . From the entrance of this river, I can plainly see Mt Jefferson which is high and covered with snow, south-east, Mt Hood, east, Mt St Helians and a high humped mountain to the east of Mt St Helians.'[1]

On the journey home the party was sadly embarrassed in its relations with the Indians it encountered by its lack of articles for gifts and trade, for almost everything of this sort had been used up before they left Fort Clatsop. Sacajawea had sacrificed her best string of beads in exchange for a specially fine sea-otter skin that the captains ardently desired to take home with them. By March 1806 Lewis computed 'Two handkerchiefs would now contain all the small articles of merchandise which we possess; the balance of the stock consists of 6 blue robes, one scarlet, one uniform artillerist's coat and hat, five robes made of our large flag, and a few old clothes trimmed with ribbon. On this stock we have wholly to depend for the purchase of horses and such portion of our subsistence from the Indians as it will be in our powers to obtain.' The sad fate of Meriwether Lewis's uniform coat well indicates the straits to which they were reduced. Sergeant Prior had purchased a much-needed canoe from the Caltlamah tribe. 'For this canoe,' Lewis wrote on 17 March 1806, 'he gave my uniform laced coat and nearly half a carrot of tobacco. It seems that nothing except this coat would induce them to dispose of a canoe which in their mode of traffic is an article of the greatest value except a wife, with whom it is equal, and is generally given in exchange to the father for his daughter. I think the United States are indebted to me another Uniform coat, for that of which I have disposed on this occasion was but little worn.'

[1] On a fine day the traveller who nowadays arrives at Portland by air sees all four of these peaks, Mt Adams and Mt St Helens to the north of the Columbia river and Mt Hood and Mt Jefferson south of the river, as well as many others in the impressive Cascade range. Mount Hood, with its symmetrical snow-covered cone, is an unforgettable sight in the dawn or sunset glow, and one wishes that the more poetically minded Lewis rather than the matter-of-fact Clark had described it in the *Journals*.

When, a little later, having decided to travel overland from where the Columbia river turned away northwards, Lewis was in sore need of horses, he had to sacrifice his sword in exchange for an 'elegant white horse' brought into camp by the Great Chief Yellepet. Yellepet had really wanted a kettle, but appeared perfectly satisfied with the sword. It would seem that the United States was very near to owing the gallant captain a whole new outfit. He almost did not need it, for on two occasions on the return journey to civilization he came nearer to losing his life than did any other member of the expedition. As recounted by him these are perhaps the most exciting incidents of the whole expedition, with the possible exception of several encounters with bears in the Rocky Mountains on the way west. The day before Lewis and his section of the party overtook Clark on the Missouri river below the mouth of the Yellowstone (down which Clark had travelled), Lewis was accidentally shot by one of his own men. On 11 August 1806 he recorded the story: 'Just opposite to the burnt hills there happened to be a herd of elk on a thick willow bar, and finding that my observation was lost for the present I determined to land and kill some of them. Accordingly we put to and I went out with Cruzatte only. We fired on the elk; I killed one and he wounded another. We reloaded our guns and took different routes through the thick willows in pursuit of the elk. I was in the act of firing on the elk a second time when a ball struck my left thigh about an inch below my hip joint. Missing the bone, it passed through the left thigh and cut the thickness of the bullet across the hinder part of the right thigh. The stroke was very severe. I instantly supposed that Cruzatte had shot me in mistake for an elk, as I was dressed in brown leather and he cannot see very well; under this impression I called out to him "damn you, you have shot me", and looked towards the place from whence the ball had come. Seeing nothing, I called Cruzatte several times as loud as I could, but received no answer. I do not believe that the fellow did it intentionally, but after finding that he had shot me, was anxious to conceal his knowledge of having done so. The ball had lodged in my breeches, which I knew to be the ball of the short rifles such as that he had, and there being no person out with me but him, and no Indians that we could discover, I have no doubt in my own mind of his having shot me.'

Lewis's encounter with a real Indian war-party was even more alarming, though it resulted in no casualties. On the upper reaches of Marias river (at what is now Cut Bank Creek, not far south of the Canadian border at the 49th parallel between Alberta and Montana) Lewis and his party of three (the scout Drouillard and the two Fields brothers) ran into eight mounted Blackfoot Indians driving a number of additional saddled horses. After spending an uneasy night in the company of these members of the most dreaded of all the Indian tribes[1] Lewis and his men awoke to a major crisis. 'This morning at daylight the Indians got up and crouched around the fire. J. Fields who was on post had carelessly laid his gun down behind him near where his brother was sleeping. One of the Indians slipped behind him and took his gun and that of his brother unperceived by him. At the same instant two others advanced and seized the guns of Drewyer [Drouillard] and myself. J. Fields seeing this turned about to look for his gun and saw the fellow just running off with her and his brother's. He called to his brother, who instantly jumped up and pursued the Indian whom they overtook at the distance of 50 or 60 paces from the camp, seized their guns and wrested them from him, and R. Fields as he seized his gun stabbed the Indian to the heart with his knife. The fellow ran about 15 steps and fell dead. Of this I did not know until afterwards, having recovered their guns, they ran back instantly to the camp. Drewyer, who was awake, saw the Indian take hold of his gun and instantly jumped up and seized her and wrested her from him, but the Indian still retained his pouch. His jumping up and crying "damn you, let go my gun" awakened me. I jumped up and asked what was the matter, which I quickly learned when I saw Drewyer in a scuffle with the Indian for his gun. I reached to seize my gun but found her gone. I then drew a pistol from my holster, and turning myself about, saw the Indian making off with my gun. I ran at him with my pistol and bid him lay down my gun, which he was in the act of doing when the Fieldses returned and drew up their guns to shoot him, which I forbad as he did not appear to be about to make any resistance or commit any offensive act. He dropped the gun and walked slowly off. I picked her up in-

[1] I spent a night at the Rocking Chair Ranch near Greenough, Montana, in 1954, as the guest of the late eminent Californian historian Robert Glass Cleland. I arrived at dusk, but in the morning he took me outside and pointed to the exact spot where Lewis and his three companions had camped overnight at the foot of a small hill, beside the Clearwater tributary of the Big Blackfoot river. Next day they had moved on towards Nine-Mile Prairie on the way to the Continental Divide and unwittingly towards the Blackfoot Indian war-party. The whole scene, as it had been in July 1806, came alive for me in July 1954 as Dr Cleland described it, quoting from memory from the Journals of Lewis and Clark. He rolled the phrase 'the river that goes to the road that leads to the land of the Buffalo' (which is what the Indians call the Big Blackfoot river) lovingly off his tongue. 'What a marvellous name!' he said.

stantly. Drewyer having about this time recovered his gun and pouch asked me if he might not kill the fellow, which I also forbad as the Indian did not appear to wish to kill us. As soon as they found us all in possession of our arms they ran and endeavoured to drive off all the horses. I now hollowed to the men and told them to fire on them if they attempted to drive off our horses. They accordingly pursued the main party who were driving the horses up the river and I pursued the men who had taken my gun, who with another was driving off a part of the horses which were to the left of the camp. At the distance of three hundred paces, they entered one of those steep nitches in the bluff with the horses before them. Being nearly out of breath I could pursue no further. I called to them as I had done several times before that I would shoot them if they did not give me my horse and raised my gun. One of them jumped behind a rock and spoke to the other who turned around and stopped at the distance of 30 steps from me, and I shot him through the belly. He fell to his knees and on his right elbow, from which position he partly raised himself up and fired at me, and turning himself about crawled in behind a rock which was a few feet from him. He overshot me. Being bareheaded I felt the wind of his bullet very distinctly.'

The Indians had decamped with some of the party's horses, but leaving their own behind. Catching four of the best of these, Lewis and his men burned the Indians' baggage as a sign of their displeasure at the unprovoked attack and departed in haste on a forced ride back to the Missouri and their companions. They travelled over ninety miles with only brief halts for rest and food. Lewis now told his men: 'That it was my determination that if we were attacked in the plains on our way to the point, that the bridles of the horses should be tied together and we would stand and defend them, or sell our lives as dear as we could.' Fortunately this was not necessary. 'We had proceeded about 12 miles on an East course when we found ourselves near the Missouri: we heard a report which we took to be that of a gun but we were not certain. Still continuing down the north east bank of the Missouri about 8 miles further, being then within five miles of the grog spring we heard the report of several rifles very distinctly on the river to our right. We quickly repaired to this joyful sound and on arriving at the bank of the river had the unspeakable satisfaction to see our canoes coming down.'

The remainder of the expedition's journey down the Missouri river and back to St Louis and civilization seemed tame by comparison. Old friends and old enemies were met and familiar scenes redescribed.

Charbonneau was paid off and departed with Sacajawea for the Upper Missouri again, promising to send the boy Baptiste down to St Louis to be educated under William Clark's supervision as soon as he was old enough. On 17 August 1806 Charbonneau received $500 and 33⅓ cents for his services to the expedition. On Wednesday, 3 September 1806, news from home was passed on to the party by 'a Mr James Airs [Aird] from the Mackinaw by way of Prarie Dechien [Prairie Duchien] and St Louis'. Wrote Clark: 'This Gentleman informed us of many changes and misfortunes which had taken place in the Illinois. He also informed us that General Wilkinson was the governor of the Louisiana, and at St Louis 300 of the American troops had been cantoned on the Missouri a few miles about its mouth. Some disturbance with the Spaniards in the Nackatosh country is the cause of their being called down to that country. The Spaniards had taken one of the United States frigates in the Mediterranean. Two British ships of the line had fired on an American ship in the port of New York, and killed the Captain's brother. Two Indians had been hung in St Louis for murder and several others in jail, and that Mr Burr and General Hamilton fought a duel, the latter was killed.' Thus did the news of the untimely death of Alexander Hamilton two years before first reach the ears of Lewis and Clark, both of whom must have known him and Aaron Burr well.

The expedition was nearly over. The men were paid off and went their several ways, Sergeant Gass to publish his diary[1] of the expedition (which was conceivably rewritten by an enterprising schoolmaster) in 1807 and to live to a great age. And when the official account of the expedition was finally issued, edited by Nicholas Biddle, in 1814, it constituted, as Bernard DeVoto had remarked, 'the first report on the West, on the United States over the hill and beyond the sunset, on the province of the American future.[2]

Lewis and Clark performed a great service to the people as well as to the President of the United States. They may not have pioneered the later emigrant trails to California or Oregon, but their journey gave heart and inspiration to the whole generation of fur traders and trappers whose journeys and discoveries really did open up these two trails. One of their own men, John Colter, was one of the earliest of the fur trappers of the Rocky Mountain West. Drouillard was another. Within

[1] Patrick Gass, *A Journal of the Voyages and Travels of a Voyage of Discovery Under the Command of Captain Lewis* (Pittsburgh, 1807).

[2] B. DeVoto, *Journals of Lewis and Clark*, Introduction, p. lii.

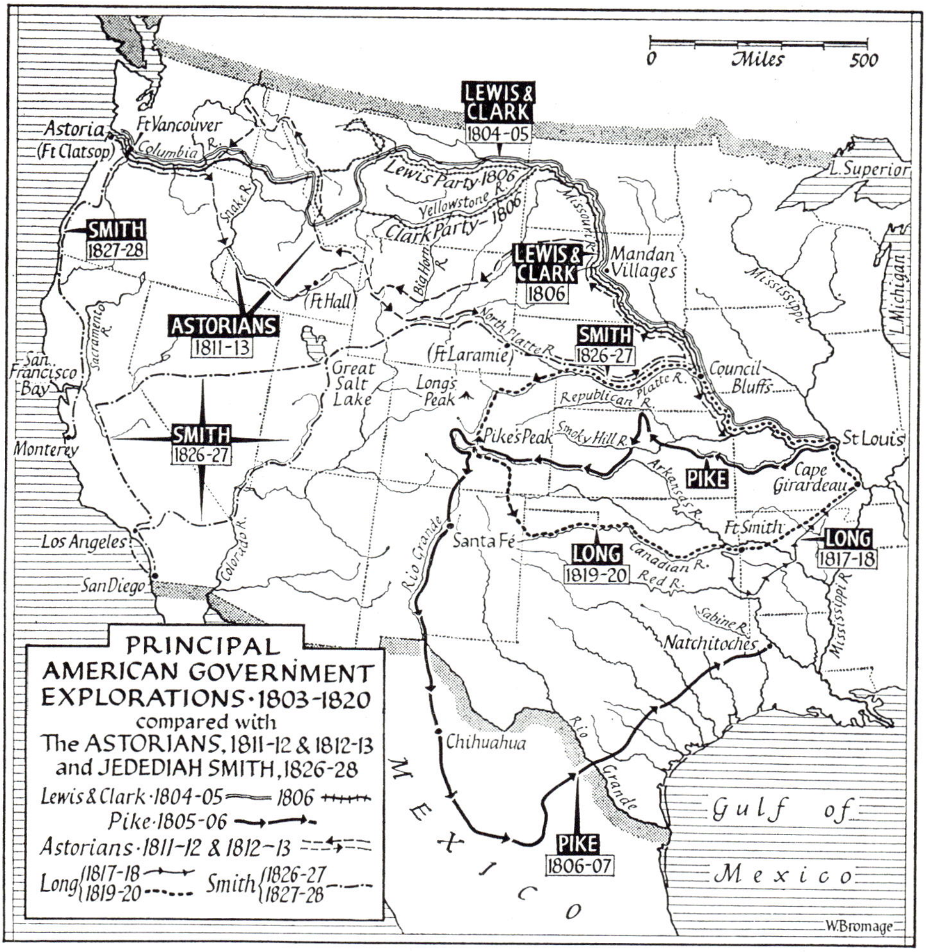

a year or two of the return of Lewis and Clark the fur trade was in full swing on the Upper Missouri and on the Yellowstone; Manuel Lisa had established his first fort (where Bighorn, Montana, now stands), and the Astorians were following in their footsteps all the way to the Pacific.

John Jacob Astor, an immigrant from Waldorf in Germany, was directly stimulated by the journey of Lewis and Clark to organize the American Fur Company and the Pacific Fur Company in 1808. In July 1810 his overland party, bound for the far West, left Montreal, and soon afterwards he sent the *Tonquin* to sail from New York round Cape Horn, to the mouth of the Columbia river. After misadventures which cast more reflection on the leadership of both parties than ever could be levelled at Lewis or Clark, a rendezvous was effected and the trading post of Astoria, a little inland from Fort Clatsop, was established. Subsequently (as Washington Irving[1] and a host of subsequent writers have chronicled) both the *Tonquin* and Astoria were quickly lost by the American and Pacific Fur Companies and the Columbia river trade abandoned to the British. But in the history of the Northwest the fact that Astoria *had* been established in 1811, and that the overland Astorians had diverged from the Lewis and Clark route sufficiently to begin the blazing of the great westward waggon trails – they are among several claimants to have first used South Pass – was to play a significant part in the eventual destiny of the Oregon country.

Like the official expedition of Lewis and Clark the achievements of the privately organized Astorians acted as an immediate stimulus to the exploitation and settlement of the Far West. The same cannot be said of the work of two other United States government explorers, Zebulon Pike and Stephen Long, who were both of the same generation as Lewis and Clark. Though both traversed many known trails and discovered much, they also both helped to generate and propagate the myth of 'The Great American Desert' lying athwart the advance of the American people westwards. Two generations of map-makers and settlers suffered from the effects of this myth, for not until the late 1860s did travellers, scientists, and railroad promoters succeed in dissipating this 'Dust Curtain', which Pike and Long had lowered just to the east of the hundredth meridian, to bog down the frontier of settlement short of the High Plains, which they considered uninhabitable. Those hurrying across them in the direction of the promised lands of Oregon and California passed them by with averted eyes, but by the end of the nineteenth century they had been converted into one of the most fertile and populous regions of the whole trans-Mississippi West.

In his inimitable way Walter Prescott Webb has traced[2] the process of 'Creating the Tradition of the "Great American Desert"' from Coronado and De Soto to Pike and Long and those who echoed them. Pike said, 'These vast plains of the western hemisphere may become in time as celebrated as the sandy deserts of Africa',[3] and James, who

[1] Washington Irving, *The Astorians* (New York, 1837).

[2] W. P. Webb, *The Great Plains*, pp. 152–60.

[3] Quoted by Webb from E. Coues (ed.), *The Expeditions of Zebulon Montgomery Pike* (3 vols, New York 1895), Vol. II, p. 523.

accompanied Long, stated categorically that 'I do not hesitate in giving the opinion that it is almost wholly unfit for cultivation and of course uninhabitable by a people depending on agriculture for their subsistence'.[1] As late as the year 1859 Horace Greeley was telling his readers of the *New York Tribune* not only that the Great American Desert existed, but that 'every day's sun is extending it'.[2]

Pike and Long were no more fortunate as explorers than they were as geographical diagnosticians. Pike, sent out at the head of a small army party by Jefferson in 1805 to explore the Upper Mississippi, missed its true source. On his second expedition, dispatched by the triple-dealing General James Wilkinson in 1806 to 'ascertain the direction, extent and navigation of the Arkansaw and Red rivers', he blundered either by accident or by design into the Upper Rio Grande valley in Spanish New Mexico, was detained by the Spanish authorities in Santa Fé, and then sent back, under escort, via Chihuahua to Nacogdoches on the Spanish–American border at the Sabine river the next year. His actual discoveries were unimportant – he sighted and named 'Pike's Peak', though he pronounced it unclimbable – but his careful observation of wide areas of the northern Spanish borderlands (which he traversed under open arrest) set down in his Journal,[3] first published in 1810, and the maps he drew, provided much useful information to the Santa Fé traders and to the Texas immigrants from the United States of the following generation. Pike himself was killed in the war of 1812.

Long's expedition of 1819–20 was the most ambitious ever to have been sent out by the Americans up to that time into the trans-Mississippi West. John C. Calhoun, Secretary of War, said 'it has for its objects the protection of our north-western frontier and the greater extension of our fur trade'. As such, it was a great fiasco, not so much on account of Long's leadership as through cheating contractors and the withholding of Congressional appropriations. 'The Yellowstone Expedition', designed to be bigger and better than that of Lewis and Clark on the Upper Missouri, had to be abandoned, therefore, and Long then led a much-reduced party (which nevertheless included pro-

[1] Quoted by Webb from R. G. Thwaites (ed.), *Edwin James's account of an Expedition from Pittsburgh to the Rocky Mountains, performed in the years 1819–1820 under the Command of Major S. H. Long* ('Early Western Travels', Cleveland 1904–7, XVII, p. 147).

[2] W. P. Webb, *op. cit.*, p. 159, note 1.

[3] *Account of Expeditions to the Sources of the Mississippi and through the Western Parts of Louisiana.*

fessional scientists and topographers and artists)[1] up the Platte to the Rocky Mountains in 1821. Pike's Peak was climbed and Long's Peak named. On the return journey, the Upper Arkansas and (by mistake for the Red river) the Canadian rivers were re-explored. Most of the scientific records of the expedition were lost, but enough remained to provide Dr James with material for his multi-volumed account of the expedition – and for his disquisition on the Great American Desert. With all its deficiencies Long's was the most important United States government expedition into the Far West that was not strictly military in object until John Charles Frémont set out in 1842. Though it played little or no part in establishing the Oregon Trail, or in making the Santa Fé Trail safer for Americans, it did at least help to persuade people to hurry on to a farther West that was now beckoning – 'beyond the sunset, in the province of the American future' – and beyond those mountains and deserts which, before the mining and the ranching frontiers had been opened up, appeared from unimpeachable official testimony (repeated in the Press, which made it doubly true) to offer them nothing at all. Nothing, that is, except hunting and trapping.

[1] S. Seymour's drawings made on the Long expedition were engraved and printed in London as early as 1823 for the first edition of James' *Account*. See plate 5 for 'Major Long holding a Council with the Pawnees'.

CHAPTER V

Fur Traders and Trappers of the Far West

North America was rich in fur-bearing animals, and the fur trade had been important since the seventeenth century; but its importance was to reach a peak in the third and fourth decades of the nineteenth century. During that time it played a leading part, perhaps the leading part, in the exploitation of the American Far West.

The fur trappers had to work beyond the farthest fringe of civilization and settlement. To sell their pelts they had to return to the frontier outposts or the fur traders had to meet them half-way and set up temporary 'rendezvous' in the wilderness. The fur trade required, therefore, capital and organization; at first its profits had been prodigious, but by the 1840s they had shrunk almost to nothing. Within the active life span of one generation, therefore – after the return of Lewis and Clark in 1806 and before the first setting out of Frémont in 1842 – the fur trade experienced its heyday and was beginning to fade away as a major phenomenon of the American frontier. Some who participated in it – Kit Carson, Tom Fitzpatrick, Jim Bridger – lived right through it into new and equally colourful careers after it was over. Others – Jedediah Smith, Harrison Rogers, Sylvester Pattie, William and Milton Sublette – died on the trail, as prisoners of the Mexicans or the Indians, or (very rarely) in their beds or blankets. Only the hardy went in for such a life. Only the hardiest, and the most fortunate, survived.

The fur trade had started in Canada[1] in the seventeenth century, first with the French and then with the British. The 'Company of Adventurers of England Trading into Hudson's Bay' had been founded in the year 1670 to pursue it, and its members and servants had followed and trapped the fur-bearing animal ever since. In its pursuit Alexander Mackenzie had, in 1793, reached the Pacific overland in the service of the rival North-west Company. In 1811 the North-west Company successfully resisted the challenge of John Jacob Astor's

[1] See H. A. Innis, *The Fur Trade in Canada* (Cambridge, Mass., 1934), *passim*.

American Fur Company, and reached an agreement with it which confined the Americans to the Rocky Mountains area, and liquidated by purchase their station, Astoria (henceforth known as Fort George), on the Columbia river, in 1813. But the Crown forced the North-west Company to merge with the Hudson's Bay Company in 1821, better to withstand the Americans. This was timely, for another threat to their monopoly was created in St Louis in 1822, when William Henry Ashley and Andrew Henry organized the Rocky Mountain Fur Company, bound by no agreement with the Canadians and willing to follow the beaver to the ends of the earth if need be. The Rocky Mountain Company stood up to both its great rivals, Canadian and American, until 1835, when, with the fur trade already beginning to decline and many of its finest leaders either dead (like Jedediah Smith) or in retirement (like General Ashley), it gave up the uneven struggle. That canny German immigrant, Astor, managed to get out of the trade in 1834 while the going was good, but Dr John McLaughlin and Sir George Simpson clung desperately to the Hudson's Bay posts at Fort Vancouver and Fort Hall, until dispossessed by the Oregon treaty of 1846 with England, which gave the United States everything up to the 49th parallel. By that time the fur trade had ceased to be an important factor in the history of the American West.

His time was short, but, as R. G. Cleland puts it in an eloquent tribute, 'in his few allotted years the trapper set his impress forever upon the map of North America and the fate of the United States. He affected the destiny of nations; he changed the future of a continent; he bequeathed to later generations of Americans a tradition of heroic exploration comparable to that of the seamen of Elizabeth or the conquistadors of Spain.'[1] At all levels of achievement – the governors, directors and factors, like Simpson, Ashley, and McLaughlin; the 'partizans' and captains like Ogden and Smith or the rank and file like Jim Baker, Jim Bridger, Jim Beckwith, and 'Uncle' Tom Wootton – these fur traders and trappers looms somewhat larger than life as it is usually lived. They called Milton Sublette 'Thunderbolt of the Rockies' and there was something of an over-display of Nature's exuberance about many of his fellows also. Imaginative writers do not need to

[1] R. G. Cleland, *This Reckless Breed of Men. The Trappers and Fur Traders of the Southwest* (New York, 1950), p. 7. Compare his tribute to the fur trapper with those of H. Chittenden, *The American Fur Trade of the Far West* (2 vols, New York, 1902), Vol. I, xiii-ix *et seq.*, and of G. F. Ruxton, *Adventures in Mexico and the Rocky Mountains* (New York, 1848) and *Life in the Far West* (reprinted, Norman, Oklahoma, 1951). See quotation on p. 106ff.

'write up' the Mountain Man; rather they have to tone him down to make him sound credible or (in some cases) to get him past the censors. A winter spent with Jim Bridger set up 'Ned Buntline'[1] for the rest of a long career as a dime novelist, and many of the stories he wrote about Jim were even true. When a British naval officer met Kit Carson – still in his thirties – at Monterey in 1846 – he paid this paladin among Mountain Men and scouts the ultimate tribute: 'Why, he is as famous here as is the Duke in Europe!'[2]

The victim of all this making of history was a harmless, compact and engaging mammal of from twenty-five to forty pounds weight full-grown. He could be made into a pet if caught young but few Mountain Men were interested in him alive. The intelligence of the beaver has been exaggerated by enthusiastic animal-tale tellers; he was not able to gnaw down a tree so that it fell neatly into place at his dam-site in a predetermined direction; nevertheless, the beaver-dam and lodge are impressive pieces of animal engineering and architecture. The beaver successfully protected himself against most of his enemies, but man proved too much for him. Using in his underhanded way the sex-gland secretions (*castoreum*) of the dead beaver as bait to attract the live one, his human enemy caught him in a steel trap and let him drown himself trying to escape. The beaver's only defence, if not drowned immediately, was to gnaw off an entrapped limb. One Mountain Man[3] reported 'Between feet and toes we took no less than 42! We put 150 traps in the water and got 15 beaver.' The beaver, if it survived so long, reached full growth at about two years old, and, as Cecil Alter says, 'the grandparents whose aging is often related to incisor trouble, finally drop away to Elysium at twelve to fifteen years of age'.[4] But

[1] 'Ned Buntline' was the pen-name of E. Z. C. Judson (1823–86), Buffalo Bill Cody's later partner and publicity agent in promoting the famous Wild West Show and other enterprises. His boisterous life reads, according to the *Oxford Companion to American Literature*, 'like one of his own dime novels, a genre of which he was a creator'.

[2] The Hon. Frederick Walpole, R.N., *Four Years in the Pacific* (London, 1851).

[3] Alexander Ross, *The Fur Hunters of the Far West* (reprint, ed. by K. A. Spaulding, Norman, Oklahoma, 1956), p. 236.

[4] J. Cecil Alter, *Jim Bridger*, Chapter 10, 'The Beaver Wonderland' (revised edition, Norman, Oklahoma, 1962), pp. 44–9, prints one of the most readable and satisfying non-scientific descriptions of the beaver and its habits. He, like many other writers on the fur trade era, made use of the classic work of Lewis H. Morgan, *The American Beaver and his Works* (Philadelphia, 1868). A famous drawing of beaver in their natural habitat is that of Charles Bodmer, first published as an illustration to Prince Maximilian's *Travels* (London, 1844), and reproduced in Cleland's *Reckless Breed*, facing p. 14, from Ackermann's engraving of the original water-colour. That attractive plate is also reproduced in this book, plate 11.

though it was easy for a beaver to become a mother, to become a grandmother (toeless and toothless at that, maybe) was a real and rare achievement, with all those fur trappers around. But then, very few Mountain Men lived to be grandfathers, either.

The cured 'plew' of the adult beaver weighed around a pound and a half and at best would fetch from four to six dollars a pound at the mountain rendezvous or trading fort. This was poor return for all the trouble and risk taken, for the prices of trade goods were very high at these places. Said John Hatcher, a typical Mountain Man, using the picturesque mountain language, 'A little 'bacca, ef its a plew a plug, an' Dupont an' Galena, a Green River or so, an he leaves for the Bayou Salade.'[1] When, however, beaver 'plew' was down to a dollar a pound, as happened in the early 1840s, the beaver was hardly worth while trapping any more, and Alexander Barclay, who was later to build Barclay's Fort at the western junction of the two branches of the Santa Fé trail at Watrous near Las Vegas, New Mexico, noted in his 'Waste Book' (kept while in the employ of the Bents at Fort William on the Arkansas), under the date 31 August 1846 'Beaver trade stopt at 90 ¢ plt [pelt]'.[2] The trade had in fact been dying for several years, though incredulous Mountain Men every season expected the price to rise again. Says G. F. Ruxton's trapper hero Killbuck in *Life in the Far West* 'Howsever, beaver's bound to rise; human natur can't go on selling beaver a dollar a pound; no, no, that ain't a going to shine much longer, I know. There was the times when this child first went to the mountains: six dollars the plew – old 'un or kitten. Wagh! but its bound to rise, I says agin . . .'[3]

[1] Quoted by W. H. Goetzmann, in *Army Exploration in the American West, 1803–1863* (New Haven, 1959, p. 29). In plain English: 'A little tobacco, even if it costs a whole beaver skin for a plug, and some gunpowder and lead, and a hunting knife or so, and he leaves for the trapping country.' Bayou Salade is a famous mountain meadow in the Colorado Rockies, near the headwaters of the Arkansas. Salida, Colorado, commemorates the name, at approximately 106° W and 39° N on the map. Bayou Salade was also known as 'Bayou Salada' and as 'South Park'. It was still a lovely spot, virtually unspoilt, near where U.S. 24 and U.S. 285 come together at Buena Vista, when I last saw it in the summer of 1964 and the winter of 1965.

[2] *Barclay Papers*. From microfilm copy in the Colorado State Archives, Denver (courtesy of the State Archivist, Mrs D. Renze). The originals now repose in the Bancroft Library at Berkeley, California, and are quoted from here with the permission of the Director, Dr G. P. Hammond.

[3] G. F. Ruxton, *Life in the Far West* (reprinted, Norman, Oklahoma, 1951), p. 18. First published, serially, in *Blackwood's Edinburgh Magazine*, June–November 1848. Many times reprinted. Killbuck is a fictional name for a real-life character, whose identity is discussed learnedly by Leroy R. Hafen in Appendix B (pp. 235–44) to

But it didn't. Their last annual rendezvous for the exchange of trade goods for skins were attended by the Rocky Mountain Fur Company in 1838 and by the American Fur Company in 1839. A fairly successful rendezvous was held on the Green river in 1840 without the participation of either of these erstwhile giants of the fur trade, but the series lapsed in 1841, the year of the first overland emigrant party to California, guided by Tom Fitzpatrick, who thus had little time for trapping. That August, Henry Fraeb had his hair lifted by an Indian war-party, and his partner Jim Bridger was busy building Fort Bridger on the Black Fork of the Green river as a permanent trading post. The year 1842 saw the very last *al fresco* rendezvous of the old type such as had been participated in with such abandon by the Mountain Men and their (or other people's) squaws.

These remarkable gatherings have been compared not too inaccurately with the great fairs of medieval times in Europe. Borrowing the idea from the fur traders of Canada, General Ashley had initiated the rendezvous system in 1823, after his first organized trapping season as head of the Rocky Mountain Fur Company. The success and convenience of the system, quite apart from providing the lonely fur trappers an opportunity for an annual debauch, made the rendezvous the high spot of each year's hunting for just on two decades. A last half-hearted effort was made in 1843 to bring the rendezvous system to life again. On 12 August that irrepressible Scottish sportsman Sir William Drummond Stewart, Baronet, wrote to Jim Bridger 'The compliments of Sir Wm. Stewart to Capt. James Bridger. Come and see us. We have been expecting you for several days, and shall wait for you a few days more to come to camp. We have commenced an extensive game of ball, and we want you to come and "keep the ball in motion", come . . . and a steed is at your service. Come – hurrah!' This letter was intended to be left on a pole for Bridger at '*The Old Rendezvous*',[1] but never reached him. In any case, Jim had trapped but few beaver that year. Indians were much more plentiful and even attacked his new fort. He had no time for fun and games with the genial baronet. In 1844 the

the Oklahoma University Press edition of 1951. The most likely candidate is John S. Smith (1810–71) who, as 'Uncle John Smith', also attracted the loving attention of Lewis H. Garrard (in *Wah-To-Ya and the Taos Trail* (1850) and Henry Inman in *The Old Santa Fé Trail* (1898).

[1] Matthew C. Field, *Prairie and Mountain Sketches* (eds K. L. Gregg and J. F. McDermott, Norman, Oklahoma, 1957), p. 126, quoted by J. C. Alter, *Jim Bridger* (1902 edn), pp. 206–7. A place near the present-day Riverton, Wyoming, actually appeared on some maps at that time as 'Rendezvous'.

situation was even worse. James Clyman found Fort Bridger all but deserted on 31 August, which should have been the height of the trading season. He didn't see much future for Jim's pride and joy, describing it as 'a temporary concern, calculated for trade with the Shoshones and Utahs, which is not very valuable. This place is likewise the general rendezvous for Rocky Mountain hunters and trappers. That once numerous class of adventurers are now reduced to less than thirty men . . .'[1] The Mountain Men had once numbered over 600! Guiding and supplying the increasing numbers of overland emigrants had now become much more profitable than trapping the beaver. But Jim Bridger at least went on trying, and in 1845 it appears that he attempted to make the best of both worlds, by going to California *and* trapping beaver. On 17 September 1843 A. R. Bouis wrote to Pierre Choteau, Jr, 'Mr James Bridger arrived at Fort John [Laramie] on the 2d. instant, and delivered Mrs [Messrs] Jos. Picotte 840 beaver skins and castorem; 675 dressed deerskins; 25 mules; 24 horses; 1400 California sea shells'.[2] Whether Jim Bridger, Mountain Man, had become Jim Bridger, Beachcomber, in an effort to diversify his business is not certain, for he may have obtained the 1,400 abalone shells (much prized by the Rocky Mountain and Plains Indians, and used as ear and nose ornaments) in trade for beaver skins, just about to become a drug on the market at '90 ¢ plt'.

George Frederick Ruxton was born at Eynsham Hall near Oxford, in England, only in July 1821, the summer before Ashley's first fur-trapping company set out from St Louis, and died in August 1848 in that very same St Louis, just as the era of the fur trade had ended – thus just spanning in his twenty-seven years the whole of that remarkable phase in the history of the American west. Although he did not visit the Rocky Mountain rendezvous until their great days were over, he is recognized as having produced the most vivid contemporary word pictures of those remarkable scenes. In his *Adventures in Mexico and the Rocky Mountains*, first published in 1847, he writes (pp. 230–1):

> At a certain time, when the hunt is over, or they have loaded their pack animals, the trappers proceed to the 'rendezvous', the locality of which has been previously agreed upon; and here the traders and agents of the fur companies await them, with such assort-

[1] *James Clyman, American Frontiersman*, 'His Diaries and Reminiscences' (San Fran cisco, 1928; reprinted, Portland, 1960), 1960 edn, p. 99.

[2] W. G. Robinson, *S. Dakota Historical Society Collections* (1918, pp. 209–10), quoted by A. Cecil Alter, *Jim Bridger* (1962 edn, p. 217).

ment of goods as their hardy customers may require, including generally a fair supply of alcohol. The trappers drop in singly and in small bands, bringing their packs of beaver to this mountain market, not unfrequently to the value of a thousand dollars each, the produce of one hunt. The dissipation of the 'rendezvous', however, soon turns the trapper's pocket inside out. The goods brought by the traders, although of the most inferior quality, are sold at enormous prices –

coffee, twenty and thirty shillings a pint cup, which is the usual measure; tobacco fetches ten and fifteen shillings a plug; alcohol, from twenty to fifty shillings a pint; gunpowder, sixteen shillings a pint cup; and all other articles at proportionately exorbitant prices. . . .

The rendezvous is one continued scene of drunkenness, gambling, and brawling and fighting, as long as the money and credit of the trappers last. Seated, Indian fashion, round the fires, with a blanket spread before them, groups are seen with their 'decks' of cards, playing at euker, poker, and seven-up, the regular mountain games. The stakes are 'beaver', which here is current coin; and when the fur is gone, their horses, mules, rifles, and shirts, hunting packs, and *breeches*, are staked. Daring gamblers make the rounds of the camp, challenging each other to play for the trapper's highest stake – his horse, his squaw (if he have one), and, as once happened, his scalp. 'There goes hos and beaver!' is the mountain expression when any great loss is sustained; and, sooner or later, 'hos and beaver' invariably find their way into the insatiable pockets of the traders. A trapper often squanders the produce of his hunt, amounting to hundreds of dollars, in a couple of hours; and, supplied on credit with another equipment, leaves the rendezvous for another expedition, which has the same result time after time, although one tolerably successful hunt would enable him to return to the settlements and civilised life, with an ample sum to purchase and stock a farm, and enjoy himself in ease and comfort the remainder of his days. . . .

This has never been bettered, but Ray Allen Billington, in his *The American Frontiersman*,[1] has equalled it. His picture supplements and complements Ruxton, and draws also upon the whole rich century of publications concerning the fur trade that have followed in Ruxton's wake.

Then the trappers from all the mountains turned their steps toward the annual rendezvous. The site had been selected a year before and the word passed around among the Mountain Men. Always some sheltered spot was chosen where towering mountain ranges protected the trappers from wind and cold, and where grass and water were plentiful. They might gather beneath the sandstone cliffs of the Wind River range where the valleys of the Popo Agie and Wind rivers were green with waving grass and bright with flaming wild flowers; perhaps Jackson's Hole was the favoured spot where the stark nakedness of the snow-dappled Grand Tetons awed even the wilderness-jaded frontiersmen; perhaps they had agreed to meet on the sun-baked plain that bordered the still waters of the Great Salt Lake. To this designated spot came flocking the bearded Mountain Men from all the West with their pack mules laden with beaver peltry, dark-skinned Mexicans from Taos and Santa Fé, French-Canadian deserters from England's Hudson's Bay Company, and whole villages of friendly Indians who pitched their tepees and settled down to join in the fun. Often more than six hundred trappers and as many Indians met together at the annual rendezvous.

Shortly after the first of July the caravan of trading goods arrived from St Louis. The Mountain Men always rode out to meet the mile-long line of laden mules, yelling like demons as they greeted the

[1] An Inaugural lecture, delivered as Harmsworth Professor of American History before the University of Oxford on 2 February 1954 (Oxford, 1954), pp. 6–7.

merchants who were willing to endure the wearisome journey for profits of 2,000 per cent. on their investments. They asked eagerly for year-old news first, then watched greedily as the merchandise was spread before them: powder from the DuPont works in Delaware, lead from the mines of the Galena district of Illinois, stubby rifles from the shops of Missouri gunsmiths, knives from the Green River country, beaver traps from England's bustling factories, beads and trinkets from Italy, coffee and sugar from South America, blankets from New England's textile mills, hanks of tobacco from Kentucky, fiery whisky from Taos or Santa Fé, and cask after cask of raw alcohol from the distilleries of Cincinnati.

Trading came first, as trappers exchanged their 'hairy bank notes', the beaver skins, for needed supplies or rare luxuries or finery for their squaws. Then the flat casks of alcohol were tapped and the rendezvous was turned into a scene of roaring debauchery. Day after day, night after night, the trappers passed metal camp kettles of the lethal fluid about, until not a sober person could be found. Some gambled recklessly when drunk, for there were no misers among men who faced death daily; often they squandered away in a few hours their entire year's earnings, their rifles, their horses, their Indian wives, and in a few cases their own scalps. Others raced their horses, or staged wrestling matches with no holds barred. Fights were common and, as drunkenness increased, often fatal. Occasionally duels were fought, usually with rifles at twenty paces, with one or both participants sure to be killed. Sometimes the fights became general, and resulted in a large loss of life. But eventually both the alcohol and the Mountain Men were exhausted. Those who had gambled away their guns and horses pledged their next year's catch for new supplies, and all stumbled away into the wilderness, their year's earnings squandered in a few days of barbaric dissipation.

Gradually the trading forts on the Upper Missouri and the Yellowstone, the Platte and the Arkansas, and other strategically situated locations began to take the place of the mountain valley rendezvous. Smaller forts there had always been, built for both defence (which the rendezvous could not provide) and trade, ever since Manuel Lisa had established himself at the mouth of the Bighorn in the footsteps of Lewis and Clark. Now, in the 1830s, the large forts began to go up on American territory (and sometimes on Mexican) after the style of the Hudson's Bay Company's Fort Vancouver, which had been established by the Canadians on the Columbia as early as 1824. Fort Union and Fort McKenzie on the Upper Missouri, Fort Laramie on the North Platte, and Bent's Fort (or Fort William) on the Arkansas were the most important of these for the fur trade. Bent's Fort, built in 1833–4 by the brothers Charles and William Bent and their partner Céran St Vrain, near the site of the present-day city of La Junta, Colorado, was visited by many travellers – Francis Parkman was there in 1846 – but let Frederick Ruxton speak again:

> Bent's Fort is situated on the left or northern bank of the river Arkansa, about one hundred miles from the foot of the Rocky Mountains – on a low and level bluff of the prairie which here slopes gradually to the water's-edge. The walls are built entirely of adobes – or sun-burned bricks – in the form of a hollow square, at two corners of which are circular flanking towers of the same material. The entrance is by a large gateway into the square, round which are the rooms occupied by the traders and employés of the host. These are small in size, with walls coloured by a white-wash made of clay found in the prairie. Their flat roofs are defended along the exterior by parapets of adobe, to serve as a cover to marksmen firing from the top; and along the coping grow plants of cactus of all the varieties common in the plains. In the centre of the square is the press for packing the furs; and there are three large rooms, one used as a store and magazine, another as a council-room, where the Indians assemble for their 'talks', whilst the third is the common dining-hall, where the traders, trappers, and hunters, and all employés, feast upon the best provender the game-covered country affords. Over the culinary department presided of late years a fair lady of colour, Charlotte by name, who was, as she loved to say, 'de onlee lady in de dam Injun country', and who moreover was celebrated from Long's Peak to the Cumbres Espanolás for slap-jacks and pumpkin pies. . . .
>
> In the corral, groups of leather-clad mountaineers, with 'decks' of 'euker' and 'seven up', gamble away their hard-earned peltries. The employés – mostly St Louis Frenchmen and Canadian voyageurs – are pressing packs of buffalo skins, beating robes, or engaged in other duties of a trading fort. Indian squaws, the wives of mountaineers, strut about in all the pride of beads and fanfaron, jingling with bells and bugles, and happy as paint can make them. Hunters drop in with animals packed with deer or buffalo meat to supply the fort; Indian dogs look anxiously in at the gateway, fearing to enter and encounter the enmity of their natural enemies, the whites: and outside the fort, at any hour of the day or night, one may safely wager to see a dozen coyotes or prairie wolves loping round, or seated on their haunches, and looking gravely on, waiting patiently for some chance offal to be cast outside. Against the walls, groups of

5. Major Long holding a Council with the Pawnees. Engraving by I. Clark after S. Seymour from Edwin James's *An Account of an Expedition to the Rocky Mountains*, London, 1823.

6*a*. Lewis and Clark and Sacajawea – an 'heroic statue' by Charlie Russell, 1917.

6*b*. The Missouri River and Council Bluffs – from a steel engraving after a sketch by F. Piercy in James Linforth's *Route from Liverpool to the Great Salt Valley*, 1846.

7*a*. Interior of the Hut of a Mandan Chief, by Karl Bodmer.

7*b*. Offering of the Mandan Indians, by Karl Bodmer.

8 (*a*) A Piekann Chief, (*b*) A Mandan Chief. (*c*) Woman of the Snake Tribe. (*d*) Dacota Woman and Assiniboin girl – all by Karl Bodmer, 1833.

9*a*. A Blackfoot Indian on horseback, by Karl Bodmer.

9*b*. Indians hunting the buffalo, by Karl Bodmer.

10*a*. The Steamer *Yellowstone* on 19 April 1833, by Karl Bodmer.

10*b*. Camp of the Gros Ventres on the Upper Missouri, by Karl Bodmer.

11*a*. Beaver Hut, by Karl Bodmer.

11*b*. Encampment of Indians on the Green River at the base of the Rocky Mountains, 1837, by Alfred Jacob Miller.

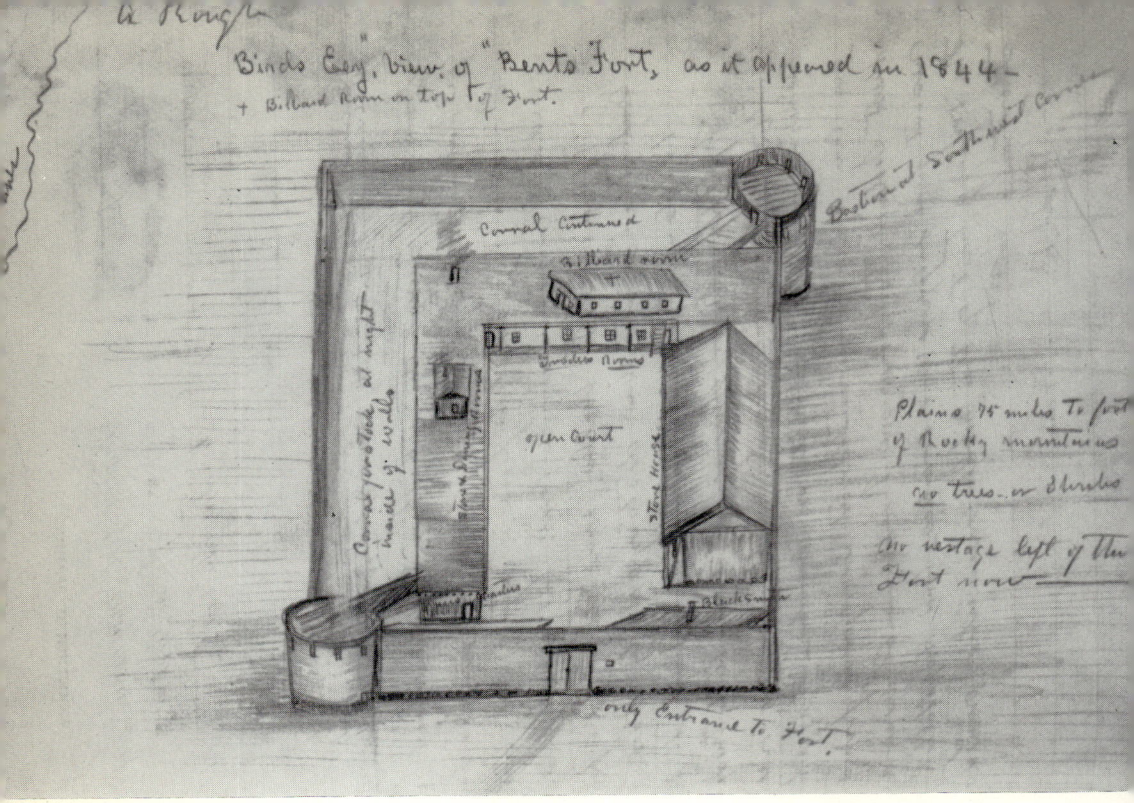

12*a*. 'Bird's Eye view' of Bent's Fort, 1844, by W. M. Boggs.

12*b*. Astor Medal, American Fur Company photograph by F. Jay Haynes.

12*c*. Jim Bridger.

> Indians, too proud to enter without an invitation, lean, wrapped in their buffalo robes, sulky and evidently ill at ease to be so near the whites without a chance of fingering their scalp-locks; their white lodges shining in the sun, at a little distance from the river-banks; their horses feeding in the plain beyond.
>
> The appearance of the fort is very striking, standing as it does hundreds of miles from any settlement, on the vast and lifeless prairie, surrounded by hordes of hostile Indians, and far out of reach of intercourse with civilised man; its mud-built walls inclosing a little garrison of a dozen hardy men, sufficient to hold in check the numerous tribes of savages ever thirsting for their blood. Yet the solitary stranger passing this lone fort, feels proudly secure when he comes within sight of the 'stars and stripes' which float above the walls.

Bent's Fort queened it for fifteen years over the whole area of the Southern Plains. With the possible exceptions of Forts Pierre and Union it was the largest in the trans-Mississippi West. It was certainly 'the largest establishment in that vast terrain between St Louis and the Pacific'.[1] Fortunately we know exactly what it looked like, though nothing of its structure has survived above ground. Not only did Ruxton, Parkman, Thomas Jefferson, Farnham, Sarah Shelby Magoffin, J. C. Frémont, Alexander Barclay, and many other visitors and residents describe it in words, but W. M. Boggs (in 1844), Lieutenant J. W. Abert (in 1845), and Edward Kern (in 1846) all made drawings of it which have survived; no photograph, though, is known to have been taken of it – this would just have been possible – before William Bent, then its sole owner, partially destroyed and then abandoned it in 1852.[2] Artists of the calibre of Bodmer, Miller, and Bierstadt did not leave paintings of Bent's Fort comparable to those made by the first of these of Fort Union, the second of Fort Laramie and the third of the rendezvous country of the Wind river valley, and elsewhere, but W. M. Boggs' annotated if crudely drawn bird's-eye-view, even showing the Bent's billiard room on the roof, allows us to imagine ourselves back where Kit Carson brought in his trophies of the hunt, where Alexander

[1] *Bent's Fort. National Historic Site.* Folder of the National Park Service of the United States Department of the Interior (1963). See also David Lavender, *Bent's Fort* (New York, 1954) *passim.*

[2] The site was partially excavated by the Colorado Historical Society in 1954, and the excavation is to be completed by the National Park Service. A reconstruction of the Fort adjacent to its original site may also be made by the Service, but meanwhile private enterprise has erected a full-scale replica near Morrison, Colorado. See also plate 12a.

Barclay wielded his telescope (specially imported from England to spy out 'hostiles' on the Plains), where Milton Sublette died of a gangrenous leg, where Susan Magoffin had her miscarriage, and where Lieutenant Emory on 2 August 1846 watched the entry of General Kearny's Army of the West.[1]

Bent's Fort was on the mountain branch of the Santa Fé trail just where it left United States for Mexican territory, and therefore was not built for the convenience of the Mountain Men alone. But they were its most picturesque denizens, even more than the Indians who pitched their lodges around its walls – for it stood at the meeting-place of the hunting grounds of the Cheyenne, Prairie Apache, Arapaho, Comanche, Ute, and Kiowa, and was also visited by bands of Shoshones, Crows, and Gros Ventres. No Indian, not even the lordly Yellow Wolf,[2] or White Thunder, Cheyenne chief and father of Owl Woman, William Bent's first wife, created such a stir as did Old Bill Williams, when he rode in from one of his lone and phenomenally successful hunting trips and ordered liquor for all – but mostly for himself. Ruxton knew him well – in so far as any man could 'know' the old coon – and has described him unforgettably.[3]

> Williams always rode ahead, his body bent over his saddle-horn, across which rested a long heavy rifle, his keen gray eyes peering from under the slouched brim of a flexible felt-hat, black and shining with grease. His buckskin hunting-shirt, bedaubed until it had the appearance of polished leather, hung in folds over his bony carcass; his nether extremities being clothed in pantaloons of the same material (with scattered fringes down the outside of the leg – which ornaments, however, had been pretty well thinned to supply 'whangs' for mending mocassins or pack-saddles), which, shrunk with wet, clung tightly to his long, spare, sinewy legs. His feet were thrust into

[1] W. H. Emory, *Notes of a Military Reconnaisance from Fort Leavenworth to San Diego . . . made in 1846–47* (U.S. Senate Documents, 30th Congress, 1st Session, Exec. No. 7, Washington, D.C., 1848). 'I looked in the direction of Bent's Fort, and saw a huge United States Flag flowing in the breeze and straining every fibre of an ash-pole planted over the centre of a gate. The mystery was soon revealed by a column of dust in the east, advancing with about the velocity of a fast walking horse. It was "The Army of the West".'

[2] 'A man of considerable influence, of enlarged views and gifted with more foresight than any man of his tribe . . .' J. W. Abert, *Examination of New Mexico in the year 1846–47* (U.S. Senate Documents, 30th Congress, 1st Session, Exec. No. 23, Washington, D.C., 1848), p. 10. Abert also sketched O-Cum-Who-Wust ('Yellow Wolf') for his report.

[3] G. F. Ruxton, *Life in the Far West* (1951 edn), pp. 178–9; pp. 112–13.

a pair of Mexican stirrups, made of wood, and as big as coal-scuttles; and iron spurs of incredible proportions, with tinkling drops attached to the rowels, were fastened to his heel – a bead-worked strap, four inches broad, securing them over the instep. In the shoulder-belt which sustained his powder-horn and bullet-pouch, were fastened the various instruments essential to one pursuing his mode of life. An awl, with deer-horn handle, and the point defended by a case of cherry-wood carved by his own hand, hung at the back of the belt, side by side with a worm for cleaning the rifle; and under this was a squat and quaint-looking bullet mould, the handles guarded by strips of buckskin to save his fingers from burning when running balls, having for its companion a little bottle made from the point of an antelope's horn, scraped transparent, which contained the 'medicine' used in baiting the traps. The old coon's face was sharp and thin, a long nose and chin hob-nobbing each other; and his head was always bent forward, giving him the appearance of being hump-backed. He *appeared* to look neither to the right nor left, but, in fact, his little twinkling eye was everywhere. He looked at no one he was addressing, always seeming to be thinking of something else than the subject of his discourse, speaking in a whining, thin, cracked voice, and in a tone that left the hearer in doubt whether he was laughing or crying.

Old Bill Williams was the most famous of the independent trappers. He sometimes condescended to join a party and occasionally acted as a guide, but never for long. He was essentially a 'loner'. In the end, old (for a Mountain Man) and ill, with even his iron constitution broken down by dissipation, this one-time preacher, who had become more Indian than the Indians, was struck down by a war-party of his own blood-brothers, the Utes, while attempting to salvage some of the equipment left behind by Frémont's ill-fated fourth expedition. His end was as dramatic and as mysterious as that of Jedediah Smith. William Brandon, in introducing a new edition of Old Bill's biography,[1] has provided him with a splendid epitaph:

> The past-master plainsman, the eccentric old-timer, the weathered rock of experience, scarred by Taos lightning and ancient demigodly deeds, the old scout, who is seldom sober and never wrong.

Though, when they discovered who he was, after killing him, the Utes are said to have given him a chief's burial, Old Bill Williams has no

[1] Alpheus H. Favour, *Old Bill Williams: Mountain Man* (Chapel Hill, 1936; new edn, Norman, Oklahoma, 1962), p. ix.

known grave. But he lives on as a type in Western fiction and Western movies without number; any time the television screen flickers on a Mountain Man it is likely, with slight variations, to be Old Bill again.

More fortunate in his biographers than Bill Williams – who hardly emerges even from Ruxton's vivid pen as a lovable figure – was Jim Bridger. Everybody liked Jim, from Sir William Drummond Stewart, who had brought out an English Life Guard's dress uniform for him to strut about in at the rendezvous,[1] to General Grenville Dodge, the Chief Engineer on the Union Pacific Railroad, who had his deeds carved in stone; and J. Cecil Alter's life of him – first published in 1925 – has become a classic.[2]

Orphaned at thirteen, apprenticed to a St Louis blacksmith at fourteen, young Jim Bridger was all of eighteen years and three days old when, on 20 March 1822, he had read out to him (for he could not as yet read, and never became adept at the art) Andrew Henry's and William H. Ashley's celebrated advertisement in a St Louis newspaper 'TO ENTERPRISING YOUNG MEN . . .'[3] Another enterprising young man to hearken to that siren song was Jedediah Strong Smith, who headed west at the same time as Jim as a member of Major Henry's fur-hunting party, 'a rifle in one hand and a bible in the other'. Jim had only the rifle, but it was a trusty snub-nosed Hawken, and with that the poor unlettered orphan was ready for any wilderness.

Forty years later Jim was still on the trail, by this time the most experienced Mountain Man and guide in all the West, and one of the very few survivors of all those enterprising young men. On 17 October 1862 another eighteen-year-old adventurer, Caspar Collins (son of Colonel William O. Collins, U.S. Army) wrote home to Mother from Fort Laramie: 'We had Major Bridger with us as guide. He knows

[1] Alfred Jacob Miller drew this remarkable scene. See also M. R. Porter and O. Davenport, *Scotsman in Buckskins* (New York, 1963), *passim*. Jim Bridger 'in armour' *faces* p. 149.

[2] J. Cecil Alter, *James Bridger: A Historical Narrative* (Salt Lake City, 1925; new and enlarged edn, Columbus, 1950; new and revised edn, entitled simply *Jim Bridger*, Norman, Oklahoma, 1962, which is the one cited here). The oft-told and greatly embroidered story of Hugh Glass and the Grizzly bear, and of Jim's alleged ignominious part in that adventure is carefully analysed by Mr Alter. But the story goes on being stock-in-trade of the 'pulp' merchants.

[3] 'TO ENTERPRISING YOUNG MEN. The Subscriber wishes to Engage one hundred young men to ascend the Missouri River to its source, there to be employed for one, two, or three years. For particulars enquire of Major Andrew Henry near the lead mines in the County of Washington who will ascend with and command the party; or the subscriber near St Louis – William H. Ashley.'

more of the Rocky Mountains than any living man. He is totally uneducated but speaks English, Spanish and French equally well, beside nearly a dozen Indian tongues . . . He has been in many Indian battles and has several arrow wounds.'[1] Young Caspar lovingly describes the fifty-eight-year-old Jim Bridger (to whom, as the context makes clear, this apparently generalized description specifically applies): 'These old Mountaineers are curious-looking fellows. They nearly all wear big white hats with beaver around it; a loose white coat of buck or antelope skins, trimmed fantastically with beaver-fur; buffalo breeches with strings hanging for ornaments along the sides; a Mexican saddle, mocassins and spurs, with rowels ten inches long, which jingle as they ride. They have bridles with, sometimes, ten dollars' worth of silver ornaments on; Indian ponies, a heavy rifle, a Navy revolver, a hatchet and a Bowie knife. They have a rawhide lasso tied on one side of the saddle . . .'[2]

Jim stayed on the trail for nearly another twenty years after this, riding his trusty horse Ruff around the fields of his Missouri farm even when almost completely blind, guided only by the horse and by the warning bark of his dog Old Sultan. He went over the final divide on 17 July 1881, and in 1904, the hundredth anniversary of his birth, his great admirer, General Dodge, had a seven-foot granite column erected to his memory in Kansas City, and pronounced an oration which, while barely this side of idolatry, was in some ways an even better memorial to the old Mountain Man: 'Unquestionably Bridger's claim to remembrance rests on the extraordinary part he bore in the explorations of the West. As a guide he was without an equal. He was a complete master of plains and woodcraft. In all my experience I never saw Bridger meet an obstacle he could not overcome.' General Dodge's *Biographical Sketch of James Bridger* (1905) expands and documents such praises, and the careful researches of J. Cecil Alter, twenty years later and in subsequent editions of his definitive biography, have carefully winnowed out the chaff (much of it resulting from Jim's own well-developed sense of humour and weakness for leg-pulling) from the Bridger story. Much that remains would seem incredible if only it had not been proved true beyond reasonable doubt by these same careful

[1] Alter, *op. cit.*, p. 301, and p. 152. One of those arrows, long ago, had been extracted on the Oregon Trail by Dr Marcus Whitman, the Rev. Samuel Parker marvelling at Jim's unflinching fortitude during the operation. See Samuel Parker, *Journal* (3rd edn, Ithaca, 1842), p. 80.

[2] *Ibid.*, p. 299.

researches. As Jim himself once remarked: 'They said I was the damnedest liar ever lived,' when he had described the marvels of what became Yellowstone National Park, now attested to by millions.[1]

One cannot have enough of Jim Bridger, but there were other Mountain Men; none nicer – except, of course, Kit Carson, unless you were an Indian – though many not so nice. 'How pleasant to meet Mr Bridger!' But what about Edward Rose, scalper extraordinary, and a white Crow 'chief' in that tribe's wars against the Blackfoot, who 'forsook civilization entirely',[2] Jim Beckwith, another Crow convert, who published his own autobiography[3] before being liquidated by poison, probably by one of his own squaws, and last, but not least, Charles Gardner, or 'Cannibal Phil', who hailed from the City of Brotherly Love, and who, taking quite literally the old Mountain Man adage 'Meat's Meat',[4] when marooned in the mountains by a snowstorm 'subsisted comfortably on the flesh of his current squaw'.[5]

At his lowest a 'case study in the reversion to the primitive' and a curiosity of American history, the fur trapper of the Far West was, at his highest, much more than this. For every Edward Rose there was a Jedediah Smith, for every Jim Beckwith there was a Joseph Reddeford Walker, for every Charles Gardner a Peter Skene Ogden. And then of course there was always Kit Carson . . . Kit Carson, who has many other claims to fame, seems, like his most famous employer, John C. Frémont (whom he helped to guide on four of his expeditions to the West), never to have blazed an entirely new trail across the Far West.

[1] Who could have been expected to believe in a river that ran cold at the top, but hot at the bottom (Fire Hole River), petrified tree-trunks still standing and a dark glass cliff (Obsidian Cliff), leave alone geysers spouting up seventy feet or more, with a terrible hissing noise, at regular intervals (Old Faithful), a waterfall three times as high as Niagara (Yellowstone Falls), and springs so hot that meat could be cooked on the top terraces and 'delightful baths' taken on the lower ones (Mammoth Hot Springs)! Needless to say, it was an army officer, John W. Gunnison, and not a Mountain Man, who took the first Mammoth hot bath. See further Alter, pp. 76–8.

[2] Billington, *American Frontiersman,* p. 10. For more gory details of Rose's career, see Z. Leonard, *Adventures of Zenas Leonard, Fur Trader and Trapper 1831–1836* (Cleveland, 1904), pp. 262–70.

[3] *Life and Adventures of James P. Beckwourth* – his 'writing name' – (New York, 1856), edited and ghosted by T. D. Bonner. Charles G. Leland's revised edn (London, 1892), pursues James to the bitter end – by arsenic.

[4] 'In their willingness to consume anything that walked, swam, wriggled or crawled, the trappers were strikingly akin to the Indians.'

[5] Billington, *Far Western Frontier* p. 50 (cf. Ruxton, *Life in the Far West,* p. 98). Billington, *American Frontiersman,* p. 10, based on the article by Leroy R. Hafen, 'Mountain Men: Big Phil the Cannibal', in *Colorado Magazine of History,* XIII (March 1936), pp. 53–8.

Truly, he has a river, a pass, a city and even a 'sink' named after him, but this, like so much of Frémont's geographical nomenclature, was a piece of topographical engineering rather than the recognition of a true discovery. Frémont even gypped Peter Skene Ogden out of the glory of having actually discovered, in 1828, the river which the latter modestly named 'The Unknown', but which his men more appropriately christened 'the Ogden' – or sometimes 'Mary's River', after Ogden's wife. Seventeen years later, points out Cleland's finger of scorn, 'John Charles Frémont, the follower of other men's trails, gratuitously dropped the name Ogden and called the river the Humboldt'.[1] Baron Alexander von Humboldt had never been within a thousand miles of it, but then Ogden was a partisan of the Hudson's Bay Company, and not an agent of Manifest Destiny and the Benton Enterprises.

Innumerable fur trappers, both famous and obscure, made contributions to the opening up of the ways to the Far West and both Jim Bridger and Old Bill Williams, each of whom had a remarkable topographical instinct, were among them; but the two men who contributed most were undoubtedly Jedediah Smith and Peter Skene Ogden, while the leader of the most remarkable single journey overland to the Pacific (when its significance for the future development of the area is considered) was Joseph Reddeford Walker. If the lines of travel of the parties led by these three men west of the Continental Divide in the one decade between 1824 and 1834 are superimposed on a map of that area[2] it is seen that they interlaced it with a network of trails, many of which they were the first, or among the first, white men to follow, and nearly all of which later proved of inestimable worth to the overland waggon parties of the 1840s and 1850s, to the railroad builders of the 1860s, to the 'tin lizzies' of the 1920s, and even to the air-conditioned Cadillacs of the 1960s.[3]

Beginning his career in the fur trade, as has been seen, in 1822,

[1] Cleland, *Reckless Breed*, p. 324. Lieut (later general) John Charles Frémont, of the U.S. Corps of Topographical Engineers, and son-in-law of the influential and aggressive 'Western' Senator Thomas Hart Benton of Missouri will reappear often in these pages (especially in Chapters VI and VII). He is one of the most controversial figures in American Western history. Even Allan Nevins has changed his mind three times about him in successive editions of his standard biography of Frémont.

[2] See maps on pages 124 and 127.

[3] J. Alexander Carroll, Western author, editor, and self-confessed 'dude', told an historical conference in 1961, 'I resolved to re-explore every nook and cranny of the West that could be reached by air-conditioned Cadillac'. But in an emergency he could not, of course, eat his horsepower, or drink his brake-fluid.

Jedediah Smith was over the Continental Divide in 1824 (at the South Pass, now beginning to come into regular use) and again in 1825 when he trapped with Ashley on the Green river and around the shores of the Great Salt Lake – which Jim Bridger had first seen, tasted, and spat out in 1824. But Smith's first great expedition into the farthest West was in 1826, when General Ashley, his fortune made, had sold out his interests in the fur trade to his three young associates Smith, Jackson,[1] and Sublette.[2] Ashley had planned this expedition before he retired, but Smith led it on behalf of the new partnership. Leaving the rendezvous on Bear river, east of Salt Lake, in August 1826, with about fourteen companions, Smith was back there again on 3 July 1827 with three of his men. 'My arrival,' he wrote, 'caused a considerable bustle in camp . . . a small cannon, brought up from St Louis, was loaded and fired for a salute.' Next day, being Independence Day, the rejoicings were redoubled 'for myself and party had been given up for lost'. He told General William Clark in a report dated 17 July 1827, 'When we arrived at the Salt Lake we had but one horse and one mule remaining, which were so feeble and poor that they could scarcely carry the little camp equipage which I had along; the balance of my horses I was compelled to eat as they gave out. The company are now starting, and therefore must close my communication. Yours respectfully Jedediah S. Smith.'[3] Despite all the hardships he had encountered in eleven months on the trail this tough young man (he was still only twenty-nine years old) was off again on 13 July, after less than a fortnight's rest,[4] to rescue and relieve the men he had left behind on the Stanislaus river in California. From this second expedition to California on which he started off with eighteen men, he returned with only one member, Arthur Black, of the combined parties of 1826 and 1827. Most of the others were

[1] David E. Jackson, after whom Jackson, Wyoming, Jackson's Hole, and Jackson Lake were named. As yet he has found no biographer, but, *si monumentum requires . . .* what's better than the Grand Teton National Park!

[2] William L. Sublette, the most famous of five brothers, all of whom were engaged in the fur trade. See further, John E. Sunder, *Bill Sublette: Mountain Man* (Norman, Oklahoma, 1959), *passim.*

[3] Maurice Sullivan, *The Travels of Jedediah Smith* (Santa Ana, 1934), printed the fragments which survive of Smith's letters and reports. Dale Morgan has now woven them into a definitive critical biography, *Jedediah Smith and the Opening of the West* (Indianapolis, 1953. Revised edition pending). Any account of Smith's career must lean heavily on Dale Morgan. The 'Bison Books' paperback edition is a reprint of the unrevised first edition of 1953.

[4] The report to Clark, cited above, seems either to have been misdated or else it was not finished until four days after he set out. See Cleland, *Reckless Breed*, p. 87.

dead. Jedediah Smith did not get back for the summer rendezvous of 1828; he and his partners were, indeed, not reunited until the summer of 1829, at Henry's Fork of the Snake river in Idaho, whence they repaired to the rendezvous at Pierre's Hole, west of the Tetons. This was attended on 20 August 1829 by about 175 trappers.[1] And what a tale Jedediah Smith and Arthur Black had to tell around the camp-fires at that rendezvous! Smith, who knew Latin as well as his Bible, may conceivably have had a more than nodding acquaintance with Homer as well. If he did he might well have compared himself to Odysseus, so remarkable and so harrowing had his adventures been in the three years since he had first set out for California, and especially on his second, more tragic, expedition to the Pacific coast.

On the 1826–7 expedition Smith had not lost a man, though he had left all but two of them behind in California when he decided to scale the high Sierras on his return journey in May 1827. On the 1827–9 expedition which followed virtually the same route from Salt Lake to southern California – via the Sevier, the Virgin, and the Colorado rivers, across the Mojave desert to the San Bernardino Mountains and the Mission farms of San Gabriel, a route later to become famous as 'the Mormon outlet' – Smith lost ten of his men in an Indian ambush while crossing the Colorado at the Mojave villages. One of these was Silas Gobel, one of the two men he had taken back with him across the Great Salt Desert to the 1827 rendezvous, an epic feat of endurance that has been called 'one of the greatest single exploits in the whole history of western exploration'.[2]

Smith left three of his nine surviving men, one of them badly wounded, in southern California, but he did not tarry there himself for another visit to the Mission of San Gabriel or to San Diego, being unsure of the welcome he would receive,[3] and hurried instead to the camp on the Stanislaus where his 1826 party awaited him, reaching

[1] Robert Newell, *Memoranda of Travel in Missouri* (Portland, Oregon, 1959), p. 31. Newell was a member of Sublette's supply party which left St Louis on 17 March 1829. He wrote a most illuminating diary, survived more than another decade of fur-trapping and rendezvous-ing and finally settled down on a farm in Oregon.

[2] Charles Kelly in *Utah Historical Quarterly*, Vol. III, No. 1, p. 27, as quoted by Cleland, *Reckless Breed*, p. 84.

[3] While the Franciscan Fathers had been friendly, Governor Echeandia had been distinctly cool towards the Americans in 1826. Smith himself has left only a fragmentary account of this first winter of a party of American fur trappers in Alta California, but his clerk and second-in-command, Harrison Rogers, kept a diary which has survived and is most revealing and entertaining reading. The account of this doughty Protestant of his friendly theological disputes with the jolly friars at what

them on 18 July. Accompanied by only two of his men – for he realized that the intrusion of the whole party into the Mexican coastal settlements once again would not be tolerated by the authorities there – he then visited the Missions of San José and Santa Clara for supplies and to attempt to establish friendly relations. He was placed under open arrest by a suspicious Father Dúran,[1] and had to visit Monterey and explain himself all over again to an even more irascible Governor Echeandia. Before he could get away and back to his men he had to post a bond for $30,000 (guaranteed by four prominent Yankee residents of Monterey) with the Mexican authorities, and had lost nearly six months. His men had relieved their enforced idleness in the San Joaquin valley by desultory hunting and trapping, though it was not good beaver country and they had but few traps with them, and by making, under Harrison Rogers, a sightseeing and shopping[2] visit to San Francisco Bay. It was the new year 1828 before they set out on their return journey. As it was far too late (or too soon) to get across the Sierras, on which snow was already falling, they sloshed their way up the flooded Sacramento valley to the Feather river. Here beaver were plentiful – one night twenty were caught[3] – and bear were almost one

---

he sometimes called 'The mansion' can be read in H. C. Dale, *The Ashley–Smith Exploration and the Discovery of a Central Route to the Pacific 1822–1829* (Glendale, California, 1941). Rogers commanded the party until Smith returned in 1827. He unfortunately perished in the massacre on the Umpqua river on 14 July 1828. He, too, must have been very pleasant to know.

[1] Dúran was to tangle some two years later with James Ohio Pattie, another American interloper, over a small matter of payment for smallpox inoculations. See James Ohio Pattie (more than assisted by Timothy Flint), *The Personal Narrative of James Ohio Pattie of Kentucky* (Cincinnati, 1831); reprinted (ed. R. G. Thwaites as Vol. 18 of *Early Western Travels*, Cleveland, 1905; paperbound edn, New York, 1962). Pattie's *Narrative* is more exciting than it is reliable, but amid exaggerations and much padding – like his (or Flint's) description of Mission San Luis Rey, lifted bodily out of La Pérouse's description of the Carmel Mission (see *supra*, Chapter III, p. 71ff) printed thirty-three years earlier – it is in essentials authentic. His was the first American book to get into print describing in detail the missions and the life of Mexican *Alta California*, and preceded Dana's *Two Years before the Mast*, for which this claim is often made, by nine years. It is equally good reading.

[2] The only 'shops' there at that time were occasional merchant ships, come to barter their very mixed cargoes for hides and tallow. The first permanent building in what is now the city of San Francisco was not put up until nearly a decade later. But they could have visited the Spanish *presidio* (fallen into decay) above the as-yet-unnamed Golden Gate, and the Mission of Saint Francis of Assisi along a cow-path about four miles away. They did find a kindly German merchant, Henry Virmond, who was willing to trade with them from his ship.

[3] 'Great trapping,' said Jedediah Smith, for 'I had but 28 traps.' Sullivan, *op. cit.* p. 68.

too many for Harrison Rogers. Elk, deer, antelope, coyotes, wolves, coons, swan, geese, brant, and wild ducks also abounded. The Indians too, were numerous, harmless and, in Smith's opinion, 'the lowest intermediate link between man and the Brute creation'. Apart from the bears – one of them nearly killed Smith's horse – this was truly a hunter's and trapper's paradise. For most of the men of this party it was to be their last paradise on earth, for when they turned towards the coast in an effort to force themselves up into Oregon the trail grew worse and worse and the Indians more hostile. They reached the sea on 8 June 1828, and the mouth of the Umpqua river on 9 July. Five days later an Indian attack decimated the party. Only Smith (who had been absent from camp reconnoitring in a canoe) and three of his men (one of whom made a lone journey all the way to Fort Vancouver on the Columbia) escaped. All their companions, all their gear, and all their furs were gone. It was utter disaster. They were succoured and re-equipped by the ever-hospitable Dr McLaughlin, who sent a most dramatic account of their misadventures back to the Hudson's Bay Company in London,[1] and immediately diverted a trapping party and some of his best hunters to salvage Smith's furs and punish the Umpqua Indians. For the jolly Harrison Rogers and his once merry men they could do nothing except bury eleven skeletons they found 'whitening in the sun'. Four bodies remained unaccounted for.[2]

But for Jedediah Smith himself this was not yet the end of the trail. Over seven hundred skins and thirty-nine horses were recovered from the Indians, and though McLaughlin had spent over a thousand dollars on the relief expedition, he and Sir George Simpson refused compensation and paid Smith $3,200 for his furs and horses. After wintering at Fort Vancouver, Smith and Black (the other two men stayed on there) set off on their own – 'sporting with Life or courting danger to madness', in the opinion of Sir George Simpson who never sent out his own men in parties of less than forty or fifty – up the Columbia valley to the Grand Coulee, across what is now eastern Washington and northern Idaho, past Lewis and Clark's 'Traveller's Rest' (Missoula, Montana) – where they did not rest – to effect their rendezvous with David Jackson and later with William Sublette. Jedediah Smith had come almost full circle of the American Far West. The cost had been high. Yet Smith's

[1] E. E. Rich (ed.), *The Letters of John McLaughlin from Fort Vancouver to the Governor and Committee, First Series, 1825–38* (Toronto, 1941), pp. 68–70. Letter dated 10 August 1828.

[2] Cleland, *Reckless Breed*, p. 113.

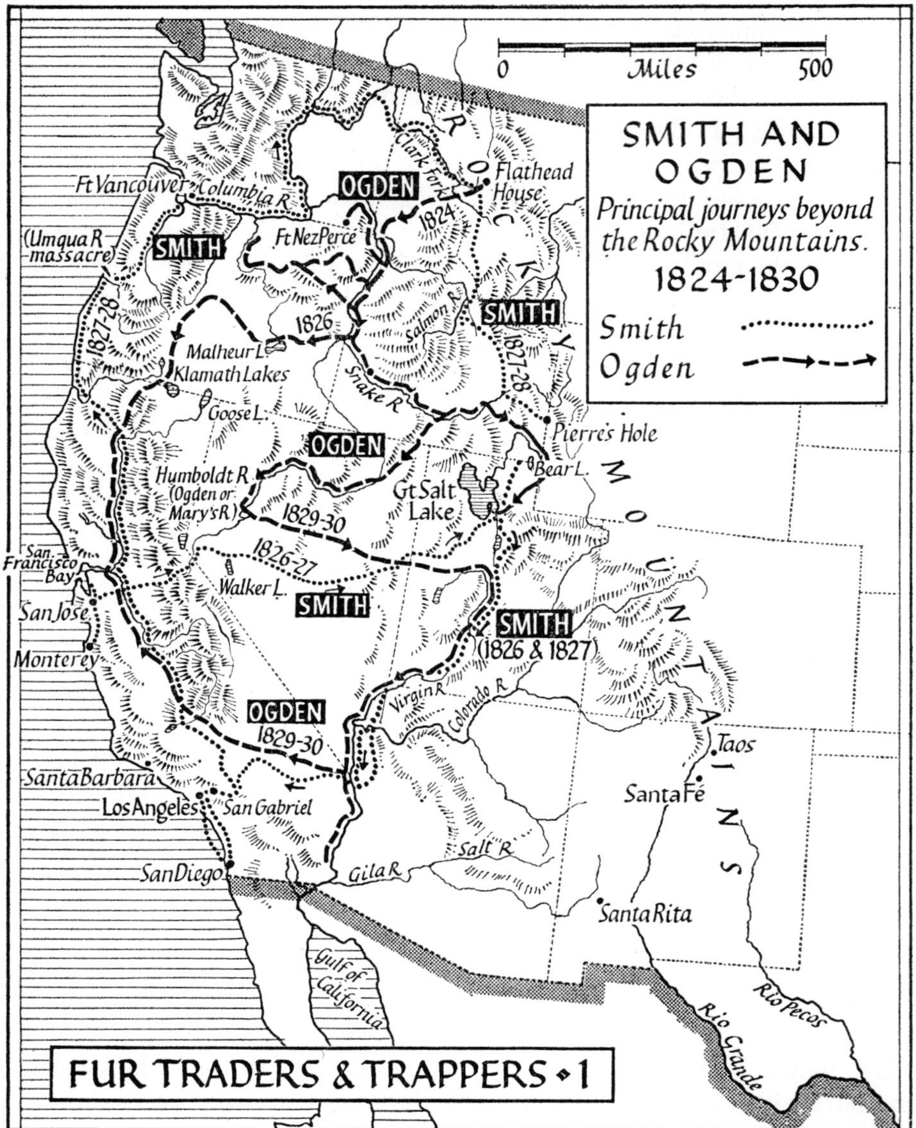

0 Miles 500
SMITH AND OGDEN
Principal journeys beyond the Rocky Mountains.
1824-1830
Smith
Ogden
ROCKY MOUNTAINS
OGDEN
SMITH
Ft Vancouver
Columbia R.
Clark Fork
Flathead House
1824
Ft Nez Perce
(Umqua R massacre)
1827-28
1826
Salmon R.
Malheur L.
Klamath Lakes
Snake R.
Goose L.
Pierre's Hole
Bear L.
Humboldt R. (Ogden or Mary's R.)
Gt Salt Lake
1829-30
1826-27
San Francisco Bay
Walker L.
San Jose
Monterey
(1826 & 1827)
Virgin R.
Colorado R.
Taos
Santa Fé
Santa Barbara
Los Angeles
San Gabriel
San Diego
Salt R.
Gila R.
Santa Rita
Gulf of California
Rio Pecos
Rio Grande
FUR TRADERS & TRAPPERS • 1

expeditions to California and the Columbia had far-reaching effects. They aroused the interest of Mountain Men and the United States Government in the Far Western territories, particularly California and the Oregon wilderness, which Smith had traversed. They also led the Hudson's Bay Company to send out reconnaissance expeditions as far south as the Gulf of California and ushered in more than a decade of profitable trapping on the watersheds of California for Dr McLaughlin and his associates.[1]

The man who led the most important of these Hudson's Bay Company expeditions was Peter Skene Ogden who stands 'second only to Smith among the field captains of the fur trade in the decade'.[2] Ogden led a party to the Great Salt Lake in May 1825, very soon after Bridger had reached it; in 1826 he went up the Deschutes and the John Day rivers into hitherto unknown country; in 1827 he visited the Klamath river and explored as far as Mount Shasta; in 1828–9 he made his celebrated discovery of the Unknown river – also known as Mary's and as Ogden's river – which Frémont was to decide should be called the Humboldt. But his name survives at Ogden's Hole, Ogden's Creek, and the City of Ogden,[3] all in Utah. Ogden's journeys took him down as far as the Gulf of California on one occasion (1829–30) and he traversed the San Joaquin and Sacramento valleys of California almost from end to end on his way back north. Taking a brigade out of Fort Vancouver every year from 1824 onwards, Ogden had encountered as many difficulties and tribulations as did Smith. He worked his men hard and the casualties among them were many.[4] This may partially explain why he lost so many by desertion to the Americans, notably in his celebrated encounter with John Gardner's party of Ashley's men at Bear Lake in 1825, as a result of which twenty-three of them went over

[1] Cleland, *Reckless Breed*, p. 116.

[2] Dale Morgan, *Jedediah Smith*, p. 131. Morgan refers scornfully to 'a folk belief which has persisted since the days of the Presidential election of 1856 that nothing of importance happened in the west before Frémont's time'.

[3] I was disappointed not to find a statue of Peter Skene Ogden in the fine square in the centre of the very pleasant city of Ogden, Utah, when I bus-stopped there in 1963. I suspect that if Ogden had been an obscure nineteenth-century Latter-Day Saint and not a Hudson's Bay captain of trappers, he would have been there on his plinth all right, bearded and frock-coated like the other elect. But, of course, Ogden did not found the city and the Mormon elders did. It is much to their credit that they have retained the name.

[4] He said, 'This life makes a man sixty in a few years. A convict at Botany Bay is a gentleman at ease compared to my trappers.' F. C. Elliott, 'The Earliest Travellers on the Oregon Trail', *Oregon Historical Society Quarterly*, Vol. XVIII, p. 80.

to the enemy. The Hudson's Bay Company never forgot or forgave this rebuff.[1]

The itinerary of Ogden's most far-ranging expedition – that of 1829–30[2] – was from the mouth of the Snake river to the Humboldt Sink across a country 'as barren as ever Christian traversed' to the Sevier river, the Virgin, and the Colorado, where twenty-six Mohave Indians were slaughtered, presumably in a move to anticipate any such attack as had been made on Smith's men in 1827. Following the Colorado to its mouth Ogden then returned through the Yuma country to the San Joaquin, where he encountered an American party under Ewing Young and travelled with it up to the Sacramento for a while. Finally, Ogden returned to the Columbia with a thousand beaver skins, only to lose most of them, nine of his men and the records of his expedition in a boat accident near the Dalles on the very last lap of his return to Fort Vancouver.[3]

Other Hudson's Bay trapping parties, notably those led by Laframboise and Work,[4] went down into California in the wake of Ogden all through the 'thirties, and as late as 1841 established a trading post at the little village of Yerba Buena on San Francisco Bay, much to the alarm of its Yankee residents. But it was Peter Skene Ogden, using to a large extent information gleaned from Jedediah Smith, who had blazed the way for them.

Both Smith and Ogden provided material for the map-makers of the 'thirties. Ogden's reports, sent back to London, were used by Aaron Arrowsmith for his map, published in 1834, and the 'J. E. Smith Route' is actually named (though very inaccurately and incompletely indicated) in Albert Gallatin's famous map published in Washington in 1836, which is so much more satisfactory than Captain Bonneville's map of 1837, made without benefit of Smith's data and drawing heavily on the gallant Captain's imagination.[5]

[1] See F. Merk, *Fur Trade and Empire* (Cambridge and London, 1931), p. 274 *et seq*, and E. E. Rich (ed.), *The Letters of John McLaughlin*, First Series, Appendix A, for this incident and its effects on Hudson's Bay policy.

[2] See map, p. 124.

[3] See further, Alice B. Maloney, 'Peter Skene Ogden's Trapping Expedition to California, 1829–30' in *California Historical Society Quarterly* [subsequently to be cited as *C.H.S.Q.*], Vol. XIX, pp. 308–16.

[4] Cleland, *Reckless Breed*, pp. 328–42, gives a detailed account of one of these expeditions and briefly refers to others.

[5] For Bonneville, see p. 128. See further, W. H. Goetzmann, *Army Exploration in the American West*, Carl I. Wheat, 'Mapping the American West, 1540–1857' (*Proceedings American Antiquarian Society*, Vol. 64 (1954)), pp. 19–194, and E. W. Gilbert,

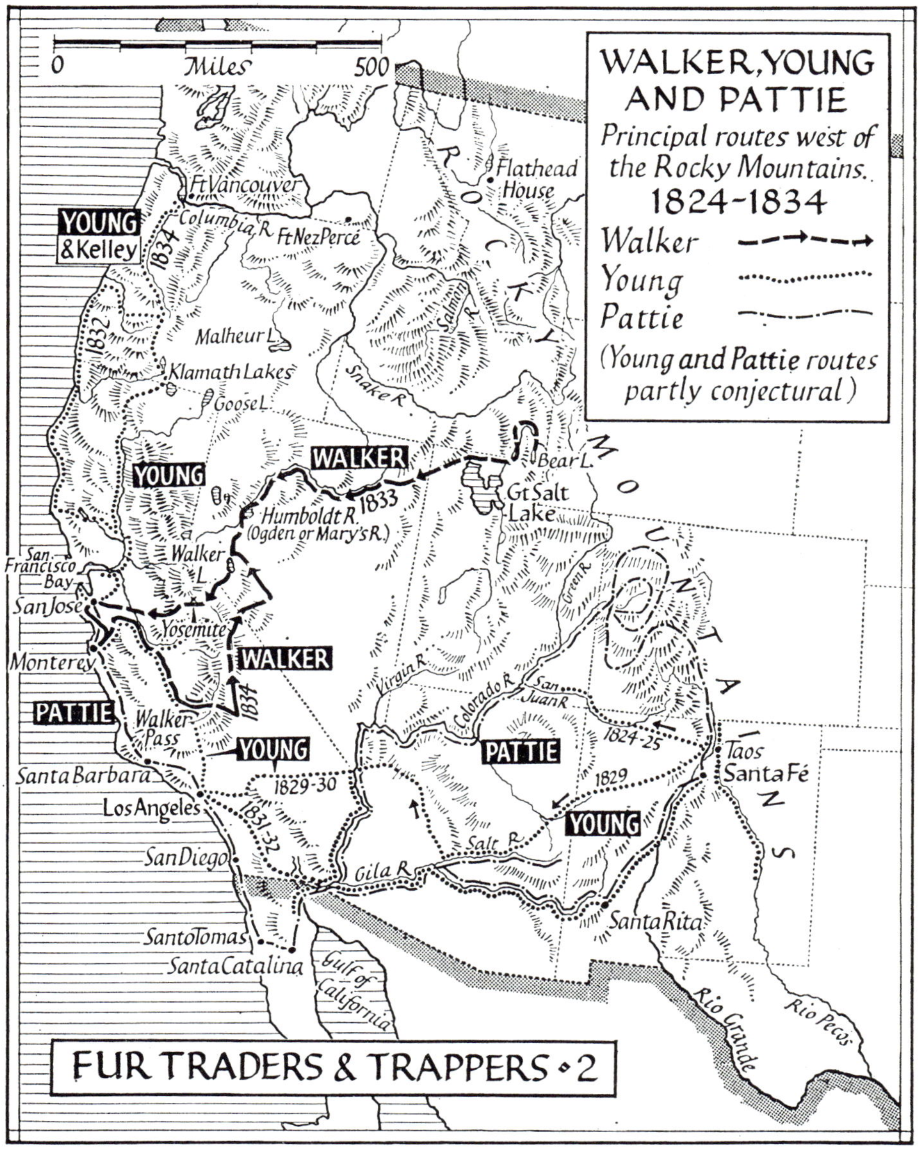
WALKER, YOUNG AND PATTIE
Principal routes west of the Rocky Mountains.
1824-1834
Walker
Young
Pattie
(Young and Pattie routes partly conjectural)
0 Miles 500
FUR TRADERS & TRAPPERS • 2
ROCKY MOUNTAINS
Ft Vancouver
Columbia R.
Ft Nez Percé
Flathead House
YOUNG &Kelley
1834
1832
Malheur L.
Salmon R.
Snake R.
Klamath Lakes
Goose L.
YOUNG
WALKER
1833
Bear L.
Gt Salt Lake
Humboldt R. (Ogden or Mary's R.)
Walker L.
San Francisco Bay
San Jose
Yosemite
WALKER
Monterey
1834
Green R.
Virgin R.
Colorado R.
San Juan R.
PATTIE
Walker Pass
YOUNG
PATTIE
1824-25
Taos
Santa Fé
Santa Barbara
1829-30
1829
Los Angeles
1831-32
YOUNG
Salt R.
San Diego
Gila R.
Santa Rita
Santo Tomas
Santa Catalina
Gulf of California
Rio Grande
Rio Pecos

Yet it was Bonneville who in 1833 was responsible for sending out Joseph Reddeford Walker's remarkable expedition – the only one to rival Smith's and Ogden's in interest and significance during the Mountain Man era. Bonneville did not accompany it beyond the Great Salt Lake and Washington Irving called it 'a disgraceful expedition', presumably because it had not followed Bonneville's limited and somewhat obscure instructions and had not brought back a wealth of furs. But it achieved a remarkable series of 'firsts' in opening up the far West. The expedition to California 'established his [Walker's] fame as an explorer and made him one of the historical pathfinders of the Great West. His trail ran from Salt Lake down the Humboldt River, across the Sierra Nevada Mountains to the coast, from the San Joaquin valley by way of Walker Pass to the Mojave–Colorado basin, up the unknown Owens valley almost to its source and back again to the Humboldt[1] and Salt Lake. His party were the first white men to see and describe the Yosemite valley and the Giant Redwoods of the Tuolumne Grove, the first to find an easy route around the south end of the high sierras (Walker's Pass, 5,250 feet above sea level). He did not pioneer a practicable waggon road to California – that was not his intention – but the first two overland parties of settlers to get through in the 1840s – those of Bidwell-Bartleson and of Chiles – followed much of his route of 1833–4, and the second of these had the advantage of Joseph Reddeford Walker himself as guide. He managed to get its waggons as far as Owens Lake and the party itself all the way to Peachtree valley and the Promised Land. His experiences of 1833–4 were of inestimable value to him and to many others in the years to follow.

A detailed and vivid narrative of the Walker expedition to California written by Zenas Leonard, one of its members, was published as early as 1839. This makes one of the great stories of the American West.[2] Leonard, a well-trained clerk, fresh out of St Louis, probably produced a better account than Walker himself would have done, for Walker, though not illiterate, was a rough-hewn Mountain Man, readier with the spoken than the written word. It is true that Leonard may have bowdlerized their adventures a little for the Pennsylvania

---

The Exploration of Western America, 1800–1850 (Cambridge, 1933), for general appreciations of the cartographical significance of Smith and Ogden. Dale L. Morgan, *Jedediah Smith and his Maps* (San Francisco, 1954), is a specialist study.

[1] Cleland, *Reckless Breed*, pp. 307–8.

[2] *Narrative of the Adventures of Zenas Leonard* 'written by himself' (Clearfield, Pennsylvania, 1839; reprinted Cleveland, 1904).

13*a*–*b*. Exterior and interior views of Fort Laramie, 1837, by Alfred Jacob Miller.

14*a*. A bourgeois, Joseph Reddeford Walker, and his squaw, by Alfred Jacob Miller.

14*b*. 'The Cavalcade' of trappers and Indians, showing Captain William Drummond Stewart on a white horse, by Alfred Jacob Miller.

carriage trade; there is no mention of horse-stealing on the side and little reference to a roistering winter spent in Monterey, California, in and out of 'Tom the Trapper's' grog shop. But Washington Irving[1] and Joe Meek,[2] who refer to such goings on both had an axe to grind, and Meek a long bow to draw. Leonard expressed great admiration for Walker as a leader of men. He had to be, for his brigade of 'forty thieves' is said to have included such indestructible characters as Bill Williams ('himself'), Joe Gale, Mark Hind, Bill Mitchell, the Meek brothers, Alexis Godey, Antoine Janise, Bill Craig, George Nidever, and John Price.[3] Walker was, says Leonard, 'a man well-hardened to the hardships of the wilderness, understood the character of the Indians very well – was kind and affable to his men, but at the same time at liberty to command without giving offense – and to explore unknown regions was his chief delight'.[4]

Walker, a fine figure of a man, over six feet tall, and a former county sheriff in Missouri[5] was, at thirty-five, already 'a great name among the Mountain Men'.[6] The squaws found him irresistible and he on his side considered them desirable though not edible. Two of Alfred Jacob Miller's most famous pictures are the head and shoulders portrait of 'Joseph Walker – The Bourgeois' and the drawing 'Bourgeois W—— and squaw',[7] while yet another, 'The Trapper's Bride', may represent Walker and his latest conquest. But of all his many adventures, the greatest moment in Walker's life was when he discovered the Yosemite valley. He asked that this alone should be commemorated on his tombstone.

[1] Washington Irving, *Adventures of Captain Bonneville* (New York, 1837; many subsequent editions, the latest and best being that edited by Edgeley W. Todd, Norman, Oklahoma, 1961).

[2] As attributed in Frances F. Victor, *The River of the West* (Hartford, 1870), to Joseph L. Meek, though Mrs Victor may have added some embroidery of her own to Joe's notorious fancy-work.

[3] Favour, *Old Bill Williams*, pp. 107–8, gives potted biographies of most of these men. Nidever stayed on in California and made quite a name for himself there. See further, *The Life and adventures of George Nidever*, by W. H. Ellison (Berkeley, 1937).

[4] Leonard, *Narrative*, p. 33. Compare Jedediah Smith's statement about himself, 'I of course expected to find Beaver, which with us hunters is a primary object, but I was also led on by the love of novelty common to all . . .' Sullivan, *Travels of Smith*, p. 26.

[5] As well as policing it he *named* the county. He called it 'Jackson', which was more respectful than Davy Crockett calling his dog 'Jackson'.

[6] George R. Stewart, *The California Trail* (New York, 1962; London, 1964), p. 5.

[7] Miller noted, 'The sketch exhibits a certain etiquette, the squaw's station in travelling is at a considerable distance in the rear of her liege lord, and never at the side of him.' H. McCracken in *The West of Alfred Jacob Miller* (Norman, Oklahoma, 1951), reproduces all three of these pictures. They also appear in many other books about the West. For one of them, see plate 14a.

'This Reckless Breed' of Mountain Men were men of action but of few words. When Dan Tobin was asked for his recollections of Kit Carson he just said, 'I et many a beaver tail with him!' They lived rough and most of them, like Jedediah Smith, died young. Those who lived into old age, growing garrulous at last in their retirement, as did Jim Bridger,[1] have left a folklore behind them which passes belief, but which is probably only a little wider than the truth. Every Mountain Man was not a John Colter – whose 'run' from his Blackfoot Indian captors, alone, unclothed and unarmed, in 1808, is one of the great 'stories' of the West and quite probably even true[2] – but most of them had adventures hardly less hazardous than his. The whole map of the Great West bears the names they gave to streams and peaks, passes and canyons, lakes and mountain meadows. 'Not a hole or corner but has been ransacked by these hardy men,' wrote Ruxton. 'From the Mississippi to the mouth of the Colorado of the West, from the frozen regions of the North to the Gila in Mexico, the beaver hunter has set his traps in every creek and stream. All this vast country, but for the daring and enterprise of these men, would be even now [1847] a *Terra Incognita* to geographers.'[3]

Beside the Mountain Man the cowboy, riding the range, repairing fences and, on rare occasions, 'Painting the Town Red',[4] seems almost tame, the train- and stage-robbing desperado petty, and the hijacking gangster of the Prohibition era a sissy. Yet the era of the Mountain Men, the heyday of the trade in the pelt of the beaver, lasted barely twenty years. By the middle 1840s the silk hat was in fashion to give it the *coup de grâce*. Those Mountain Men who survived settled down, grumbling, on farms, went into the cattle industry, became guides and scouts to the overland parties and the armies of the West, or just faded away, as silently as they habitually moved.

[1] Jim Bridger was known in his early days as 'Old Gabe' not because he had the gift of the gab but because the Bible-toting Jedediah Smith likened him to the Archangel Gabriel, top sergeant of the Lord's brigade and transmitter of his orders to the *engagés*.

[2] See B. Harris, *John Colter* (New York, 1952).

[3] Porter and Hafen, *Ruxton of the Rockies*, p. 228. In the less-dignified language of the typical Mountain Man (Black Harris): 'I've trapped beaver on Platte and Arkansa, and away up on Missoura and Yallar Stone; I've trapped on Columbia, on Lewis Fork, and Green River; I've trapped, marm, on Grand River and the Heeley [Gila] . . . I've trapped in heav'n, in airth, and hell . . .' Ruxton, *Life in the Far West*, p. 8.

[4] The title of a famous painting and of a bronze by Frederic Remington. See also his drawing on p. 297.

CHAPTER VI

Breaking the Waggon Trails West

The trail to Santa Fé, the first of the three great trails across the trans-Mississippi West, may be said to have opened in 1821, fully twenty years before the California and Oregon trails. It could have opened earlier but for the Spanish prohibition on trade between New Mexico and the British and French settlements in the Mississippi valley. Independent Mexico relaxed this ban, and William Becknell, the involuntary 'father of the Santa Fé trade', Thomas James, and the Glenn–Fowler parties, trading warily in the American–Spanish border country on the Upper Arkansas river, were then all invited to visit Santa Fé, and reached it before the end of the year. In 1822, on a second expedition, Becknell pioneered the 'Cimarron cut-off', shorter but more hazardous than the better-watered 'Mountain route' on which Bent's Fort was to be established a decade later. His were the first American waggons to reach Santa Fé. The longer Raton Pass route, used by the pack-trains hitherto, was too steep for the wheeled vehicles of the day. By 1831 one caravan of a hundred waggons carried over $200,000 worth of goods to the New Mexican capital and it was ceasing to be a mere outpost of civilization. The trade had its ups and downs, but it continued every year until 1843, after which, in an atmosphere of ever-worsening relations between Mexico and the United States, General Santa Anna, President of Mexico, reimposed the ban. It was to be finally and triumphantly swept aside by the U.S. 'Army of the West' in 1846.

The Santa Fé Trail has had many chroniclers, but pre-eminent among those of a literary turn of mind who actually participated in the trade was Dr Josiah Gregg. His *Commerce of the Prairies*, first published in 1844,[1] is a vivid and erudite work, on which many later writers have leaned heavily. Gregg himself took part in the trade only between 1831 and 1841, but in his book he surveys its whole development (from the

[1] Josiah Gregg, *Commerce of the Prairies* (2 vols, New York, 1844). Many times reprinted. The reprint edition of the Southwest Press, Dallas, Texas, 1933, is the one cited here. A paperback edition is now available. See also *Diary and Letters of Josiah Gregg*, ed. M. G. Fulton. Introd. by Paul Horgan (2 vols, Norman, Oklahoma, 1941).

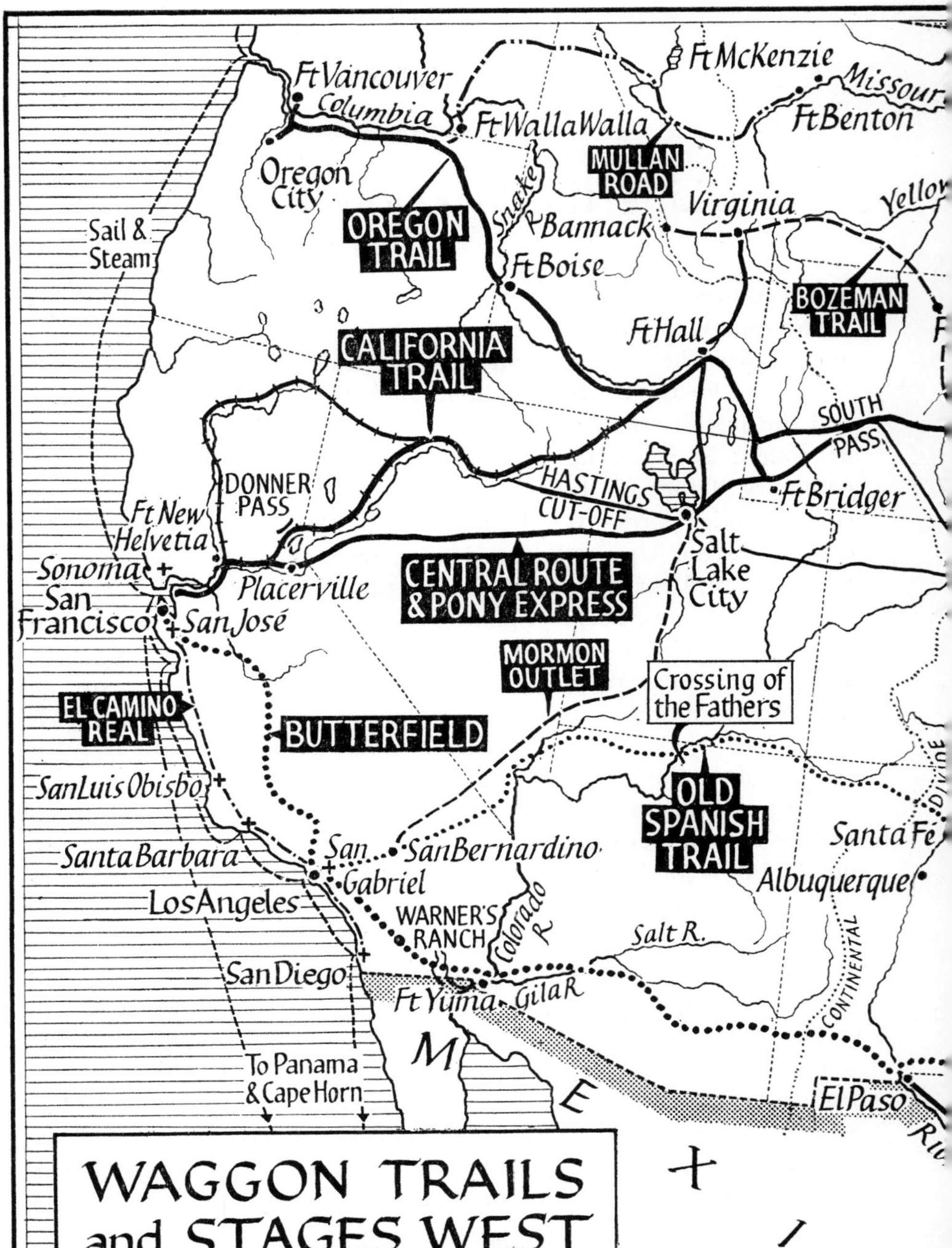

WAGGON TRAILS and STAGES WEST 1821–1869

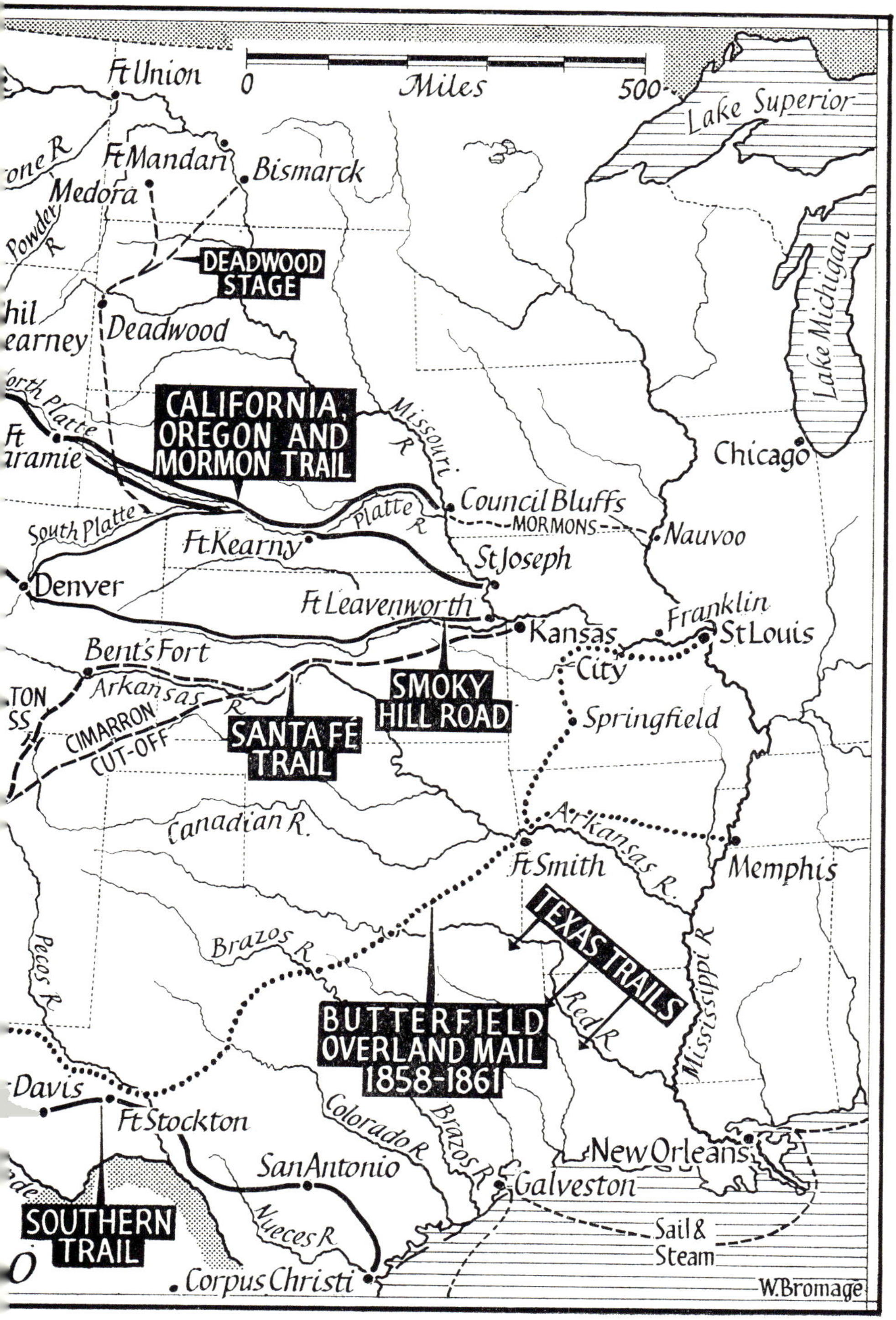

0
Miles
500
Ft Union
Ft Mandan
Bismarck
Medora
Powder R
DEADWOOD STAGE
Deadwood
CALIFORNIA, OREGON AND MORMON TRAIL
North Platte
South Platte
Platte R
Missouri R
Council Bluffs
MORMONS
Nauvoo
Ft Kearny
St Joseph
Denver
Ft Leavenworth
Kansas City
Franklin
St Louis
Bent's Fort
Arkansas R
CIMARRON CUT-OFF
SANTA FÉ TRAIL
SMOKY HILL ROAD
Springfield
Canadian R.
Arkansas R.
Ft Smith
Memphis
TEXAS TRAILS
Red R
Brazos R
Pecos R
BUTTERFIELD OVERLAND MAIL 1858-1861
Mississippi R
Davis
Ft Stockton
Colorado R
Brazos R
San Antonio
Nueces R
New Orleans
Galveston
Sail & Steam
SOUTHERN TRAIL
Corpus Christi
Lake Superior
Lake Michigan
Chicago
W.Bromage

first organized caravan of 1822 on which seventy men took about $15,000 worth of merchandise on pack-animals to Santa Fé) until 1843, when three hundred and fifty men and two hundred and thirty waggons participated and took $430,000 worth to Santa Fé, of which no less than two-thirds was shipped on to Chihuahua in Old Mexico.[1] Gregg's account of the arrival of the caravan at Santa Fé is deservedly famous:[2]

> A few miles before reaching the city, the road again emerges into an open plain. Ascending a table ridge, we spied in an extended valley to the northwest, occasional groups of trees, skirted with verdant corn and wheat fields, with here and there a square block-like protuberance reared in the midst. A little further, and just ahead of us to the north, irregular clusters of the same opened to our view. 'Oh, we are approaching the suburbs!' thought I, on perceiving the cornfields, and what I supposed to be brick-kilns scattered in every direction. These and other observations of the same nature becoming audible, a friend at my elbow said, 'It is true these are heaps of unburnt bricks, nevertheless they are *houses* – this is the city of SANTA FÉ.'
>
> Five or six days after our arrival, the caravan at last hove in sight, and wagon after wagon was seen pouring down the last declivity at about a mile's distance from the city. To judge from the clamorous rejoicings of the men, and the state of agreeable excitement which the muleteers seemed to be laboring under, the spectacle must have been as new to them as it had been to me. It was truly a scene for the artist's pencil to revel in. Even the animals seemed to participate in the humor of their riders, who grew more and more merry and obstreperous as they descended towards the city. I doubt, in short, whether the first sight of the walls of Jerusalem were beheld by the crusaders with much more tumultuous and soul-enrapturing joy.
>
> The arrival produced a great deal of bustle and excitement among the natives. '*Los Americanos!*' – '*Los carros!*' – '*La entrada de la caravana!*' were to be heard in every direction; and crowds of women and boys flocked around to see the newcomers; while crowds of *léperos* hung about as usual to see what they could pilfer. The wagoners were by no means free from excitement on this occasion. Informed of the 'ordeal' they had to pass, they had spent the previous morning in 'rubbing up'; and now they were prepared, with clean faces, sleek combed hair, and their choicest Sunday suit, to meet the 'fair eyes' of glistening black that were sure to stare at them as they passed.

[1] Gregg, *Commerce of the Prairies* (1933 edn), p. 322.
[2] *Ibid.*, pp. 66–8.

There was yet another preparation to be made in order to 'show off' to advantage. Each wagoner must tie a bran new 'cracker' to the lash of his whip; for, on driving through the streets and the *plaza pública*, every one strives to outvie his comrades in the dexterity with which he flourishes this favorite badge of his authority.

Our wagons were soon discharged in the ware-rooms of the Custom-house; and a few days' leisure being now at our disposal, we had time to take that recreation which a fatiguing journey of ten weeks had rendered so necessary. The wagoners, and many of the traders, particularly the novices, flocked to the numerous fandangoes, which are regularly kept up after the arrival of a caravan. But the merchants generally were anxiously and actively engaged in their affairs – striving who should first get his goods out of the custom-house, and obtain a chance at the 'hard chink' of the numerous country dealers, who annually resort to the capital on these occasions . . .

The arrival of a caravan at Santa Fé changes the aspect of the place at once. Instead of the idleness and stagnation which its streets exhibited before, one now sees everywhere the bustle, noise and activity of a lively market town. As the Mexicans very rarely speak English, the negotiations are mostly conducted in Spanish.

In its early days, when the caravans were still small, the Santa Fé trade was not greatly hampered by Indians, but before the end of the twenties they had become a major menace to it. Gregg gives several quite literally hair-raising accounts of Indian attacks and white parties' reprisals, and mentions the notorious *Proyecto de Guerra*, adopted in 1837 by the people of Chihuahua, the neighbouring province to New Mexico, which paid 'a hundred dollars . . . for the scalp of a full-grown man, fifty for that of a squaw, and twenty-five for that of every papoose!'[1] to deal with constant Apache depredations. Old Bill Williams, the Mountain Man, was brought in to utilize his knowledge of Indian languages and his skill in negotiating with the Indians to make safer the passage along the Santa Fé Trail. The treaty of Sibley and his fellow United States Government Commissioners with the Osage Indians – also Bill Williams' blood brothers and the tribe of his first squaw – at Council Grove (from which this famous spot derived its name) on 10 August 1825 was largely Bill's achievement, and so was that a little later with the Kansas Indians. The Comanche were another matter, and nobody managed to come to terms with these 'Spartans of

[1] Gregg, *op. cit.*, p. 199. Gregg called the Indians 'The *Unconquered Sabaeans* of the Great American Desert'.

the Plains' on the Santa Fé Trail or anywhere else. In 1829 a large caravan, despite a military escort under Major Bennett Riley as far as the Mexican border and consisting of sixty men and thirty-six waggons led by Charles Bent and the fiery Colonel Marmaduke, was attacked by Comanches during its first unescorted day inside New Mexican territory. Ninety-five hunters under Ewing Young, 'who might be considered equal to five hundred inexperienced men', turned up to convoy the battered caravan into Taos, to which it had to be deflected instead of going straight to Santa Fé. On the way back this caravan was protected by a force of Mexican cavalry under General Vizcarra, but though the caravan itself got through, the military escort was badly carved up on the Cimarron while returning to its base.[1] It was near the Cimarron that, two years later, the Comanches caught up with Jedediah Smith, separated from his party and searching for water, and put an end to his short but spectacular career. That year Josiah Gregg's caravan (it was his first crossing of the Plains) was travelling about a month behind that of Smith and William Sublette, and he is somewhat critical, in his account of this tragedy, of the precautions taken by these perhaps over-confident Mountain Men. He writes:

> Capt. Smith and his companions were new beginners in the Santa Fé trade, but being veteran pioneers of the Rocky Mountains, they concluded they could go anywhere; and imprudently set out without a single person in their company at all competent to guide them on the route. They had some twenty odd wagons, and about eighty men . . . every kind of fatality seems to have attended this little caravan.[2]

Sublette finally struggled into Santa Fé after parleying his way through an 'immense horde of Blackfeet and Gros Ventres', a sadder and a wiser man.[3]

These were the teething troubles of the Santa Fé trade but Gregg points out that 'since the year 1831, few or none of the difficulties or dangers which once environed the Santa Fé adventures have been encountered. No traders have been killed by the savages on the regular route, and but few animals stolen from the caravan. On the whole, the rates of insurance upon adventures in this trade should hardly be as

[1] Gregg, *op. cit.*, p. 50.

[2] *Ibid.*, pp. 54–5.

[3] *Ibid.*, p. 56. If Gregg's identification is correct, these 'treacherous savages' were rather far from their usual hunting grounds.

high as upon marine adventures between New York and Liverpool.[1] But political difficulties increased as the Indian menace faded, and it was these which ground the trade to a halt in 1843, the very year that the Oregon migration began on a large scale. The trouble came mainly from the direction of the Republic of Texas, which claimed New Mexico up to the Rio Grande at least, and would have been prepared to expand westward to the Pacific Ocean, given support and encouragement by the United States. The disastrous Texas–Santa Fé expedition of 1841 had greatly increased tension in the borderlands, and when a party of freebooters, some of whom were Texans, robbed and murdered a prominent Mexican merchant named Chavez in February 1843, near the Little Arkansas, and at least a hundred miles inside the territory of the United States, Mexican indignation greatly increased, despite the fact that the murderers were afterwards brought to trial and condemned in St Louis. The last straw was the ignominious Sniveley expedition of one hundred and seventy-five men out of north Texas, who, after defeating General Armijo's vanguard inside Mexican territory in the summer of 1843, caused that worthy to retreat with his main force to Santa Fé, but was soon afterwards disarmed, when it returned to United States territory, by Captain Philip St George Cooke, U.S. Army, under orders to keep peace along the trail. This 'Second Santa Fé Expedition' resulted in a Mexican Government protest and demand for damages to Waddy Thompson, United States Minister to Mexico, whose efforts towards maintaining good relations were as much hampered by such things as these Santa Fé Trail incidents as by the recent seizure, in October 1842, of Monterey, California, 'by mistake'. Santa Anna's decree of 7 August 1843 closed the customs houses at Taos, El Paso, and Chihuahua.

Though these ports of entry were reopened on 31 March 1844, and a certain amount of trade went over the Santa Fé Trail in 1844, the whole enterprise was about to be swallowed up by the onward march of Manifest Destiny and the war between the United States and Mexico.[2] In 1845 Colonel Stephen Kearny led his dragoons on a military reconnaissance as far as the border to show the flag and the might of the United States; and in 1846 (now a general) he led the 'Army of the West' to occupy New Mexico and make it American. After the war, though Bent's Fort faded out of the picture, the army established an important new supply depot at Fort Union, near the western juncture at Watrous of the Mountain and Cimarron routes of the Santa Fé Trail,

[1] Gregg, *op. cit.*, p. 326.

[2] See further, p. 153.

and the trade along it increased vastly once again. Heavier 'Murphy' waggons than those used previously followed both branches, now greatly improved, and by 1860 freighting over the trail employed nearly ten thousand men and regularly used three thousand waggons. Large fortunes continued to be made (and lost) and the Indians remained intermittently troublesome, but the era of Becknell and Gregg had passed. Charles Bent was dead, William Bent abandoned the old fort in disgust when the Government would not buy it from him, but the prosaic army of sutlers and quartermasters at Fort Union, which was just another army camp, indicated that the pioneering days of the famous trail were over. 'In the early and middle forties' Bent's Fort had 'assumed the combined proportions of a great Oriental caravanserai and an Occidental mercantile house. Here it stood on the plains, the central point of interest, the isolated refuge of wanderers on a wide-spread danger-abounding region. Here dwelt the scout, guide, and protector of travelers in a strange land. Here at intervals for several years, Kit Carson was a resident hunter supplying the Fort with buffalo meat.'[1]

The physical difficulties of the Santa Fé Trail were never very great for well-organized and well-armed parties, only the crossing of the Cimarron desert by the one route and the long rough pull over the Raton Pass by the other were memorable impediments on the way. But for the danger from Indians the mountain route could have been one long picnic for younger and more carefree travellers, journeying at the right season and with proper equipment.

The way to Texas from the American settlements of the Mississippi valley was even easier, and cannot really be described as a 'trail' at all. From 1820 onwards, in the wake of the first party of settlers taken in under the *empressario* contracts of Moses and Stephen Austin, the Americans poured across the Sabine river by a variety of routes, and many others went by sea to Texas ports and by roadsteads from New Orleans. This was a mass migration which Spanish and Mexican Government regulation or prohibition could not stem or control.

Apart from the ordinary American citizens who just went to Texas to get land, and with no ulterior motives, there were a few active political agitators whose unavowed intention it was to end Mexican rule there and to bring the province into the United States. These were

[1] A. J. Flynn, 'Furs and Forts of the Rocky Mountain West' in *The Colorado Magazine* (March 1932), Vol. IX, No. 2, p. 35.

not necessarily agents of the American Government, though there is reason to believe that Sam Houston, the most famous of these 'activists', was carefully briefed by President Andrew Jackson before he emigrated to Texas in 1832.[1] Some of these men were just free-wheeling souls who believed that the rule of the United States ought to extend all over the American continent, and who enjoyed a fight anywhere. The dedicated agitators, the born trouble-makers and the genuinely disgruntled American settlers who had suffered from the vacillations of Mexican policy and the harshness of Santa Anna's recent measures in Texas, together provided more than enough tinder to produce the revolution of 1835. The heroic resistance by small groups of Americans cut off at the Alamo in San Antonio and in Goliad, and their massacre by superior Mexican forces, hardened the resistance of the insurgent Americans and helped to lead them to their eventual victory on the field of San Jacinto (near Houston City), where Sam Houston's amateur soldiers defeated Santa Anna's professionals, captured the proud peg-legged Mexican dictator, and sent him as a gift to Andrew Jackson. Houston survived to become twice President of the Texas Republic and eventually Senator in Washington for the State of Texas, but the toll of the 'patriots' had been heavy. Jim Bowie ('The Knife') and Davy Crockett had both died in the siege of the Alamo, which Texans have never permitted the world to forget.

After Texas became a republic in 1836 (by which year fully thirty thousand immigrants from the United States had arrived there), and even more so after the economic depression of 1837 in the United States had added an even more compelling incentive, 'Gone to Texas'[2] scrawled up on the barns and outhouses of abandoned farms and on the doors of shanties was a common sight throughout the American South. An oft-told tale[3] of the period is of

> Nightfall and a drizzling rain drove an elderly horseman traveling a road to Vicksburg to seek shelter near a roadside fire. As he approached, he saw around it the encampment of a family 'a-moving' to Texas – a very common sight in Mississippi in the year 1841. Two bodies wrapped in blankets lay close to the blaze. Near them a

[1] The somewhat unsatisfactory evidence for and against this assumption is discussed in the biographies of Jackson and of Houston by Marquis James. See Bibliographical Note, p. 380.

[2] Often abbreviated into 'G.T.T.'.

[3] As retold by W. Hogan, *The Texas Republic* (Norman, Oklahoma, 1946), p. 3.

tow-headed boy, crying loudly, leaned against a front wheel of a waggon.

The old horseman rode up and addressed him in a mollifying voice, 'What's the matter, son?'

'Matter!' roared the piney-woods lad. 'Fire and damnation, stranger! Don't you see Mammy there shaking with ager! Daddy's gone a-fishing! Jim's got every cent of money there is, playing poker at a bit ante! Bob Stokes is gone on ahead with Nance! Sal's so corned she don't know that stick of wood from seven dollars and a half! Every one of the horses is loose! There's no meal in the waggon! The skillet's broke! The baby's in a bad fix, and it's half a mile to the creek. I don't care a damn if I never see Texas!!!'

The cost of the removal of family and stock and worldly goods to Texas was slight. Asa Hoxey, who went to the Austin colony at San Felipe in 1833, estimated it as not more than ten dollars a head. Would-be emigrants were even recommended to make reconnaissances into Texas to select suitable locations and then go back for their families,[1] but it is unlikely that any *empresario* or land agent offered them the cost of the journey or free chicken dinners in the style of later real-estate operators. The really classy way of emigrating to Texas seems to have been as a cabin passenger on the steam packet *Columbia* from New Orleans to Galveston, where:

> The Captain's a gentleman – always at the head of his table – set out in the best style – silver forks, or what looks like silver – large and small, with ivory knives. White waiters, neat and orderly – French Cook . . . and Bedding the finest and whitest linen – water-closets – and lady-like chambermaid, everything nice.[2]

The same enraptured passenger found the *New York* of the same line (by which this ecstatic lady seemed to commute) even more sybaritic. As she lay on her 'luxurious couch' in her stateroom, surrounded by 'blue satin damask and dimity' and by walls of mahogany 'polished like the finest pianos' she could 'think of nothing but Cleopatra'.[3] 'Gone to Texas' indeed!

No wonder the Texas immigrants caused the population of the Lone Star Republic to quadruple in ten years. By the census of 1850 the State

[1] *Texas in 1840, or the Emigrant's Guide to the New Republic* (*anon.*, n.d.), quoted by Hogan, *op. cit.*, p. 4.

[2] Mrs Mary Austin Holley to Mrs William M. Brand, 19 Dec. 1837. Holley Papers (University of Texas Library). Quoted by Hogan *op. cit.*, p. 8.

[3] *Ibid.*, p. 9.

of Texas had over 212,000 inhabitants – including 58,000 slaves, all of whom (or their parents) had been brought in from the United States, for slavery had been abolished in Mexico. The foreign-born population at this time was only 12,000, most of whom were Germans imported by the *Adelsverein*, and other German settlement societies,[1] directly from Europe.

The way to Texas was wide open; but the way to California and Oregon was beset with difficulties, especially for wheeled vehicles. Quite apart from badlands and deserts, well-nigh impenetrable forests and deep canyons, none of which had to be crossed on the way to Texas, two high mountain systems and many minor ranges had to be surmounted or circumvented by those who were bound for the Sacramento or the Willamette. An even harder task confronted those hardy souls who sought to extend the Santa Fé Trail to southern California. Indeed, the last way was so difficult that it never was established as a route for waggons and at one point even pack-horses and mules had to be unloaded before they could be led up and down the man-made stone steps at the crossing of the Great Colorado river which had first been blazed by Fathers Dominguez and Escalante in 1777.[2]

Although it had previously been brought back into use in places by fur trappers, including the parties of Pattie and of Jedediah Smith, this 'Old Spanish Trail' was pioneered in 1829 as a trade route by an enterprising New Mexico merchant, Antonio Armijo, who was later to lead a successful revolution in that province and was to be its last governor under Mexican sovereignty. Other pack-trains may have reached California by the route earlier, but Armijo's is the first that

[1] For the organized German immigration into the Texas Republic and its importance, see J. A. Hawgood, *The Tragedy of German–America* (New York, 1940), Chap. V.

[2] 'The Crossing of the Fathers' is still a remote and romantic spot. Robert Glass Cleland visited it in 1946. 'I left the small rowboat in which two companions and I . . . were floating down the Colorado, and made an overland reconnaissance. Without trail or landmarks, we wandered over a high, barren mesa, climbed in and out of a deep canyon, crossed rough naked ridges, and came at last to the crude steps that Father Escalante fashioned a hundred and seventy years before and Citizen Antonio Armijo successfully used a long generation later. They were not steps in the ordinary sense of the word, but shallow grooves, makeshift devices that weary men had cut out of grudgingly yielding rock to check the momentum of their mules and let the slipping, sliding animals regain their balance. Off in the lonely distance we saw a valley, silent, old and vast, that brooded for ever over the ruins and remnants of a broken world . . . a world where Time had never wakened and the centuries and ages lay sleeping in the sun.' Cleland, *Reckless Breed*, p. 268. But now man-made dams threaten to obliterate this idyllic scene.

can be authenticated.[1] Armijo's diary of the expedition, published in Mexico City in 1830, said, 'On the 6th of November of the past year, there left from the village of Abiquiu 31 men . . . wishing to discover a route to Upper California and to sell therein some manufactures of their country.'[2] It was a round-about route, striking first north-west from Abiquiu to the 'Four Corners' region near Mesa Verde, and then via the Goose Neck Gorge of the San Juan river to the 'Crossing of the Fathers', which was made with great difficulty on 8 December. The Virgin river was reached on 1 January 1830, and San Gabriel Mission, via the Mojave river and the Cajon Pass, on 31 January. The journey from the New Mexico to the Californian settlement was thus achieved in under three months. After some profitable trading in California the expedition did even better on its return journey, the advance party getting back to Santa Fé in forty days and Armijo himself in two months of travel.

This became an important route over the next twenty years, taking silver, woollen goods, and blankets to California, and bringing back horses and mules and even 'small quantities of goods of Chinese and New England manufacture'.[3] Unfortunately many of the horses and mules had not been paid or bartered for, but just rounded up and driven off from the extensive Californian *ranchos*. This tended to give the caravans from New Mexico a bad name in California, especially as 'it is known that the greater part of these *Chaquanosos* . . . are American and English'.[4] This was certainly an activity of 'Peg-leg' Jack Smith, and possibly of Jim Baker, Old Bill Williams, and other Mountain Men as well, as, just possibly perhaps, Joseph Reddeford Walker.[5]

The California–New Mexico trade over Armijo's Old Spanish Trail languished under this blight. The sleepy *Alta California* administration

[1] Cleland, *Reckless Breed*, discusses this claim, pp. 264–5.

[2] *Ibid.*, p. 263, from translation by Leroy R. Hafen in *Huntington Library Quarterly*, Vol. XI, No. 1, pp. 87–101.

[3] *Ibid.*, p. 270.

[4] E. Lawrence, 'Horse Thieves on the Spanish Trail', in *Touring Topics* (later *Westways*, published monthly by the Automobile Club of Southern California, and a mine of popularly-presented but often valuable information based on original research, about early California history), Vol. XXIII, No. 1, pp. 22–5, cited by Cleland, himself a frequent contributor to this magazine, in *Reckless Breed*, p. 271.

[5] Walker may conceivably have been confused with one 'Chief Joseph Walkara, the Ute – perhaps the greatest horse-thief the West ever knew'. Cleland (*Reckless Breed*, p. 301) accepts this somewhat circumstantial alibi, and exonerates his hero Joe Walker, that 'figure of heroic proportions in the history of the West, a man of integrity, courage, and simplicity' (*ibid.*) from the charge of being a despised *Chaquanoso*.

tried to control the trade by means of licences and by an official inspection of the horse-herds before they left for New Mexico. The Government of New Mexico also attempted to give the trade a better character, vesting in caravan captains special authority and punitive powers to enable them to 'lead the caravan with as much order as if it were in national service'.[1] But the fatal flaw of the Old Spanish Trail was that it could not be transformed into a waggon route with comparative ease, like the Santa Fé Trail, or even after surmounting many difficulties, like the California and Oregon Trails. No covered waggons followed in 'the steps of the Fathers', no railroad was to be built along Armijo's route; and although United States Highways 30 and 40 now stretch along much of the Oregon and California Trails, and U.S. 50 and 350, U.S. 56 and 85 and the even more recent interstate highways ribbon most of the old waggon roads from the broad Missouri to Santa Fé, Armijo's trail to Mesa Verde and the San Juan valley is still only covered by state roads at the best; while the long haul from Medicine Hat and the Great Goose Necks of the San Juan, to Lee's Ferry and Marble Canyon on the Colorado – more than a hundred miles as the eagle flies, but much farther as those two writhing rivers wind – is still traversed by no road at all. You still have to 'pack-in' to the Crossing of the Fathers. Escalante's (and Cleland's) wilderness remains undefiled by that importation from a bad Old World, the wheel.

Even as late as 1846 no practicable waggon route existed from Santa Fé to California for Stephen Kearny and his Army of the West to follow. General Kearny himself and his hundred dragoons arrived in California without a waggon train, but he sent Captain St George Cooke back to command the Mormon Battalion and to make a road.[2] This was achieved (though at one point the waggons had to be dismantled to get them through a narrow mountain defile) when Cooke pushed and creaked his way into San Diego on 29 January 1847 after an epic march.[3] Needless to say, both Kearny and Cooke kept well to the south

[1] Cleland, *Reckless Breed*, p. 275, quoting from the Ritch manuscripts, a valuable collection of documents on New Mexican history in the Huntington Library, San Marino, California which he uses extensively.

[2] The Mormon Battalion was recruited, with Brigham Young's full approval, from among young Mormons already assembled for the great migration westward. These men served in the Army of the West for a year, and sometimes longer, and saw much campaigning. The tithes from their pay helped to swell the coffers of the Church during the early lean years. The military skills they learned were of permanent value after they returned to Zion.

[3] R. Bieber, *Exploring Southwestern Trails, 1846–1854* prints Cooke's own account of this expedition. Henry W. Bigler, one of his Mormon volunteers, who was later

of the Crossing of the Fathers, and used two variants of the much longer Gila river route, crossing the Colorado near Yuma.

It was not until 1843 that wheeled vehicles reached the Dalles of the Columbia river in the Oregon country, and not until 1844 that the first waggon train managed to cross the Sierras (at Truckee Pass) into the great valley of California. All previous attempts, and there had been many, had failed. Not until the waggons came through was a mass emigration of settlers to these two areas practicable, though a number of pioneering parties had previously struggled through on horse- or mule-back or on foot – like the Bidwell–Bartleson company of 1841, with Nancy Kelsey, the eighteen-year-old wife of Benjamin Kelsey and their one-year-old daughter Ann, the only woman and the only child to cross the whole way with this 'first company of American emigrants to enter California overland'.[1]

Naturally, the 1843 and 1844 parties which first took the waggons

---

to assist in Marshall's first discovery of gold at Sutter's Mill, wrote an illuminating (and oddly spelled) diary of the march which is partially printed in 'Extracts from the Journal of Henry W. Bigler' in the *Utah Historical Quarterly*, Vol. V (1932).

[1] George R. Stewart, *The California Trail*, p. 28. Nancy and Ann Kelsey thus occupy a niche in the Wilderness hall of fame very close to that of Sacajawea and Baptiste Charbonneau. Unlike Baptiste, Ann 'having established herself as the first American child to cross the Sierra Nevada and enter California by the central route . . . disappears from history' (Stewart, p. 29), but Nancy lived on until 1895. 'Enough incidents happened to me to make a book,' she told the Press in 1893. 'I have seen U. S. Grant when he was little known. I have baked bread for General Frémont and talked to Kit Carson. I have run from bear and killed most all other [*sic*] kinds of small game.' (*Ibid.*, p. 29.)

There is no book about The Kelseys, but Stewart, the historian of *U.S. Highway 40* (New York, 1953) which follows so much of the California trail, and the chronicler of the tribulations of the Donner overland party of 1846 (in *Ordeal by Hunger*) has collected in the first chapter of *The California Trail* – written on the Berkeley campus of the University of California, almost within a long shadow of Mount Diabolo – most interesting biographical information not only about Nancy and her child but about the thirty-one men who made up the rest of the party. Several of them became famous and one or two will reappear in these pages. James Bidwell, a young schoolmaster from Ohio, and the real spark-plug of the party, went on to serve as John Augustus Sutter's right-hand man at New Helvetia, to become a California millionaire, to found the city of Chico, to help nominate Lincoln in the Republican Convention of 1860, to serve in Congress and to run for President (but as the Prohibition Party candidate) in 1892. He died in 1900 (*ibid.*, p. 28). *The California Trail* not only gives the route of the overland party of 1841 in great detail, but discusses the development of the trail year by year until 1849 with equal care, summarizing its progress and its variations up to 1859, and bridges the era between 1859 and the completion of the first transcontinental railroad along its route, in 1869, in a final chapter.

through have a high and honourable place in the annals of the westward migration. Elijah Stevens, a typical Mountain Man, led the one into California and Dr Marcus Whitman, a Presbyterian medical missionary, led the other into Oregon. It takes all sorts to make a New World. The old pattern of Conquistador and Friar was repeating itself in a slightly different design on other frontiers and in another century.

The Oregon Trail began with Columbus, says David Lavender,[1] and Captain Gray, who had discovered the mouth of the Columbia river, was engaged in the China trade. Because they used water-routes wherever possible, neither Mackenzie nor Lewis and Clark may be said to have contributed much, other than in inspiration, to the pioneering of a waggon trail to the Oregon country. Hunt's Astorians in 1811 and Stuart's returning Astorians in 1812 were the first overland parties to traverse substantial portions of the Oregon Trail proper, though it is uncertain whether either of them actually used the South Pass over the Continental Divide. Ogden's parties explored its western portions between 1824 and 1829, and Ashley's and Henry's men made more familiar its eastern sections (especially the passage of the South Pass) from 1823 onwards. But though the *Missouri Gazette* of St Louis had, as early as 15 May 1813,[2] said optimistically, '. . . it appears that a journey across the continent of N. America might be performed with a waggon, there being no obstruction in the whole route that any person would dare to call a mountain', more than two decades were to pass before the first waggon passed over the Oregon Trail all the way from the Mississippi valley to the Columbia river. Thirty years were to pass before the first waggon travelled all the way overland to the great central valley of California.

'From Independence,' founded in 1832, 'to the mouth of the Walla Walla was the original Oregon Trail, parent of all the central routes to the Pacific. . . . This great highway ran through a wilderness . . . there was nowhere along its line, at the beginning of 1832, even a cabin.'[3] The fur-trapping parties of the 1820s and early 1830s, and even the fur-trading caravans which pursued them to the *rendezvous*, needed to travel too rapidly to want to experiment with wheeled vehicles. It was the missionaries who first tried to use this cumbersome and much slower means of transportation and even they did not succeed,

[1] Lavender, *Westward Vision*, p. 3.

[2] Quoted in W. J. Ghent, *The Road to Oregon* (London and New York, 1929), p. 18.

[3] *Ibid.*, p. 24.

until after many heartbreaking failures, in getting a waggon into the Oregon country. Dr Marcus Whitman and Henry Spalding first took their missionary wives, riding side-saddle, all the way from western New York to Fort Vancouver in 1836, and the Reverend and Mrs Elkanah Walker, the Reverend and Mrs Cushing Eels, the Reverend and Mrs Asa Smith and the Reverend and Mrs William Grey followed, equally uncomfortably, in 1838. These hardy women (some of whom were pregnant for part of the journey) rode distances of up to forty-five miles a day, and four, at least, out of six, still had enough energy left to write diaries and journals on the way. From these we learn what 'an unheard-of journey'[1] it was for a woman in those days. The first waggon train followed only in 1843, seven years after Narcissa Whitman and Eliza Spalding. Never underestimate the power of a woman!

These first waggons were taken through by Marcus Whitman, by now a veteran of the trail. He had first traversed it with Samuel Parker (who prudently returned by sea) in 1835, but had turned back near the Three Forks of the Missouri to recruit more assistants and to finish his wooing of Narcissa Prentiss, who had wished to join the 1835 expedition in her own right. Their marriage solved an awkward problem of etiquette, though it created another, for Henry Spalding, chosen as Whitman's fellow-missionary by the Presbyterian Board in 1836, had been an unsuccessful suitor of Narcissa, and though he now married Eliza Hart, he still harboured some resentment. It speaks well for the good sense of the two women that this potentially explosive situation was kept under control throughout the long trek of 1836, and eventually sublimated in the course of converting the heathen. Even in 1836 Marcus Whitman had attempted to take a waggon over the trail. At Fort Hall it had to be cut down to a two-wheeled vehicle. Narcissa had noted in her diary a week earlier, 'Husband has had a tedious time with the wagon today . . .' and by 28 July she was only too willing to see the last of it: 'One of the axle-trees of the wagon broke today; was a little rejoiced, for we were in hopes that they would leave it, and have no more trouble with it. Our rejoicings are in vain for they are making a cart of the back wheels this afternoon and lashing the forewheels to it – intending to take it through in some shape or other.'[2] Finally, at Fort Boise, even

[1] C. M. Drury, *First White Women over the Rockies. Diaries, Letters and Biographical Sketches of the Six Women who made the Overland Journey in 1836 and 1838* (3 vols, Glendale, 1963, 1966), quoting Narcissa Whitman, Vol. I, p. 20.

[2] *Ibid.*, Vol. I, p. 75.

the stubborn Marcus Whitman gave up and the cart was abandoned. It had not been used to any extent, as he had intended, for the ladies to ride in when they grew weary of the side-saddle. When they finally reached Fort Vancouver, Whitman left Narcissa there while he retraced his steps to Walla Walla to establish his Waiilaptu Mission.

When the fur trappers Caleb Wilkins, Robert Newell, and Joseph Meek brought the bare *chassis*, or running gear without waggon beds, of three carts that had been abandoned at Fort Hall by other parties, as far as the Columbia river in 1840, Whitman praised their achievement in characteristic language:

> Oh, you will never regret it! You have broken the ice, and when others see that wagons have passed, they, too, will pass, and in a few years the valley will be full of our people.[1]

There were in 1840 about a hundred Americans in the Oregon country. The 'Great Emigration' was yet to come, but Whitman was right. When it did come it came on wheels, and he came with it.

The Elijah White-Lansford Warren Hastings parties of 1842 abandoned some of their waggons at Fort Laramie (Frémont says that they sold them 'at the prices they had paid for them in the States', which is doubtful) and the remainder at Fort Hall, but the wheel-obsessed Whitman was not with them. When the Hudson's Bay Company official at Fort Hall tried to persuade the much larger party of 1843 to do likewise, Whitman, who had joined these emigrants when returning from his famous 'ride' eastward through the winter of 1842–3, was foremost among those who refused to take this loaded advice, and the waggons went through. This emigration consisted, according to Whitman, of 'no less than 200 families, consisting of 1,000 persons of both sexes', with over 200 waggons, 694 oxen, and 773 loose cattle. No sheep were taken, which omission Whitman considered to be a mistake The famous Mountain Man, Captain John Gannt, was their guide as far as Fort Hall (from there Joseph Reddeford Walker led some of them down into California), Peter H. Burnett (who was to become the first Governor of California under the Constitution of 1849) was their first captain, and James W. Nesmith (later Senator for Oregon) his orderly sergeant. But it was Marcus Whitman who got the waggons through to the Columbia. Jesse Applegate, captain of the slower 'Cow Column' after the emigration of 1843 split up into two sections, has testified to this. He wrote, in his classic account of this migration, published in

[1] Quoted by Ghent, *op. cit.*, p. 46.

1876[1] '... it is no disparagement to others to say that to no other individual are the emigrants of 1843 so much indebted for the successful conclusion of their journey, as to Dr Marcus Whitman'. Applegate also calls Whitman 'that good angel' of the emigrants.

The Protestant missionary impulse in the Oregon country had by this time almost exhausted its momentum. The Methodist pioneers in the Willamette valley, Jason and Daniel Lee, had turned to farming; Jason as 'promoter, developer, business adviser and constant advocate of the Americanization of the country'[2] played a leading part in the Champoeg constitutional convention which provided a ready-made 'American' form of government for the emigrants of 1843. The American Board had sought in 1842 to liquidate the Presbyterian missions and only the persuasiveness of Whitman had given these a reprieve. The Indians, never very co-operative after their first inquisitiveness about the White Man's religion had been satisfied, were now growing positively unfriendly. This unfriendliness and suspicion finally culminated in the massacre of the Whitmans in 1847. Only Father de Smet and his fellow Roman Catholics continued to work with success among the North-western Indians after this, but it was the Protestant missionaries who had spearheaded the settlement of the Oregon Territory from the United States.

The Oregon treaty of 1846 between Great Britain and the United States belongs rather to diplomatic history than to the history of the Westward Movement, but it was the Oregon migration of 1834–46 which made that treaty so favourable to the Americans. Although they had put hardly a settler *north* of the Columbia river by the treaty year, they had by then so many in the Willamette valley, and had been so active in the Walla Walla region, that Sir George Simpson and Dr McLaughlin, the factor, decided that the Hudson's Bay Company – 'H.B.C. – Here Before Christ' as the trappers said – should evacuate not only Fort Boise and Fort Hall but also Fort Vancouver, their headquarters on the north bank of the Columbia, and retire to Fort Victoria on Vancouver Island. This cut the ground from under the feet of a vacillating British Government. Lord Aberdeen had never said 'The

[1] Jesse Applegate, 'A Day with the Cow Column', *Transactions* of the Oregon Pioneer Association (1876), reprinted in the *Oregon Historical Society Quarterly* (December 1900), by the Caxton Club, edited by Joseph Schafer (Chicago, 1934) and by the Champoeg Press, edited by Dorothy Johansen (Portland, Oregon, 1952), p. 17.

[2] W. J. Ghent, *Dictionary of American Biography* (New York, 1933), Vol. X, p. 112. Article on 'Jason Lee'.

Columbia River line or Fight', as the Americans had said 'Fifty-Four Forty or Fight', and he now persuaded his colleagues and the British people to accept the 49th parallel as the mainland border all the way to the Straits of Juan de Fuca. McLaughlin, broken and disappointed, took up residence in Oregon City, in 'enemy territory', and even applied for United States citizenship, but a crude and insensitive generation of American frontiersmen cold-shouldered in his old age the man who had done so much for them, more even than Whitman. Jedediah Smith, the Lees, the Whitmans, Nathaniel Wyeth, even Hall Jackson Kelley and William Slacum (whom, he rightly suspected, were up to no good), Lansford Warren Hastings and Elijah White (who, whether he suspected it or not, were also active and conscious agents of Manifest Destiny), all these men and women – and others – were succoured, supplied, or protected by Dr McLaughlin. Many of them testified to his kindness and generosity. But he could also be fierce! When the Reverend Herbert Beaver, an Englishman who came as Anglican chaplain to the Fort, made insulting remarks about Mrs McLaughlin – who was of mixed Scottish and Indian blood – McLaughlin booted him around the compound and probably regretted that he could not do the same to Mrs Beaver, who was as bigoted and obnoxious as her spouse. Narcissa Whitman formed an unfavourable impression of Beaver, saying, in a letter dated 25 October 1836,[1] 'He seldom draws the line of distinction between the righteous and the wicked, and when he does it is so faintly that it is scarcely perceptible.' She also did not like the way he conducted his services. He, on his side, objected to Narcissa conducting the singing of hymns out of church. And so it went on. The good Presbyterian ladies obviously preferred the Papist McLaughlin to their fellow-Protestant. These squabbles must have enlivened a long wet winter.

The 'Great Migration' of 1843, piloted on wheels to the promised land by Marcus Whitman and his Cayuse Indian assistant, Stickus, was followed in 1844 by three parties containing in all about 1,500 persons, despite the admonition of the *Missouri Republican* of 11 June 1844 that 'no man of information or in his right mind, would think of leaving such a country as this, to wander over a thousand miles of desert and

[1] C. M. Drury, *op. cit.*, p. 106 (note 49). The Rev. H. Beaver's viewpoint can be appreciated (though hardly admired) by reading *Reports and Letters of Herbert Beaver 1836–38*, edited by T. E. Jessett (Champoeg Press: Portland, Oregon, 1959). This volume also prints the James Douglas report on the 'Beaver Affair' dated 5 October 1838.

five hundred of mountains to reach such as that . . .'[1] The old Mountain Man James Clyman (tired of farming and shopkeeping in the Middle West) helped to guide one of the parties, along with his companion of many a trail, 'Black' Harris, and he has left a vivid and impressionistically spelled diary of the journey.[2] The 1845 guide was Stephen Meek, who recklessly led one caravan by a mythical 'short cut' through the Cascades, and fifty to seventy persons lost their lives before the party could be extricated from this 'worst disaster of the Oregon road',[3] comparable to the Donner disaster on the California Trail the next year[4] – and Meek was nearly lynched by irate survivors. But upwards of three thousand emigrants had taken the trail that year and the great majority came through, and brought their hundreds of waggons with them. The Oregon Trail, though still difficult, was now becoming a beaten track.

Only about 1,350 persons went to Oregon in 1846 – the Mexican War had broken out and the news of the Oregon Treaty came through too late to exert much influence – but still it was many more than went to California despite the propagandist efforts of Caleb Greenfield at Fort Hall, and the exhortations in print of Lansford Warren Hastings that California must be Americanized, as Oregon had been, by sheer weight of numbers. Hastings even cast himself in the role of 'President of California' when the Texas game should have been played there, but he was on the wrong side of the Sierra Nevada Mountains, as it happened, when the Bear Flag Movement,[5] which might have given him his chance briefly to achieve this ambition, broke out in June. It was in 1846 that he changed from an Oregon booster to a California booster[6]

[1] Quoted by David Lavender in *Westward Vision*, p. 388, where he also discusses the estimates of the size of the 1844 emigration to the Oregon country. Ghent (*The Road to Oregon*, p. 83) estimates the migration to Oregon of 1844 as much smaller.

[2] C. L. Camp has edited this diary in *James Clyman, Frontiersman* (Portland, Oregon, 1960).

[3] Lavender, *op. cit.*, p. 395.

[4] See further, next page.

[5] See Chapter VII, p. 167.

[6] So much did the Oregon settlers fear the effects of Hastings' efforts that they called a public meeting (*Oregon Spectator*, Oregon City, 25 June, 1846) on 15 June 1846, 'for the purpose of sending an express to meet the emigration from the United States to this country, in order to prevent their being deceived and led astray by the misrepresentation of L. W. Hastings, who is now on his way from California for that object . . .' Quoted in C. H. Carey's introduction to the reprint of L. W. Hastings, *The Emigrants' Guide to Oregon and California*, reproduced in facsimile from the original edition of 1845 (Princeton, 1932, p. xviii).

and started trying to persuade California-bound emigrants to take the fateful 'Hastings Cut-off' across the deserts of Utah and Nevada; but his book, originally published in 1845, had already compared Oregon unfavourably with California, even though, in it, he was still seeking to attract emigrants to both. By the time Hastings wrote (though not when he had himself first crossed the continent in 1842) waggons had won their way through to the Columbia and the Sacramento valleys without benefit of his advice. This advice tended to be recklessly inaccurate. Elisha Stevens led the first waggon train safely across the Sierras into California in 1844, but did not write a book about it. In consequence, perhaps, less than two hundred emigrants reached California overland in 1845, but they had an easier time than Stephen Meek's 'cut-off' section of the Oregon emigrants. In 1846 the number reaching California rose to around five hundred,[1] excluding the survivors of the Donner party.

The story of the Donner party is one of the best known and most spine-chilling in the history of the West. George Stewart has retold it well in his *Ordeal by Hunger*.[2] Losing time by bad organization and judgement and over-heavy but inadequate equipment, the party – named after its wealthiest and most 'solid' rather than its most active member (George Donner and his wife, Tamsen, were both to lose their lives) – was also weakened by dissensions. James Reed, a natural leader in times of difficulty, was 'banished' for having killed another member in a brawl, and forced to go on ahead to California alone. After struggling over the dreadful 'Hastings Cut-off' across the grim Nevada desert, the party was caught by unusually early snowfalls in the California Sierras near the present Truckee Pass (not far from Squaw valley, famous today as a winter sports area) and forced to camp there until rescue parties could arrive from the Sacramento valley in the spring of 1847. Food ran out and some members of the party managed to subsist on the hides of their dead cattle, which at first they had used to roof their tents and dug-outs. Others resorted to cannibalism, to some extent at least, though it has never been proved that any member of the party was actually killed in order to be eaten. Enough, anyway, died of starvation and exhaustion. The diaries and accounts of survivors and rescuers (including two transparently honest and very vivid letters

[1] Ghent, *Trail to Oregon*, p. 87. Compare with Stewart, *California Trail*, pp. 143–84.

[2] George R. Stewart, *Ordeal by Hunger* (Berkeley, 1936; new edition, New York, 1960; also published in the *Frontier Library*, London, 1962, with an introduction by Marcus Cunliffe).

written by a girl of twelve, Virginia Reed, along with the diary of the Irishman, Patrick Breen) authenticate the *fact* of cannibalism though they do not establish all its *circumstances*. Without its practice some of the children, at least, who were rescued, may not have lived through the ordeal.

That 'Year of Decision', 1846, in which the Donner party set out for California, also saw the outbreak of the Mexican War. The aggressive diplomacy of Andrew Jackson was followed up by actions on the part of

both the Tyler and the Polk administrations and their servants which thoroughly, and understandably, alarmed Mexico – already put on her guard by the Texas revolution of 1835, by the two Texan 'invasions' of New Mexico and by the premature and mistaken seizure of Monterey, capital of Upper California, by an American naval squadron under Commodore Thomas ap Catesby Jones in 1842. Countermeasures were taken on the Texas border, in New Mexico, and in California, but these did not stop further 'Yankee' infiltration into these regions. Mexico sought the assistance of European powers against the United States, but the price she would have had to pay was too high, even had effective help been available against a now powerful nation, very conscious of its 'Manifest Destiny' to dominate the whole North

American continent. The presidential election of 1844 had brought this sentiment into the open in the United States in its crudest and most extreme forms – as the calls for 'All Mexico' in the South and for 'Fifty-four Forty or Fight' in the North demonstrated. The term 'Manifest Destiny' was not coined until 1845,[1] but the feeling which it crystallized had long existed – even back to the days of John Adams and Thomas Jefferson – and between 1844 and 1846 this was translated into action, leading to the outbreak of the Mexican War in May 1846. Though an armed clash with Britain was avoided (and British Columbia and Alberta saved for the Crown) by the Oregon Settlement, Mexico declared that she would regard the American annexation of Texas as a *casus belli*. She had already withdrawn her Minister from Washington and refused to receive a special envoy from President Polk, when a minor clash between Mexican and American soldiers on the Rio Grande – towards which river General Taylor had moved his forces forward from the Nueces, which the Mexicans claimed to be the true border of Mexico and the Texas Republic – gave Polk his opportunity to declare war in self-righteous terms. Even without a formal declaration a state of war already virtually existed, and fresh 'incidents' were continuing to occur at frequent intervals in New Mexico, and in California as well. Kearny had 'shown the American flag' to Governor Armijo in the former in 1845, and Frémont to General Castro in the latter in the spring of 1846. The Army of the West and the 'California Volunteers' were soon to come into existence. American naval squadrons were equally active and the Navy was, in fact, to beat the Army in the race to occupy Upper California and rule it as conquered territory.[2]

By the Treaty of Guadalupe Hidalgo, in January 1848, Mexico was

[1] 'Manifest Destiny' was a phrase first used by the Irish-American newspaper editor, John L. O'Sullivan, in July 1845, with regard to the crisis caused by the proposed annexation of Texas. It immediately gained wide currency. The use, meaning, and origins of the term are discussed exhaustively by S. K. Weinberg, in *Manifest Destiny* (New York, 1925), and re-examined more recently, and somewhat less mordantly, by Frederick Merk, in *Manifest Destiny and Mission* (Cambridge, Mass., 1962). See also John A. Hawgood, articles on 'Manifest Destiny' in *British Essays in American History* (eds H. C. Allen and P. Hill, London, 1957), and in *Collier's Encyclopaedia* (New York, 1963–).

[2] The complicated campaigns of the Mexican War can be followed in summary form in O. A. Singletary, *The Mexican War* (Chicago, 1960), and in much greater detail in the older J. H. Smith, *The War with Mexico* (New York, 2 vols, 1919), which is still the standard treatment. John A. Hawgood's article in *Collier's Encyclopaedia* attempts to relate the planning and execution of the campaign of the Mexican War to the ideas of American expansionists and to assess its importance in the history of the West.

formally to cede the conquered provinces of New Mexico (then much larger than the present State) and Upper California, and to recognize the annexation of Texas, but she did not lose Lower California or Sonora or Chihuahua or Coahula, and, apart from the small and peaceable Gadsden Purchase (1853), the integrity of her northern borders, as established in 1848, have been respected by the Government of the United States ever since. 'Punitive' expeditions sent into Mexico against the Apaches, or against Mexican 'border ruffians' such as Pancho Villa, were withdrawn when the trouble ended.

The Mexican War, and the extension of United States territory in which it resulted, ranks in importance with the Louisiana Purchase in the history of the American West. It brought not only California and New Mexico into the Union, eventually as states, but also Arizona and major portions of Colorado, Nevada, and Utah; it gave to the United States her Empire on the Pacific for which she had for so long striven.

In 1847 only ninety waggons headed for California, half the number of 1846, though twice the 1845 figure. The war with Mexico was the cause of this slump. 'We can only wonder that anyone at all started' in 1847, as Stewart says. The news of what had happened to the Donner party would also have had its dampening effect. Many more waggons and people went to Oregon that year, and most of the emigrants who made their way there now took the 'Applegate Road' through Southern Oregon into the upper Willamette valley, but some of those who took the earlier route over the Blue Mountains gave the measles to the Cayuse Indians, and thus indirectly caused the Whitman massacre of 29 November 1847. The traditional fate of the medicine man who could not cure his patient was death, and Marcus Whitman, Narcissa, and the others who died at the mission that day were victims of this stern aboriginal law. The news of the massacre all but stopped further emigration to Oregon by the more northerly route for a time. Joe Meek rode to St Louis and Washington, D.C., as 'Envoy Extraordinary and Minister Plenipotentiary of the Republic of Oregon to the Court of the United States' (as the Press wrote him up)[1] and this resulted in the organization of the Oregon Territory and the arrival there, via Santa Fé and Los Angeles (where he heard all about the gold discoveries) and by sea, of Governor Lane in March 1849. For very obvious reasons – like the discovery of gold in California in January 1848–1847 was to be the last year in which the emigration to Oregon was larger than that to

[1] Lavender, *Westward Vision*, p. 399.

California, although 'No one setting out for California in the spring of 1848 knew about the finding of gold'.[1] Neither did the news that the war with Mexico was over and California officially ceded to the United States reach the emigrant parties which set out from the Missouri assembly points in the spring of 1848. The avalanche did not begin, therefore, until 1849. Then, 'In a single year the numbers so increased that for *one* person who travelled the trail to California in '48, *fifty* travelled it in '49'.[2]

In the gold rush years every possible variant on the California and Oregon Trails that had not been used before was explored and adopted, or found wanting and abandoned. The Lassen route, the Carson route, and the Salt Lake cut-off had, like the Hastings cut-off, been used before the gold rush. The Mormons in 1847 followed the way blazed by the Donner party through the Wasatch Mountains to Salt Lake, improving upon the route of Brigham Young and his advance party of 1846. It was, indeed, the earlier waggon parties who made things easier and quicker for the later parties, just as the pack-mule parties and the parties on foot, guided by the know-how of Mountain Men, pointed the way for the first waggon parties.

It is a complete myth that John Charles Frémont, whose first United States Government expedition of 1842 did not even reach the Sierras, and whose second in 1843 met but did not lead the first waggon parties on their way West,[3] was either the Pathfinder or the Pathmarker of the West; though he, and his wife (who never went West until 1849, and then by sea), may well be claimed as the West's greatest popularizers. Brigham Young had read Frémont's *Report* of the expedition of 1843–4 and was influenced by it to settle his people around the Great Salt Lake, but[4] the Mormon Trail was just another variant – using the

[1] Stewart, *California Trail*, p. 193.

[2] *Ibid.*

[3] But this myth is an old soldier that never dies. On 11 April 1945 Senator Capper of Kansas had printed in the *Congressional Record* (79th Congress, 1st Session) the claim by the popular novelist Paul Wellman concerning Frémont's Second Expedition, that 'it was this expedition, with the consequent publicity attending it, which more than any other single factor led to the great rush of immigrants to the West'. Yet Wellman goes on to disclose that 'nearly 1,200 immigrants' were already assembled at Kansas City in 1843 when Frémont arrived there at the beginning of his expedition! Who came first, the pioneer or the publicist?

[4] Frémont's first Report was published as a Senate Document in 1843 and his second in 1845. They were many times reprinted, as by Henry Polkinhorn, in one volume of 278 pages, in Washington, D.C., in 1845. The *National Intelligencer* newspaper had somewhat uncritically claimed 'The Great Salt Lake, the Bear River Valley, and the rivers, the valleys and the mountains of Upper California, may

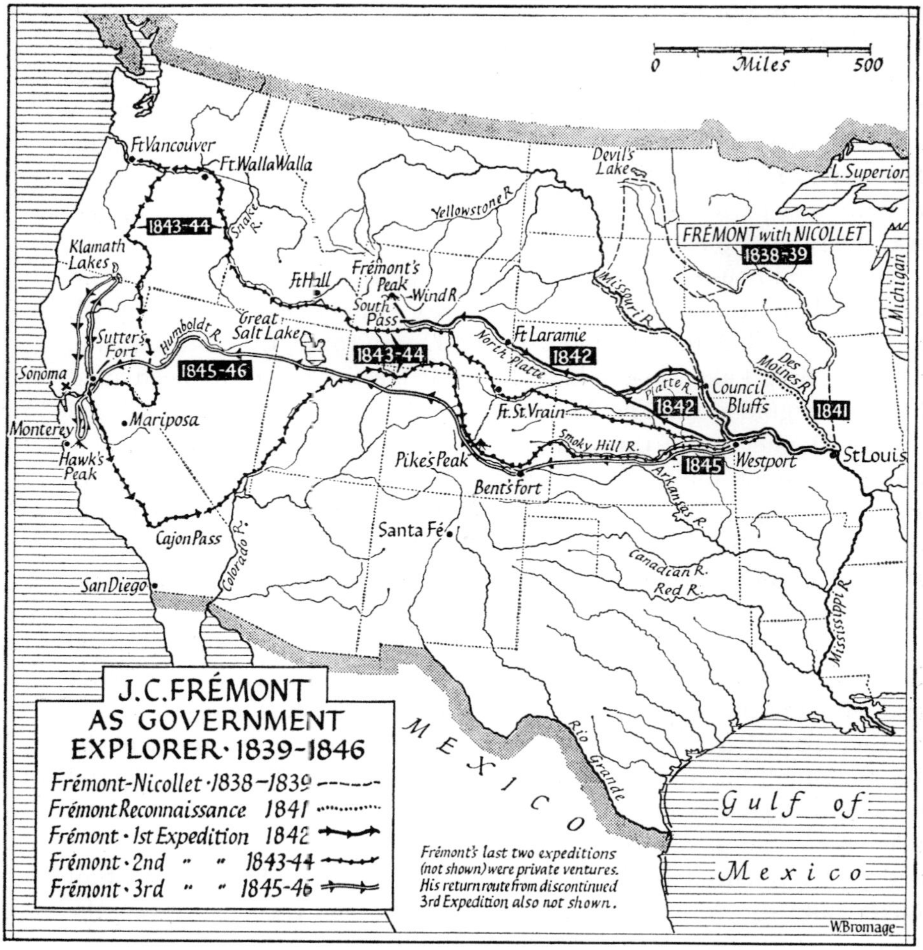

north bank of the Platte river instead of the south bank – of the trail followed by Oregon and California pioneers for the past twenty years, and by hundreds of waggons for the past ten years, for Fort Hall, where waggons tended to be abandoned in the early days, was beyond the Salt Lake. Frémont 'located no new pass or any new route to Oregon'[1] or indeed to California. Frémont's Peak was not the highest

be said to be now first brought to the knowledge of civilized man by these expeditions' and Brigham Young, in an interview with the *New York Times* (which Frémont quotes in his *Memoirs of my Life*, Vol. I – no other was published – pp. 415–16) acknowledged his debt to Frémont, though saying Frémont had 'made a mistake' in describing the great Salt Lake as 'partially fresh'. This Frémont denied.

[1] Goetzmann, *Army Explorations*, p. 93.

in the Rockies, as he claimed, and had in all probability been previously climbed by Bonneville's men. The Sierras had previously been crossed in winter by Jedediah Smith. In fact, it is difficult to discover any real 'first' in the discovery and opening up of trails to and through the West for Frémont. He only caught up the 'Great Migration' of 1843 as Jesse Applegate's cow column floated down the Columbia river on flatboats on the last weary lap of its long journey. But he wrote it all up incomparably and his *Reports* became best-sellers. 'For a whole generation of people his report and map were to serve as guides for their trek to the promised empire of the Pacific.' Boys of all ages had their imaginations fired by the Frémont reports. The pulp poet Joaquin Miller tells how his family read them on their Ohio farm by candlelight, 'I never was so fascinated. I never grew so fast in my life . . . I fancied I could see Frémont's men, hauling the cannon up the savage battlements of the Rocky Mountains, flags in the air, Frémont at the head, waving his sword, his horse neighing wildly in the mountain wind, with unknown and unnamed empires on every hand . . . I began to be inflamed with a love for action, adventure, glory and great deeds, away out yonder under the path of the setting sun.'[1]

The waggon trails west were thus all firmly established before the era of the gold rush put an almost impossible strain on their much-travelled ways, despite the fact that a majority of the Argonauts were to arrive in California by sea. Down to 1857 more than 165,000 people crossed the continent to California overland. The number of animals they took with them must have approached a million.

It was in 1857 that a new phenomenon appeared upon the plains, providing a singular contribution to the history of Western transportation. This was the handcart, the little brother as it were of the covered waggon, and it was Mormon ingenuity and doggedness that produced the remarkable handcart experiment of 1857–60. During those years approximately 3,000 people walked the whole distance from Iowa City, the assembly point, to Salt Lake City, pushing or pulling handcarts until they reached the promised land. During the same period

[1] Joaquin Miller, *Overland in a Covered Waggon* (ed. S. G. Firman, New York, 1930), pp. 42–3, as quoted by Goetzmann, *op. cit.*, p. 84. The family went West to the Willamette valley in 1852, and 'Joaquin', as he now began to call himself (after another of his heroes, Joaquin Murieta, the Mexican–Californian bandit) went to California in 1856. See further *Dictionary of American Biography*, Vol. XII, pp. 621–2.

only 5,200 migrated to Utah by waggon team.[1] It was a time of tribulation and near-bankruptcy for the Church of Jesus Christ of Latter Day Saints, and during these years the whole desert kingdom was in jeopardy. First came the crop-failures and famines of the 'grasshopper years' 1855–6, and then the 'declaration of war' on the Mormons by President Buchanan's Government and the occupation of the Territory by United States troops. The handcart experiment did not save the day, but it contributed a great deal towards maintaining morale and in preventing the inward migration from falling to an insignificant trickle, which might have resulted in disaster for the missions abroad and spelled ruin to the Church at home. Brigham Young, the Head of the Mormon Church, initiated the handcart experiment with brave words which he himself could hardly have entirely believed, saying: 'If it is once tried, you will find that it will become the favourite method of crossing the plain', and it was, of course, by far the cheapest. Three of the five handcart companies organized in 1856 reached their destination in good order, welcomed on their last day's tramp 'home to Zion' by enthusiastic 'Saints', weeping and 'speechless with joy'. Two other companies, starting later, ran into bad weather and 67 of the 500 in the Willie company, and no fewer than 135 of the 567 in the Martin contingent died on the way. 'With more than 200 dead it was a far greater disaster than that which overcame the oft-publicized Donner Party.'[2]

It was partially to prevent the recurrence of such disasters that the Brigham Young Carrying and Express Company (popularly known as the 'X.Y. Company') was formed in 1857 to carry the mails 'by swift pony express' and to prepare a waggon line to haul freight. A successful bid was made to carry a monthly United States mail from Independence to Salt Lake City and the first mail went through in twenty-six days. Staging points were set up and a number of regular settlements established along the route, mostly by using labour and materials supplied free by the 'Saints', at the behest of Brigham Young. A new class of 'express missionaries' was created, and these young men were strung out along the trail, outfitted and supplied by wealthier and older members of the Church.[3] Unfortunately this enterprising development, anticipating in many ways the great express and staging enterprises

[1] G. E. Larson, *Prelude to the Kingdom: Mormon Desert Conquest – A Chapter in American Co-operative Experience* (Francetown, N.H., 1947), pp. 235–6.
[2] L. Arrington, *Great Basin Kingdom*, p. 158.
[3] *Ibid.*, pp. 167–8.

of the 1860s,[1] was brought to an end by the cancellation by the United States Government of the four-year mail contract on 10 June 1857 – barely six months after it had been signed – and by the 'Utah War' of 1858, which resulted in the evacuation of all the outposts of Zion outside the Salt Lake Basin, and indeed, a brief 'Exodus' from the capital itself by its entire Mormon population as the United States Army marched in.

For a short time it appeared that the tragic history of the Mormon Church during the 1830s and 1840s might now be continued after a decade of promise and achievement in Utah. But the steady hand of Brigham Young (contrasting with the somewhat unsteady policy of President Buchanan in Washington) was at the helm, and the Saints returned to resume their remarkable colonization work.[2]

The tragedies of earlier days had shown that religious fervour was not enough to found and consolidate a new settlement and to put into operation revolutionary social and economic ideas there, unless accompanied by organizing ability of a very high order. Joseph Smith, the prophet and founder of the Church, lacked this ability and he was constantly at

[1] See further, Chapter VIII. [2] See further, Chapter XIII, *passim*.

loggerheads, right up to his assassination in 1844, with his associates in the Church as well as with the hostile 'gentiles' outside it. Brigham Young was an organizing genius, who not only had vision but could compel the loyalty of his people, and even secure the grudging admiration and aid of the world outside. Founded in New York State in 1830, the Mormon sect, gaining adherents and enemies as it went, moved its headquarters first to the Western Reserve of Ohio (1831) and then to Jackson County on the Missouri frontier. In 1833 they were banished to Clay County across the river and many returned to Kirtland, Ohio. The next 'Zion' was to be Far West, Missouri (1837), and Kirtland was then evacuated. Again the building of 'a Kingdom of God in the Wilderness' by the new sect encountered implacable local opposition despite the economic progress made. In 1839, the whole community was moved back across the Mississippi to Quincy, Illinois, and Joseph Smith established his new – and last – capital at nearby Nauvoo ('beautiful place' in Hebrew), as he rechristened a swampy village hitherto known as 'Commerce'. By 1844 there were over twenty-five thousand Mormons living in Nauvoo and the adjacent area. Nauvoo was to be a model city; it was planned on a grand scale and several imposing buildings (for a frontier community) were completed. Then disaster struck again. The almost open practice of polygamy (despite numerous 'official denials' that it existed) by Joseph Smith and other members of the Mormon hierarchy undoubtedly served to increase the opposition of the 'gentiles' in neighbouring communities, and this led to the rioting and demonstrations in which Joseph Smith and his brother Hyrum lost their lives in 1844 – and also to the final exodus to an even 'farther west' in 1846–7, led by Brigham Young, the new Head of the Church.

The move into the Salt Lake valley was to get away from the United States and from interference by its intolerant citizens and officials, whereas most other Americans who migrated to the Far West in those days fervently hoped that the Stars and Stripes would soon follow them – into Oregon, into New Mexico, into Texas, and into California, and even beyond. Indeed, many of these other Americans had been motivated, in part at least, by such patriotic sentiments, in that age of 'Manifest Destiny', in deciding to make the difficult journey across the Plains or round the Horn. How different it was with the Mormons! Their religious fervour and iron discipline took them into the 'Great Basin Kingdom' when it was still an uninhabited (and believed to be uninhabitable) region nominally owned by Mexico. Here, within a

15. Comanche Village, by George Catlin (1834), showing women preparing buffalo hides which, when sewn together, covered tipis up to 25 feet in diameter.

16*a*. Arrival of the Caravan at Santa Fé, from *Commerce of the Prairies* by Josiah Gregg (1844).

16*b*. Emigrant train attacked by Comanches, by Seth Eastman, *c*. 1849.

year, Manifest Destiny had caught up with them, and within two years 'that damn flag', as one Mormon elder called it,[1] was flying over their latest 'Zion'; for, by the treaty of Guadalupe Hidalgo all of the Utah Territory, the proposed 'State of Deseret' of the Mormon planners, became part of the United States.

But this time the Mormons were not to be dislodged. Utah had to wait a half-century for statehood,[2] but long before that time the Mormon economic and social experiment had succeeded, and though the religious beliefs and practices of the Saints (even after the complete banning of polygamy by the Church) continued to arouse opposition (though also to secure converts, all over the world) the United States had learned how to live with them and they with the United States.

It cannot be said that, but for the Mormon example, the inhospitable Great Basin area between the Rockies and the Sierras and Cascades could *never* have been settled, and that Americans and immigrants alike would have continued to leap-frog over it to Oregon and California. But Mormons were the first to *prove* that it could be settled and could support a large, self-sufficient, and growing population. This was their greatest contribution to the history of the American Far West, and it was a very impressive one. They were there before the railroads, before the overland stages, even before the Gold Rush. Never in the history of human migration have a dedicated people more decisively made the desert blossom like a rose.

The three great trails across the trans-Mississippi West, therefore, before the building of the transcontinental railroads, were the Santa Fé Trail, the Oregon Trail, and the California Trail. The Santa Fé Trail continued across from the Rio Grande valley to the Pacific as the Old Spanish Trail to Los Angeles, the Gila river being a less-used alternative to San Diego. An even more southerly trail was developed from Memphis across Arkansas, the Indian Country (Oklahoma) and Texas to El Paso, Yuma, and San Diego, to be used as the route of the overland stage coaches. The outbreak of the Civil War soon put an end to its usefulness. It was too roundabout ever to have been an emigrant trail. It carried mail, important small-bulk freight, and affluent or expense-account passengers at considerable speed and in great discomfort.

Even less important for the overland migration was the short-lived (1860–1) but spectacular Pony Express, from St Joseph to Sacramento and San Francisco, carrying, of course, no passengers, but mail at

[1] See Chapter VII, p. 169. [2] See Chapter XIII, p. 329.

$5.00 per half ounce at first – always at a loss, both in money and in men. The opening of the transcontinental telegraph put paid – if that is the word – to this experiment in 1861. The Pony Express route, which was no new way but just a streamlined version of the by that time very much cluttered-up California Trail, closed an era which may be said to have begun, on that particular trail, on the memorable evening when Nancy Kelsey put her one-year-old daughter Ann to bed on 'Dr' John Marsh's ranch under Mount Diabolo – less than twenty miles short of San Francisco Bay, one November day in the year 1841.

CHAPTER VII

By Land and Sea to Eldorado

In 1839 an elderly Scotsman, who had never been there, published the first *History* in the English language of little-known California.[1] His book was widely read on both sides of the Atlantic and received favourable notice in the London *Times*.[2] In 1840 a young Harvard student, who had shipped for two years before the mast in the trade between Boston and Pacific coast ports, printed his experiences and his book became a best-seller[3]; he described the uninhabited mist shrouded shores of San Francisco Bay, the high cliffs of Capistrano, the desolate wasteland of the San Pedro anchorage, the pleasant social life of the rustic provincial capital, Monterey. In the years 1841 and 1842, a young French attaché from his country's legation in Mexico City visited the two Californias and described the Franciscan missions one by one, visited the Russian establishments at Fort Ross and Bodega Bay, and penetrated as far as the outpost of civilization – New Helvetia – recently established on the upper Sacramento by an enterprising Swiss emigrant, John Augustus Sutter; his book, too, attracted considerable attention.[4] On 12 November 1842 a Prussian diplomat in New York wrote to a colleague in London 'Upper California is one of the finest countries in the world . . . It is only necessary that it should be in the possession of an active, industrious and energetic people.'[5]

[1] Alexander Forbes (of Tepic), *A History of Upper and Lower California*, from their first discovery to the present time, comprising an account of the climate, soil, natural productions, agriculture, commerce, etc. A full view of the Missionary Establishments and condition of the free and domesticated Indians. With an appendix relating to Steam Navigation in the Pacific . . . (London, 1839).

[2] *The Times*, 6 September 1839. See also this Chapter, note 1, p. 167.

[3] R. H. Dana, Jr, *Two Years before the Mast* (Boston, 1840; many subsequent editions).

[4] M. Duflot De Mofras, *Exploration du Territoire de L'Orégon, des Californies, et de la Mer Vermeille*, executée pendant les Années 1840, 1841 et 1842 . . . (4 vols, Paris, 1844; English trans. by M. Wilbur, San Francisco, 1937; 2 vols).

[5] Friedrich von Roenne (Prussian Minister in Washington) to a fellow-Prussian diplomat in London (Minister Christian von Bunsen). Manuscript letter in German in Prussian Secret State Archives, Merseburg, D.D.R. Photostat copy in Library of Congress, Washington, D.C. – Roenne mentions Forbes' book as the latest authority on Upper California. See John A. Hawgood, 'A Projected Prussian Purchase of California' (*Southern California Quarterly*, Dec. 1966).

Such a people (though the Prussian diplomat thought that the Germans would qualify) were the citizens of the United States, a certain number of whom had already found their way, by sea or overland, to California by the year 1840. The 'Yankee Exodus' of the generation after the war of 1812 brought a number of men from Massachusetts and other parts of New England into this remote pastoral Utopia, some to trade and go away, others to stay. John Cooper came to Santa Barbara in 1823, and also had a residence and store in Monterey. He married into the powerful Spanish-Californian Vallejo family; Abel Stearns came to the pueblo of Los Angeles in 1829 and married Arcadia, beautiful daughter of Juan Bandini; Thomas Oliver Larkin, Cooper's half-brother, came to Yerba Buena and then to Monterey in 1832, and after a shipboard romance on the long voyage from Boston to California via the Sandwich islands, married an American widow, Rachel Holmes. Theirs were the first all-American children to be born in Mexican *Alta California*. Meanwhile trappers were seeping over the mountains and deserts, seeing California and finding that it was good. Some of these, like William Wolfskill and Isaac Graham, decided to stay. Not until 1841 was the first organized immigrant party (that of Bidwell and Bartleson)[1] to find its way into the California valleys overland, but individuals, like John Marsh, Harvard graduate and amateur physician and surgeon, who went by way of Santa Fé in 1836, had arrived earlier. A few other foreigners also arrived before 1840, but the Americans predominated. There were, in that year, still fewer than three hundred alien residents in Upper California.[2]

Upwards of a hundred of these foreigners were summarily arrested in April 1840 at the orders of Governor Alvarado (who had seized power in a revolution in 1836, assisted by some of these very same foreigners) and deported in irons to Tepic, in western Mexico, in order to be sent for trial in Mexico City. Although[3] his motives are still somewhat obscure, Alvarado was certainly influenced by his fear that these

[1] See *supra*, Chapter VI, p. 144.

[2] Thomas Oliver Larkin, in 1856, compiled a list, which he made as complete as possible, of 'Names of British Subjects and Citizens of the United States who resided in Alta California – prior to 1840'. He calculated that 'during this period, there were living in California, a few French, Germans, Portuguese, and Italians (not forty) and thirty to forty natives of the Sandwich Islands and Foreigners of Color'. His list contained the names of 162 persons identified as Americans, 60 as English, 21 as Irish and 15 as Scots. This list is printed as an appendix to *First and Last Consul* (ed. J. A. Hawgood, San Marino, California, 1962), pp. 109–18.

[3] They were released in Tepic, as a result of the intervention of Eustace Barron, the British Consul there, and were afterwards repatriated.

W. Bromage
OREGON
IDAHO
NEVADA
(STATE · 1864)
(formerly Carson County, California)
UTAH
ARIZONA
MEXICO
Crescent City
Eureka
SHASTA DAM
Redding
LASSEN VOLCANIC
Sacramento R.
Pyramid Lake
Humboldt R.
Humboldt Sink
Carson Sink
Donner Pass
Reno
L. Tahoe
Carson City
Marysville
Ft. Ross
Sacramento
Stockton
YOSEMITE
KING'S CANYON
Mt. Whitney 14,495 ft
DEATH VALLEY
Las Vegas
L. Mead
BOULDER DAM
DAVIS DAM
SEQUOIA
Fresno
San Joaquin R.
Salinas R.
Monterey
San Jose
San Francisco
Bakersfield
Mojave Desert
JOSHUA TREE
Colorado R. Aqueduct
PARKER DAM
Colorado R.
San Gabriel
San Bernardino
Los Angeles
Salton Sea FORMED 1905-07
IMPERIAL DAM
Gila R.
Yuma
San Diego
Sonoma · 1823
San Rafael · 1817
Dolores · 1776
San José de Guadalupe · 1797
Santa Clara · 1777
Santa Cruz · 1791
San Juan Bautista 1797
Carmel · 1770
Soledad · 1791
San Antonio de Padua · 1771
San Miguel · 1797
San Luís Obispo · 1772
La Purísima Concepción · 1787
Santa Inéz · 1804
Santa Barbara · 1786
San Buenaventura · 1782
San Fernando · 1797
San Juan Capistrano · 1776
San Luís Rey · 1798
San Diego de Alcala · 1769
97
40
99
101
50
6
91
80
MODERN CALIFORNIA
U.S. Highways
National Parks & Monuments
Franciscan Missions
Santa Inez · 1804
(some names shortened)
0
Miles
200

foreigners, and particularly the Americans among them, were gaining too much influence in Upper California, and might eventually take it over, as had so recently happened in Texas. The Government of the United States had for some time been casting longing eyes on San Francisco Bay, which most Americans considered to be the only part of the province worth having, and two of the United States' envoys in Mexico, Anthony Butler (1835) and Waddy Thompson (1842) unsuccessfully opened negotiations for the purchase of all or part of California, to include the coveted bay. Between these two attempts Lieutenant Charles Wilkes, of the U.S. Navy, visited the bay in the course of his exploring expedition, and added his praises of it to those of others; and a year after Wilkes, Commodore Thomas ap Catesby Jones actually took possession of Monterey, the Californian capital, on behalf of his country, on 20 October 1842, under the mistaken impression that war had broken out between the United States and Mexico and that a British naval squadron was on its way to put California under the protection of Her Majesty Queen Victoria. Though he evacuated the port within two days, apologized to the newly arrived Mexican Governor, Micheltorena, and sailed away after participating in a *fiesta* held in his honour at Los Angeles by the fun-loving Californians (who never let either business or politics interfere with pleasure), the incident distinctly worsened Mexican–American relations, already embittered by the arrest of Isaac Graham and his fellow-foreigners in 1840, and everybody now knew that the first action of the United States Navy in the event of actual war breaking out would be to seize California and keep it. In this trigger-happy atmosphere men of good will, such as Thomas Oliver Larkin on the side of the American residents – he had been appointed U.S. Consul in the Californias in 1843 by Tyler's administration – and General Mariano Guadalupe Vallejo, the leading landowner in the north of the province, on the side of the Californians, worked against time to settle California's destinies in a peaceful way. Both of them realized that California's future lay with that of the United States, and Larkin worked openly to this end. His appointment in 1845 as Confidential Agent (while remaining Consul) by the Polk administration, underlined and redoubled his efforts. He was to be overtaken by the events of the spring and summer of 1846, when first of all J. C. Frémont, in California (without explicit orders) on his third 'exploring' expedition, defied the Californian authorities for a time after General Castro had ordered him to withdraw his force of very warlike-looking 'topographical engineers', and then lent covert encouragement to an insurrection among the

American settlers known as the Bear Flag Revolution. The American-dominated 'California Republic' set up in Sonoma (where Vallejo, although the Americans' best friend, had been captured and imprisoned by the insurgents) lasted only three weeks, but it justified all the worst fears of the Spanish-Californians and alienated many of them who had hitherto been friendly towards the United States.[1]

On 7 July 1846 the American Navy did reoccupy Monterey and take possession of Upper California, this time for keeps, for the war with Mexico had finally broken out on the Rio Grande and Commodore Sloat now felt justified in obeying his secret orders without risking a repetition of the Ap Catesby Jones fiasco of 1842. Within days the Stars and Stripes were also flying over Yerba Buena, New Helvetia, and (replacing the short-lived Bear Flag) Sonoma. Frémont and the 'messenger of destiny' who had chased after him into the Oregon, Lieutenant Archibald Gillespie of the U.S. Marines,[2] organized the California Volunteers, who marched to Monterey and were then shipped down south to complete the American conquest of California. This was not accomplished quite so easily as the almost bloodless occupation of the north, and General Kearny's hundred Dragoons suffered a technical reverse, at least, at San Pasqual (when they arrived there after a long march from Santa Fé) at the hands of the Californians, who had previously rallied and thrown the high-handed Gillespie out of the *pueblo* of Los Angeles. Resistance ended at the capitulation of Cahuenga Pass,[3] early in 1847, although the American commanders, Commodore Stockton, J. C. Frémont (whom he had appointed Military Governor of California), and Stephen Kearny, who had come over the mountains and deserts to 'pull rank' on them both, continued their private war against each

[1] For the background of the American infiltration and conquest of California, see R. G. Cleland, *The Early Sentiment for the Annexation of California . . . 1835–1846* (Austin, Texas, 1915); J. A. Hawgood, 'Patterns of Yankee Infiltration in Mexican California' (*Pacific Historical Review*, February 1858, Vol. XXVII), pp. 27–37, and 'J. C. Frémont and the Bear Flag Revolution: A Reappraisal' (Univ. Birmingham Hist. Journal, 1959, Vol. VII, pp. 80–100; reprinted in revised form in *Southern California Quarterly*, June 1962, Vol. XLIV, No. 2, pp. 67–96). More general works on the subject are R. G. Cleland, *From Wilderness the Empire* (New York, 1944), Chapter 12, pp. 193–205, and Chapter 13, pp. 206–21, and Norman Graebner, *Empire on the Pacific* (New York, 1953), *passim.*

[2] See Werner Marti, *Messenger of Destiny* (San Francisco, 1960), for a full treatment of the thrilling and mystifying mission of this dashing and choleric leatherneck secret agent and courier, licensed – and only too happy – to kill.

[3] A 'location' where many a subsequent 'army' has bitten dust.

other for some months longer. The consequence of this dispute was the famous Frémont court martial of 1847–8.[1] With the departure of Stockton, Frémont (under open arrest), and Kearny, the Military Government settled down to its proper business of completing the absorption of Upper California as part of the United States, under Colonel R. B. Mason and his Adjutant, Lieutenant William Tecumseh Sherman, who had arrived by sea in 1847. The Treaty of Guadalupe Hildalgo, negotiated by Nicholas Trist in Mexico City in February 1848 (though news of its terms took several months to reach Monterey) handed over California officially to the United States.

Two weeks earlier gold had been discovered by James Marshall in the tail-race of John Augustus Sutter's saw-mill at Coloma on the south branch of the American river, a tributary of the Sacramento.

After that, California was never the same again. 1848 saw also the year of revolutions in Europe. Marshall made his great discovery on 24 January; the Treaty of Guadalupe Hildalgo was signed on 2 February; King Louis Philippe lost his throne on 24 February; Prince Metternich fell from power in Vienna on 13 March; on 15 March the daily *Californian*, San Francisco's first newspaper, had an item at the bottom of the third column of the second page which read:

GOLD MINE FOUND

> In the newlymade raceway of the Saw Mill recently erected by Captain Sutter on the American Fork, gold has been found in considerable quantities. One person brought thirty dollars worth to New Helvetia, gathered there in a short time. California, no doubt, is rich in mineral wealth; great chances here for scientific capitalists. Gold has been found in almost every part of the country.

Nobody paid much attention, even in San Francisco, to this obscure item, but an era had ended on the shores of the Pacific and a new age had begun, just as assuredly as at the Hofburg and at Versailles, in Frankfurt and in Prague. Not until early in May, when Sam Brannan,

[1] Frémont was convicted of insubordination and dismissed from the Army; but President Polk set the penalty aside. Frémont nevertheless resigned his commission. The published report of this *cause célèbre* reads like a novel and it is remarkable that it has never been dramatized or filmed. Extensive extracts from the proceedings appeared in the Press, but the full report took the form of a *Message* from President Polk (Executive Document No. 33, 30th Congress; 1st Session [Senate], Washington, D.C., 1848, 447 pp.).

a recusant Mormon elder, who had led a shipload of 'Saints' round Cape Horn to California two years earlier, ran through the streets of San Francisco (still, despite its grand new name, a tiny village of several hundred inhabitants, on Yerba Buena Cove) flourishing in his hand a bottle of dust that glinted in the sun, and shouting 'Gold! Gold! Gold from the American river!' did even a local gold rush begin. It was to

take another half-year for the East and the outside world to realize the extent and the importance of the gold discoveries initiated by James Marshall.

A half-hearted attempt on the part of its first discoverers and their immediate associates to keep the gold mining secret was ended by Brannan.[1] Within a month of his action San Francisco was emptied of its able-bodied men and boys: its two newspapers (one recently transferred from Monterey) ceased publication, and the furniture of its only hotel (the owner of which, former U.S. Vice-Consul William Leidesdorf, had recently died) was put up for auction; the complete crews of most merchant vessels in the harbour deserted, and naval vessels had to put out to sea to avoid a similar immobilizing fate. The American Army of Occupation soon consisted only of officers. The military

[1] He had taken the gold dust in trade from a thirsty and garrulous miner at his general store at Sutter's Fort on the Sacramento. Compare account on p. 188.

governor had to cook his own dinner. His adjutant went out on horseback to head off enlisted men escaping inland towards the mines. James Marshall and Sam Brannan had really started something.

It had not been until 1842 that the United States Government first openly showed its intention to secure California by force if necessary. Less than four years later California was American-occupied territory, and seven years later it was the most desirable place on earth for millions of people, hundreds of thousands of whom faced every imaginable hardship to reach the Eldorado it had become. A sleepy Mexican province, with under fifteen thousand white and near-white inhabitants in 1845, was to become by 1850 a State of the American Union, humming with every kind and sort of human activity and enterprise – but with the pick and shovel, the pan and sluice, the 'long-tom', the 'cradle', and the flume[1] dominating the scene – and containing a population of close on a hundred thousand. Another quarter of a million, at least, were converging on California from all parts of the world, from China, from Chile, from the Antipodes, and from the Cape of Good Hope, from Samarkand and, possibly, from Timbuctoo and Kamchatka, from Madagascar and Sarawak. The great Rush was on.

The 1848 Gold Rush was a local one. The settlements on or near the coast emptied and most of their able-bodied inhabitants departed for the diggings. This is how (in the words of Walter Colton)[2] it happened in Monterey. 'June 20, 1848 . . . My messenger has returned with specimens of gold; he dismounted in a sea of upturned faces. As he drew forth the yellow lumps from his pockets, and passed them around among the eager crowd, the doubts, which had lingered till now, fled. . . The excitement produced was intense; and many were soon busy in their hasty preparations for a departure to the mines. The family who had kept house for me caught the moving infection. Husband and wife were both packing up; the blacksmith dropped his hammer, the carpenter his plane, the mason his trowel, the farmer his sickle, the baker his loaf, and the tapster his bottle. All were off for the mines, some on carts, some on horses, and some on crutches, and one went in a litter . . .' From San Francisco, Thomas Larkin, the American Consul, wrote to the Secretary of State in Washington, on 28 June 1848:[3] 'Three fourths of the houses in the town on the Bay of San Francisco are deserted . . . every blacksmith, carpenter and lawyer is leaving; brickyards, saw-

[1] See illustrations, pp. 177 and 180.
[2] Walter Colton, *Three Years in California* (New York, 1850), pp. 246–7.
[3] G. P. Hammond (ed.), *The Larkin Papers* (Berkeley, 1951–64), Vol. VI, pp. 301–4.

mills and ranches are left perfectly alone. A large part of the volunteers at San Francisco and Sonoma have deserted . . . vessels are losing their crews . . . both our newspapers are discontinued . . . San Francisco has not a justice of the peace left . . . Every bowl, tray, warming pan and pigin has gone to the mines. Everything in short that has a scoop in it that will hold sand and water. All the iron has been worked up into crow-bars, pick-axes and spades . . .' The story was the same in Sonoma, San José, and Santa Cruz. The fever was somewhat slower to reach San Luis Obispo, Santa Barbara, Los Angeles, and San Diego, but well before the end of the year these little towns had emptied of their folk too, and migrant miners had begun to come up out of Mexico. John Charles Frémont, leading the remnants of his disastrous fourth expedition by the southern route from Santa Fé to begin a new life on the property he had purchased, through Thomas Larkin, in California, met on the Gila river, in February 1849, 'A large party of Mexicans from Sonora, several hundred in number . . . From them was received the news of the discovery of gold in California, and this large party were on their way to California to hunt for Gold.'[1] Frémont persuaded the Sonorans to go with him to his Mariposa grant, for which he had paid Larkin $3,000. It proved (Jessie Frémont was to claim,[2] with, in this case, pardonable exaggeration) 'the richest gold-bearing estate in the country. Soon the bags of gold, in lumps, in dust, in rich bits of rock, began to accumulate in inconvenient quantities' filling up all the drawers and cupboards (when taken to Monterey) of the house the Frémonts shared with Señora Alvarado.

It will be noted that the news of the gold discoveries had not yet reached Santa Fé when Frémont left that city in January 1849 after the failure of his fourth expedition. It had reached the east coast a little earlier, but the extent of the discoveries was not fully realized until President Polk published, in his annual Message on 5 December 1848, a glowing account of them, based upon the special report of Colonel Mason, the Military Governor of California, and on other information received through official channels. He said:

[1] 'Great Events during the Life of J. C. Frémont and Jessie Benton Frémont,' written by Lt Francis and Jessie Frémont. Typescript with MS. revisions in Bancroft Library, Berkeley, California (Document CB 397, Pt I, Vol. 1, p. 97). Although not itself published, this narrative was extensively used by Mrs Frémont in her various publications, and by Allan Nevins in his biography of Frémont. The original narrative is quoted from here with the permission of the Director of the Bancroft Library, Dr G. P. Hammond.

[2] *Ibid.*, p. 101.

It was known that mines of the precious metals existed to a considerable extent in California at the time of its acquisition. Recent discoveries render it probable that these mines are more extensive and valuable than was anticipated. The accounts of the abundance of gold in that territory are of such an extraordinary character as would scarcely command belief, were they not corroborated by the authentic reports of officers in the public service, who have visited the mineral district, and derived the facts which they detail from personal observation. Reluctant to credit the reports in general circulation as to the quantity of gold, the officer commanding our forces in California visited the mineral district in July last, for the purpose of obtaining accurate information on the subject. His report to the War Department of the result of his examination, and the facts obtained on the spot, is herewith laid before Congress. When he visited the country, there were about four thousand persons engaged in collecting gold. There is every reason to believe that the number of persons so employed has since been augmented. The explorations already made warrant the belief that the supply is very large, and that gold is found in various places in extensive districts of country.

Information received from officers of the navy, and other sources, though not so full and minute, confirm the accounts of the commander of our military force in California. It appears also, from these reports that mines of quicksilver are found in the vicinity of the gold region. One of them is now being worked, and is believed to be among the most productive in the world.

The effects produced by the discovery of these rich mineral deposits, and the success which has attended the labours of those who have resorted to them, have produced a surprising change in the state of affairs in California. Labour commands a most exorbitant price, and all other pursuits but that of searching for the precious metals are abandoned. Nearly the whole of the male population of the country have gone to the gold district. Ships arriving on the coast are deserted by their crews, and their voyages suspended for want of sailors. Our commanding officer there entertains apprehensions that soldiers cannot be kept in the public service without a large increase of pay. Desertions in his command have become frequent, and he recommends that those who shall withstand the strong temptations, and remain faithful, should be rewarded.

This abundance of gold, and the all-engrossing pursuit of it, have already caused in California an unprecedented rise in the price of the necessaries of life.[1]

[1] This famous Message has been reprinted many times. It is to be found, of course, in Richardson, *Messages of the Presidents*, but in more convenient form was included,

Colonel Mason's own account, dated 17 August 1848, told of his visit in June to 'twenty-five miles up the American Fork, to a point now known as the Lower Mines or Mormon Diggins [*sic*]'. He described how

> The hill sides were thickly strewn with canvas tents and bush arbours; a store was erected, and several boarding shanties in operation. The day was intensely hot, yet about two hundred men were at work in the full glare of the sun, washing for gold – some with tin pans, some with close woven Indian baskets, but the greater part had a rude machine, known as the cradle.
>
> This is on rockers, six or eight feet long, open at the foot, and at its head has a coarse grate or sieve; the bottom is rounded, with small cleets nailed across. Four men are required to work this machine; one digs the ground in the bank close by the stream; another carries it to the cradle and empties it on the grate; a third gives a violent rocking motion to the machine; whilst a fourth dashes on water from the stream itself. The sieve keeps the coarse stones from entering the cradle, the current of water washes off the earthy matter, and the gravel is gradually carried out at the foot of the machine, leaving the gold mixed with a heavy fine black sand above the first cleets.
>
> The sand and gold mixed together are then drawn off through augur holes into a pan below, are dried in the sun, and afterwards separated by blowing off the sand. A party of four men thus employed, at the lower mines, averaged $100 a day. The Indians, and those who have nothing but pans, or willow baskets, gradually wash out the earth, and separate the gravel by hand, leaving nothing but the gold mixed with sand, which is separated in the manner before described. The gold in the lower mines is in fine bright scales, of which I send several specimens.[1]

The *New York Courier and Enquirer* published a letter written by a naval officer on the U.S. ship *Dale*, and dated San José, Lower California, 17 November 1848, which told the results of several more months of the local Californian Gold Rush of that year:

> The *rancheros* have left their farms, and unless supplies are sent into the country there must be a famine. I *saw* a man who paid six hundred dollars for a barrel of flour.
>
> Every thing in the shape of goods and provisions commands the

---

together with a number of other valuable documents, as an appendix to J. C. Frémont, *Geographical Memoir*, p. 68.

[1] Frémont, *Geog. Mem.* (1849), p. 69.

highest prices at the mines, payable in gold – which has been sold at the mines for five dollars per ounce, *Troy* weight, and in some cases for even less. At San Francisco and Monterey it sells for from ten to twelve dollars in trade. A vessel sailed a short time before our arrival at Monterey, for Mazatlan, with twelve hundred pounds of this gold, which I found upon our arrival sold for over sixteen dollars per ounce, *avoirdupois* weight. The gentleman who owns this gold came out to this country in January, 1847, in one of the store-ships chartered in Boston, to bring out provisions for the squadron; he brought out with him between four and five thousand dollars worth of goods, which he bought at auction for a venture. He located in San Francisco, and in August of the same year, he told me that with the goods he brought out, and his purchase of two lots, he was worth thirty thousand dollars. Lots bought originally for fifteen dollars are now worth five or six thousand dollars; all of this took place before the discovery of the mines. This gold has been assayed and found to be twenty-three and a half carats fine – pure virgin gold. The largest piece found weighs twenty-five pounds, in one solid block; the next weighs seven pounds, and so on, down to fine black sand.[1]

A ship sailed from Boston for San Francisco the day after Polk's Message was published, and thus had the honour of carrying the first of the Argonauts around the Horn. Already before the end of the year, three weeks later, 335 people were on their way to the mines of California by the 'short' sea route via Panama, and in 1849 over six thousand (including members of John Augustus Sutter's own family) used this difficult and fever-ridden route. One of these trans-Isthmian Forty-Niners, named Collis P. Huntington, paused at Panama City to open a store and earn the first instalment of what was to become one of the greatest fortunes to be earned by a California resident during the next half-century. He was later to move on to Sacramento and to become the biggest of the fabulous 'Big Four'. Meanwhile people were pouring around the Horn and overland, by every established trail and a few novel ones, to the mines. The first steamship, the *California*, to open William H. Aspinwall's Pacific Steamship Navigation Company's 'regular' service left New York on 6 October 1848, before the gold fever had really started, and reached San Francisco on 28 February 1849, to find it in full swing. This ship carried Jessie Frémont to a dramatic reunion with her 'lost' husband (at Chagres she had been told that he had probably not survived his fourth expedition), although she had

[1] Frémont, *Geog. Mem.* (1849), p. 78.

travelled overland from Panama to Chagres, and hers is one of the most vivid descriptions of the sea-and-Isthmian route in 1849.[1] The *California* had a royal reception at the Golden Gate and at Yerba Buena Cove, where 'A few low houses, and many tents, such as they were, covered the base of some of the wind-swept treeless hills, over which the June fog rolled its chilling mist. Deserted ships of all sorts were swinging with the tide.'[2] The *California* was itself almost immediately to lose nearly all its own crew.

By early 1849 from four to five thousand persons (nearly all of them men) had reached the mines from outside California. By the end of 1849 the figures had reached between forty and fifty thousand, including many foreigners. By the middle of 1850 there were at least twenty thousand foreigners in California out of a population of around a hundred thousand. Of these hundred thousand only about eight in each hundred were women. Not all of these women were housewives. 'The miners came in '49, the whores in '51' runs the ribald old song, but even by 1851 resolute, literate (as will be seen), and respectable women were coming around the Horn, across the Isthmus and along the overland trails to upstage and to outnumber the 'soiled doves' of the cribs and the honky-tonks. Mrs Megquier, Mrs Clappe ('Dame Shirley'), and Mrs Sarah Royce, all women of unassailable virtue and high moral tone,[3] were among the vanguard of these ladies.

California's population explosion by immigration was phenomenal, and, in a comparable period of time, can hardly be said to have been matched in recorded statistical history. Before the end of 1852 – the peak year of the California gold boom – the state had a quarter

[1] J. B. Frémont, *A Year of American Travel* (New York, 1878, reprinted San Francisco, 1960), *passim*. Another eloquent traveller, the Swiss Carl Meyer (who was probably a mining engineer, so accurate and detailed are his technical descriptions of the diggings) left New Orleans in February 1849, reached Monterey, California, in July, and spent the autumn and winter at the mines. He met the Frémonts at Mariposa, and stayed in California until 1852. Henry R. Wagner had edited the translation by Ruth F. Axe of Carl Meyer, *Bound for Sacramento* (Claremont, California, 1938). It was originally published as *Nach dem Sacramento* in Aarua, Switzerland, in 1856. He also published there (in 1852) a *Prospectus to form a Society for Emigration to California*, which was also translated into English by Ruth F. Axe, and published in Claremont, California, in 1938.

[2] J. B. Frémont, *A Year of American Travel* (1878 edn), p. 97. This was the *California*'s second voyage to San Francisco, returning under-crewed and over-passengered from Panama, where she had returned after the first outward voyage, to start the projected service.

[3] All three wrote valuable diaries or letters which have been published. See Bibliographical Note, p. 382.

of a million inhabitants (or over fifteen times as many as at the beginning of 1848) and by the census of 1860 the figures had risen to 380,000 (or half as many again). By 1860 the population of Oregon had crept up only to 52,000 (from a population approximating to that of California's in 1848) and that of Utah, despite the Mormon church's tremendous efforts to colonize and settle its chosen land, to just over 40,000.[1] The increase in each of these rich and attractive territories was

thus only fourfold in the twelve years, whereas California's was nearly thirtyfold.

Not all the California immigrants became miners, and many who went to the mines ceased to remain there. By the end of 1848 there were approximately still only 5,000 men at the mines, by the end of 1849 the number was about 40,000, by the end of 1850 about 50,000; by the end of 1852 certainly 100,000. Even in 1860, after the bonanza days were long over, fully 82,573 men returned their occupations as 'miner' in the United States census. Of the 35,000 Chinese in California in 1860 perhaps three-quarters were still living in the mining counties and 'reworking placer ground sold to them or abandoned to them by discouraged white men . . . It is entirely possible that by the close of the decade of the fifties one quarter of the working miners may have been Chinese.'[2]

The mining population of California did not fall spectacularly after

[1] Rodman W. Paul, *Mining Frontiers of the Far West* (New York, 1963) p. 15, gives the 1848 figures for California as 'about 14,000 other than Indians', and of Oregon (including Washington) as 'perhaps 10,000–12,000 whites and half-breeds'. Utah's census figures for 1850 and 1880 were 11,380 and 40,273. For further details see R. W. Paul, *California Gold* (Cambridge, Mass., 1947), pp. 23–5.

[2] Paul, *Mining Frontiers*, pp. 35–6.

the early gold rushes – as it did in so many other states and territories – because the mines remained rich, even though the gold was becoming harder and more expensive to get year by year. The peak year was 1852 when over $81 million worth of gold came out of California mines. In 1853 and 1854 the 'take' was down to just under $70 million each year; between 1865 and 1885 the yearly figures fluctuated between $15 million and $20 million, and the lowest figure of any year up to 1900

was just over $11 million. California thus entered the twentieth century still very much the golden state, with a half-century's production of that precious metal totalling over $1,300 million, or an average of $26 million's worth a year. These are heady figures, and those $1,300 million have played no inconsiderable part in swaying the destinies of America and of the world ever since. Parlayed into much greater sums by astute financial manipulators of the type of Collis and Henry Huntington, Leland Stanford and George Hearst they have created 'empires' for them or their families no less considerable than those of the Caesars of old; their hard-bitten faces have launched a thousand ships and woven – and unwoven – a hundred thousand miles of railroad. They have founded universities, created great research libraries, assembled fabulous collections of Old Masters, piled newspaper upon newspaper, bought presidents, sold senators, purchased crown jewels for their wives and crown princes for their daughters and built themselves palaces to live in, and mausoleums to lie dead in, which rival (or at least mimic) Knossos, Tivoli, Helicarnassus, and the Taj Mahal.

Hardly any of the great California millionaires of the half-century after 1848 had actually *worked* in the mines – four of the greatest fortunes were made by men who, with unnecessary denigration, have been labelled 'the four grocers of Sacramento' – but it all began with Sutter's roving enterprise, Marshall's discovery in the tail-race, Sam Brannan's Town Cry, Colonel Mason's report and President Polk's Message. 'Gold! Gold! Gold from the American river' (and, of course, gold from all the other places where men, encouraged and emboldened by this discovery, sought for and found precious metals and other riches throughout the American Far West) was what built Nob Hill, bought 'The Blue Boy' and reassembled a Spanish monastery stone by stone (but with all modern conveniences added, including a carved and panelled elevator for the tycoon and gold-plated waste-pipes for his mistress' bathroom) on a high hill overlooking the coast of California. But not every California (or Nevada, or Colorado, or Arizona) millionaire, or his heir, was like Dorothy Parker's 'Wealthy son of a bitch'. The astronomical vulgarity of San Simeon[1] and the poor (but at least pious) taste of the Stanford Memorial Chapel[2] are cancelled out by the restraint with which are displayed the wonders of Henry Huntington's San Marino,[3] the tomes of Adolph Sutro,[4] the treasure-houses of the De Youngs,[5] and the gifts and foundations of many other equally public-spirited and even more publicity-shy California plutocrats. Not all their gold came out of the South Fork of the American river, but there a page of history was turned to disclose many leaves of gold that would follow after.

1 Now a State Historical Monument, viewable by the public at $2 a head, but with an extra $2 fee for the private – and most vulgar – parts.

2 Mistakenly rebuilt after an Act of God – and who can blame Him – had knocked it about a bit in April 1906.

3 The Henry E. Huntington Library and Art Gallery at San Marino, California.

4 What survived the 1906 earthquake and fire of the magnificent library of this German–Jewish immigrant engineering genius is now housed in a special building on the campus of the Roman Catholic University of San Francisco, to the credit of all concerned.

5 The De Young Museum and Art Gallery in Golden Gate Park, San Francisco, is one of the West's finest. The De Young money was greatly augmented by newspaper publishing as was – at first – the Hearst fortune.

Not every gold-rush merchant became rich. One moderately successful member of that profession, S. C. Davis,[1] on his second venture in California (the first, in 1850–1, was not successful at all, but he fell in love with the country and returned there in 1852) amassed 190 ounces of gold dust and a cheque for $350 as 'the result of my two years labor' before he finally returned home to Nashua, New Hampshire, in 1854. The gold dust he guarded with his colt revolver and a fierce dog in California and 'slept with my money under me' while crossing the steamy Isthmus of Panama (on board ship the pursers took charge of it, at a commission of 1 per cent of its value on each voyage). He finally sold it in New York. 'We went down to Wall St to sell our dust . . . I had 170 oz's which I sold at 17.60 . . . I took a check on Gilbert & Sons, of Boston for $2,900, Ward [his more cautious companion] taking all his in cash.' Davis' earnings were thus at a rate of under $1,500 a year and the cost of his outward passage had to be deducted from that. His return trip was paid for in gold dust out of the 190 ounces he started back with. Stephen Chapin Davis (who was to die in 1856 at the age of twenty-four after another mercantile adventure selling 865 barrels of New Hampshire apples in Liverpool, England, at a profit of nearly 900 per cent, far better than he had ever done with California's gold, and netting him and his partner nearly $5,000 each) was certainly a more typical gold-rush merchant, in his ups and downs of fortune, than Collis P. Huntington, who died in 1900 a multi-millionaire.

Possession or lack of business ability was a big factor in the success or failure of a gold-rush merchant, but whether a miner struck it rich or not seems to have been sheer luck. Even the most skilled tin or lead miner from the Middle West or from Europe or the most experienced and hard-working silver miner from Mexico tended to do no better than the merest greenhorn straight from college, plough, or office-stool, or from behind a counter. Charles Pancoast, the Quaker 'forty-niner'[2] who stuck to mining (with a little ranching and shopkeeping on the side) for five years until he returned to Philadelphia and the drug business for which he had been trained in 1854, not only records his own lack of success –

[1] B. B. Reynolds (ed.), *California Gold Rush Merchant. The Journal of Stephen Chapin Davis* (San Marino, California, 1956), *passim.*

[2] Hannum, A. P. (ed.), *A Quaker Forty-Niner. The Adventures of Charles Edward Pancoast on the American Frontier.* An account written by himself. Foreword by J. B. McMaster (Philadelphia and London, 1930), *passim.*

My loss of $1,600 in the turning of the Stanislaus; the high cost of living without production on the Merced; and now the loss of my Mules, with other expenses, had so reduced my capital that after paying my passage from San Francisco [to try his luck afresh at Trinity river, in northern California] I had now about ten dollars. My continued Misfortunes and the prospect before me were enough to crush the spirits of almost any man; but Youth, Health, Spunk, Energy and Perseverence are not readily subdued. . . .[1]

[Published at the WIDE WEST OFFICE, 181 Clay Street, San Francisco.]

RIVER MINING.

– but he also recounts the remarkable good fortune of another:

We then went out prospecting to Mt Ophir, and reached a point where we could see the Yosemite Valley; but as it was reputed to have no Gold in it we did not regard it as worthy of our attention. We had no luck the first day; but as we were returning I found an abandoned Claim with a good show of Gold, and the next day we carried our clumsy heavy rocker up a high mountain to these Diggings. We left our Tent where it was and climbed this Mountain, averaging $12.00 to $16.00 each per day. In front of our Tent was a small Boulder, that we were in the habit of using as a seat. One Sunday a young Miner who was making us a friendly visit remarked 'This stone has Gold in it; I see a speck.' He washed off the dirt and we could see another speck or two. He asked if he might have the stone and we answered in the affirmative. He then went up to a speculative Store Keeper on the Flat [Big Oak Flat] and brought

[1] Hannum, A. P. (ed.), *op. cit.*, p. 306. 'Uncle Charlie' Pancoast was then thirty-three years old. He lived until 1906, his eighty-eighth year.

him down to look at it. The Store Keeper gave him $200 for it, broke it up, and obtained $3,000 worth of Gold – a prize we lost from our ignorance.[1]

Tales like these, true and false – and Charles Pancoast was a particularly reliable narrator, though he set down his reminiscences many years later and his memory often played him false on place-names and dates – have been preserved by innumerable forty-niners and by those who followed them in search of 'the elephant'[2] in later years. One example of such late-comers was the Englishman J. D. Borthwick, who was not only a skilled observer but a gifted artist. His book *Three Years in California* illustrated by himself appeared as early as 1857.[3] Almost casually he states: 'In May 1851 I happened to be residing in New York, and was seized with the California fever. My preparations were very soon made and a day or two afterwards I found myself on a small barque about to sail for Chagres with a load of California emigrants.'[4] By the time he had arrived at the mines, after sundry adventures, many of the diggings had been 'worked out' by the crude methods then still employed, but 'every place in the mines had its tradition of Wonderful events which had occurred in the olden times; that is to say, as far back as '49 – for three years in such a fast country were equal to a century'.[5]

Without exaggeration, Borthwick remarked in 1857, 'Certainly no country ever so rapidly advanced to so high a position as California;

[1] Hannum, *op. cit.*, p. 291. This, at one fell swoop, was as much as Stephen Davis made in two years of storekeeping. Once again, though, it was not the miner who struck it rich.

[2] 'I have seen the elephant,' or – according to the *Oxford English Dictionary* – 'I have seen the elephant from trunk to tail' was the picturesque forty-niner way of saying that one had seen everything. P. T. Barnum probably inspired the phrase.

[3] The edition here cited is that published in 1857 by William Blackwood in Edinburgh and London 'with eight illustrations by the Author'. For one of these, see plate 17b.

[4] Borthwick, *op. cit.*, p. 3.

[5] *Ibid.*, p. 322. Two longer extracts from Borthwick's book are included in the invaluable little anthology *Pictures of Gold Rush California*, edited by M. M. Quaife, in the Lakeside Classics series (Chicago, 1949). Other contemporary works quoted from *in extenso* in this anthology include H. R. Helper, *The Land of Gold;* D. B. Woods, *Sixteen Months in the Gold Diggings;* Bayard Taylor's *Eldorado*, and Alonzo Delano's *Life on the Plains and among the Diggings*. An article from the *New York Herald* (1 September 1848) on 'California in 1848', and one from *Harper's Monthly Magazine* (April, 1860) on 'How the Gold was mined', are also included, as well as selections from the works of Walter Colton (*Three Years in California*) and Louise Clappe (*The Shirley Letters*), already cited in this chapter. A comprehensive gold-rush bibliography is Carl Wheat, *Books on the Gold Rush* (San Francisco, 1949).

but it is equally true that no country ever commenced its career with such effective population, or with the same elements of wealth to work upon . . . the attractions offered by California were such as draw to it a complete ready-made population of active and capable men, of every trade and profession.'[1] When Sir Richard Burton reached California overland via Salt Lake City in 1860 he found 'At Sacramento – the newer name for New Helvetia – a capital mass of shops and stores, groggeries and hotels', but it was San Francisco, the 'Eldorado of the West', where a tolerable opera, a superior supper, and the society of friends made the arrival exceptionally comfortable and where 'Mr Consul Booker placed my name on the lists of the Union Club, which was a superior institution to that of Leamington',[2] that most excited his admiration. A generation later James Bryce found San Francisco equally impressive and very much larger. But the most dramatic account of the mushroom growth of that metropolis of the West under the stimulus of the Gold Rush was recorded by that 'pioneer of pioneers' Richard Henry Dana. To the 1869 edition of his classic *Two Years Before the Mast*, first published in 1840, he added an appendix entitled 'Twenty-Four Years After'.[3] Here are its opening paragraphs:

> It was in the winter of 1835–6 that the ship *Alert*, in the prosecution of her voyage for hides on the remote and almost unknown coast of California, floated into the vast solitude of the Bay of San Francisco. All around was the stillness of nature. One vessel, a Russian, lay at anchor there, but during our whole stay not a sail came or went. Our trade was with remote missions, which sent hides to us in launches manned by their Indians. Our anchorage was between a small island, called Yerba Buena, and a gravel beach in a little bight or cove of the same name, formed by two small projecting points. Beyond, to the westward of the landing-place, were dreary sandhills, with little grass to be seen, and few trees, and beyond them higher hills, steep and barren, their sides gullied by the rains. Some five or six miles beyond the landing-place, to the right, was a ruinous presidio, and some three or four miles to the left was the Mission of

[1] Borthwick, *op. cit.*, p. 381–2.

[2] Richard F. Burton, *The City of the Saints and Across the Rocky Mountains to California* (London, 1861). The new edition with introduction and notes by Fawn M. Brodie (Frontier Library, London, 1964) is the one cited here (pp. 557–8).

[3] This appendix occupies pp. 356–87 of the reprint of *Two Years Before the Mast* in the Penguin Travel and Adventure series (London, 1948) and is to be found on pp. 341–71 of the Signet Classics edition (New York, 1964). The passage given here follows pp. 356–8 of the former.

Dolores, as ruinous as the presidio, almost deserted, with but few Indians attached to it, and but little property in cattle. Over a region far beyond our sight there were no other human habitations, except that an enterprising Yankee, years in advance of his time, had put up, on the rising ground above the landing, a shanty of rough boards, where he carried on a very small retail trade between the hide ships and the Indians. Vast banks of fog, invading us from the North Pacific, drove in through the entrance, and covered the whole bay; and when they disappeared we saw a few well-wooded islands, the sand-hills on the west, the grassy and wooded slopes on the east, and the vast stretch of the bay to the southward, where we were told lay the Missions of Santa Clara and San José and still longer stretches to the northward and north-eastward, where we understood smaller bays spread out, and large rivers poured in their tributes of waters. There were no settlements on these bays or rivers, and the few ranchos and missions were remote and widely separated. Not only the neighbourhood of our anchorage, but the entire region of the great bay was a solitude. On the whole coast of California there was not a lighthouse, a beacon, or a buoy; and the charts were made up from old and disconnected surveys by British, Russian, and Mexican voyagers. Birds of prey and passage swooped and dived about us, wild beasts ranged through the oak groves, and as we slowly floated out of the harbour with the tide, herds of deer came to the water's edge, on the northerly side of the entrance, to gaze at the strange spectacle.

On the evening of Saturday, the 13th of August 1859, the superb steamship *Golden Gate*, gay with crowds of passengers, and lighting the sea for miles around with the glare of her signal lights of red, green, and white, and brilliant with lighted saloons and state-rooms, bound up from the Isthmus of Panama, neared the entrance to San Francisco, the great centre of a world-wide commerce. Miles out at sea, on the desolate rocks of the Farallones, gleamed the powerful rays of one of the most costly and effective lighthouses in the world. As we drew in through the Golden Gate, another lighthouse met our eyes, and in the clear moonlight of the unbroken Californian summer we saw, on the right, a large fortification, protecting the narrow entrance, and just before us the little island of Alcatraz confronted us – one entire fortress. We bore round the point towards the old anchoring-ground of the hide ships, and there, covering the sand-hills and the valleys, stretching from the water's edge to the base of the great hills, and from the old presidio to the mission, flickering all over with the lamps of its streets and houses, lay a city of one hundred thousand inhabitants. Clocks tolled the hour of midnight from its steeples, but the city was alive from the salute of our guns, spreading the news that the fortnightly steamer had come, bringing mails and passengers from the Atlantic world. Clipper ships of the largest size lay at anchor in the stream, or were girt to the wharves; and capacious high-pressure steamers, as large and showy as those of the Hudson or Mississippi, bodies of dazzling light, awaited the delivery of our mails, to take their cruises up the bay, stopping at Benicia and the United States Naval Station, and then up the great tributaries – the Sacramento, San Joaquin, and Feather rivers – to the far inland cities of Sacramento, Stockton, and Marysville.

The dock into which we drew, and the streets about it, were densely crowded with express-wagons and hand-carts to take luggage, coaches and cabs to take passengers; and with men – some looking out for friends among our hundreds of passengers – agents of the press, and a greater multitude eager for newspapers and verbal intelligence from the great Atlantic and European world. Through this crowd I made my way, along the well-built and well-lighted streets, as alive as by day, where boys in high-keyed voices were already crying the latest New York papers; and between one and two o'clock in the morning found myself comfortably abed in a commodious room in the Oriental Hotel, which stood, as well as I could learn, on the filled-up cove, and not far from the spot where we used to beach our boats from the *Alert*.

Sunday, August 14th. When I awoke in the morning, and looked from my windows over the city of San Francisco, with its storehouses, towers, and steeples; its court-houses, theatres, and hospitals; its daily journals; its well-filled professions; its fortresses and lighthouses; its wharves and harbour, with their thousand-ton clipper ships, more in number than London or Liverpool sheltered that day; itself one of the capitals of the American Republic, and the sole emporium of a new world, the awakened Pacific; when I looked across the bay to the eastward, and beheld a beautiful town on the fertile, wooded shores of the Contra Costa; and steamers, large and small, the ferry boats to the Contra Costa, and capacious freighters and passenger-carriers to all parts of the great bay and its tributaries, with lines of their smoke in the horizon – when I saw all these things, and reflected on what I once was and saw here, and what now surrounded me, I could scarcely keep my hold on reality at all, or the genuineness of anything, and seemed to myself like one who had moved in 'worlds not realised'.

HUTCHINGS'
CALIFORNIA MAGAZINE.

VOL. II. NOVEMBER, 1857. No 5.

THE DISCOVERY OF GOLD IN CALIFORNIA.

GEN. JOHN A. SUTTER.
[From an Ambrotype by R. H. Vance.]

THE DISCOVERY OF GOLD IN CALIFORNIA.

Ours is the age of gold,
And ours the hallowed time.—*Mellen.*

To the lovers of history, nothing can be more welcome and valuable than the unvarnished narrative of events, from the actors themselves: therefore, we feel the greater pleasure in presenting our readers with the following statements, with which we are favored: one from the good old pioneer, Gen. John August Sutter; and the other from Mr. James W. Marshall, the favored discoverer of the gold—and who, unitedly, are the fathers of *The Age of Gold.*

It was in the first part of January, 1848, when the gold was discovered at Coloma,* where I was then building a saw-mill. The contractor and builder of this mill was James W. Marshall, from New Jersey. In the fall of 1847, after the mill seat had been located, I sent up to this place Mr. P. L. Wimmer with his family, and a number of laborers, from the disbanded Mormon Battalion; and a little later I engaged Mr. Bennet from Oregon to assist Mr. Marshall in the mechanical labors of the mill. Mr. Wimmer had the team in charge, assisted by his young sons, to do the necessary teaming, and Mrs. Wimmer did the cooking for all hands.

I was very much in need of a saw-mill, to get lumber to finish my large flouring mill, of four run of stones, at Brighton, which was commenced at the same time, and was rapidly progressing; likewise for other buildings, fences, etc., for the small village of Yerba Buena, (now San Francisco.) In the City Hotel, (the only one) at the dinner table this enterprise was unkindly called "another folly of Sutter's," as my first settlement at the old fort near Sacramento City was called by a good many, "a folly of his," and they were about right in that, because I had the best chances to get some of the finest locations, near the settlements; and even well stocked rancho's had been offered to me on the most reasonable conditions; but I refused all these good offers, and preferred to explore the wilderness, and select a territory on the banks of the Sacramento. It was a rainy afternoon when Mr. Marshall arrived at my office in the Fort, very wet. I was somewhat surprised to see him, as he was down a few days previous; and when, I sent up to Coloma a number of teams with provisions, mill irons, etc., etc. He told me then that he had some important and interesting news which he wished to communicate secretly to me, and wished me to go with him to a place where we should not be disturbed, and where no listeners could come and hear what we had to say. I went with him to my private rooms; he requested me to lock the door; I complied, but I told him at the same time that nobody was in the house except the clerk, who was in his office in a different part of the house; after requesting of me something which he wanted, which my servants brought and then left the room, I forgot to lock the doors, and it happened that the door was opened by the clerk just at the moment when Marshall took a rag from his pocket, showing me the yellow metal: he had about two ounces of it; but how quick Mr. M. put the yellow metal in his pocket again can hardly be described. The clerk came to see me on business, and excused himself for interrupting me, and as soon as he had left I was told, "now lock the doors; didn't I tell you that we might have listeners?" I told him that he need fear nothing about that, as it was not the habit of this gentleman; but I could hardly convince him that he need not to be suspicious. Then Mr. M. began to show me this metal, which consisted of small pieces and specimens, some of them worth a few dollars; he told me that he had expressed his opinion to the laborers at the mill, that this might be gold; but some of them were laughing at him and called him a crazy man, and could not believe such a thing.

* The Indian name and pronunciation is Cul-lumah, (beautiful vale,) now Americanized Coloma.

SUTTER'S FORT IN 1848.

After having proved the metal with aqua fortis, which I found in my apothecary shop, likewise with other experiments, and read the long article "gold" in the Encyclopedia Americana, I declared this to be gold of the finest quality, of at least 23 carats. After this Mr. M. had no more rest nor patience, and wanted me to start with him immediately for Coloma; but I told him I could not leave, as it was late in the evening and nearly supper time, and that it would be better for him to remain with me till the next morning, and I would travel with him, but this would not do: he asked me only "will you come to-morrow morning?" I told him yes, and off he started for Coloma in the heaviest rain, although already very wet, taking nothing to eat. I took this news very easy, like all other occurrences good or bad, but thought a great deal during the night about the consequences which might follow such a discovery. I gave all my necessary orders to my numerous laborers, and left the next morning at 7 o'clock, accompanied by an Indian soldier, and vaquero, in a heavy rain, for Coloma. About half way on the road I saw at a distance a human being crawling out from the brushwood. I asked the Indian who it was: he told me "the same man who was with you last evening." When I came nearer I found it was Marshall, very wet; I told him that he would have done better to remain with me at the fort than to pass such an ugly night here; but he told me that he went up to Coloma, (54 miles) took his other horse and came half way to meet me; then we rode up to the new Eldorado. In the afternoon the weather was clearing up, and we made a prospecting promenade. The next morning we went to the tail-race of the mill, through which the water was running during the night, to clean out the gravel which had been made loose, for the purpose of widening the race; and after the water was out of the race we went in to search for gold. This was done every morning: small pieces of gold could be seen remaining on the bottom of the clean washed bed rock. I went in the race and picked up several pieces of this gold, several of the laborers gave me some which they had picked up, and from Marshall I received a part. I told them that I would get a ring made of this gold as soon as it could be done in California; and I have had a heavy ring made, with my family's coat of arms engraved on the outside, and on the inside of the ring is engraved, "The first gold, discovered in January, 1848." Now if Mrs. Wimmer possesses a piece which has been found earlier than mine Mr. Marshall can tell,* as it was probably received from him. I think Mr. Marshall could have hardly known himself which was exactly the first little piece, among the whole.

The next day I went with Mr. M. on a prospecting tour in the vicinity of Coloma, and the following morning I left for Sacramento. Before my departure I had a conversation with all hands: I told them that I would consider it as a great favor if they would keep this discovery secret only for six weeks, so that I could finish my large flour mill at Brighton, (with four run of stones,) which had cost me already about from 24 to 25,000 dollars—the people up there promised to keep it secret so long. On my way home, instead of feeling happy and contented, I was very unhappy, and could not see that it would benefit me much, and I was perfectly right in thinking so; as it came just precisely as I expected. I thought at the same time that it could hardly be kept secret for six weeks; and in this I was not mistaken, for about two weeks later, after my return, I sent up several teams in charge of a white man, as the teamsters were Indian boys. This man was acquainted with all hands up there, and Mrs. Wimmer told him the whole secret; likewise the young sons of Mr. Wimmer told him that they had gold, and that they would let him have some too; and so he obtained a few dollars' worth of it as a present. As soon as this man arrived at the fort he went to a small store in one of my outside buildings, kept by Mr. Smith, a partner of Samuel Brannan, and asked for a bottle of brandy, for which he would pay the cash; after having the bottle he paid with these small pieces of gold. Smith was astonished and asked him if he intended to insult him; the teamster told him to go and ask me about it; Smith came in, in great haste, to see me, and I told him at once the truth—what could I do? I had to tell him all about it. He reported it to Mr. S. Brannan, who came up immediately to get all possible information, when he returned and sent up large supplies of goods, leased a larger house from me, and commenced a very large and profitable business; soon he opened a branch house of business at Mormon Island.

Mr. Brannan made a kind of claim on Mormon Island, and put a tolerably heavy tax on "The Latter Day Saints." I believe it was 30 per cent, which they paid for some time, until they got tired of it, (some of them told me that it was for the purpose of building a temple for the honor and glory of the Lord.)

So soon as the secret was out my laborers began to leave me, in small parties first, but then all left, from the clerk to the cook, and I was in great distress; only a few mechanics remained to finish some very necessary work which they had commenced, and about eight invalids, who continued slowly to work a few teams, to scrape out the mill race at Brighton. The Mormons did not like to leave my mill unfinished, but they got the gold fever like everybody else. After they had made their piles they left for the Great Salt Lake. So long as these people have been employed by me they have behaved very well, and were industrious and faithful laborers, and when settling their accounts there was not

* Mrs. Wimmer's piece weighs about five dollars and twelve cents. The *first piece*, Mr. Marshall says, weighed about fifty cents.

SUTTER'S FORT. IN 1857.

one of them who was not contented and satisfied.

Then the people commenced rushing up from San Francisco and other parts of California, in May, 1848: in the former village only five men were left to take care of the women and children. The single men locked their doors and left for "Sutter's Fort," and from there to the Eldorado. For some time the people in Monterey and farther south would not believe the news of the gold discovery, and said that it was only a '*Ruse de Guerre*' of Sutter's, because he wanted to have neighbors in his wilderness. From this time on I got only too many neighbors, and some very bad ones among them.

What a great misfortune was this sudden gold discovery for me! It has just broken up and ruined my hard, restless, and industrious labors, connected with many dangers of life, as I had many narrow escapes before I became properly established.

From my mill buildings I reaped no benefit whatever, the mill stones even have been stolen and sold.

My tannery, which was then in a flourishing condition, and was carried on very profitably, was deserted, a large quantity of leather was left unfinished in the vats; and a great quantity of raw hides became valueless as they could not be sold; nobody wanted to be bothered with such trash, as it was called. So it was in all the other mechanical trades which I had carried on; all was abandoned, and work commenced or nearly finished was all left, to an immense loss for me. Even the Indians had no more patience to work alone, in harvesting and threshing my large wheat crop out; as the whites had all left, and other Indians had been engaged by some white men to work for them, and they commenced to have some gold for which they were buying all kinds of articles at enormous prices in the stores; which, when my Indians saw this, they wished very much to go to the mountains and dig gold. At last I consented, got a number of wagons ready, loaded them with provisions and goods of all kinds, employed a clerk, and left with about one hundred Indians, and about fifty Sandwich Islanders (Kanakas) which had joined those which I brought with me from the Islands. The first camp was about ten miles above Mormon Island, on the south fork of the American river. In a few weeks we became crowded, and it would no more pay, as my people made too many acquaintances. I broke up the camp and started on the march further south, and located my next camp on Sutter creek (now in Amador county), and thought that I should there be alone. The work was going on well for a while, until three or four traveling grog-shops surrounded me, at from one and a half to two miles distance from the camp; then, of course, the gold was taken to these places, for drinking, gambling, etc., and then the following day they were sick and unable to work, and became deeper and more indebted to me, and particularly the Kanakas. I found that it was high time to quit this kind of business, and lose no more time and money. I therefore broke up the camp and returned to the Fort, where I disbanded nearly all the people who had worked for me in the mountains digging gold. This whole expedition proved to be a heavy loss to me.

At the same time I was engaged in a mercantile firm in Coloma, which I left in January, 1849 — likewise with many sacrifices. After this I would have nothing more to do with the gold affairs. At this time, the Fort was the great trading place where nearly all the business was transacted. I had no pleasure to remain there, and moved up to Hock Farm, with all my Indians, and who had been with me from the time they were children. The place was then in charge of a Major Domo.

It is very singular that the Indians never found a piece of gold and brought it to me, as they very often did other specimens found in the ravines. I requested them continually to bring me some curiosities from the mountains, for which I always recompensed them. I have received animals, birds, plants, young trees, wild fruits, pipe clay, stones, red ochre, etc., etc., but never a piece of gold. Mr. Dana, of the scientific corps of the expedition under Com. Wilkes' Exploring Squadron, told me that he had the strongest proof and signs of gold in the vicinity of Shasta Mountain, and further south. A short time afterwards, Doctor Sandels, a very scientific traveler, visited me, and explored a part of the country in a great hurry, as time would not permit him to make a longer stay. He told me likewise that he found sure signs of gold, and was very sorry that he could not explore the Sierra Nevada. He did not encourage me to attempt to work and open mines, as it was uncertain how it would pay, and would probably be only profitable for a government. So I thought it more prudent to stick to the plow, notwithstanding I did know that the country was rich in gold, and other minerals. An old attached Mexican servant who followed me here from the United States, as soon as he knew that I was here, and who understood a great deal about working in placers, told me he found sure signs of gold in the mountains on Bear Creek, and that we would go right to work after returning from our campaign in 1845, but he became a victim to his patriotism and fell into the hands of the enemy near my encampment, with dispatches for me from Gen. Micheltorena, and he was hung as a spy, for which I was very sorry.

By this sudden discovery of the gold, all my great plans were destroyed. Had I succeeded with my mills and manufactories for a few years before the gold was discovered, I should have been the richest citizen on the Pacific shore; but it had to be different. Instead of being rich, I am ruined, and the cause of it is the long delay of the United States Land Commission, of the United States Courts, through the great influence of the squatter lawyers. Before my case will be decided in Washington, another year may elapse, but I hope that justice will be done me by the last tribunal — the Supreme Court of the United States. By the Land Commission and the District Court it has been decided in my favor. The Common Council of the city of Sacramento, composed partly of squatters, paid Alpheus Felch, (one of the late Land Commissioners, who was engaged by the squatters during his office), $5,000, from the fund of the city, against the will of the tax-payers, for which amount he has to try to defeat my just and old claim from the Mexican government, before the Supreme Court of the United States in Washington.

SUTTER'S MILL, IN 1848.

Unfortunately for Gen. Sutter, he had one failing—*his heart was too large and confiding.* The men who shared most largely in his princely hospitality and confidence, were the first to take advantage of it, by stealing away his possessions. His generous nature taught him to feel that all *white men* were *honest*—but he did not find them so;—a mistake to which is attributable his present impoverished circumstances. Now, when he should be enjoying the fruit of his long and enterprising labors in peace, he is annoyed with contentions and lawsuits innumerable—simply *in trying to hold his own!* Even the quiet and pleasant Hock Farm—his homestead—(a spot which is ever sacred to the heart of an American)— was sold, not long since, under the hammer of the sheriff. Recently, however, it has been redeemed, at a great sacrifice. And this is the man to whom we are so much indebted for the gold discovery. May God forgive us Californians, for our shameful indifference to the Old Pioneer.

—

The following is Mr. Marshall's account of his discovery of the gold:—

Being a millwright by trade, as there was a ready cash sale for lumber, I concluded to seek a location in the mountains and erect a mill, to supply the valley with lumber. Some time in April, 1847, I visited New Helvetia, commonly known as the "Fort," where I made my resolution known to John A. Sutter, sen., and requested of him an Indian boy, to act as an interpreter to the mountain Indians in the vicinity of the American river—or Rio del los Americanos, as it was then called. At first he refused, because, he said that he had previously sent several companies, at various times, and by different routes, for that purpose, all of whom reported that it was impossible to find a route for a wagon road to any locality where pine timber could be procured, and that it was the height of folly to attempt any such thing.

Capt. Sutter at length, however, promised me the desired interpreter, provided I would stock some six or eight plows for him first, of which he was in immediate want, which I readily agreed to do. While I was employed upon this job there was much talk at the Fort concerning my contemplated trip to the mountains; and Messrs. Gingery, P. L. Wimmer and McLellan having resolved also to take a trip, with the same object in view, came where

I was working, and asked me where I expected to find a road and timber, and I promptly gave them my views and directions.

They departed, I believe in company, but finally separated, and P. L. Wimmer found pine timber and a road, on what is now known as the Sacramento and Diamond Springs road, and about the 12th of May, Gingery and Wimmer commenced work, about thirteen miles west of the (now called) Shingle Spring House.

On the 16th of May, having completed my work for Capt. Sutter, I started, with an Indian boy, —— Treador, and W. A. Graves, (who is now residing in Butte county, and who had assisted me in my work, and heard the conversation between myself, Gingery, Wimmer and McLellan,) accompanied me for the purpose of seeing the mountains. On the 18th of May we entered the valley of Culluma [Coloma]; and on the 20th Gingery joined our company. We then traveled up the stream now called Weber creek—the Indian name of which is Pul-Pul-Mull—to the head of the creek; thence higher in the mountains until we arrived at the South Fork of the American river, where it divides into two branches of about equal size; from whence we returned by Sly Park and Pleasant Valley to the Fort.

On my arrival I gave Capt. Sutter an account of my trip, and what I had discovered. He thereupon proposed to me a partnership; but before we were ready to commence operations, some persons who had tried, in vain, to find Culluma, reported to Sutter that I "had made a false representation, for they could find no such place." To settle matters, Capt. Sutter furnished me with a Mission Indian, who was Alcalde of the Cosumnes tribe, as an interpreter and guide—trusting partly to the Indian's report, as to the propriety of the proposed co-partnership.

The report which I had made on my first trip having been fully confirmed by observations on the second, the co-partnership was completed, and about the 27th of August we signed the agreement to build and run a saw-mill at Culluma. On the third day (I think) afterwards, I set out, with two wagons, and was accompanied by the following persons, employed by the firm of Sutter & Marshall, viz.: P. L. Wimmer and family, James Barger, Ira Willis, Sidney Willis, Alex. Stephens, Wm. Cunce, James Brown, and Ezekiah Persons.

On our arrival in the Valley we first built the double log cabin, afterwards known as Hastings & Co.'s store. About the last of September, as Capt. Sutter wanted a couple of capable men to construct a dam across the American river at the grist-mill—near where the Pavilion now stands—I sent the two Willis', as the most capable; (Wm. Cunce being in feeble health, left about the same time;) and I received Henry Bigler, Israel Smith, Wm. Johnston and —— Evans in return; and shortly afterwards I employed Charles Bennet and Wm. Scott, both carpenters. The above named individuals, with some ten Indians, constituted my whole force.

While we were in the habit at night of turning the water through the tail race we had dug for the purpose of widening and deepening the race, I used to go down in the morning to see what had been done by the water through the night; and about half past seven o'clock on or about the 19th of January—I am not quite certain to a day, but it was between the 18th and 20th of that month—1848, I went down as usual, and after shutting off the water from the race I stepped into it, near the lower end, and there, upon the rock, about six inches beneath the surface of the water, I DISCOVERED THE GOLD. I was entirely alone at the time. I picked up one or two pieces and examined them attentively; and having some general knowledge of minerals, I could not call to mind more than two which in any way resembled this —*sulphuret of iron*, very bright and brittle; and *gold*, bright, yet malleable; I then tried it between two rocks, and found that it could be beaten into a different shape, but not broken. I then collected four or five pieces and went up to Mr. Scott (who was working at the carpenter's bench making the mill wheel) with the pieces in my hand, and said, "I have found it."

"What is it?" inquired Scott.

"Gold," I answered.

"Oh! no," returned Scott, "that can't be."

I replied positively,—"I know it to be nothing else."

Mr. Scott was the second person who saw the gold. W. J. Johnston, A. Stephens, H. Bigler, and J. Brown, who were also working in the mill yard, were then called up to see it. Peter L. Wimmer, Mrs. Jane Wimmer, C. Bennet, and J. Smith, were at the house; the latter two of whom were sick; E. Persons and John Wimmer, (a son of P. L. Wimmer), were out hunting oxen at the same time. About 10 o'clock the same morning, P. L. Wimmer came down from the house, and was very much surprised at the discovery, when the metal was shown him; and which he took home to show his wife, who, the next day, made some experiments upon it by boiling it in strong lye, and saleratus; and Mr. Bennet by my dirertions beat it very thin.

Four days afterwards I went to the Fort for provisons, and carried with me about three ounces of the gold, which Capt. Sutter and I tested with *nitric acid.* I then tried it in Sutter's presence by taking three silver dollars and balancing them by the dust in the air, then immersed both in water, and the superior weight of the gold satisfied us both of its nature and value.

About the 20th of February, 1848, Capt. Sutter came to Coloma, for the first time, to consummate an agreement we had made with this tribe of Indians in the month of September previous, to wit:—that we live with them in peace, on the same land.

About the middle of April the mill commenced operation, and, after cutting a few thousand feet of lumber was abandoned; as all hands were intent upon gold digging. In December, '48, Capt. Sutter came again to Coloma, and some time in that month sold his interest in the mill to Messrs. Ragley & Winters, of which new firm I became a member. The mill was soon again in operation, and cut most of the lumber of which the town of Coloma was built.

The *first piece of gold* which I found, *weighed about fifty cents.* Mr. Wimmer, having bought a stock of merchandise some time about May or June, 1848; and Mrs. Wimmer being my treasurer, used four hundred and forty dollars of my money to complete the purchase; and among which was the first piece of gold which I had found. Where that went, or where it is now, I believe that nobody knows.

J. W. Marshall.

This is the unvarnished statement which the writer received from the lips and pen of Mr. James W. Marshall himself; and being unacquainted with him personally, I went to several gentlemen in Coloma—among whom were several old pioneers still resident there—to ascertain, if possible, whether or not Mr. M.'s statements were true and trustworthy, and the answer invariably was, in substance, "Whatever Mr. Marshall tells you, you may rely upon as correct." I moreover read the affidavits of several of the men who were present when the gold was discovered by Marshall, and which affidavits were affirmatory of the facts which are stated.

There is another fact I wish here to mention, that it may be recorded in the remembrance of the English, as well as the American public. It is this: Mr. Hargraves, the discoverer of gold in Australia, was mining in Coloma in the summer of 1849, and went to Sutter & Marshall's mill for some lumber; and as he and Marshall were leaning against a pile of lumber, conversing, Mr. H. mentioned the fact that he was from Australia. "Then why," replied Marshall, "don't you go and dig gold among your own mountains? for, what I have heard of that country, I have no doubt whatever that you would find plenty of it there."

"Do you think so, indeed?" inquired Hargraves.

"I do," was the answer.

"If I thought so I would go down there this very autumn," was Hargraves' reply. He went; and with what result, the millions of pounds sterling which have since poured into the British treasury can give the history.

Mr. Hargraves, for this discovery, received from the British Government the sum of £5,000, (or twenty-five thousand dollars,) and from the Australian government £10,000, or $50,000, making $75,000.

Mr. Marshall is almost denied the credit of the discovery, by some unprincipled persons, and his reward from the United States Government is, alas! what? At this very moment wronged of every dollar and every foot of land which he possessed, he would not have, but for the daily charity of comparative strangers, even a cabin in which to lay his head to rest at night—and, is this, kind readers, *gratitude?—our* gratitude? to the man by whose instrumentality a new age—THE GOLDEN AGE—has been inaugurated.

In August last, anxious to obtain an excellent portrait of Mr. Marshall, I journeyed to Coloma for that purpose; and, although Mr. M. cheerfully gave every information in a very simple and straightforward manner concerning the history of the country and of the men who figured in it around Coloma, at an early day, he could not be prevailed upon to allow his likeness to be taken. After returning to this city, a letter was penned to him, urgently asking for it, and the following answer was received, which, while it denies the request, will also show the just bitterness of his spirit at the treatment he has received:—

Coloma, Sept. 5th, 1857.

DEAR SIR:—In reply to your note received three days ago, I wish to say that I feel it a duty I owe to myself to retain my likeness, as it is in fact *all I have that I can call my own*, and I feel like any other poor wretch—I want *something* for self. The sale of it may yet keep me from starving; or, if may buy me a dose of medicine in sickness; or pay for the funeral of a—dog—and such is all that I expect, judging from former kindnesses. I owe the country nothing. The enterprising energy of which the orators and editors of California's early golden days boasted so much, as belonging to Yankeedom, was not national, but individual. Of the profits derived from the enterprise, it stands thus—

Yankeedom,..................	$600,000,000
Myself Individually,..........	$000,000,000

Ask the records of the country for the reason why; they will answer—I need not. Were I an Englishman, and had made my discovery on English soil, the case would have been different. I send you this in place of the other. Excuse my rudeness in answering you thus.

I remain, most respectfully,

J. W. MARSHALL.

Is this, then, the reward befitting the dignity and gratitude of a great nation and people—like our own—for that discovery which has poured hundreds of millions of wealth into the laps of the people and the treasury of our country; and, in addition to giving us the stability consequent upon the establishment of a metallic currency, (which is the desire and envy of all nations) has spread prosperity across the broad acres of every State in the Union? while *the individual* who has been the cause of this, is allowed almost to starve of hunger and exposure in our mountains! Who, then, is there among us that does not feel his cheek glow with shame at such ungrateful neglect? Let him answer, for he needs our pity. If the Executive ear is closed against a fit reward for such an important service, let you and I, gentle reader, put our hand into our own pocket, and if we find it empty, let us deny ourselves some little luxury, if needs be, that we may yet, in some measure, wipe out the disgraceful stain from our history, by seeing that James W. Marshall, the discoverer of gold in California, has at least a fertile farm which he can call his own, and where he may spend his remaining days in comparative ease,—without the humiliation of dependence upon strangers, after the benefit he has conferred upon our country, and the world.

CHAPTER VIII

The Mining Boom moves Inland

'What a clover field is to a steer, the sky to the lark, a mudhole to a hog, such are newer diggings to a miner,' wrote the *Daily Oregonian* on 12 July 1862,[1] and by that date this irresistible urge had taken California's argonauts – and many others who followed them more directly – to fresh fields all over the trans-Mississippi West and up even into Canada and Alaska. Nevada and Colorado had become mining territories almost as fabulous as the golden state itself, and were experiencing a similar hothouse growth and efflorescence. Miners were also finding the precious metals, though in much smaller quantities, in Oregon and the Washington Territory (resulting in a backwash of population *from* California, which had stolen so many of the Oregon country's early immigrants in 1849) as well as in Idaho, Montana and Arizona. These territories were still largely in the hands of the Plains Indians, proud tribes who resented, and reacted to, every advance of the white man, and many a lone prospector or small under-guarded party lost their hair at the hands of Sioux, Blackfoot, or Apache war-parties, instead of hitting pay dirt and striking it rich, before the inland mining empire became firmly established. But established it was, and new discoveries in the Dakotas, in Utah, and in the centre and extreme south of Arizona, as well as the discovery of fresh bonanzas in Nevada and Colorado – such as the revival of Virginia City's Comstock boom in the 1870s and the Cripple Creek rush at the beginning of the 1890s – kept the mineral empire expanding and the roving miners on the move, almost to the end of the century. Even then, some of these old-timers (who had often been boys in their teens in 1849, and could still heft a pick, or at least stake a claim and dream) were off to Dawson City in the frozen North of Alaska and the fabulous Klondyke. The Manuel brothers, Fred and Moses, present a case in point.[2] Starting off from their home in Minnesota they reached Montana in 1866 and 1867

[1] Quoted by W. J. Trimble, *The Mining Advance into the Inland Empire* (Madison, Wis., 1914), p. 158.

[2] As Rodman Paul summarizes their story in *Mining Frontiers*, pp. 183–5.

respectively when Moses was only nineteen. Not striking it rich there they next tried Utah, then thought of going to Arizona, but changed their minds and tried their luck in Idaho. 'Finding more Indians than gold' there they next trekked down through the Nevada and eastern California deserts (prospecting all the way) into Arizona. Then in 1874 Moses went by sea up to British Columbia and the Alaska border and found some gold, but even more cold, at Great Slave Lake. Retreating from the inhospitable climate he thought he'd try South Africa next (where the Rand was beginning to boom), but was deflected at Portland, Oregon, to the Black Hills of South Dakota. He rejoined his brother (who had not taken part in the Alaskan adventure) in Helena, Montana, then beginning to blossom out of the notorious 'Last Chance Gulch'. Pursued by hostile Indians and nearly buried by snowstorms, they made it across Wyoming to the new promised land and started working three claims known as The Homestake, Old Abe (Fred was a Union Army Veteran!), and Golden Terra. These they made yield enough to be able to sell them in 1876 for $70,000, $45,000, and $35,000, respectively, to interests connected with the ubiquitous George Hearst (who in these days picked up and threw away mines with almost as much abandon as later his son did newspapers). Fred and Moses then 'retired' back to Minnesota with their hard-gotten gains. But the itch was still upon Moses –now an old-timer of twenty-nine. He went back to Helena, Montana, and was eventually blown up in a mine explosion there in the year 1905 – on the move to the last. Fred took a line of less resistance and joined the health-seekers in southern California. Like Wyatt Earp he eventually died peaceably in his bed at Los Angeles. There is no monument anywhere – except the mine itself, which continues to produce – to these sibling discoverers of the Homestake Mine, one of the richest in all the West.

The California Argonauts dispersed to the four winds – wherever they smelled metal – in search of daughter lodes. They were tough and they died hard. Mark Twain has idealized them in a magnificently over-written epitaph, as

> erect, bright-eyed, quick-moving, strong-handed young giants – the strangest population, the finest population, the most gallant host that ever trooped down the startled solitudes of an unpeopled land. And where are they now [1871]? Scattered to the ends of the earth – or prematurely aged and decrepit – or shot or stabbed in street

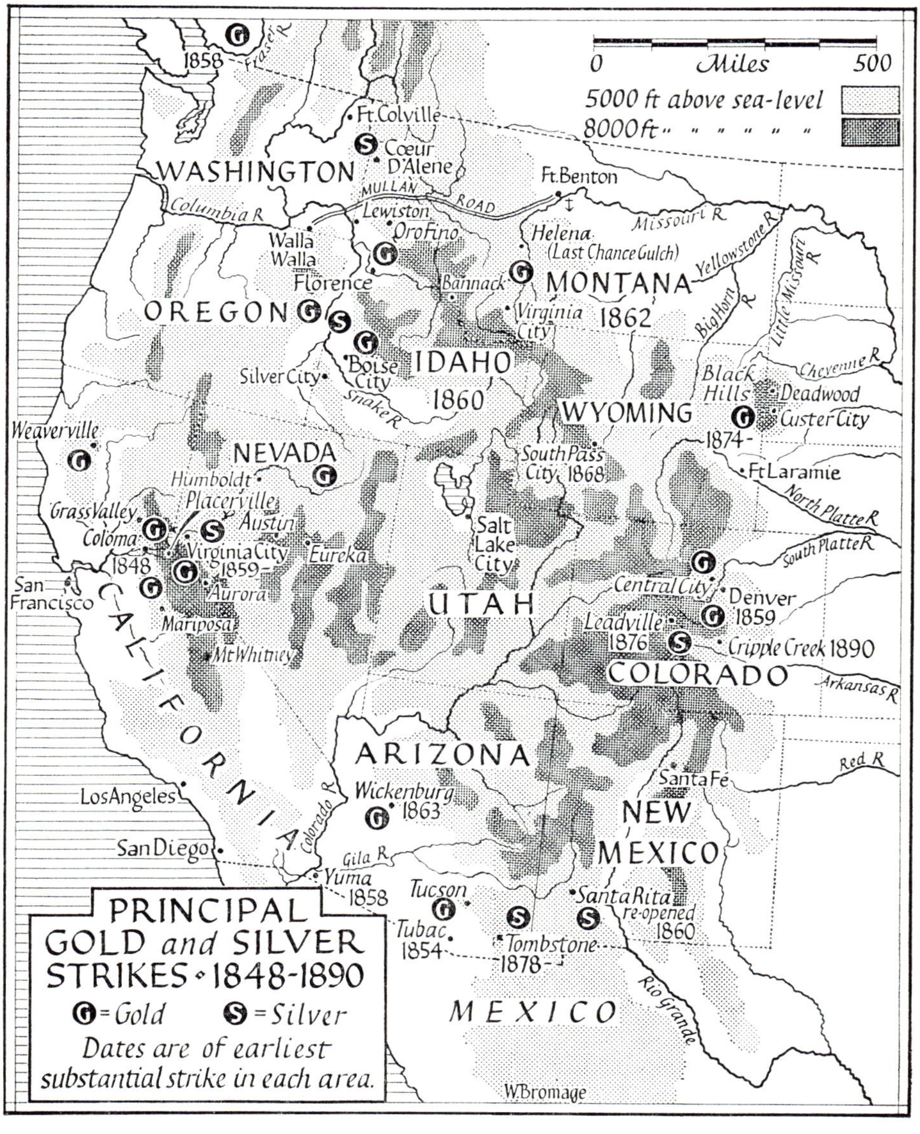

0 Miles 500
5000 ft above sea-level
8000 ft " " " " "
1858
Fraser R
Ft. Colville
Cœur D'Alene
WASHINGTON
MULLAN ROAD
Ft. Benton
Columbia R
Lewiston
OroFino
Walla Walla
Florence
Helena (Last Chance Gulch)
Missouri R
Yellowstone R
Little Missouri R
Bannack
MONTANA 1862
OREGON
Virginia City
Big Horn R
Boise City
IDAHO 1860
Silver City
Snake R
Cheyenne R
Black Hills
Deadwood
Custer City
1874
WYOMING
Weaverville
NEVADA
South Pass City 1868
Humboldt
Ft Laramie
North Platte R
Placerville
Grass Valley
Austin
Coloma
Virginia City 1859
Eureka
Salt Lake City
South Platte R
1848
San Francisco
Aurora
Central City
Denver 1859
UTAH
Mariposa
Leadville 1876
Cripple Creek 1890
Mt Whitney
COLORADO
Arkansas R
CALIFORNIA
ARIZONA
Red R
Santa Fé
Los Angeles
Colorado R
Wickenburg 1863
NEW MEXICO
San Diego
Gila R
Yuma 1858
Tucson
Santa Rita re-opened 1860
Tubac 1854
Tombstone 1878
Rio Grande
MEXICO
PRINCIPAL GOLD and SILVER STRIKES • 1848-1890
G = Gold S = Silver
Dates are of earliest substantial strike in each area.
W. Bromage

affrays – or dead of disappointed hopes and broken hearts – all gone, or nearly all . . .[1]

Mark Twain was to meet some of the Argonauts, not yet so decrepit as they were later to become, when he arrived in Carson City, the territorial capital of Nevada, as 'Mr Secretary's secretary', one eventful summer's day in 1861. He describes in *Roughing It* how 'In 1858 silver lodes were discovered in "Carson County" [then part of Utah] and then the aspect of things changed. Californians began to flock in . . Congress passed a bill to organize "Nevada Territory". At this time the population of the territory was about twelve to fifteen thousand [about the same as California before the Gold Rush] . . . By and by I was smitten with the silver fever. "Prospecting parties" were leaving for the mountains every day, and discovering and taking possession of rich silver-bearing lodes and ledges of quartz. Plainly this was the road to fortune. The great "Gould and Curry" mine was held at three or four hundred dollars a foot when we arrived; but in two months it had sprung up to eight hundred . . . The Gould and Curry claim comprised twelve hundred feet and it all belonged originally to the two men whose name it bears. Mr Curry owned two-thirds of it – and he said that he sold it out for twenty-five hundred dollars in cash, and an old plug horse that ate up his market value in hay and barley in seventeen days by the watch. And he said that Gould sold out for a pair of second-hand government blankets and a bottle of whiskey that killed nine men in three hours, and that an unoffending stranger that smelled the cork was disabled for life. Four years afterwards the mine thus disposed of was worth in the San Francisco market $7,600,000 in gold coin.'[2]

Even more fabulous than the Gould and Curry mine was the Comstock. Indeed, Comstock was the name given not only to one famous mine but also to a whole mining area. It is ironic that the man after whom this immensely rich lode was named was himself just a claim-jumper on it, though others were to benefit from his claim enormously more than did he or the original discoverers. He was to die a failure and by suicide years later in Montana, once again in search of the crock of gold that had eluded him in Nevada. The story of H. T. P.

[1] Mark Twain, *Roughing It* (first published 1871). Signet Classics edition (New York, 1962), pp. 309–10.

[2] *Ibid.*, pp. 146–7 and 242.

Comstock has been superlatively told by 'Dan de Quille' (William Wright):[1]

In the evening of the day on which the grand discovery was made by O'Riley and McLaughlin, H. T. P. Comstock made his appearance upon the scene.

'Old Pancake', who was then looking after his Gold Hill mines, which were beginning to yield largely, had strolled northward up the mountain, toward evening, in search of a mustang pony that he had out prospecting for a living among the hills. He had found his pony, had mounted him, and, with his long legs dragging the tops

of the sagebrush, came riding up just as the lucky miners were making the last clean-up of their rockers for the day.

Comstock, who had a keen eye for all that was going on in the way of mining in any place he might visit, saw at a glance the unusual quantity of gold that was in sight.

When the gold caught his eye, he was off the back of his pony in an instant. He was soon down in the thick of it all – 'hefting' and running his fingers through the gold, and picking into and probing the mass of strange-looking 'stuff' exposed.

[1] D. de Quille (William Wright), *The Big Bonanza – An authentic account of the Discovery, History and Working of the World-Renowned Comstock Lode of Nevada . . .* (Hartford, Conn., 1876). Reprinted with original illustrations (New York, 1947), ed. by Oscar Lewis, pp. 25–7. The best, and best-known, contemporary account of the Nevada mining boom.

Conceiving at once that a wonderful discovery of some kind had been made, 'Old Pancake' straightened himself up, as he arose from a critical examination of the black mass in the cut wherein he had observed the glittering spangles of gold, and coolly proceeded to inform the astonished miners that they were working on ground that belonged to him.

He asserted that he had some time before taken up 160 acres of land at this point, for a ranch; also that he owned the water they were using in mining, it being from the Caldwell spring, in what was afterwards known as Spanish Ravine.

Suspecting that they were working in a decomposed quartz vein, McLaughlin and O'Riley had written out and posted up a notice, calling for a claim of 300 feet for each and a third claim for the discovery, which extra claim they were entitled to under the mining laws.

Having soon ascertained all this from the men before him, Comstock would have 'none of it'. He boisterously declared that they should not work there at all unless they would agree to locate himself and his friend Manny (Emmanuel) Penrod in the claim. In case he and Penrod were given an interest, there should be no further trouble about the ground.

After consulting together, the discoverers concluded that, rather than have a great row about the matter, they would put the names of Comstock and Penrod in their notice of location.

This being arranged to his satisfaction, Comstock next demanded that one hundred feet of ground on the lead should be segregated and given to Penrod and himself for the right to the water they were using – he stoutly asserting that he owned not only the land, but also the water, and, as they had recognized his right to the land, they could not consistently ignore his claim to the water flowing upon it. In short, he talked so loudly and so much about his water-right that he at last got the hundred feet, segregated, as he demanded. This hundred feet afterwards became the Spanish or Mexican mine, and yielded millions of dollars.

Dan de Quille's account of Comstock's later misfortunes is in the vintage style of the man who gave Mark Twain his basic training as a reporter:

After Comstock's wife ran away with the strolling miner[1] he thought best to let her continue on her travels unmolested. He

[1] *The Big Bonanza*, p. 48. The whole of Chapter IX (pp. 45–8) is hilariously devoted – apart from its unhappy ending – to 'Comstock's Matrimonial Venture'. Old Pancake literally *bought* his wife from a Mormon, who found her surplus to require-

opened a store at Carson City with the money received for his mining interests in Virginia City and also had a branch store at Silver City, a town on Gold Canyon, about three miles below Gold Hill, which was laid out in the summer of 1859.

He soon broke up in the mercantile line, losing everything. He trusted everybody – all went to his stores and purchased goods without money and without price, and at last his old friends the Paiute Indians came in and carried away the remnants. Comstock made them all happy, male and female, by passing out to them armfuls of red blankets and calico of brilliant hues.

His stock in the Carson store was as good as was seen in most trading establishments of the kind at that day, but his Silver City branch never amounted to much, the stock consisting principally, as the miners said, of blue cotton overalls, pick-handles, rusty bacon, 'nigger' shoes, and 'dog-leg' tobacco.

After losing all of his property Comstock left Nevada and went to Idaho and Montana, through which countries he wandered and prospected for some years, always hoping that some day he would come upon a second Comstock lode. He was always ready to join every expedition that was fitted out to explore new regions, as the 'big thing' seemed to him to be ever just ahead.

In 1870 he joined the Big Horn expedition in Montana, and this was his last undertaking. When near Bozeman City, on September 27, 1870, he committed suicide by shooting himself in the head with his revolver. The Montana papers said it was supposed that he committed the act while laboring under temporary aberration of mind, and this was doubtless the case, as his was by no means a sound or well-balanced brain.

In his later years Comstock wrote a long and somewhat lugubrious autobiographical letter, which was published in part in the St Louis *Republican* newspaper, giving a well-edited version of how he discovered and then lost the Comstock lode. Here is the middle part of that letter, as reproduced in *The Big Bonanza*.[1]

Riley and McLaughlin were working for me at the time of the Ophir discovery. I caved the cut in and went after my party to take

---

ments, in return for 'a horse, a revolver and sixty dollars' and he demanded and received a regular bill of sale. She soon ran away from him with a 'seductive youth of the town', but Comstock offered $100 reward for her apprehension, which was won by a 'dead-broke' Placerville miner. 'By practising eternal vigilance Comstock managed to keep his wife that winter, but in the spring . . . she ran away with a long-legged miner . . . finally [she] came to anchor in a lager-beer cellar in Sacramento.'

[1] *The Big Bonanza*, pp. 50–1.

up the lead and form my company. Manny Penrod, Peter Riley, Patrick McLaughlin, 'Kentuck', or Osborne, and myself formed a company. With my party I opened the lead, and called it Comstock lode; that is the way they came by their interests; I gave it to them.

We started to rocking with my water; had only a small quantity to rock with. We made from five to ten and twelve pounds a day, and the dust was from $9 to $12 an ounce – went that at Brewster's bank, Placerville, California, where I did my business.

I continued owning the claim, locating 1,400 feet out for myself, for the use of my water to the company. I also located the Savage claim; showed the ground to old man Savage. I located the Gould & Curry – went into the valley and got old Daddy Curry to come down, and put him in possession of it.

I also owned the Hale & Norcross, and kept Norcross for a year to work in that ground. I also owned the principal part in Gold Hill and leased it out to Walsh and Woodruff – leased to them 950 or 760 – don't now remember which. Now I will tell you how I sold it; it has never been told as it ought to be told throughout the United States for my benefit, and it shall be.

Sandy Bowers, I gave him his claim of 20 feet in Gold Hill. Bill Knight, I gave him his claim; Joe Plato, I gave him his. Joe is dead now, and his widow is awful rich.

I was working this claim, the Ophir, and taking out a good deal of ore; I did not know what the ore was worth, being in the wilderness then, with no road to get out or into from California. It was an awful wilderness! I took several tons of the ore and transported it by ox-teams, to best advantage, through the mountains of California, and Judge Walsh was my agent and helped me.

Now during this time I was taking out large gold and silver specimens, and took one specimen, weighing 12 pounds, and boxed it up and ordered it sent to Washington City. I instructed John Musser, a lawyer at Washoe, to send it; I don't know whether it ever reached there or not. I wanted Congress to see it, and the President, for it was the first gold and silver ore mixed ever found in the United States.

I went on working, and Judge Walsh and Woodruff were there for two months, trying every day to buy me out. My health being bad I sold the claim to them on these terms: I was to get $10,000, and did get it at last; and I was to receive one-eleventh of all that ever came out of the claim during my natural life, and at my death was to will it to whoever I pleased; also, to receive $100 per month.

That was the contract; and two men, Elder Bennett and Manny Penrod, witnessed it; but my health was bad, and before I had the contract of sale recorded, Woodruff and Walsh sold it out. Having taken no lien on the property, I never got a dollar, from that day to this except what was at first received.

I am a regular born, mountaineer, and did not know the intrigues of civilized rascality. I am not ashamed to acknowledge that. Well, I had a store in Carson City and was lying in the back room sick and helpless. I told Ed. Belcher to take all my papers, and the contract between Judge Walsh and Woodruff and myself, and put them under my pillow. I could speak, but couldn't help myself a bit. They all said I would die, and said: 'Boys, let's pitch in and help ourselves!' And they did pitch in; and I never saw the papers afterwards. And the Gold Hill I leased to Walsh and Woodruff; and then Frink and Kincaid got it, and I never got anything for it; and the 160 acres of ground on which Virginia City is built is my old recorded ranche. I used to raise all my potatoes and vegetables on it, and had the Indians do the work for me.

Virginia City was first called Silver City. I named it at the time I gave the Ophir claim its name. Old Virginia and the other boys got on a drunk one night there, and Old Virginia fell down and broke his bottle, and when he got up he said he baptized that ground Virginia – hence Virginia City.

So much for Henry Thomas Paige Comstock and his lode of mischief! 'Old Virginia' was an equally colourful character and came to an equally violent end. Says Dan de Quille:[1]

James Fennimore, better known as James Finney and familiarly called 'Old Virginia' by all the old settlers of Washoe, he being a native of the state of Virginia, came to the mines on Gold Canyon in 1851. He came from the Kern River country, California, where he had a 'difficulty' with a man and, believing he had killed him, took a little walk across the Sierra Nevada Mountains, dropping the name of Fennimore and calling himself James Finney.

Although fond of the bottle, Old Virginia was by no means a loafer. He had his sprees, but these were generally followed by seasons of great activity.

He was very fond of hunting, and when not engaged in mining or prospecting he was ranging the mountains and valleys in search of deer, antelope, and mountain sheep. He was interested in nearly all the enterprises of the early Johntown and Gold Hill, mines, but missed being in the Ophir at the time of the discovery of silver, having sold his interest in the Six-mile Canyon diggings the previous season.

[1] *The Big Bonanza*, pp. 52–3.

> He was killed in the town of Dayton, in July 1861, by being thrown from a 'bucking' mustang that he was trying to ride while a good deal under the influence of liquor. He was pitched head-first upon the ground, suffered a fracture of the skull, and died in a few hours. At the time of his death he was possessed of about $3,000 in coin and had been talking of returning soon to his native state.

An old Paiute brave who had known both Comstock and Fennimore pronounced a joint epitaph on them to de Quille.[1]

> Hoss kill um Ole Birginey, Comstock he kill heself. Comstock owe me fifty-five dollar; Old Birginey owe me forty-five dollar! Me think . . . maybe both too much whisky.

Though the first discoverers failed to make great fortunes out of them, the Western Nevada mines proved to be enormously rich. Between 1859 and 1869 about $100 million worth of gold and silver – the latter constituting two-thirds of this in value – was extracted from them, but by the late sixties their productivity was beginning to decrease. The Comstock lode produced $16½ million worth of precious metals in 1867 alone, but only $8 million worth in 1869. While it was estimated[2] that the Ophir mine 'has taken out $13 million, but used it nearly all up in expenditures, and probably not returned to the stockholders so much as they have paid in', it was his one-sixth share in the Ophir mine, acquired in 1859, that brought to George Hearst his first fortune. People like Judge Walsh and Almarin B. Paul also did very well out of coming to Washoe in 1859 and buying out Comstock and company. But the first ten years of production and the fortunes made therein constituted only a small bonanza beside the 'Big Bonanza' of 1873 and the following years, when the Comstock lode, recapitalized, and exploited by new and more scientific methods and benefiting from the completion of the transcontinental and feeder railroads, became 'the richest spot in the world',[3] made men like John Mackay, William Ralston, William Sharon, James Fair, James Flood, Samuel Curtis, William O'Brien, and J. P. Jones as rich, everyone of them, as Croesus.[4]

[1] *The Big Bonanza*, p. 53.

[2] By Samuel Bowles in *Our New West* (Hartford, Conn., 1869), p. 289.

[3] The title of Chapter LXIV of de Quille's *The Big Bonanza.*

[4] 'Although Mr Mackay is now [1876] worth fifty or sixty million dollars, yet like Mr Fair ["worth thirty or forty million dollars"], he spends much of his time, when at Virginia City, in the lower levels. Almost every morning at six o'clock he descends into one or another of his mines,' says de Quille (*op. cit.*, p. 398), who makes Mackay the hero of his book and dedicates it to this 'Prince of Miners and "Boss" of the Big

The four 'bonanza kings' comparable to the 'big four' of California, were Mackay, Fair, Flood, and O'Brien. They all came via California and were of Irish extraction. Mackay was born in Dublin and had been a ship's carpenter. Fair was born in Ulster, but they always worked very closely and amicably together. 'The pair generally hold a grand council on all matters of moment. When this council is in session at the private office of the works [of the Consolidated Virginia and California Mining Companies] the miners, in passing back and forth, hold up their fingers to one another as a sign that no noise is to be made . . .'[1] The silences of John Mackay and of James G. Fair were worth about $50,000 a day at the height of the big bonanza. A dividend of $10 per share, or over $1 million, was being paid *every month* after all mining expenses had been met. 'Out of the first bonanza, into the top of which O'Riley and McLaughlin luckily struck their picks, was taken about $20,000,000 before the deposit was exhausted; out of the consolidated Virginia mine alone has already been taken $15,500,000 and as yet [1876] they have hardly begun working in real earnest.'[2] Peter's and Pat's celebrated water-hole of 1859 was only about four feet deep; the big bonanza of 1873 had to be worked at the 1,500-foot level below the surface, and James G. Fair estimated the cost of mining and milling as high as $17 a ton of ore. But it was worth between $100 and $200 a ton, so why worry!

Eventually the Comstock lode was to produce over $300 million worth of ore (between 1859 and 1880) and the Virginia City and Gold Hill area became 'an industrial suburb of California and particularly of San Francisco'.[3] The boom city which R. H. Dana had beheld with eyes of wonder in 1859 boomed again, after California's own gold rush had petered out, under this shower of Comstock gold and silver. Had Dana returned again, in 1883, after another twenty-four years, he would once more not have recognized San Francisco. The mansions of the rich were no longer festooned around George Gordon's elegant

---

Bonanza'. Unlike so many of the mineral nabobs, Mackay remained unspoilt and unassuming. It remained for his ambitious wife and extravagant children to discover the primrose path. His grand-daughter Ellen Mackay married the famous song-writer Irving Berlin. Mackay himself lived until 1902 and after his death his business manager told the press, 'I don't suppose he knew within twenty millions *what* he was worth.'

[1] *The Big Bonanza*, *op. cit.*, p. 401.

[2] *Ibid.*, p. 380.

[3] Paul, *Mining Frontiers*, p. 56.

South Park[1] but were climbing to the crest of 'Nob Hill' (on California Street) in ever-increasing grandeur. There the Fair and the Flood mansions were beginning to look even the ornate palaces of 'Boss' Crocker and Leland Standford in the eye. Among lesser men great wealth was no longer rare in this true 'City of Gold'. Joseph L. King, Chairman of the San Francisco Stock and Exchange Board for many years once remarked[2] in all seriousness:

> Prior to the Civil War, extremely wealthy men in California were not so numerous . . . and one could name our millionaires on his finger ends. Men possessing $100,000 were considered well off, while a $50,000 citizen was always addressed with the prefix of 'Mister'.

To be called 'Mister' after the wealth of the big bonanza hit town one presumably had to be worth at least a million!

The whole of Nevada (mushroomed into a State of the Union in 1864) had a smaller population at all times – in 1859, in 1879 and also in 1959 – than had the city of San Francisco at the same dates. Every advance of the Western mining frontier advanced the fortunes of San Francisco's already rich 'Misters', lent prestige to its mint and its stock exchange and expanded its port facilities. It was not only the principal outlet for all this wealth (though after 1869 the trans-continental railroad permitted some of it, more expensively, to move more directly eastward) but the principal source of the ever-increasing need for capital to keep the mines working productively and to develop new ones.

Not so Virginia City, the metropolis of the Comstock lode, which was to fade almost into a ghost town in the 1880s when the big bonanza was over, and to survive, a shrunken remnant of its former splendid self, frequented only by tourists and their exploiters. In the 1860s and 1870s everybody tried to visit Virginia City, and many people wrote books about it, whether they were residents (if literate) or in transit. Not only its famous local chroniclers, Twain and de Quille and John Hittell, but Easterners like Horace Greeley, Samuel Bowles, and Henry Vil-

[1] Conceived by George Gordon, an English forty-niner, who brought George H. Goddard, the architect of the Holland Park Estate in London, out to design and develop South Park. South Park's houses no longer exist, but Mount Goddard in the High Sierras, which was named after him, constitutes a more enduring monument to their architect. Dr Albert Shumate, Past President of the California Historical Society is engaged on a study of Gordon's South Park, the buildings of which strikingly resembled those of the Holland Park Estate, which, unlike Holland House itself, survived the London 'blitz'.

[2] Joseph L. King, *History of the San Francisco Stock and Exchange Board* (San Francisco, 1910), pp. 256–7, quoted by Paul in *Mining Frontiers*, p. 57.

lard, and Europeans like Sir Richard Burton and Charles Dilke, all had something to say about the phenomenon that was Virginia City. Dilke, fresh down from Cambridge and on a world tour that was to produce his influential book *Greater Britain* in 1869, to help spearhead his country's revived interest in empire, wrote:

> To see Virginia City and Carson since I first heard their fame in New York had been with me a passion . . . Virginia City has passed through its second period – that of 'vigilance committees' and 'historic trees' – and is entering the third, the stage of churches and 'city officers' or police.
>
> The population is still a shifting one. A by-law of the municipality tells us that the 'permanent population' consists of those who reside more than a month within the city. At this moment [autumn 1867] the miners are pouring into Washoe from Montana, from Arizona and from Utah, coming from the gayeties of the largest mining city, to spend their money during the short, fierce winter.[1]

[1] C. W. Dilke, *Greater Britain* (London and Philadelphia, 2 vols, 1869), Vol. I, p. 166.

'From Montana, from Arizona and from Utah. . . .' The mining frontiers of the Far West were already extended far beyond the Mother Lode and the Comstock by the middle sixties. Half-way across Nevada, in the middle of nowhere, Samuel Bowles, journeying by stage coach in the party of Schuyler Carfax, later Vice-President of the United States, found in the summer of 1865 'the most representative mining town we had yet seen'.[1]

> Beginning in 1863, Austin had in a year's time a population of six to eight thousand, fell away in 1865 to four thousand, and now probably has no more than three thousand. Its houses are built anywhere, everywhere, and then the streets get to them as best they can; one side of a house will be four stories the other one or two – such is the lay of the land; not a tree, not a flower, not a blade of green grass anywhere in town; but the boot-blacks and baths and barbers are of European standards; it has a first-class French restaurant and a daily newspaper; the handsomest woman, physically, I ever saw presided, with almost comic queenliness, over one of its lager beer saloons; gambling went on openly, amid music, in the area of every 'saloon' – miners risking to this chance at night the proceeds of the scarcely less doubtful chance of the day; while the generally cultivated and classical tone of the town may be inferred from this advertisement in the daily paper: 'Mammoth Lager Beer Saloon, in the basement, corner Main and Virginia streets, Austin, Nevada. Choice liquors, wines, lager beer and cigars, served by pretty girls, who understand their business and attend to it. Votaries of Bacchus, Gambrinus, Venus or Cupid can spend an evening agreeably at the Mammoth Saloon.'

A little earlier than Dilke, Samuel Bowles also discerned signs that this once wild mining camp – 'the "cussedest" town in the States, its citizens expecting "a dead man for breakfast" every day', as Dilke had put it – was beginning to settle down.[2]

> We found in Virginia, the original 'Washoe' of mining history, many contrasts to and improvements upon Austin. It is three or four years older; it puts its gambling behind an extra door; it is beginning to recognize the Sabbath, has many churches open, and closes part of its stores on that day; is exceedingly well built, in large proportion with solid brick stores and warehouses; and though the fast and fascinating times of 1862–63 are over, when it held from fifteen to twenty thousand people, and Broadway and Wall street were not

[1] Bowles, *op. cit.*, p. 279.

[2] *Ibid.*, pp. 280–1.

more crowded than its streets, and there are tokens that its great mines are nearly dug out, it still has the air of permanence and of profit, and contains a population of seven or eight thousand, besides the adjoining town or extension of Gold Hill, which has about three thousand more.

The situation of Virginia is very picturesque; above the canyon or ravine, it is spread along the mountain side, like the roof of a house, about half-way to the top. Directly above rises a noble peak, fifteen hundred feet higher than the town, itself about six thousand feet high; below stretches the foot-hill, bisected by the ravine; around on all sides, sister hills rise in varying hights, rich in roundness and other forms of beauty, but brown in barrenness, as if shorn for prize fight, and fading out into distant plain, with a sweet green spot to mark the rare presence of water and verdure.

For a whole decade, from 1865 to 1874, the Comstock lode was, as the miners put it, in 'borrasca', or clouded over. But the clear sky of the biggest 'bonanza' of all was just around the corner. The shares of the Consolidated Virginia Mine, organized by Washoe's new 'big four' out of several earlier workings that were now considered to be worthless by other mining experts, stood at $1 each in 1870, but had skyrocketed to $700 by 1875. That was when the mine was bringing in $50,000 a day. Dividends of nearly $75 million were paid by the Company between 1875 and 1881.[1] Then the skies clouded over again for Virginia City, this time for good. The $38 million production of the Comstock lode in 1875 alone fell to less than $1½ million in 1881. As early as 1878 unemployment among the Washoe miners had become a serious problem and they began to drift away, and Comstock skills and mining know-how, like Comstock capital, were to be exported all over the United States, indeed all over the world. But the population of Virginia City was still over fifteen thousand in 1880 (a figure it had first reached as long ago as 1863) compared with about twenty thousand in the peak year 1875. It never did quite become a ghost town and by the time of its centennial in 1959 it had been rescued from oblivion by tourism.[2]

[1] Paul, *Mining Frontiers*, p. 80, quoting G. H. Smith, *The History of the Comstock Lode, 1850–1920* (Reno, 1943), p. 259. Smith's figures are more reliable as well as more up to date than those in E. Lord, *Comstock Mining and Miners* (Washington, D.C., 1883; reprinted Berkeley, California, 1959, ed. by D. F. Myrick).

[2] And by a pair of entrepreneurs of bygone glamour named Lucius Beebe and Charles Clegg, co-authors of *Virginia and Truckee* and of *Legends of the Comstock Lode* (Stanford and Oxford University Presses, 1950). Beebe (who died early in 1966) told how some of the great mining fortunes were used in *The Great Spenders* (New York, 1966.)

For obvious reasons the mining rush into western Nevada from 1858 onwards was from the west. Not so the almost simultaneous rush into the Colorado Rockies. This came mainly across the plains from the Middle West and the East, and therefore contained a much higher proportion of 'Greenhorns', though most of the early discoveries were made by seasoned miners, and Horace Greeley, the famous editor of the *New York Herald*,[1] reckoned that three out of every ten participants in the Pike's Peak gold rush had previously worked in California.

The Colorado Rockies were virtually uninhabited in 1858; the Indians whose hunting grounds they were still lived in the stone age and would have had little use for precious metals had they found any; the Mountain Men who roamed its slopes and found the way through its passes were after beaver, not gold. But a whole new profession, that of 'prospector', had been created by 'the California experience' since 1848 – men who sought to locate new mines rather than to exploit them, and who were willing to take quick and moderate payments for their 'claims', as has been seen in Nevada. A member of the fraternity, one W. G. Russell, a disappointed forty-niner who had returned, still not rich, to his native Georgia, organized a party to prospect the Pike's Peak region of Colorado in the summer of 1858. On Cherry Creek near its confluence with the South Platte, considerably to the north of Pike's Peak itself, they found small quantities of placer gold. This was not enough to satisfy them, and they moved on, prospecting the eastern slopes of the Rocky Mountains, all the way to what is now Wyoming. But travellers' tales exaggerated their successes and the newspapers of the Middle West, which was still economically stagnant under the influence of the 'Panic of 1857', filled their columns and spread their headlines with stories of A NEW ELDORADO IN KANSAS TERRITORY. After a winter of feverish preparation about a hundred thousand gold-seekers, nearly all of them greenhorns, started to rush across the plains from Kansas City and Independence and Omaha and many other assembly points, as soon as – in some cases even before – the snow was off the prairie. Meanwhile Russell's party had returned to winter on Cherry Creek, where a party from Lawrence, Kansas, meanwhile arrived and also found but little gold, and the two groups turned to the frustrated frontiersman's favourite off-season pastime, the laying-out of town lots and the creation of metropolises on paper. Denver and Aurora – one might as well have gold in the

[1] H. Greeley, *An Overland journey from New York to San Francisco in the summer of 1859* (New York, 1860), p. 15.

name even if there was none in the creek – were laid out, and so were two other more ephemeral cities around where Cherry Creek and the South Platte converged. When the fifty-niners began to swarm in the following spring they found plenty of real estate but no gold awaiting them. Of the hundred thousand who started out it is reckoned that one half never even arrived – having turned back discouraged by those returning from Pike's Peak (or thereabouts) 'busted'. Of those who did reach the region, one half had left before the end of 1859. This was the greatest fiasco in American gold-rush history, but nevertheless an entirely unpopulated area did acquire a population of about twenty-five thousand in one year, and those who failed at mining, real-estate dealing, and politics[1] turned to the ever-present last resort of agriculture, for unlike most parts of the California and Nevada mountains, the Eastern Rockies contained many fertile high valleys (like the remarkable series of 'Parks' the Mountain Men had used and Ruxton and Frémont had so eloquently described), while the plains just to the east, including the Cherry Creek–South Platte area itself, were level and ready for the plough.

While the empire-builders of Cherry Creek wrote prospectuses and banged gavels in their winterized log-cabins, an experienced 'miner-forty-niner' named George A. Jackson went out and found gold in usable quantities in January 1859 at Chicago Creek, but kept the news dark until April. Meanwhile John H. Gregory, another far-ranging Georgian – perhaps there was too much Abolitionist talk around the settlement camp fires – hiked in mid-winter up the nearby north branch of Clear Creek, also west of Denver. In the early spring, on 6 May, just when the earliest would-be-argonauts of 1859 were

[1] Politics was the third-largest industry in early Colorado – long before the territory had even acquired that name – and a perfect pastime for the short, cold winter days and colder, longer winter evenings of 1858–9. When the Cherry Creek settlements had no more than a hundred inhabitants these elected thirty-five delegates to petition Congress for territorial status. By the spring of 1859 their ambition had grown to the extent of proclaiming themselves 'The State of Jefferson'. An unsympathetic Congress kept them waiting until 1861 even for territorial status, and until 1876 for statehood, but there was no harm in trying. It was his observation of the situation in Colorado at this time which prompted Albert D. Richardson, in his entertaining *Beyond the Mississippi* (Hartford, Conn., 1867, p. 77) to coin the often-quoted aphorism, 'Congregate a hundred Americans anywhere beyond the settlements and they immediately lay out a city and apply for admission into the Union, while twenty-five of them become candidates for the United States Senate'. This was almost literally true of the settlers along Cherry Creek in 1858. See further W. and W. H. H. Larimer, *Reminiscences of General William Larimer and His Son . . .* two of the Founders of Denver City (Lancaster, Penn., 1918), *passim.*

catching their first glimpse of Pike's Peak, he really struck it rich in a quartz vein. He panned out nearly a $1,000 worth of gold in a few days. True footloose prospector that he was, Gregory sold out his claim quickly for a mere $21,000 and disappeared from history.[1] But unknown to the elusive Gregory, 'angels' were hovering around his head that chilly May day in 1859, and as these angels included such well-known Eastern journalists as Horace Greeley, Henry Villard, and Albert D. Richardson, all of whom descended on Gregory Gulch in June, the resultant publicity was enormous. Though their books took some time to appear – Greeley's and Villard's in 1860, and Richardson's[2] not until 1867, their articles were in print within weeks of their visit, and they dropped their rivalry to combine in a remarkable and enthusiastic joint-statement[3] which materially helped to turn the ebb-tide back from Colorado in 1859 into a real gold rush of the traditional Californian pattern during the latter half of the year.

The Gregory diggings did not turn out to be very rich and were soon exhausted, but their discovery set men, with renewed hope, prospecting all over the eastern slopes of the Colorado Rockies and before the year was out a number of other equally promising strikes had been made. Colorado's mineral 'belt' was found to be almost as extensive, though by no means as rich (gold was never found in the same profusion as, for instance, at Mariposa) as the Mother Lode of California, and it stretched about two hundred miles from north-east (in Boulder County) to south-west (in San Juan County), as far east as South Park,[4] and as far west as the Upper Colorado river.

Colorado's gold brought an inordinate number of people there considering that only $25,000,000 worth was taken out in the whole decade of 1858–67. The best years were 1862 and 1863, with nearly $3,500,000 worth each, but 1864 to 1868 were slump years, in which

[1] For the little that is known of him, see C. Bancroft, 'The Illusive Figure of John H. Gregory, Discoverer of the First Gold Lode in Colorado', in the *Colorado Magazine*, Vol. XX (1943), pp. 121–35.

[2] For all three see further, Bibliographical Note, p. 383.

[3] Reprinted by Leroy R. Hafen in *Colorado Gold Rush Contemporary Letters and Reports, 1858–59* (Glendale, California, 1941), pp. 376–82.

[4] Said Samuel Bowles (*op. cit.*, p. 187), who prayed that it would not be done, for he loved the place: 'An intelligent investigator of the subject tells me that the whole of South Park would pay three to four dollars a day for the labor of washing it over.' This may well have been true, for an old-timer, for a wager, panned enough gold to pay for drinks all round out of the dust in the main street of Dutch Flat, California, just outside the old gold-rush-period hotel, in 1963, over a hundred and ten years after the gold rush there.

population seeped away again from the mines and from the territory as a whole. The population of Colorado had exceeded thirty-four thousand by 1860, but it was only thirty-nine thousand by 1870, a mere net gain of five thousand, for it has been estimated that fully sixty per cent of the territory's immigrants of the sixties failed to stay there. Even Denver, the supply metropolis of the local mining areas, had only 4,759 inhabitants by 1870. Samuel Bowles was an acute first-hand observer of Colorado's recession of the middle sixties; he wrote of the territory as having been saved by agriculture, though he discerned an upward turn in her mining fortunes by 1868. He wrote[1] in 1869:

> When we first visited the country, in 1865, the original era of speculation, of waste, of careless and unintelligent work, and as little of it as possible, of living by wit instead of labor, of reliance upon eastern capital instead of home industry, was, if not at its hight, still reigning, but with signs of decay and threatening despair. In the next two years, 1866 and 1867, affairs became desperate; the population shrunk; mines were abandoned; mills stopped; eastern capital, tired of waiting for promised returns, dried up its fountains; and the secrets of the rich ores seemed unfathomable. Residents, who could not get away, were put to their trumps for a living; and economy and work were enforced upon all. Thus weeded out, thus stimulated, the population fell back on the certainties; such mining as was obviously remunerative was continued; the doubtful and losing abandoned; the old and simple dirt washing for gold was resumed, and followed with more care; and farming rose in respectability and promise. The discovery and opening of specially rich silver mines near Georgetown kept hope and courage alive, and freshened speculation in a new quarter; but the main fact of the new era was that the people went to work, became self-reliant, and, believing that they 'had a good thing' out here, undertook to prove it to the world by intelligent and economic industry.
>
> These were the kernel years of Colorado; they proved her; they have made her. Her gold product went down, probably, to say a million dollars, in each of 1866 and 1867; but it began at once, under the new order of things, to rise; and agriculture also at once shot up and ahead, and directly assumed, as it has in California, the place of the first interest, the great wealth. No more flour, no more corn, no more potatoes at six cents to twelve cents a pound freight, from the Missouri River; in one year Colorado became self-supporting in food; in the second an exporter, the feeder of Montana,

[1] Bowles, *op. cit.* pp. 179–81.

> the contractor for the government posts and the Pacific Railroad; and now, in the third year (1868), with food cheaper than in 'the States', she forces the Mississippi and Missouri Valleys to keep their produce at home or send it East. She feeds the whole line of the Pacific Railroad this side the continental divide, and has even been sending some of her vegetables to Omaha. Her gold and silver product ran up to at least two millions in 1868, got out at a profit of from twenty-five to fifty per cent., and is certainly to be at least three millions in 1869. Her agricultural products were near twice as much, certainly three millions for 1868, and perhaps four millions; though it is difficult to make as certain estimates in this particular, and the Indians worked great mischief with the ingathering of the crops the past fall.
>
> Central City, in the midst of the mountains on the north branch of Clear Creek, continues to be the center of the gold quartz-mining; and business there was never more healthily prosperous than now, though the population is not so large (in 1868–9) as in 1864–5. But all its stamp mills were in operation in the fall of 1868, and more were being erected; for after wearily waiting through two or three years for more effective processes for reducing the ores, their owners have set these in operation again, simplified, perfected and economized their working, and, from about forty mills and seven hundred and fifty stamps, were then producing near fifty thousand dollars of gold a week, at a cost for both mining and milling of from two-thirds to three-quarters that sum. This season is expected to see say fifty mills and one thousand stamps at work in that valley. The most valuable ores of the neighboring mines are not put through this process, but are sold at about one hundred dollars a ton to Professor Hill's smelting or Swansea works, now established there, and working the richer and sulphuretted ores with an economy and completeness that the plain stamp mills cannot do.

The perspicacious and well-informed Bowles (as befitted a vice-presidential adviser and public relations man in the Age of Johnson) had already discerned that silver as well as agriculture might come to the rescue of Colorado. He was proved right, for by 1874 the annual value of her silver production exceeded $3 million and had passed that of her gold. Though her older and most prosperous mining camps, such as Georgetown and Central City, continued to produce silver as well as gold ('indeed, there is silver in all the gold ores and gold in all the silver ores of the State', wrote Bowles) but at increasing cost as more and more expensive ore-crushing and separating machinery was introduced, the most spectacular silver mines in all Colorado were not opened up until 1877, when Leadville, well to the south of most of the other diggings, began to boom directly a smelter was established there by a German-trained metallurgist named August Meyer, and jumped in size in eighteen months from a tiny hamlet to a large city. By 1880 Leadville had nearly fifteen thousand inhabitants, twenty-eight miles of streets and an opera house, and the railroad had reached it up the Arkansas valley from the south. Only Denver, with over thirty-five thousand inhabitants (nearly a tenfold increase during the decade and

now the state capital) was larger. Leadville's phenomenal prosperity was floated on a sea of silver and it soon took the title of America's chief silver-producing centre away from Virginia City and Gold Hill: its \$2 million worth of silver in 1878 rose to \$9½ million in 1879 and \$11½ million in 1880. It also produced lead (worth nearly \$2 million in 1879) copper and zinc, and its richness in these baser metals was to carry its prosperity on even into the twentieth century. The silver princes of Leadville's heyday excelled in picturesqueness, if not in out-and-out wealth, the big four of the big bonanza. The most fabulous of these was H. A. W. Tabor, a semi-illiterate miner who bought himself an actress ('Baby Doll' eventually became his second wife, and survived in reduced circumstances until 1935), an opera house for her to perform in, and a seat in the United States Senate for his own performances; but the Dexter family and the Healys ran the Tabors close. And all this happened over ten thousand feet above sea level!

Leadville put Colorado back on the map as a leading producer of precious metals, but it was Cripple Creek on the western slopes of Pike's Peak that kept her there. Not until 1890 was its gold first found but thenceforward it almost literally poured out, and 'Cripple Creek became Eldorado, a miniature California with modern conveniences'[1] including (by 1894) the telephone, electric light and power, and two railroads. By this time it had a population of 10,000 and was still growing fast. This was a very sophisticated gold rush indeed. Even its *demi-monde* came, by Pullman, straight from Paris.

After 1894 gold 'attained an overwhelming primacy'[2] over silver in Colorado, and, during the decade 1895–1904, $229 million worth of it was produced in the Centennial State. By the year 1897 Colorado was producing more gold annually than was California. The production of silver had dropped spectacularly after its virtual demonetization, and the repeal of the Sherman Act[3] in 1893 had both curbed domestic demand and lowered its price. It was down to under $7 million worth by 1905, compared with over $23 million in Colorado's best silver year. But the state entered the twentieth century as America's top producer of the two precious metals combined and accounted for one third of the country's total production. It was still possible to say in 1910, over fifty years after the 'Pike's Peak' gold rush and the strike at Gregory's Gulch, that 'Colorado is pre-eminently a mining region, and to this fact it owes its colonization'.[4]

The biggest bonanzas of California, Nevada, and Colorado were nowhere matched in the other states and territories of the Union, but this was not for want of trying, especially in Montana and Idaho, in Utah, Arizona, and New Mexico, and, finally, in the Dakotas. For brief spells the gold or silver mines in one or other of these regions topped the production of California, Nevada, and Colorado, as when the Boise Basin of Idaho alone did better than all Colorado between 1863 and 1866.[5] Idaho's mining frontier moved rapidly southward from the first discoveries on the Clearwater river in 1860 to the Sal-

[1] Paul, *Mining Frontiers*, pp. 132–3.

[2] Article on Colorado in *Encyclopaedia Britannica*, 11th edn (1910), Vol. VI, p. 720.

[3] An Act forced through Congress by the 'Silver Bloc' in 1890, under which the United States Government had to purchase 4½ million oz of silver a month at a fixed ratio of 16 oz of silver being worth 1 oz of gold.

[4] *Encyclopaedia Britannica, loc. cit.*

[5] According to the *U.S. Geological Survey* for 1896–7, Part III, p. 655, cited by Paul, *Mining Frontiers*, p. 139.

mon river valley in 1861, and then to the Boise Basin in 1862. Mining camps like Oro Fino and Florence lived and died in rapid succession during these years, for 'The miners of Idaho were like quicksilver', who 'ran after any atom of gold in their vicinity'.[1] The Boise Basin contained most gold, so they stayed there longest. By the summer of 1864 it had a population of over sixteen thousand. The relative inaccessibility of these Idaho mining camps, especially from the east, tended to make them the resort of the roughest and toughest elements from the California, the Nevada, and the Oregon Territory's fields. 'Before these adventurers, now eastbound and no longer facing west, there arose the vast and formidable mountain ranges which in their time had daunted even the calm minds of Meriwether Lewis and William Clark. But the prospectors and the pack-trains alike penetrated the Salmon River range . . . Here the indomitable packer from the West, conquering unheard-of difficulties, brought in whiskey, women, pianos, food, mining tools. Naturally all these commanded fabulous prices. The price for each and all lay underfoot . . .' says the inimitable Emerson Hough.[2] Life was short as well as brutish in Oro Fino, Florence, Placerville, Centreville, and Boise City in those days, and by the mid-sixties the survivors had begun to move on to a new Eldorado, reputedly far more rich. By 1870 the bloom was off the Boise Basin. 'The decline in the production of Idaho is due to the exhaustion of the creek and gulch claims of the older placer-mining districts of the Boise Basin. The greater portion of these claims have been turned over to Chinamen, who are content with small earnings and who will maintain, no doubt for many years to come, a moderately productive industry in these abandoned fields,' wrote L. W. Raymond, the United States Commissioner of Mining Statistics in March 1871.[3] The California story was thus repeating itself in the Territory (as it now was, since 1863) of Idaho and 'the heathen Chinee' took over what the white man disdained. 'The fact is,' continued Raymond,[4] 'that new fields of mining nearer the railroad are draining Idaho of her nomadic mining population.' Quartz mining, requiring fewer men and much more expensive

[1] H. H. Bancroft, *Works*, Vol. XXXI, p. 427, quoted by Paul, *Mining Frontiers*, p. 139.

[2] E. Hough, *The Passing of the Frontier* (Chronicles of America Series, Vol. XXVI, New Haven, Conn., 1918), pp. 59–60. This picturesque writer is great fun, but must be read with some restraint.

[3] R. W. Raymond, *Statistics of Mines and Mining . . . West of the Rocky Mountains* (Washington, D.C., 1872), p. 187.

[4] *Ibid.*, p. 191.

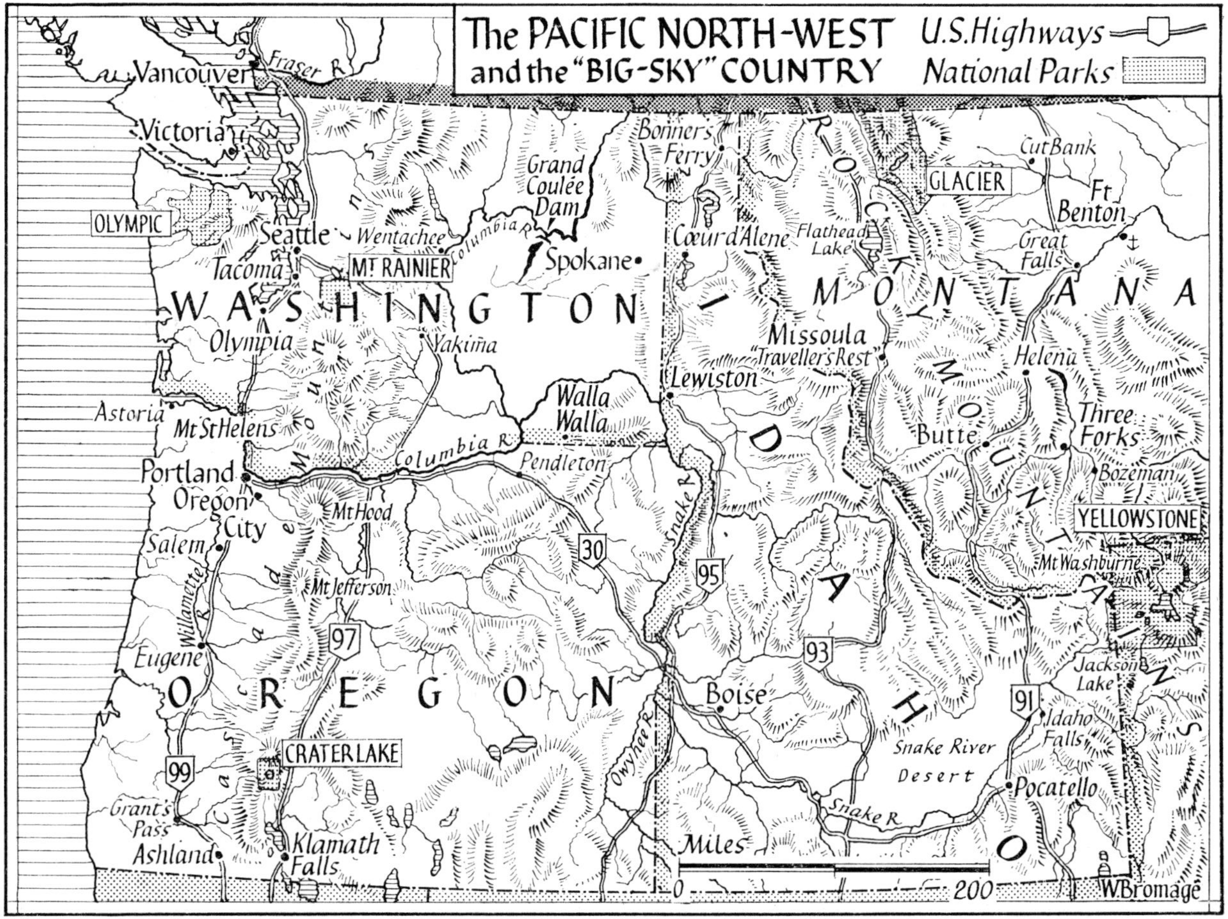
The PACIFIC NORTH-WEST
and the "BIG-SKY" COUNTRY
U.S.Highways
National Parks
Vancouver
Fraser R.
Victoria
OLYMPIC
Seattle
Tacoma
Wentachee
MT RAINIER
Columbia R.
Grand
Coulée
Dam
Spokane
WASHINGTON
Olympia
Yakima
Astoria
Mt St Helens
Walla
Walla
Columbia R.
Portland
Oregon
City
Salem
Mt Hood
Pendleton
Mt Jefferson
Willamette R.
Eugene
OREGON
CRATER LAKE
Grant's
Pass
Ashland
Klamath
Falls
Cascade Mountains
Owyhee R.
Bonners
Ferry
Cœur d'Alene
Lewiston
Snake R.
IDAHO
Boise
Snake River
Desert
Snake R.
Pocatello
Miles
0
200
Flathead
Lake
GLACIER
Cut Bank
Ft
Benton
Great
Falls
MONTANA
Missoula
"Traveller's Rest"
Helena
Three
Forks
Butte
Bozeman
YELLOWSTONE
Mt Washburne
ROCKY MOUNTAINS
Jackson
Lake
Idaho
Falls
W.Bromage

machinery, was still in its infancy there. The agent of the ubiquitous Wells Fargo Company in Boise City, W. A. Atlee, estimated the Territory's total yield of gold and silver for the year 1870 to have been worth only $6 million. His estimate for 1869 had been $2 million higher.[1] But there were compensations. Sixty years after Lewis and Clark this area had at last been opened up to settlement. Depots created for the miners on the supply route from the Columbia river, like Walla Walla and Lewiston, burgeoned as cities, and did not die when the mining boom was over. The area contained much fertile land in addition to the impassable ranges of the Bitterroot mountains and the unnavigable rapids and falls of the Clearwater – 'the River of No Return'. 'As the placer mines decline,' said the *Boise Statesman* on 1 July 1870, 'persons forsake them for the more permanent pursuits of farming and stock-breeding . . . the grain, hay and vegetable crop of Boise and other agricultural districts is better than ever.' Those who had seen enough of the elephant could now settle down and raise cattle, but those who still wanted to raise hell (and strike it rich in the bargain) went 'over the hill' again into what is now Montana, the next magnet for the footloose miner.

In Montana the tough miners of Idaho, who had, many of them, been the dregs of more westerly and earlier mining areas, met and mingled explosively with more sedentary and law-abiding elements from the Mississippi valley or up from Utah and Colorado, who were part of the orthodox westward movement and not the backwash of California, Nevada, and British Columbia. Again an earlier mining frontier pattern repeated itself and a vigorous and ruthless vigilante movement came into being to rid Montana – on the end of a rope – of men like the notorious Henry Plummer (who, in true 'Western' style, first managed to get himself elected Sheriff of Bannack) and the somewhat over-publicized desperado Slade.[2]

Minor gold discoveries had been made in Montana as early as 1852, and James and Granville Stuart[3] tried their luck at Gold Creek

[1] Raymond, *op. cit.*, p. 187.

[2] Two well-known frontier classics have glamorized both the villains and the vigilantes of Montana. Though somewhat over-written, both were the work of eyewitnesses. These are T. J. ('Professor') Dimsdale, *The Vigilantes in Montana* (Virginia City, Montana, 1866. Reprinted Norman, Oklahoma, 1953), and N. P. Langford, *Vigilante Days and Ways* (2 vols, Boston, 1890). For the true, but still not too sober, facts, see M. G. Burlingame and K. Ross Toole, *A History of Montana* (3 vols, New York, 1957). Mark Twain, in *Roughing It*, made, from hearsay, a sort of hero-villain of Slade.

[3] See Granville Stuart, *Journals and Reminiscences* (ed. P. C. Phillips, Cleveland, 2 vols, 1925), *passim.*

in 1858, but Bannack (1862) Alder Gulch (1863) and Last Chance Gulch (1864) were the really big strikes that gave the Montana goldfields national and international fame. Parties which had set out for Idaho from the east and from Colorado were deflected to this area in 1862, and one company of Oregon-bound settlers from St Paul left half its members behind prospecting the Grasshopper Diggings (Bannack), the first large-scale Montana mining camp. Meanwhile the Idaho miners were seeping in over the mountains, the Plummer gang among them. On his first day in Bannack Henry Plummer killed a man and won the usual speedy acquittal. 'Life in Bannack at this time was perfect isolation from the rest of the world,' wrote Nathaniel Langford. '. . . All the great battles of the season of 1862 – Antietam, Fredericksburg, Second Bull Run – all the exciting debates of Congress, and the more exciting battles at sea, first became known to us on the arrival of the newspapers in the spring of 1863.' The news of the organization of the Territory of Idaho (including Montana and Wyoming) on 3 March, 1863 must have trickled into Bannack almost as slowly. Alder Gulch, less remote and much richer, had a more rapid growth. Its chief camp, the nostalgically named (after its Nevada namesake) Virginia City, had a population of ten thousand within two years of the first discovery there in May 1863. The first year's yield of gold out of Alder Gulch was worth over $10 million. Eventually over $120 million worth came out of the Gulch. When young 'J. Sidney Osborn' (James Knox Polk Miller)[1] first reached Virginia City, Montana Territory, on 6 June 1865, just turned twenty-one and with only $2 left out of his original $3,500, the place was not yet very prepossessing, but the vigilantes had done their work. The robbers were dead, the people felt safe, the crack of pistols had ceased and they could walk the streets without constant exposure to danger, according to Langford's testimony. Young Miller wrote down in his diary a first impression of Alder Gulch:

[1] A pseudonym taken from Thackeray's *Vanity Fair*, which this omnivorous reader greatly admired. His 'name in the States' had been James Knox Polk Miller. Born on 26 April 1845, just after the inauguration of the 'dark horse president' from Tennessee, Miller had absconded from New York in 1864, with $3,500 he abstracted from the funds of a business in which he was partner with an uncle, and, after trying his luck, with little success, as a merchant – selling cigars to the 'gentile' minority – in Salt Lake City, he moved on to booming 'Virginia' just under a year later. His frank and illuminating diary has been published as *The Road to Virginia City*, edited by Andrew F. Rolle (Norman, Oklahoma, 1960), whose researches into Miller's career provided the information used here.

From Nevada's [Nevada City's] west end to the east end of Virginia City is about 3 miles. The houses and stores are mostly on one street and are built of logs, mud and stones with dirt roofs. The street runs along 'Virginia Gulch' where, for a width of 500 to 1000 feet, shovelled, uplifted & piled, it looks as if an enormous Hog had been uprooting the soil. My board and lodging at the Missouri House[1] are to cost me $14 pr. week. Mr Ray is proprietor of the establishment. 'Puss' Ray, a very friendly girl, is one of the *attractions* of the house.[2]

Miller's first Sunday in Virginia City (11 June 1865) was an eye-opener after the austerities of his months in Salt Lake City.

There was nothing visible to remind a person in any degree that it was Sunday. Every store, saloon and dancing hall was in full-blast. Hack running, auctioneering, mining, and indeed every business, is carried on with much more zeal than on week days. It made me heartsick to see it.[3]

But even Miller was deflected from going to church that day by being asked to take tickets at the door of 'The Montana Theatre' for his friends of the road north, 'The Keystone Gymnastic Troupe'. 'I spent the evening at the Montana Theatre,' he confessed. 'Today showed me an entirely new phase of life.' Failing next day to get a bookkeeping job he had been promised, Miller almost decided to throw up the sponge after this first discouraging week in Virginia City and to move on to San Francisco. But he soon afterwards obtained a good position. Nevertheless, by 8 June 1866 he was still '$5 worse off than nothing, after a year's work in such a country as this, $3,500 worse off than when I left the states. I much doubt whether the Lord ever intends to let me make another "Pile".'[4] But this young man of failing faith had, ten days later, netted 'a gain of $563.14 since June 8' by a successful speculation in salt, and after this he did not look back. By 18 June 1867 he was in St Louis, staying at the Southern Hotel, visiting the theatre with a pair of rented opera glasses, to see *The Black Crook*[5]

[1] There were also a California Hotel, a Virginia Hotel, a Wisconsin House, an Idaho Hotel, and a Nebraska House. All carried advertisements in the *Montana Post*, according to Rolle (*op. cit.*, p. 75, n.4).

[2] Rolle, *Road to Virginia City* (Miller's diary for 7 June, 1865), p. 75.

[3] *Ibid.*, p. 77.

[4] *Ibid.*, p. 96.

[5] 'I found that the play was one which owed its popularity to the scenic effects, the beautiful dancing, and the scant amount of clothing covering the dancer.' Diary, 17 July 1867 (Rolle, p. 131). *The Black Crook*, by Charles M. Barras, was described on its title-page when published in Philadelphia in 1866 as 'A Most Wonderful History Now being Performed With Immense Success in All the Principal Theatres Throughout the United States'.

and with enough money ($2,000) saved up for a year of carefree travel.[1] Miller had taken French lessons while still in Virginia City, and he was Paris-bound. By 29 June 1867 he was departing from New York on a French steamer, 'a slight thumping in my heart as even to a matter-of-fact person the ocean is a wide gulf to separate one from his friends'. But 'the elephant' had the last laugh, for after visiting not only Paris but also Rome, Alexandria, Cairo, and Jerusalem, he was back in Montana (at Helena) a year to the day after he had left.[2] He set up business at Deer Lodge, but moved on to Deadwood, South Dakota, the centre of a new gold rush, in 1876. He turned from storekeeping to building and became very successful as a real-estate developer and President of the Deadwood Central Railroad Company. It will be noticed that, in all his career, James Knox Polk Miller never once staked a claim, panned for gold or tunnelled for silver. But he struck it rich and made his 'pile' nevertheless. He was to die in Santa Barbara, California, in 1891, at the age of forty-six, of tuberculosis. If one ignores his trips to Paris, Rome, Cairo, and Jerusalem and his weakness for Charlotte Bronte,[3] his was a not untypical life of America's mining frontier.

The last boom year in Montana was 1868 and the gold and silver production of the Territory only worth just over $9 million in 1870,[4] but by that time Last Chance Gulch had managed to get itself re-christened 'Helena' and called 'cosmopolitan' (in 1868) by a newly arrived episcopal bishop. His wife was amazed at the opulence of the local ladies who called on her 'arrayed in silk and adorned with gold and jewels', and she and her husband either did not guess or did not care to inquire how some of these adornments had been earned in this community still over eighty per cent male in 1870.[5] Helena went on to become the Territorial and eventually the State Capital of Montana, while its displaced rival, Virginia City, went into decay. The latter, with

[1] He had thought of going to college instead, but after correspondence with Princeton University and obtaining its prospectus he decided that it would cost him at least $3,000 to attend that seat of learning.

[2] *Ibid.*, p. xii.

[3] Diary, 24 August 1865. 'Business dull, my work heavy as usual. After supper took up "Jane Eyre" by Currer Bell. Became very interested in it and read until 2 or 3 o'clock in the morning . . . Poor Jane, you have loved as only passionate characters can . . . Mr Rochester, how I felt the similarity of many points of his character, as drawn, and my own.' (Rolle, p. 79).

[4] Cf. Bowles, *op. cit.*, p. 402. 'The present [1869] gold production of the Territory is about eight millions of dollars a year, and the population twenty-five thousand.' *Op. cit.*, p. 204.

[5] Daniel S. Tuttle, *Reminiscences of a Missionary Bishop*, as quoted by Paul, *Mining Frontiers*, pp. 140–1.

its neighbour Nevada City, has been restored for the tourists of the twentieth century. Butte too, nearly died as a gold-mining centre, but was saved by silver mining and then, even more spectacularly, by copper.

The mining frontier moved eastward again in the 1870s – like J. K. P. Miller – into the Black Hills of the Dakota Territory. This was Sioux Indian country, guaranteed to the tribe by a treaty concluded in 1868. As early as 1874, according to a San Francisco editorial[1] of that year 'the glowing reports of Custer's expedition to the Black Hills have had the effect of exciting a lot of prospectors who want some new country to work in'. Prospectors were already in the Territory, dodging both the Indians and the Army, before the end of 1875, and they were not deterred by the defeat and death of 'General' George Custer and his 7th Cavalry at the Little Bighorn in the summer of 1876. Finally, in the spring of 1877, the Indian title was extinguished and the region officially opened to exploitation. But by that time several thousand eager miners or prospectors had 'jumped the gun'. Deadwood Gulch and neighbouring Lead were the richest mining camps. Here the familiar frontier patterns of 1849 and 1859 and of 1862 were repeated. The area was over two hundred miles from the nearest railroad until the 1890s, so stagecoach days appeared again in this hitherto uninhabited area. 'The Attack on the Deadwood Stage' by road agents became a nationally famous bar-room picture almost rivalling 'Custer's Last Stand'. A theatre was opened in Deadwood as early as June 1876;[2] a Methodist (who was killed by Indians) and a Congregationalist preacher arrived before the end of the year; a Roman Catholic priest quickly followed. The Salvation Army was also soon on the scene. In June 1877 George Hearst and his fellow-California capitalists moved in on the new bonanza and purchased the Homestake and associated mines from the Manuel brothers.[3] 'Wild Bill' Hickok arrived, briefly to bestride the narrow gulch like a colossus until he was shot in the back in a tavern brawl. 'Calamity Jane' reached the height of her reputation in Deadwood and lived on, like 'Baby Doll', long after she had lost both her man and her looks. Even as early as July 1878 Deadwood City was said by a

[1] San Francisco *Mining and Scientific Press*, 19 September 1874, quoted by Paul, *Mining Frontiers*, p. 177. See also *Custer's Gold* by Donald Jackson (New Haven, 1966).

[2] At the Gem Theatre *The Mikado* was to run for 130 nights, the Lord High Executioner being especially appreciated, but 'the theatre was ruined by such competition as street carnivals, dance halls, bar room quartets, and the Salvation Army', says Riegel, in *America moves West.*

[3] See *supra*, p. 196.

leading mining engineer, who had visited many other similar areas in his early days, to be no longer a rough camp, but already a place of some refinement where 'all the conveniences and even the luxuries of life can be obtained . . . in no other district is justice more ably administered or greater security afforded to life and to property'.[1] If Janin's assertion – and it does seem that Wells Fargo conveyed $60 million worth of bullion out of Deadwood without loss – can be accepted, then it seems that mining frontiers developed with great precocity in the late 1870s com-

pared with 'the days of Forty-nine'. Indeed, a similar rapid advance to sophistication, sobriety and sabbatarianism of Leadville, at the same time, and of Cripple Creek somewhat later also occurred. By 1880 there were 3,570 professional miners in the Dakota Territory, according to the census figures, which indicated that the Black Hills gold rush was not at any time on the scale of those in California, Nevada and Colorado, or even of the smaller ones in Oregon, Idaho and Montana. But, once again, population had been rapidly drawn to a remote and hitherto entirely unsettled area, and though Deadwood was to fade to a pale shadow of its former self before the end of the century, the Homestake mine, at Lead, remains famous and productive to this day.[2] And out

[1] Louis Janin, *Report on some of the Leading Mining Claims . . . in the Black Hills* (n.p., 1879), quoted by Paul, *Mining Frontiers*, p. 181, from a typescript copy of the rare original publication in the possession of James A. Noble of Pasadena, California.

[2] Nearly $6½ million worth of gold and silver came out of South Dakota's mines in 1902. Gold production alone was worth nearly $7¾ million in 1908 'the greater part coming from the Homestake Mine' according to the *Encyclopaedia Britannica, op. cit.* Vol. XXV, p. 508.

of this frontier, in addition to Wild Bill (who had also flourished his gun elsewhere) came yet another, and somewhat more mythical, folk 'hero' – Deadwood Dick, darling of the dime novelists.

South Dakota and southern Arizona rival each other in the history books, in Hollywood and in tourist literature as the 'last and wildest' of the American mining frontiers. This was not strictly true of either, but Tombstone and Deadwood did perhaps run in roughly parallel grooves during the late 1870s and early 1880s.

Arizona had experienced earlier mining boomlets, even in Spanish and Mexican days, and the ubiquitous *Norte Americano* prospectors were at last on their own country's ground there after 1848 and (in the extreme south) 1853. Men from California 'struck it' but somewhat poorly, near Yuma and Ehrenburg in the late 1850s and moved on up to Prescott and Wickenburg (named after a veteran miner) in the early 1860s. Tucson, near the famous mission of San Xavier del Bac, was Arizona's first 'wide-open' mining town, but more as a place to roister and obtain a grub-stake in than as the centre of a very productive region. Tucson was still, in the 1860s, liable to have to stand siege at the hands of raiding Apache Indians.

Ed Schieffelin, the discoverer of the famous 'Lucky Cuss' silver mine at Tombstone, which started that community on its heady career, was not an itinerant forty-niner or fifty-niner. Indeed, he had only been born (in Pennsylvania) in 1848, months after James Marshall's great find, but had been taken to California as a boy of ten and by the age of seventeen was working a claim in Jackson, Oregon.[1] After trying his luck in Nevada and Utah and Idaho, Schieffelin drifted down to Arizona. Other prospectors, including one Bronkaw, in 1858, had made some discoveries already in the extreme south of Arizona and then lost their hair to the Apaches. The Army did not want Schieffelin to go into this dangerous country even in 1878, but he did so and it provided him with his fortune rather than the 'tombstone' the soldiers warned him it would mean for him. In the best prospecting tradition he sold out in 1880 and moved to the fleshpots of Los Angeles.[2]

The 'Lucky Cuss' was the first Tombstone silver mine to be worked but others were soon opened up. The 'Contention' mine alone pro-

[1] See further, H. H. Bancroft, *Works*, Vol. XVII, p. 589 n.

[2] Schieffelin Hall in Tombstone, named after him and built in 1881 (*see over*), was one of the largest adobe structures in the United States. It was the most famous theatre between El Paso and San Francisco and it still stands today, exhibiting a 45-minute 'Historama' of Tombstone's past.

duced $1,676,000 in 1882, and by May 1883 had yielded over $5 million worth and paid out nearly half that amount in dividends, an exceedingly high net yield. The early 1880s were the heydey of Tombstone, when the population rose to some thirteen thousand and the Earps and the Clantons stalked each other along Frémont Street at the back of (but not inside) the O.K. Corral, while the young Reverend Endicott Peabody gave exhibitions of fisticuffs[1] in the Crystal Palace Saloon in aid of his Episcopal Church funds, before returning east to

become headmaster of Groton and mentor of the young Franklin Delano Roosevelt. But about the time that the Apache menace was finally removed by the surrender and internment of Geronimo, the flooding of the Tombstone mines and the demonetization of silver administered the *coup de grâce* to the prosperity of the area. Fitful attempts to restart the silver mines were made, but Tombstone's great days were over. Its fifteen city blocks shrank to two or three, its magnificent town hall (built in 1881 and now a National Historical Monument) and its massive court house echoed with emptiness. Finally, Tombstone even ceased to be a county seat and began to fall apart at the seams. Rescued from oblivion in the 1920s and 1930s by writers like Stuart N. Lake and Walter Noble Burns[2] and restored to the public eye by Hollywood and the television networks in more recent years, Tombstone sadly diminished, may now be said to ride again, but on the silver screen rather than on a silver stallion.

[1] A science acquired at Cheltenham College in England, where he had been educated until 1876, although he was a New Englander by birth.

[2] See Bibliographical Note, p. 384. See also J. Gilcriese (ed.) *It Happened in Tombstone* (Flagstaff, Arizona, 1965).

CHAPTER IX

The Revolution in Western Transportation

Just as the American colonists were still building Queen Anne houses in Virginia and New England in the 1750s, so was the American West still extensively using stage coaches in the 1880s, nearly half a century after they were beginning to be supplanted by railroads east of the Mississippi. By 1865 there were still only 3,272 miles of railroad in the whole of the trans-Mississippi West, but a network of over ten times that mileage (35,085) east of the river. The first railroad to reach the Mississippi had come to it in 1854; the Missouri was not touched on its middle course (opposite Hannibal) until 1859; all Oregon still had only nineteen miles of rail at the close of the Civil War. By then California had 214 miles of railroad, but the California Stage Company alone 'operated 28 daily stage lines covering over 1,970 miles of California road. On these it used 1,000 horses and 134 coaches, and employed 184 agents, drivers, and hostlers.'[1] Between 1858 and 1890 over six hundred of the renowned and elegant 'Concord coaches' were manufactured by Abbot, Downing and Company, of Concord, New Hampshire 'and it may be presumed that the largest share of these found service on Far West roads'.[2] It was not until well after the Civil War that railroad transportation began to play any significant part on Far Western frontiers. When it did it tended to follow the lines of older trails.

Frederick Jackson Turner, father of the 'frontier hypothesis',[3] pointed out long ago that 'The buffalo trail became the Indian trail, and this became the trader's "trace"; the trails widened into roads and the roads into turnpikes and these in turn were transformed into railroads.'[4]

[1] O. O. Winther, *Express and Stage Coach Days in California* (Stanford, 1936), pp. 153–6, and his *Transportation Frontier. Trans-Mississippi West, 1865–1890* (New York, 1964), p. 46.

[2] Winther, *Transportation Frontier*, p. 61.

[3] See Chapter XIV.

[4] F. J. Turner, Collected essays on *The Frontier in American History* (New York, 1920), p. 14. The famous 'title essay', in which this passage occurs was first published in 1893. It proved to be of seminal importance.

In the trans-Mississippi West this pattern was not invariably followed – turnpikes, for instance, could hardly be established on the Oregon Trail across the Plains, though toll-ferries and bridges may be said to have taken their place – but normally it was the sequence. The first trans-continental railroad followed almost exactly the route of the old Oregon–California Trail of the 1840s and Promontory Point in Utah, where the Union Pacific and the Central Pacific were finally joined, was right in the middle of Jim Bridger's old fur-hunting and Indian-fighting ground, above Bear River Bay of the Great Salt Lake. The Atcheson, Topeka, and Santa Fé Railroad was to follow approximately the line of the old Santa Fé Trail, and Southern Pacific Railroad up from San Diego to San Francisco that of the *Camino Real*, past the Franciscan missions of San Juan Capistrano, San Gabriel, San Fernando, San Buenaventura, Santa Barbara, San Luis Obispo, San Miguel, and Santa Clara. The great Union Station at Los Angeles stands on the edge of the old Spanish Plaza; passengers detrain now from the *Chief* and *Super-Chief* at the Pasadena Depôt of the Santa Fé line just two or three miles from where Jedediah Smith and his men staggered into the San Gabriel Mission after crossing the American wasteland; the Third Street Rail Terminal at San Francisco is even nearer to Mission Dolores, built in 1776 in honour of Saint Francis of Assisi.[1]

But before all this could happen pack-horses and covered waggons innumerable would have to stamp and rut these trails; the handcarts of the Mormons, the stage coaches, and the Pony Express would follow them; railroad surveys, both government- and privately-sponsored, would have to be made; the Indian menace would have to be met and countered and the bandit-gangs and lone road agents such as the colourful Black Bart, dealt with by the 'suspended sentences' of vigilantes, the rough 'equalizing' justice of frontier marshals and the relentless sleuthing of the 'Pinkertons'.[2]

Owing to the nature of the rivers of the West and of the terrain beyond the Mississippi, besides the fact that little of this area began

[1] See map, p. 165.

[2] 'Black Bart' the most celebrated and successful stage coach robber in all the West was finally traced, by an assiduous Wells Fargo detective, through his laundry mark on a dropped pocket-handkerchief. The hilarious and true story of this elderly, engaging, and poetically inclined Raffles is well told by O. O. Winther in *Via Western Express and Stage Coach*, pp. 86–90. The anticlimactic nature of Black Bart's capture and consignment to St Quentin jail can almost be regretted. The Scarlet Pimpernel betrayed by his blood group! Dick Turpin identified by his palm-prints! Achilles fatally scratched by a bobby-pin! Siegfried catching his death of cold! The reward poster is reproduced as plate 18.

to be settled before the age of railroads, canals did not play a conspicuous part in its transportation history. In 1840 the United States had almost exactly as many miles of canals (3,326) in use as of railroads (3,328), but west of the Mississippi the mileage of each was nil. By 1850 canal-building even east of the Mississippi had virtually stopped – the Chicago and Illinois Canal, opened in 1848, being the last important one – and the total national canal mileage was only 3,698. Railroad mileage had risen to 8,879. West of the Mississippi there were still only four miles of railroad (in Missouri) and no canals at all. There were still no canals in 1860; but trans-Mississippi railroad mileage was now 1,814.[1]

If canals can be ignored in the trans-Mississippi West, river traffic cannot. Lewis and Clark tried to get by water all the way to the Pacific in 1804–5, when the country between the middle-Missouri and the mouth of the Columbia river was still unexplored. They found the Missouri fairly easily navigable as far as Great Falls, and the Columbia uneasily and intermittently navigable from its confluence with the Snake down to the ocean. Columbia river navigation, indeed, owing to the many rapids and gorges, never became easy. The first small steamboat on its waters, the Hudson's Bay Company's *Beaver*, plied from 1836 onwards between Fort Vancouver and the ocean and up and down the Willamette, but could not penetrate beyond the Dalles. Only after 1850 did steamboats become important in the Columbia river and Puget Sound areas, and finally 'combination steamer, wagon-freighting, pack train and stage coach services were established that effectively linked the Columbia River watershed with that of the Missouri'.[2] This was quite obviously a transitional and somewhat makeshift 'transportation chain', awaiting the completion of the Northern Pacific Railroad, which was not until 1883. Meanwhile, the Oregon Steam Navigation Company, organized in 1860, managed to establish a virtual monopoly of river transportation in the Pacific North-west, and had to be bought up at the high price of $5 million by Henry

[1] From a table in G. R. Taylor, *The Transportation Revolution 1815–1860* (Vol. IV of *The Economic History of the United States*, New York, 1951), p. 79, based on *Hunt's Merchant's Magazine*, and H. V. Poor, *Manual of the Railroads of the United States*. Louisiana is not considered to be a trans-Mississippi state in the figures given here. It had fourteen miles of canals and eighty-nine of railroad in 1850. By 1860 it had 335 miles of rail. Minnesota (not a state until 1859) is excluded from the table and so is Oregon.

[2] Winther, *Western Transportation*, p. 83, and more fully, in his *The Old Oregon Country* (Stanford, 1950), Chapter 12.

Villard, the promoter of the Northern Pacific, in 1879, when he sought to establish a co-ordinated rail and steamboat empire, which he was able to do with considerable success.[1]

Nothing entirely adequate could be done about bridging the bulk-transportation gap between the Missouri and the Columbia rivers until the rail came through in 1883, but the Mullan Road, built from Fort Benton, at the head of navigation of the Missouri, to Fort Walla Walla near the confluence of the Columbia and the Snake, became a major freighting route, and waggon roads like this, and the Bozeman Trai from Fort Laramie on the North Platte to Virginia City and Bannack in Montana carried many thousands of tons of goods between the Atlantic and the Pacific drainage areas before the N.P. came through. These supplemented the older Oregon and California Trails, and the more recently established Central Overland Road going more directly westward from Denver through Salt Lake City to the Nevada mines and the Pacific.

Missouri river-transportation became big business as soon as steamboats arrived to replace the cumbersome 'pirogues' and keelboats, which were well-nigh impossible to navigate upstream without superhuman efforts. The first steamboat puffed its way laboriously upstream in 1819, but it required another forty years before the tortuous 3,100 midstream mileage from St Louis to Fort Benton was completely spanned by steam. After 1860 Fort Benton became for a few years a major river port.[2] From the 1840s onwards regular steamship lines were in operation north of Council Bluffs, but as early as 1832 the American Fur Company's *Yellowstone* had struggled up to Fort Union at the mouth of the river after which she was named. Thence, in 1833, she carried a German Prince, Maximilian of Wied-Neuwied, his huntsman-valet Dreidoppel, and the Swiss artist he had under contract, Karl Bodmer, on a sightseeing and scientific expedition into the Far West. They managed to get by steamboat as far as Fort McKenzie, just east of the Great Falls, but had to complete their journey on from Fort Union by keelboat. Prince Maximilian's published *Travels* and Bodmer's drawings and paintings have preserved a remarkable picture of life on the Upper Missouri in those early days. Both the *Yellowstone* and the *Assiniboin*, the steamboats they used, appear in Bodmer's portfolio, and

[1] See further, J. B. Hedges, *Henry Villard and the Railways of the Northwest* (New Haven, Conn., 1930), *passim.*

[2] Paul Sharp, *Whoop-Up Country. The Canadian American West, 1865–1885* (Minneapolis, 1955), *passim.*

he made a splendid sepia-tone water-colour of an episode during the keelboat journey.[1] George Catlin, a much cruder painter, had preceded Bodmer up the Missouri on the *Yellowstone* in 1832, but though he did make a picture of the little steamer, he was much more interested in Indian portraits for his famous 'Gallery' than in river scenery. Alfred Jacob Miller did not paint the Missouri journey, but he has left pictures of many other western rivers, including, notably, the Green and the Platte.

Even before 1860 the lower half of the Missouri had become very busy indeed, rivalling even the Mississippi itself in density of traffic. An average of nearly one steamboat a day tied up at Fort Leavenworth in 1859. On the eve of the Civil War St Louis had outstripped even New Orleans as a steamboat passenger centre (over a million passengers used it annually from 1855 onwards) and 'it is significant to note that more of these vessels operated between St Louis and the Upper Mississippi and Missouri river points than between the city and New Orleans and other lower Mississippi River ports'.[2] After 1860, with the pushing of steam navigation up to Fort Benton and the opening of the gold and silver mines of Idaho, Montana, and the Dakotas, Missouri river traffic boomed as never before. Young James Knox Polk Miller's embarkation for Cythera at Fort Benton on the *Waverly* on 2 June 1867 bound for St Louis (and Paris) took him to Omaha in ten days and ten hours,[3] and the *Waverly* passed forty-seven other vessels between Fort Benton and Yankton alone. The journey was not without other incidents:

[1] *Maximilian of Wied-Neuwied* (Prinz zu Wied) *Reise in das innere Nord-Amerika in den Jahren 1832 bis 1834* (Koblenz, 1839); English translation, London and New York, 1843. Reprinted by R. G. Thwaites (ed.) as *Travels in North America*, in the 'Early Western Travel' series, Cleveland, 1905. Bodmer's *Atlas* or portfolio of drawings was issued as a separate volume, and was reissued in the Thwaites edition (the most easily accessible) on a reduced scale and in black and white. The original folio *Atlas* was issued in black and white, in three colours, in full colour (now very rare) and part-coloured (the costumes only). Some editions appear to have been pirated, according to Bernard DeVoto, *Across the Wide Missouri* (New York, 1947, London, 1948), p. 453. DeVoto prints a useful critical essay on 'The First Illustrators of the West' (*ibid.*, pp. 391–415), and reproduces ten of Bodmer's plates, six of them (not very satisfactorily) in colour. *American Heritage* magazine (April 1963) reproduced in colour twenty-nine of Bodmer's original water-colours painted on the expedition, from the collection owned by the Northern Natural Gas Company, now on permanent loan to the Joslyn Art Museum in Omaha, Nebraska. See also Chapter V, p. 105, note 4.

[2] Winther, *Transportation Frontier*, p. 25.

[3] Rolle (ed.), *The Road to Virginia City*, pp. xx and 128.

June 4. . . . This morning a negro, one of the boat hands, fell overboard. No effort was made to save him . . .

June 5. . . . Passed a point and saw the remains of a trading post . . . burned by the Indians . . .

June 6. . . . rushed on deck, found the entire force of the boat engaged . . . in shooting buffalo . . . they were hoisted aboard and duly skinned and cleaned for the table . . . Shortly after dinner we passed a war party of Indians about 75 in number . . . a passenger shot at a beaver but missed him.

July 7. . . . a sharp trial of speed took place, which was soon brought to a close by the collision of our boat with the bank of the river, thereby disabling one of the paddle wheels and causing a detention of four hours . . .

July 8. . . . Started at daylight. Our first exploit was to run into the *G. A. Thompson*, smashing their cookhouse and seriously disarranging their breakfast . . .

July 9. . . . Passed the bank today where the Indians attacked the 'Big Horn', and killed one man, while wooding a few weeks since.

July 10. . . . It blew so fiercely that the boat was turned round and round, frequently driving us against the bank. We were finally forced to tie up. A soldier taken with delirium tremens is howling hideously below the hurricane deck upon which I am watching the sun set . . .

July 11. . . . reached Choteau Agency where, for the first time since leaving Benton, I saw some signs of cultivation.

July 12. . . . Passed Sioux City and reached Decatur . . . purchased . . . butter at .25¢. Quite different from the price at Benton, where we paid $2.50 per lb.[1]

Never a dull moment! And, to end up with, the *Waverly* left Miller behind in Omaha as he tarried too long at 'Shoat's Billiard Saloon, a beautiful hall with twelve tables and a splendid bar'. He chased after the boat (which had his gold dust on board) in the *Stonewall*, but did not catch up with her at St Joseph, so took a train 'by Northern Missouri R.R. from St Joseph to Weston, thence by ferry at $1.00 apiece fare to Leavenworth' and by train on to Jefferson City, where he 'Found that the *Waverly* had passed ten hours ago.' Finally he reached St Louis, by train, two hours ahead of the *Waverly*. His gold dust recovered, he went out 'on the town' and here occurred the already related incident[2] of the opera glasses and the scantily clad dancer.

[1] Rolle, *op. cit.*, pp. 120–5.

[2] See Chapter VIII, p. 221, n. 5.

17*a*. 'How California Mines are worked', by Charles Nahl.

17*b*. Monte in the Mines, by J. D. Borthwick, from *Three Years in California* 1857.

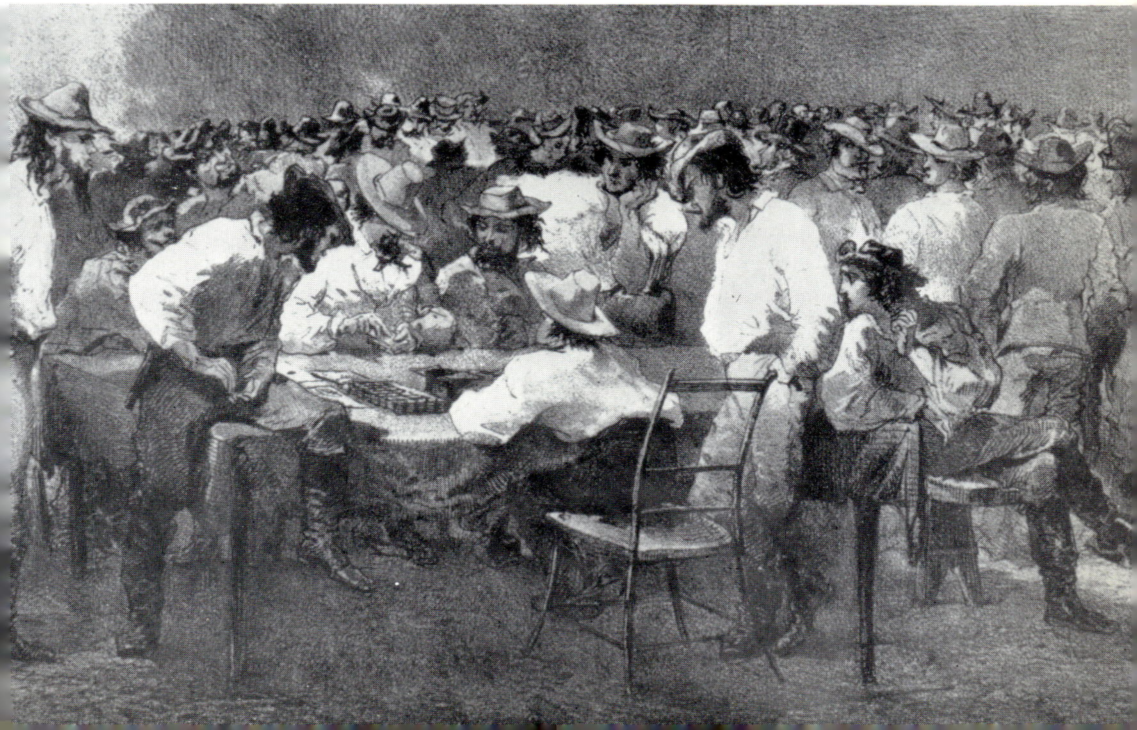

ARREST. STAGE ROBBER.

These Circulars are for the use of Officers and Discreet Persons only.

About one o'clock P. M. on the 3d of August, 1877, the down stage between Fort Ross and Russian River, was stopped by a man in disguise, who took from Wells, Fargo & Co.'s express box about $300 in coin and a check for $205 32, on Granger's Bank, San Francisco, in favor of Fisk Bros. On one of the way-bills left with the box, the robber wrote as follows :

I've labored long and hard for bread—
For honor and for riches—
But on my corns too long you've trod,
You fine haired sons of bitches.
BLACK BART, the Poet.

Driver, give my respects to our friend, the other driver; but I really had a notion to hang my old disguise hat on his weather eye.

Respectfully
B. B.

It is believed that he went into the Town of Guernieville about daylight next morning.

About three o'clock P. M, July 25th, 1878, the down stage from Quincy, Plumas Co., to Oroville, Butte Co., was stopped by one masked man, and from Wells, Fargo & Co.'s box taken $379 coin, one diamond ring said to be worth $200, and one silver watch valued at $25. In the box when found next day, was the following : [Fac simile.]

here I lay me down to sleep
to wait the coming morrow
perhaps success perhaps defeat
And everlasting sorrow
I've labored long and hard for bread
for honor and for riches
But on my corns too long you've trod
You fine haired sons of bitches
let come what will I'll try it on
My condition can't be worse
and if there's money in that Box
Tis munny in my purse
Black Bart
the Po8

About eight o'clock A. M. of July 30th, 1878, the down stage from La Porte to Oroville was robbed by one man, who took from express box a package of gold specimens valued at $50, silver watch No. 716,996, P. S. Bartlett, maker.

It is certain the first two of these crimes were done by the same man, and there are good reasons to believe that he did the three.

There is a liberal reward offered by the State, and Wells, Fargo & Co. for the arrest and conviction of such offenders. For particulars, see Wells, Fargo & Co.'s "Standing Reward" Posters of July 1st, 1876.

It will be seen from the above that this fellow is a character that would be remembered as a scribbler and something of a wit or wag, and would be likely to leave specimens of his handwriting on hotel registers and other public places.

If arrested, telegraph the undersigned at Sacramento. Any information thankfully received.

J. B. HUME, Special Officer Wells, Fargo & Co.

18. Black Bart Reward poster (see page 228).

After this his progress was rapid. 'Having breakfasted in Missouri, lunched in Illinois, dinned [*sic*] in Indiana and supped in Ohio' and having purchased a ticket by the Baltimore and Ohio R.R. for $36 to New York and Washington, Miller reached the national capital on 21 June, just nineteen days out of Fort Benton. 'I visited the Smithsonian Institution and in the evening went to see Ben Zoub Zoub Arab Jugglers. I was delighted with the Capitol buildings . . .' He had left Helena, Montana, by Wells Fargo stage coach on 28 May. Had he not missed the *Waverly* at Omaha, the whole trip from Fort Benton to New York would have cost him just $137 in fares.

The year of Miller's downstream trip, 1867, was Fort Benton's peak year for arrivals from the east by river. Forty-three steamers tied up and disgorged 'ten thousand passengers, eight thousand tons of mining equipment and seven thousand tons of foodstuffs and other goods . . . twenty-five hundred men, three thousand teams, twenty thousand oxen and mules and six hundred waggons were needed to transport all this on from Fort Benton'.[1] Fort Benton retained some importance until 1890, long after the lower Missouri river traffic had been driven to the wall by the railroad network. Sioux City, Yankton, and Bismarck all had their days as river ports as the railroads reached these cities from the east, by-passing the older, slower water route (even for heavy freight) via St Louis, Independence, St Joe, and Omaha. Bismarck also became an important staging point down to Deadwood and the Black Hills, and at this metropolis, where river, road, and rail met, the young British scholar and politician, James Bryce, found an amazing mirage of future greatness when he visited the Dakota territorial capital in 1883.[2]

> I happened [he wrote] to be at the city of Bismarck in Dakota when this young settlement was laying the corner-stone of its Capitol, intended to contain the halls of the legislature and other State offices of Dakota when that flourishing Territory becomes, as it soon must, a State, or perhaps, for they talk of dividing it, two States. The town was then only some five years old, and may have had six or seven thousand inhabitants. It was gaily decorated for the occasion, and had collected many distinguished guests – General U. S. Grant, several governors of neighbouring States and Territories, railroad potentates, and others. By far the most remarkable

[1] Winther, *Transportation Frontier*, p. 80.

[2] James Bryce, *The American Commonwealth* (London and New York, first edn, 1888; revised edn, London, 1904), Vol. III, pp. 643–5.

> figure was that of Sitting Bull, the famous Sioux chief, who had surprised and slain a detachment of the American army some seven years before. Among the speeches made, in one of which it was proved that as Bismarck was the centre of Dakota, Dakota the centre of the United States, and the United States the centre of the world, Bismarck was destined to be 'the metropolitan hearth of the world's civilization', there came a short but pithy discourse from this grim old warrior, in which he told us, through an interpreter, that the Great Spirit moved him to shake hands with everybody. However, the feature of the ceremonial which struck us Europeans most was the spot chosen for the Capitol. It was not in the city, nor even on the skirts of the city; it was nearly a mile off, on the top of a hill in the brown and dusty prairie. 'Why here?' we asked. 'Is it because you mean to enclose the building in a public park?' 'By no means; the Capitol is intended to be in the centre of the city; it is in this direction that the city is to grow.' It is the same everywhere from the Mississippi to the Pacific. Men seem to live in the future rather than in the present; not that they fail to work while it is called to-day, but that they see the country not merely as it is, but as it will be, twenty, fifty, a hundred years hence . . .

But alas (eighty years later), Bismarck only had a population of a little over twenty thousand and was still not the centre of the world. The Capitol, rebuilt as a fine skyscraper, remained on the edge of town.

While the Missouri was the longest navigable and most important river of the trans-Mississippi West, many other rivers saw a busy steamboat traffic until the railroads reached them and took away their freight and passengers. Everywhere they helped to advance the frontier. Both the Arkansas and the Red rivers of the South were navigable for nearly a thousand miles. The Minnesota river, meandering across the state of that name to St Paul, on the Mississippi, was linked up to the Red river of the North for freighting purposes by a giant 'portage' of cart-trails, past Pembina, Minnesota, into Canada, and navigation on the Red river was financed from the Twin Cities, which benefited mightily. By 1874 the Red River Transportation Company was operating five steamers and twenty barges. St Paul still had nearly two million tons of river freight and nearly one and a half million river passengers as late as the year 1884. Some river traffic even survived there into the twentieth century.[1]

In the Far West even the Colorado was found to be navigable for steamers as far inland as the desert outpost of Fort Yuma. The first

[1] Winther, *Transportation Frontier*, pp. 77–8.

steamer in San Francisco Bay was a little tub belonging to the American Vice-Consul William Leidesdorff, a former sailing-boat captain who died early in 1848. She did not survive her owner, but the gold rush brought the *Pioneer* up the Sacramento and steamboats began to ply regularly on both that river and the San Joaquin. Sacramento and Stockton soon became important river ports. By the early 1850s luxurious steamboats such as could have graced the Mississippi itself kept regular schedules between San Francisco and Sacramento City and ports higher up both the Sacramento and the Feather rivers. John Augustus Sutter, the founder of New Helvetia and the squire of Hock Farm, wrote to an old school friend in Germany, who in 1852 had inquired about how he and his family could emigrate to California:

> Each day steamers go from San Francisco to Marysville, and they all halt here at Hock Farm . . . every day four large steamboats pass by the house, and stop on request. I myself use them a lot as it is so convenient to get here in this way. Just two miles above us is the flourishing town of Marysville, sixty miles below is Sacramento City where my Fort still stands, and we are about 150 miles from San Francisco, the great metropolis [*Weltstadt*]. If I leave here about midday, and stop a while at Sacramento, I can still be in San

Francisco early the next morning. When I first arrived there, it had only four houses.[1]

It had also taken eleven days for Sutter to reach the site of Sacramento, where he built his fort, from San Francisco Bay, when he had arrived as the first white pioneer in the Upper Sacramento valley in August 1839. He must also have had in mind his odyssey of five years (1834–9) spent in reaching California from Switzerland when he advised his friend, in the same letter:

> The journey via the Isthmus of Panama or via San Juan de Nicaragua by steamer would not only cost a lot for a large family, but the long stay in Panama is very expensive, and one also risks catching Panama fever, as was the case with my wife and my younger son. It would therefore be best to make the journey from Boston or New York in a clipper ship round Cape Horn. This sort of sailing ship is very big, sails remarkably fast and makes the journey in 90 to 100 days from New York or Boston to San Francisco.[2] You are much more comfortable on these ships and much less exposed to danger than on the steamships, and the cost of living is barely one third as much. These fine ships have not long been in service and not very long ago the journey round Cape Horn lasted from 5 to 6 months. There is a House in Boston which each month sends one of these ships here with passengers, and it comes to another House in San Francisco which has business connections with the first. It can therefore be arranged that one can pay in advance and make sure of a passage or reservation for one's friends. If it is all right by you I will, directly after receiving your letter, pay the fares in San Francisco and immediately send the documents that will secure a passage for seven persons. You will then have simply to pay for the journey as far as Boston or New York . . . An Emigration will be coming here overland this summer and autumn which it is reckoned will be at least 75,000 strong. This journey would be too troublesome for you, as it needs waggons and cattle and the necessary supplies of food have to be transported, while it requires at least 5 to 6 months for the journey from Missouri here.

[1] The letter from which this passage is translated (the original is in German) was written on 1 May, 1852 at 'Hock Farm, Sutter County, California' and addressed to Jakob Friedrich Hess, of Kandern, Baden, Germany. It is quoted from there with the kind permission of Jacob Frederick Hess, Jr, of Canton, Ohio, great-great-grandson of the addressee. It has been printed in full in the *University of Birmingham Historical Journal* (Birmingham, 1965), Vol. X, No. 1, pp. 90–4.

[2] The fastest run of the famous clipper ship *Flying Cloud* from Boston to San Francisco (in 1854) was eighty-nine days and eight hours. See R. A. Rydell, 'The Clipper Ship Era', in *Pacific Historical Review*, Vol. XVIII, No. 1 (1949), pp. 70–83.

Sutter's letter gives a very good idea of the improvement in communications between the East and the Sacramento valley of California in the four years since the first gold discovery, when Leidesdorff's little launch had been the only steamship in Californian waters. The clipper ships remained the most comfortable, if not the fastest means of making this journey, until the trans-Isthmian railroad was completed in 1855, by which time luxurious steamships were running regularly down from east-coast and Gulf ports to the Isthmus of Panama and up from there

to California. The overland stage coaches were to carry passengers and mail from St Louis to San Francisco between 1858 and 1861 even faster, though at considerably more discomfort for the former, than the steamer and Isthmian railroad route.[1]

The story of Western stage-coaching would be a romantic one even if a stage had never been robbed by a road agent. The drivers were colourful characters, written about by Western travellers with almost Dickensian zest. Billy Carll, Billy Hamilton, Clark Foss, Charlie Parkhurst, Hank Monk, and men who were known simply as 'Sage Brush Bill', 'Cherokee Bill', and even more simply as ' "Alfred" – just plain Alfred',[2] were among the best known of them. Hank Monk keeps

[1] The first Butterfield Overland Mail, which left St Louis on 16 September 1858, reached San Francisco at 7.30 a.m., on 10 October. The steamer, *John L. Stephens*, carrying mail which had also left St Louis on 16 September, and gone east by train, arrived in San Francisco from Panama at 5.0 p.m. on 16 October. L. H. Wright and J. M. Bynum (eds), *The Butterfield Overland Mail* (San Marino, 1942 and 1955), p. 133, n. 154, and *passim*. This is an annotated reprint of dispatches printed in the *New York Herald* from Waterman L. Ormsby, its special correspondent and the only through passenger on the first Westbound stage. Ormsby and the overland mail went through in twenty-three days and twenty-three hours.

[2] Winther, *Via Western Express*, p. 69.

getting into literature – including Mark Twain's *Roughing It* – as the driver who gave the great and pompous Horace Greeley his come-uppance on a celebrated occasion on which was based perhaps the most oft-told tale of the Far Western frontier, ending (however it began, and however the different versions varied in between) with 'keep your seat, Horace, and I'll get you there on time', when Greeley's head was jolted through the roof of the coach. If Hank Monk was the most famous Jehu in all the West, the polite, profane, laconic 'baccy-chewing, cigar-smoking, 'one-eyed Charlie' Parkhurst was the most singular. It was discovered only when he died in 1879 that 'he' had been a woman!

The 'stage coach kings', the men who organized the Western Express routes and turned them into big business during the 1850s and 1860s, were almost as colourful as their drivers. Men of great ability and much ruthlessness, most of them came from the East with the gold rushes and had been in the business there. The first 'regular' stage coach service in California, started in the autumn of 1849, was anything but an express. One John Whistmann drove an old French omnibus the fifty miles from San Francisco to San José in nine hours when the weather was fair. He charged 'thirty-two dollars or "two ounces" ' for the trip. At about the same time James Birch took passengers from Sutter's Fort to Mormon Island and Coloma (where gold had first been discovered) on the American river for the same fare. He was his own driver and promised to be 'Through by Daylight!' The newly founded Sacramento *Placer Times* wrote up Birch's stage on 9 March 1850 as '*the* line to get to the Mines in a hurry'[1] – which was what every forty-niner wanted. Birch, who was to be one of the earliest magnates of the road, soon discovered the publicity value of a long and impressive-sounding title for his stage operations. In 1851 he founded 'The Telegraph Line of the United States Mail Stages' to run from Sacramento to the diggings at Rough and Ready, Grass Valley, and Nevada City. Continuously expanding his activities Birch merged with his competitors in northern California to become president of the California Stage Company on 1 January 1854. By 5 January 1855 Governor John Bigler was able to announce proudly to the Stage Legislature that 'Inland travel between all the principal parts of the State by means of stages has . . . been rendered expeditious and comfortable'.[2] It had also become much cheaper. The fare from Sacramento to Coloma was now down to five dollars. By 1860 the California Stage Company had extended its services to Port-

[1] Winther, *Via Western Express*, p. 7. [2] *Ibid.*, p. 12.

land, Oregon, 710 miles from Sacramento, on a daily schedule. In 1857 Birch had also won a post office contract to convey mails and passengers twice a month between San Diego and San Antonio, Texas. The 1,500-mile pull, across inhospitable deserts most of the way and through even more actively inhospitable Apache country (where a military escort had to be provided), took thirty days. James Birch himself would have been wiser to stick to his own slow 'Jackass Mail' and brave the Apache arrows, but instead he took the steamship *Central America* out of San Diego, bound for New York, and was drowned when she sank on 11 September 1857.[1] The first mail had left San Antonio on 9 August, and had reached San Diego on the 31st.

By 1857 many other hands were already grasping at the torch that James Birch let fall. As early as 1851 a mail and passenger route was established to run each month from Salt Lake City to Sacramento. From Independence via Salt Lake City to Sacramento mail now could be conveyed in an elapsed time of two months, and from the East Coast to the West Coast in about ten weeks. A monthly mail service had been started along the Santa Fé Trail from Independence and on from Santa Fé to San Antonio, Texas, in 1850, via El Paso. Birch's San Antonio to San Diego line, also via El Paso, was a logical completion of this network, but it was much too slow to satisfy those who wanted really rapid transit from the Mississippi valley to the Pacific slopes and for this reason the famous Butterfield Overland Mail was born in 1858. After a tremendous struggle between the proponents of rival routes and a good deal of lobbying in Washington, President Buchanan's Postmaster-General Brown awarded a contract on 16 September 1857 (just a week after Birch's demise) to John Butterfield[2] of New York, a founder of the American Express Company, to take the United States mails from St Louis and from Memphis to San Francisco by a roundabout southern route which, after reaching El Paso, roughly coincided with Birch's route as far as San Diego, but then continued up through California, by Los Angeles and the San Joaquin valley to San Francisco Bay. The distance was more than 2,750 miles and the contract was a rich one – a mail subsidy of $600,000 for six years. But Butterfield was a friend of President Buchanan, Postmaster-General Brown's home town was Memphis, and Jefferson Davis (from Mississippi), the Secretary of War, threw all his powerful weight in favour of the Overland Mail passing through southern and not central states and

[1] Wright and Bynum, *Butterfield Overland Mail*, p. 145 n.

[2] For Butterfield, see further, *Dict. Am. Biog.*, Vol. III, pp. 174–5.

territories. Associates of Butterfield in the venture were the Western Stage Coach pioneers W. B. Fargo and W. D. Dinsmore. Eastern capitalists put up most of the money. Beginning on 16 September 1858, as specified in the contract, the Butterfield Overland Mail was a resounding success from the start. By 1860 it was carrying more mail than the inter-ocean steamers. It never did get mail or passengers through from St Louis to San Francisco in under twenty-one days ('inside of twenty-five days' was required by the mail contract) as Butterfield prophesied that it would, but came pretty near to it. Waterman Ormsby's twenty-three days and twenty-three hours on the first westward run[1] stood as a record for a long time. The trip seems to

have shaken up that intrepid young journalist somewhat. Despite his statement on arrival at San Francisco that he felt fine and was willing to return East in the same way, he seems, in fact, to have gone back to New York by steamer.[2]

Even had the Overland Stage reduced its time to twenty days it would not have satisfied a generation craving for even greater speed of communication. To meet that craving the Pony Express was born on 3 April 1860. It took mail (and not much of that) but nothing else from St Joseph, Missouri, to Sacramento, California, in under ten days, at the exceedingly high rate of from two to ten dollars an ounce. The Pony Express carried 34,753 items of mail before it was discontinued

[1] See *supra*, pp. 221–2. [2] Wright and Bynum, *op. cit.*, p. ix.

on 26 October 1861, just two days after the even more speedy transcontinental telegraph line was completed. The Pony Express made no very significant contribution to the transportation revolution in the West; it carried far too little mail, and no passengers; it was ruinously expensive to its promoters and lost them a fortune; but as 'promotion' for the West it was, in every way, a fabulous achievement. It went to the heads of contemporaries[1] and has been keeping old men from the chimney corner and young men from the office desk ever since.

The Pony Express was one of the many enterprises of Russell, Majors and Waddell. William H. Russell and William B. Waddell began their Western activities as government freight contractors on the Santa Fé Trail in the early 1850s. They provisioned the United States Army's Utah expedition to subdue the Mormons and 'for about five years . . . dominated the freighting business on the plains'.[2] Then they branched out – disastrously, as it was to prove – into stage-coaching and mail-carrying. Their Leavenworth and Pike's Peak Express ran to the new mining frontier in Colorado from February 1859, and they also began carrying the mails (and some passengers) from St Joseph to Salt Lake City at about the same time. The Leavenworth and Pike's Peak company went into liquidation before the year was out and was

[1] For one of many ecstatic contemporary accounts of the Pony Express and its riders, see the illustrated article in *Hutchings' California Magazine* (Vol. V. No. 1, July 1860). Even Mark Twain – in *Roughing It* – was sufficiently overawed by the Pony Express to write an unusually dead-pan and entirely worshipful account of it. It is one of his best pieces of reporting – and probably his straightest.

[2] Winther, *Transportation Frontier*, p. 26. Their story is told in detail by R. W. and M. L. Settle, in *Empire on Wheels* (Stanford, California, 1949).

absorbed in the new and grandly titled Central Overland California and Pike's Peak Express Company, another Russell enterprise. The aim was to dominate all stage- and freight- and mail-carrying services between the Missouri and the Pacific coast and the froth on this heady idea was the Pony Express. On 6 March 1861, two days after President Lincoln's inauguration, the Butterfield Overland Mail (which ran through no fewer than four of the eleven southern states which were to secede from the Union and through only one state – California – which did not) ground to a halt. Congress and the Post Office Department had already taken steps to transfer the Overland Mail to the central route, entirely through Northern-dominated territory. Jefferson Davis was no longer in Washington to say them nay; he was off in Richmond, organizing a rival government. The new Overland Mail contract provided for a daily service between St Joseph and Sacramento, taking thirty-five days or less. It was hoped to get the time down to twenty-three days, to match Butterfield's achievement further south. The Central Overland Company was to operate the section between the Missouri river and Salt Lake City, but the Butterfield Company (now presided over by Dinsmore) retained the lucrative Salt Lake to Virginia City, Nevada, route for itself – this was the period of the earlier Comstock boom. The western end of the route from Virginia City to Sacramento was sublet to the Pioneer Stage Company. From there to San Francisco the river-steamer service was by this time so good that even the Pony Express used it – on the first run the ship carried both rider *and* horse in order that they could gallop up from the embarcadero to the post office in Portsmouth Square and be subjected to a civic reception. The pony, it was reported by onlookers, by this time appeared somewhat dazed. Soon, of course, a railroad was to be completed up the Sacramento valley. Had it been open by 1861 the unfortunate quadruped would probably have been put on board the train! Indeed, when the new Central Overland Stage Coach service began on 18 July 1861, it started at Hannibal, Missouri, and ended at Folsom, California, because by this time these two places had become railheads. Mails and passengers completed their westward safari by train on the newly opened Folsom to Sacramento railroad, the first in the state of California. The Central Overland California and Pike's Peak Express sank under the weight of its Pony Express deficit and its none too profitable working of the Missouri to Salt Lake stage, and the gibe levelled at the company by its restive employees and by a heartless press that C.O.C. & P.P. stood for 'Clean Out of Cash and Poor Pay' was soon no exaggeration. Early in

1862 bankruptcy was reached and the chief creditor, one Benjamin Holladay, moved in for the kill. Holladay was to become the biggest stage and express tycoon of them all in the years that followed. The discredited C.O.C. & P.P. had its name shortened to a more manageable 'Overland Stage Company', and in case anybody should doubt who was now really boss, it soon became 'The Holladay Overland Mail and Stage Company'. Nobody dared to make a play on words with those initials.

Benjamin Holladays' tentacles were now all over the West. He had a line up from Salt Lake City to Virginia City (Montana) on a new mining frontier, and others to Boise City (Idaho), Walla Walla (Washington), and into the Columbia river valley. Hardy travellers could now go by stage all the way from Hannibal (reached by rail from eastern points) to the Dalles of the Columbia, courtesy of Ben Holladay. He constantly travelled his own stages to keep up standards and to improve the service.[1] His competitors were impressed, but not overawed. The Butterfield interests counter-attacked in 1865 by founding the 'Butterfield Overland Despatch' – the industry seemed to be running out of names – to ply between Atchison, Kansas (by now an important railroad town) and Denver by the Indian-infested Smoky Hill Road, a variant on the old Leavenworth and Pike's Peak route. Holladay, scenting danger from the competition, made the B.O.D. an offer and bought it out in March 1866, when it was in temporary financial difficulties and was growing tired of pulling arrows out of the coachwork and the upholstery. But he continued to operate the Smoky Hill route and his empire had now grown so big that people were beginning to call him 'the Napoleon of the West'. He didn't seem to mind! But what he did mind was the progress of the first transcontinental railroad, started by virtue of the Pacific Railroad Act of 1864, and now laying its inexorable ribbons of steel westward from Omaha and eastward from Sacramento.

The Holladay Overland Mail and Stage Company did not operate directly west of Salt Lake City, and the California Stage business had been dominated by Wells, Fargo and Company after the failure of Adams and Company (a bank as well as an express company) in 1855. Wells Fargo bought out the Pioneer Company and was operating in Nevada as well as California, and soon it controlled the stage and express routes all the way east to Salt Lake City itself. By 1866 the two

[1] See further, J. V. Frederick, *Ben Holladay: The Stagecoach King* (Glendall, California, 1940), *passim.*

giants stood face to face across the Bonneville salt flats and it was only a question of which would swallow up the other. Holladay, when he took over the Butterfield Overland Despatch Company appeared to be the more likely winner, but in an abrupt about-face almost as dramatic as the other Napoleon's action in the matter of the Louisiana Purchase, he sold out to Wells Fargo in November 1866 for a million and a half in cash, $300,000 worth of Wells Fargo stock, and a directorship in their company. This *douceur* no doubt made it easier for him to contemplate another change of corporate image and to see his name dropped from the title of the routes he had established or taken over. Henceforth 'Wells, Fargo and Company' operated all the way from the Missouri to the Pacific and it was this great enterprise, and not the astute Ben Holladay, which had to make the agonizing reappraisal of its operations that the completion of the first transcontinental rail link in 1869 rendered necessary. Wells Fargo survived, but not, probably, in a form of which Ben Holladay would have approved.

The driving of the gold and silver spikes at Promontory Point near Ogden, Utah, on 10 May 1869, by Leland Stanford and Thomas C. Durant, amid the puffs and snorts of the Central Pacific's 'Jupiter' No. 60 and the Union Pacific's No. 119, standing face to face on that memorable day, was the culmination of a long struggle to achieve a transcontinental railroad, stretching right back into the 1840s. What had been a dream to Asa Whitney, an unrealized ambition of Thomas Hart Benton, and a will o' the wisp for John C. Frémont (on his disastrous fourth expedition of 1848), became a reality only when the first train went through from Omaha to Sacramento. A journey which had never been completed by stage-coach passengers in less than twenty-one days, and which the Pony Express riders had brought down by superhuman efforts to just under nine days (carrying only a small *mochila* of gold-plated mail) could now be completed in a week by anybody who had the fare – and the stamina to go through without a break. In American transportation history 10 May 1869 was more important than any date since the opening of the Erie Canal in 1825, and was not to be matched until Wilbur Wright wobbled across the sands of Kitty Hawk and made the first sustained powered flight in a heavier-than-air machine in 1903, and Henry Ford, with more immediate practical effects, produced the first 'Model T' automobile in 1907. General Grenville Dodge, Chief Engineer of the Union Pacific describes the memorable occasion:[1]

> The Central Pacific had made wonderful progress coming east, and we abandoned the work from Promontory to Humboldt Wells, bending all our efforts to meet them at Promontory. Between Ogden and Promontory each company graded a line, running side by side, and in some places one line was right above the other. The laborers upon the Central Pacific were Chinamen, while ours were Irishmen, and there was much ill-feeling between them. Our Irishmen were in the habit of firing their blasts in the cuts without giving warning to the Chinamen on the Central Pacific working right above them. From this cause several Chinamen were severely hurt. Complaint was made to me by the Central Pacific people, and I endeavored to have the contractors bring all hostilities to a close, but, for some reason or other, they failed to do so. One day the Chinamen, appreciating the situation, put in what is called a 'grave' on their work, and when the Irishmen right under them were all at work let go their blast and buried several of our men. This brought about a truce at once. From that time the Irish laborers showed due respect for the Chinamen, and there was no further trouble.
>
> When the two roads approached in May, 1869, we agreed to connect at the summit of Promontory Point, and the day was fixed

[1] Grenville M. Dodge, *How We Built the Union Pacific Railway and other Railway Papers and Addresses* (n.p., n.d.), pp. 15–16.

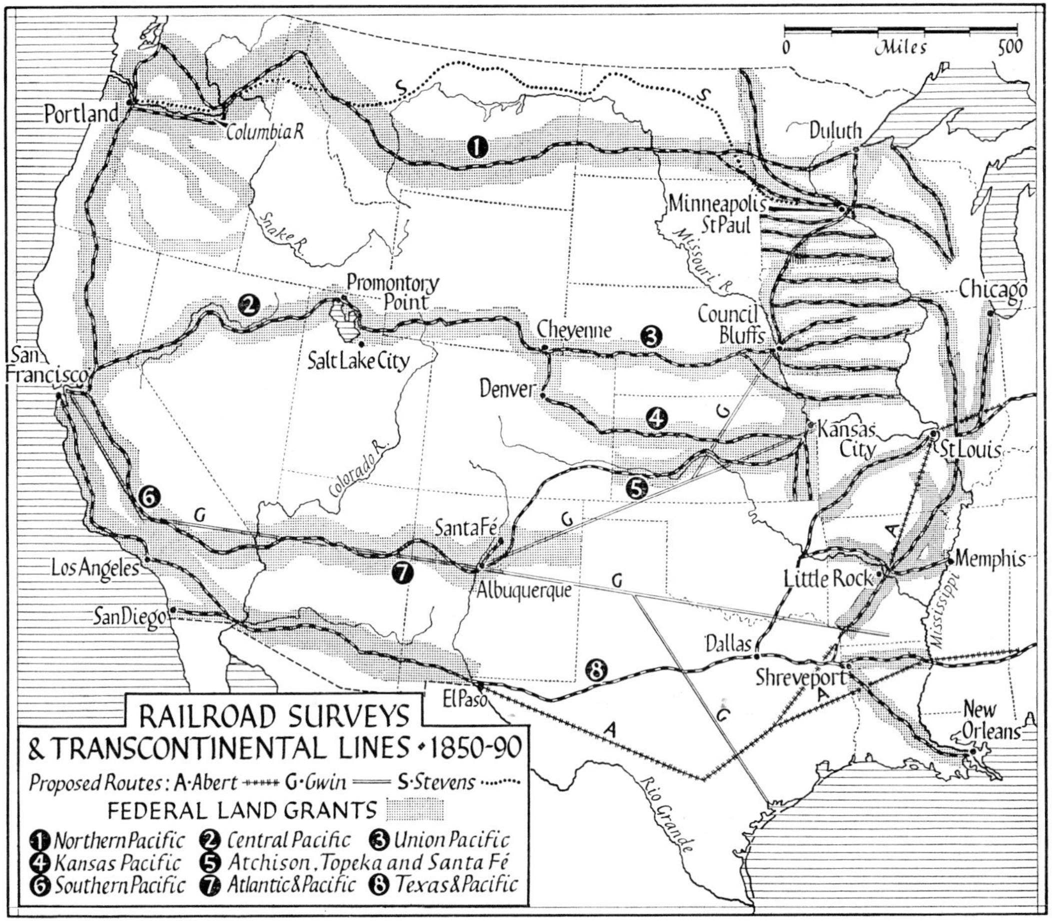
RAILROAD SURVEYS
& TRANSCONTINENTAL LINES • 1850-90
Proposed Routes: A·Abert G·Gwin S·Stevens
FEDERAL LAND GRANTS
1 Northern Pacific
2 Central Pacific
3 Union Pacific
4 Kansas Pacific
5 Atchison, Topeka and Santa Fé
6 Southern Pacific
7 Atlantic & Pacific
8 Texas & Pacific
0 Miles 500
Portland
Columbia R
Snake R.
Duluth
Minneapolis
St Paul
Missouri R.
Chicago
Promontory Point
Salt Lake City
Cheyenne
Council Bluffs
San Francisco
Denver
Kansas City
St Louis
Colorado R.
Santa Fé
Albuquerque
Los Angeles
San Diego
Memphis
Little Rock
Mississippi
Dallas
Shreveport
El Paso
New Orleans
Rio Grande

so that trains could reach us from New York and California. We laid the rails to the junction point a day or two before the final closing. Coming from the East, representing the Union Pacific, were Thomas C. Durant, Vice President, Sidney Dillon, who had taken a prominent part in the construction of the road from the beginning, and John R. Duff, directors, together with the consulting engineer and a carload of friends. From the West the representatives of the Central Pacific were its President, Leland Stanford, Mr Collis P. Huntington, Mr Crocker, Mr Hopkins,[1] Mr Colton, and other members of that company, and Mr Montague, chief engineer, and a detachment of troops from Camp Douglass, Salt Lake City. The two trains pulled up facing each other, each crowded with workmen who sought advantageous positions to witness the ceremonies, and literally covered the cars.

'It was a bright but cold day,' he added. 'After a few speeches we all took refuge in the Central Pacific cars, where wine flowed freely, and many speeches were made.' Samuel Bowles, writing in 1869[2] described the whole journey on the new railroad from Omaha to San Francisco Bay and compared it with his stage-coach ride over the same route in 1865. He spared no superlatives: 'There will speedily be other railroads across our continent. The rivalries of sections, the temptations of commerce, the necessities of our political system, will add at least two more through lines within a generation's time. But this, the first, will forever remain the one of history; the one of romance. Its construction in so short a time was the greatest triumph of modern civilization, of all civilization, indeed. The work was seriously begun on the California side in 1864; on the eastern end in 1866; and the early part of the year 1869 witnessed its entire completion.'[3]

The second transcontinental railroad link to be completed was across the great American south-west and was due to the enterprise and initiative of the promoters and builders of the Atcheson, Topeka, and Santa Fé Railroad, which also followed an historic trail. Said to 'start nowhere and go nowhere' it is true that it had to veer southwards down the Rio Grande valley through Albuquerque rather than continue west from the transportation 'dead end' of Santa Fé, New Mexico's capital. It is also true that it could only get running rights to the Pacific coast by making costly and often disadvantageous agreements with the

[1] The 'Big Four' grocers of Sacramento. See *supra*, p. 178.

[2] Bowles, *Our New West*, Chapter III, pp. 45–74.

[3] *Ibid.*, p. 68.

monopolistic Southern Pacific (successor to the Central Pacific) and its president, the inflexible Collis P. Huntington. But Santa Fé trains did run through. They were over the Raton Pass (after an epic struggle for track-laying priorities with the Denver and Rio Grande Railroad) in 1878 and into 'La Ciudad de la Santa Fé de San Francisco' itself by 1878; by 1883 the Atlantic and Pacific Railroad (now a subsidiary of the Santa Fé Company) had been pushed as far as Needles on the Colorado river at the California–Arizona border; joint-tracking rights were secured with Huntington's Southern Pacific from Mojave to San Francisco, and a line from Barstow down to San Diego was completed by the California Southern, another Santa Fé subsidiary. Thus by blood, sweat, and not a few tears (shed in chagrin at Mr Huntington's hard terms and his even more exacting interpretation of agreements) the Atcheson, Topeka, and Santa Fé Railroad system reached the Pacific coast a decade and a half after the U.P.–C.P. joint enterprise. The Santa Fé Railroad eventually was extended at both ends to run rom Chicago to the Pacific coast over its own lines. It also reached the Gulf of Mexico at Galveston and even right across Old Mexico from Nogales to the port of Guaymas on the inner side of the Gulf of California. Its attempt to control and complete a more ambitious route across Mexico via Chihuahua to Topolobampo failed.[1]

The way to finance transcontinental railroads through government aid had been pointed to by Senator T. H. Benton in his unsuccessful bill of 1849, which advocated the sale of public land to assist the building of a line from St Louis to San Francisco, and in 1850 the first federal grant of land to a railroad – though not a transcontinental one – was

[1] These two Mexican subsidiaries of the Santa Fé were both in Kino country (see Chapter III, p. 62 ff.). If he could have lived to 1882 and travelled up from the Gulf to his missions at Magdalena and Tubac by the Sonora Railway, this unflappable Jesuit would probably only have remarked, 'I told you so', and he would have shown Christian sympathy for another promoter and dreamer, one A. E. Stilwell, who in 1912 wrote: 'The Kansas City, Mexico, and Orient Railroad' – surely the grandest of all those grand railroad names, but to be absorbed by the Santa Fé in 1928 – 'is one of the greatest enterprises of today; it opens one of the treasure houses of the world in the mines of Mexico; it will build a port that will rival any on the Pacific coast . . . the port of Topolobampo . . . will have its line of steamers to the Orient, Central and South America, New Zealand and Australia . . . and the one hundred miles of the Fertile river valley [Rio de la Fuerte], as rich as the Nile, will contribute great earnings to the road.' Quoted by L. L. Waters in *Steel Trails to Santa Fé* (Lawrence, Kansas, 1950), pp. 367–8. Alas, the line was never completed across the Sierra Madre, and Topolobampo remains a sleepy little Mexican fishing village. A rusty nationalised single track runs up the Rio de la Fuerte as far as San Pedro, to the dead end of A. E. Stilwell's ambitions.

19. Deadwood – a photograph by F. Jay Haynes.

20*a*. Laying the Track of the Pacific Railroad, from *Our New West*.

20*b*. Ceremony at Promontory Point, 10 May 1869, when the Union Pacific and Central Pacific railroads were joined near Ogden in Utah.

made. By 1853 the clamour for railroads to the Pacific from different parts of the Union caused Congress to pass the Pacific Railroads Survey Act. This act called for four possible routes – between the 49th and the 47th parallels, between the 38th and the 39th, along the 35th, and along the 32nd – to be explored and reported on by the topographical engineers of the Army. These four surveys were much more detailed and scientific than Frémont's better-written but far more impressionistic reports of the 1840s.[1] Each one worked out a practicable route from the Mississippi valley to the Pacific, but not one of them was to be followed very closely by any of the five transcontinental railroads that were actually completed between 1869 and 1893, because the promoters of these made their own surveys, and often, for political or financial or other reasons, diverged considerably from the shortest, the easiest, or the most logical routes. But some were better than those which had been officially surveyed, for 'the routes selected for survey were those with the most political support'.[2]

The Central and the Union Pacific benefited from the two Pacific Railroad Acts passed by Congress in 1862 and 1864, and signed by President Lincoln, to the extent of many millions of acres of land[3] and also received substantial cash subsidies, in the form of government bonds,[4] for every mile of line. The generous terms made millionaires of both the constructors and the operators of the first transcontinental railroad, and notably of Sacramento's 'Big Four', who acted in both capacities for the Central Pacific.

The next transcontinental railroad project to receive a federal subsidy was not quite so generously treated. An act passed on 4 July

[1] Enormous amounts of data were collected by these surveys, published in eleven huge and sumptuously illustrated volumes between 1855 and 1860. The surveys have been described and evaluated by G. L. Albright, *Official Explorations for Pacific Railroads* (Berkeley, California, 1921), and in W. H. Goetzmann, *Army Exploration in the American West 1803–1863* (New Haven, Conn., 1959), Chapter 7. The 47th–49th parallel survey is typical of all four. It was led by Isaac Stevens, the first Territorial governor of Washington, and its principal artist was John Mix Stanley, who in some eighty engravings published in the volumes has left a striking and imperishable picture of the American West along its northern borders, from Lake Superior to Puget Sound and the Columbia river valley, as it appeared in the 1850s.

[2] Goetzmann, *op. cit.*, p. 277.

[3] For each mile built ten alternate (odd-numbered) sections of government land on either side of a 200-foot right-of-way were granted to the railroad.

[4] These bonds were interest-bearing and redeemable in thirty years, but were also instantly negotiable, so could be used to finance the laying of the tracks. The subsidy per mile varied from $16,000 across the Nebraska prairies to $48,000 in the stretches over the Rocky Mountains and the Sierras.

1864 authorized the construction of a line from Lake Superior to Puget Sound, to be called the Northern Pacific. This line received twice as much land per mile as the C.P.–U.P., but no cash subsidy. It was short of money from the start, and although authorized by Congress in 1869 to mortgage its assets, it fell into the hands of Jay Cooke, the Philadelphia financier to whom a railroad was strictly a speculation and not a public service, and was involved in his bankruptcy in 1873, when it had reached only as far west as Bismarck, in the Dakota Territory. Henry Villard, another eastern promoter (whose interest in the West dated from his visit to the gold mines at Gregory Gulch in 1859 as a journalist),[1] took over the ailing Northern Pacific and pushed it through to Portland by 1883, and to Seattle in 1887. By it the real 'Lewis and Clark country' was at last opened up to large-scale settlement, for the Northern Pacific not only passed the site of the Mandan villages near Bismarck but ran up the Yellowstone river, over the Bozeman Pass, past the Three Forks of the Missouri to Missoula (Traveller's Rest), while one branch ran down from west to Spokane to the Dalles and Portland, Oregon. At the other end of the line Minneapolis and St Paul (Duluth was the second eastern terminal) went mad in 1873 in a huge celebration graced by the presence of President Chester A. Arthur, General U. S. Grant, General Phil Sheridan, and Carl Schurz. It was Henry Villard's finest hour, and 'within four years St Paul's population had doubled'.[2]

Yet another transcontinental line, the Great Northern, was to be built without any federal subsidy at all, either in land or in cash. This was nearer to the Canadian border than the Northern Pacific and approximated more closely to the route surveyed in the 1850s by Isaac Stevens. This was achieved by the financial genius of James J. Hill – the 'Jim' Hill of the famous *Railroad Bum Song*[3] – and it was completed from Duluth to Seattle in 1893. It was to be economically one of the most successful of all the great trunk lines, despite the competition of the privately-owned Canadian Pacific and the government-sponsored Canadian Trunk, both spanning the continent not far north of the border. The Great Northern, ninety years after, pursued the

[1] See *supra*, Chapter VI, p. 212.

[2] Winther, *Transportation Frontier*, p. 116.

[3] 'Oh I like Jim Hill; he's a
good friend of mine
And that's why I'm hiking
down Jim Hill's main line'
etc., etc.

ghosts of Lewis and Clark, and the fur traders who followed them, even further, for it ran along the Upper Missouri valley where Forts Union and McKenzie had once stood and past Cut Bank on Maria's river near where Meriwether Lewis and four of his men had once stood off a Blackfoot war-party. Browning, the Blackfoot tribal capital, is now a station on the Great Northern just before it climbs over the Continental Divide through the Lewis Range and descends Pacificwards to Columbia Falls above Flathead Lake in the land of the Big Sky.[1]

The 32nd parallel route, along or near the Mexican border and through Texas, was a gigantic battle-ground of the Western and Eastern railroad tycoons Collis P. Huntington of the Southern Pacific and Thomas Scott of the Pennsylvania Railroad; the apple of Scott's eye was the Texas and Pacific project, which was chartered in 1871 and started from Marshall, Texas. He linked his eastern railroad empire up with this line at Dallas in 1873 and started pushing it across the northern Texas plains. Meanwhile the Southern Pacific had bridged the Colorado and reached Yuma, Arizona. Without federal aid or sanction, it then struck across the Arizona and New Mexico Territories to El Paso. The Texas and Pacific, which had meanwhile come under the control of another 'robber baron', Jay Gould, connected up with the Southern Pacific in an uneasy, and somewhat unholy, alliance in 1882. Once again Collis Huntington was to welsh on his agreements and to establish control over a more direct route across Texas to New Orleans before the end of the same year. Thus was established the famous 'Sunset Route'. The fifth of the great transcontinental railroads had two prongs across Texas, one pointing through Fort Worth and Dallas at what was to become oil-rich north and east Texas, and the other, through San Antonio, at the cattle and staple-crop empires of the sub-tropical Gulf Coast area.

The Texas and Pacific thus never went beyond Texas; the Atlantic and Pacific (starting from Springfield, Missouri) had also been squeezed between the upper grindstone of the Atcheson, Topeka, and Santa Fé and the nether grindstone of the Southern Pacific, and it, too, never reached the promised land. The mills of Collis P. Huntington also ground exceeding small and at one time he controlled or part-controlled all the transcontinental roads except the Great Northern. Another ambitious project, the Kansas Pacific, promoted by the by now ill-starred

[1] A. B. Guthrie, Jr, gave the name *Big Sky* to his best-selling, Pulitzer Prize winning novel of the fur-trading era (New York and London, 1947; republished in the Frontier Library, London, 1965).

John Charles Frémont, reached Denver, connected with the Union Pacific at Cheyenne in 1871, and then gave up.

A sixth transcontinental railroad did not join the original five across the United States from the Mississippi to the Pacific until the twentieth century, when the Chicago, Milwaukee, St Paul, and Pacific railroad reached Seattle in 1909. New routes, but not through routes, had been built from Chicago as far as Montana (the Chicago, Burlington and Quincey, and the Chicago and Northwestern) from Salt Lake City to the Columbia river (the Oregon Short Line continuing the U.P.) from Pueblo to Salt Lake City (a branch of the Denver and Rio Grande)[1] from San Francisco to Portland (the California and Oregon, a subsidiary of the S.P.), down the San Joaquin valley from Mojave to San Francisco (an extension of the Atlantic and Pacific–Santa Fé system), from Los Angeles to Salt Lake City (the San Pedro, Los Angeles and Salt Lake Line), and finally (in 1911) the Western Pacific, more or less paralleling the half-century-old Central Pacific, from San Francisco to the Salt Lake. The opening of the Panama Canal in 1915 may be said to have effectively ended all dreams of new transcontinental railroads, though, as has been seen, A. E. Stilwell still had one more magnificent dream in his pipe as late as 1912.

By 1915 it was already possible to cross the continent hopefully, and sometimes even to arrive, by automobile. The Lincoln Highway Association had been founded in 1914 to promote what is now U.S. 40 into a hard-surfaced route all the way. This, and the other transcontinental highways of the next quarter-century, brought to an end the great age of the railroads, just as these in their time had ended the era of the stage coach and the covered waggon. One man, however, managed to straddle the whole transportation revolution. Jay Monaghan has told his story:[2]

> Out in the State of Washington a seventy-six-year-old man with long white hair and beard started east with an ox-team along the road he had traveled westward in 1852. He intended to stop at all the small towns, organize civic-minded citizens and enlist their help to mark the once famous trail. His trip elicited immediate response. In the East great crowds lined the roads to see him. He drove into New York City and stopped his ox-team to be photographed in Wall Street. He went to Washington and shook hands with the great

[1] For the trials, tribulations and triumphs of this remarkable intramontane narrow-gauge line, see R. Athearn, *Rebel of the Rockies* (New Haven, 1962), *passim.*

[2] Epilogue (pp. 412–13) to Jay Monaghan, *The Overland Trail* (New York, 1947).

Rough Rider. Ezra Meeker had achieved his mission, but he had only begun to be famous as an overland pioneer. In 1916 – aged eighty-six – he made the trip again in an automobile with a covered wagon top and camp outfit. The daring experiment of crossing the continent in a motor car, he said, was one of his ambitions in life. And it was an achievement, surely enough. The Lincoln Highway Association had not been organized until 1914, and people still wrote books about motoring from coast to coast. The dusty, rutted roads bore no resemblance to the modern highways tourists travel today on U.S. 40 to the Northwest or U.S. 30 through the Donner Pass to San Francisco. . . .[1]

The Covered Wagon, with accompanying strains of 'Oh, Susanna', proved one of the most popular pictures of the silent screen, and with its success the Overland Trail became an American epic. The year following the picture's opening on Broadway, an aviation meet was held in Dayton, Ohio. An old biplane appeared in the western sky. It sailed down to the field, circled, came to the ground and taxied along the track before the grandstands. Two goggled figures sat in the tandem cockpit. They pulled off their helmets, and the crowd beheld white-haired Ezra Meeker, aged ninety-four. He had made his last trip, high in the air, above the Oregon Trail.

That was 1926. A year later a young man, almost as young as Ezra Meeker had been when he drove an ox-team west in 1852, started out from St Louis eastwards. Like James Knox Polk Miller in 1867 he was Paris-bound. On the wings of 'The Spirit of St Louis' Charles August Lindbergh was to make the first solo flight across the Atlantic. Ezra Meeker, at ninety-five, lived into yet another transportation era in which the wheels of Marcus Whitman had come full circle.

[1] In fact it is U.S. 40 that goes through the Donner Pass to San Francisco and U.S. 30 to the Pacific North-west. See Stewart, *U.S. 40, passim.*

CHAPTER X

The Indian Problem and its Solution

The Woodland Indians of the East had sometimes fought the colonists and sometimes had allied themselves with them against other foes. In the struggles between the French and the Spaniards, the French and the British, the Royal forces and the revolted colonists, the Indians had been used by both sides. From time to time Indian leaders, such as King Philip and Pontiac, had put up a broader resistance to the white man than the usual sporadic defence or attack of the chiefs of individual tribes. Various attempts had been made to end Indian warfare by treaty or by insulating the Indian hunting grounds from the settlements of the white men and the most ambitious of these was the 'Proclamation Line' drawn by the Government of King George III along the crest of the Appalachians in 1763 at the end of the Seven Years War. All beyond this line was to remain Indian hunting grounds in perpetuity. Almost immediately Edmund Burke perceived that the Proclamation Line would be useless to stop the westward surge of the white settlers, who, already restive under British rule, would only find it a new grievance. His eloquent prophecy[1] was very soon to come true.

> Already they have topped the Appalachian Mountains . . . they could change their manners with the habits of their life; would soon forget a government by which they were disowned; would become hordes of English Tartars . . . Such would be the unhappy result of an endeavour to keep, as a lair of wild beasts, the earth which God, by an express Charter, has given to the children of men . . .

Burke's philosophy, put more crudely, was also that of the colonial and American settler who equated the Indians with the wild beasts, due for extermination as the wilderness was tamed. Unlike the Middle American Indians, those of the North did not provide the white man with a labour force for the fields or the mines, nor were they suitable except to a very limited extent as house-servants. Even when converted to Christianity they tended to cling to their tribal ways and continued

[1] *The Works of Edmund Burke* (12 vols, London and Boston, 1866–7), Vol. II, pp. 131–2.

to live in their tribal long-houses, tepees, pueblos, or hogans. There were just enough of them – perhaps half a million at the time of the Mexican War of 1846, when their systematic extermination may be said to have commenced – to be a nuisance to the white man, but not enough of them to be his tool to enrich him and help him to create a new and powerful nation. So Negro slavery was introduced and the willing, cheerful, malleable, and prolific 'darkie' became the hewer of wood and the drawer of water for the American South – remaining so even after emancipation. The North, with a different climate and economy, was able to draw upon ever-increasing immigration from Europe for its basic labour force. In neither section was any serious attempt made to integrate the Indian with the economy or the social institutions of the white communities. This even applied to such adaptable peoples as the 'Five Civilized Tribes' of the East and the Pueblo Indians of the Rio Grande valley, who were far from being the wild Stone Age savages that many white men imagined every Indian to be. Oddly enough a 'tame' Indian was no more highly regarded than a wild Indian in white circles; indeed, he was not given the respect sometimes accorded to such untameable figures as Tecumseh or Sitting Bull, Chief Joseph or Geronimo. If an Indian 'came over' into a white community he remained too often a second-class citizen (and in the civic sense he rarely if ever was able to exercise a citizen's rights); in white communities intermarriage with Indians was rare; between white woman and red men it was virtually non-existent. Most of the 'squaw men' of the farthest frontier concluded only strictly temporary alliances with Indian brides and made full use of the looseness of the marriage tie among the tribes. They often lived part of each year as Indians, in the villages of their squaws, adopted as members of the tribe. Stable communities of squaw men, like the Hudson's Bay head-quarters at Fort Vancouver on the Columbia river, were rare, and greatly resented by bigoted white visitors like the Reverend Mr Beaver.[1] When the Mountain Men visited Bent's Fort and similar establishments to trade and carouse they tended to leave their Indian wives outside the walls. 'A wife in the tepee' was a well-understood term. Sometimes the Mountain Men in question would have another more favoured squaw, or a Mexican wife, waiting for him inside – an additional reason for parking the other one extra-murally, as if she were one of his ponies or mules. An Indian man living in a white community tended to be looked upon with the sort of suspicion that

[1] See *supra*, Chapter VI, p. 149.

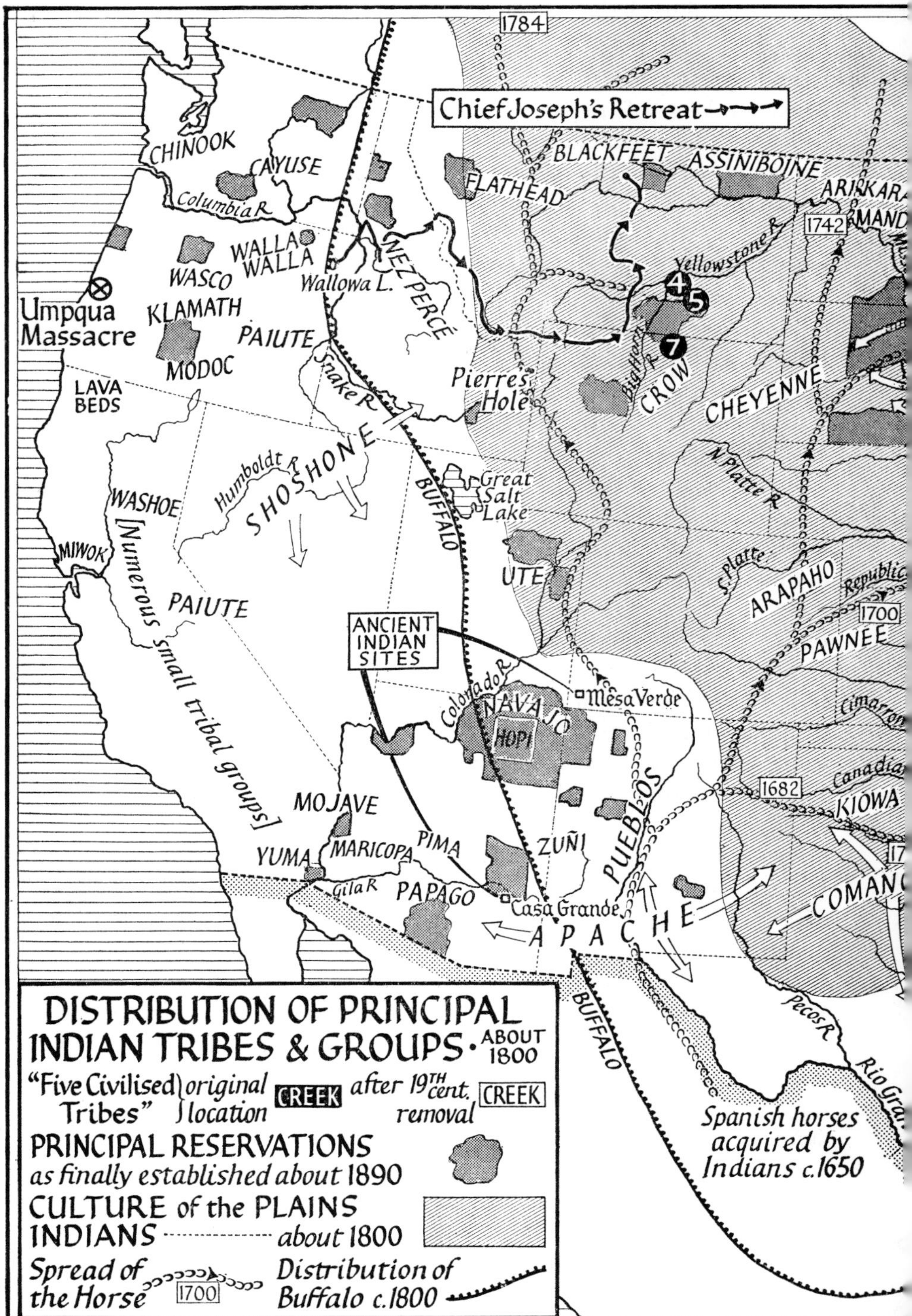
DISTRIBUTION OF PRINCIPAL INDIAN TRIBES & GROUPS · ABOUT 1800
"Five Civilised Tribes" original location CREEK after 19th cent. removal CREEK
PRINCIPAL RESERVATIONS as finally established about 1890
CULTURE of the PLAINS INDIANS about 1800
Spread of the Horse 1700
Distribution of Buffalo c.1800
Chief Joseph's Retreat
1784
1742
1700
1682
CHINOOK
CAYUSE
Columbia R.
WALLA WALLA
WASCO
Wallowa L.
NEZ PERCÉ
Umpqua Massacre
KLAMATH
PAIUTE
MODOC
LAVA BEDS
Snake R.
Pierre's Hole
BLACKFEET
ASSINIBOINE
FLATHEAD
Yellowstone R.
Big Horn R.
CROW
CHEYENNE
SHOSHONE
Humboldt R.
BUFFALO
Great Salt Lake
WASHOE
MIWOK
Numerous small tribal groups
PAIUTE
UTE
N. Platte R.
S. Platte
ARAPAHO
PAWNEE
ANCIENT INDIAN SITES
Colorado R.
NAVAJO
HOPI
Mesa Verde
PUEBLOS
MOJAVE
YUMA
MARICOPA
PIMA
ZUÑI
Gila R.
PAPAGO
Casa Grande
APACHE
KIOWA
Pecos R.
Spanish horses acquired by Indians c.1650

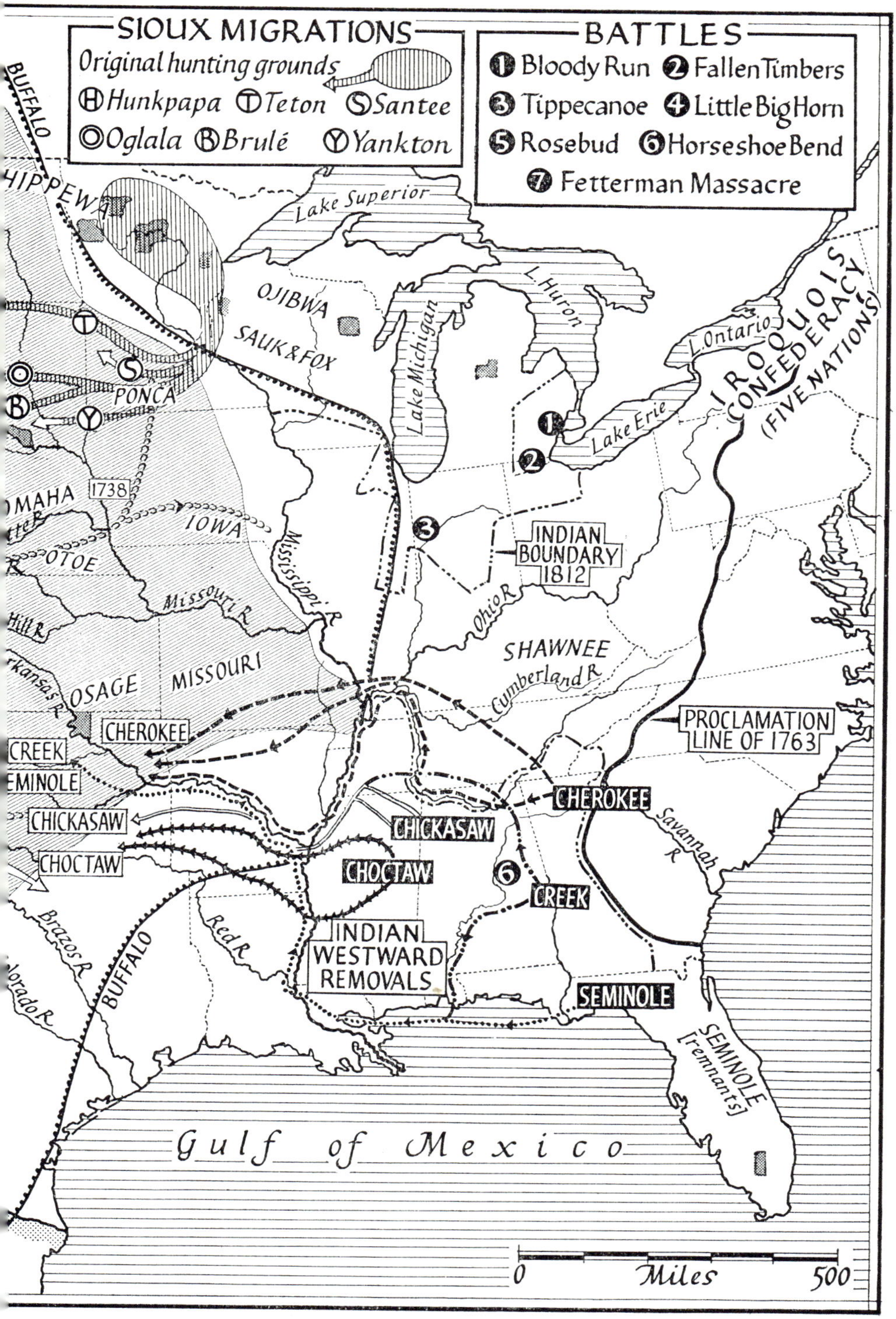
SIOUX MIGRATIONS
Original hunting grounds
Ⓗ Hunkpapa Ⓣ Teton Ⓢ Santee
◎ Oglala Ⓑ Brulé Ⓨ Yankton
BATTLES
1 Bloody Run 2 Fallen Timbers
3 Tippecanoe 4 Little Big Horn
5 Rosebud 6 Horseshoe Bend
7 Fetterman Massacre
BUFFALO
CHIPPEWA
Lake Superior
OJIBWA
SAUK & FOX
L. Huron
Lake Michigan
L. Ontario
Lake Erie
IROQUOIS CONFEDERACY (FIVE NATIONS)
PONCA
OMAHA
1738
IOWA
OTOE
Mississippi R
Missouri R
INDIAN BOUNDARY 1812
Ohio R
SHAWNEE
Cumberland R
MISSOURI
OSAGE
Arkansas R
CHEROKEE
CREEK
SEMINOLE
CHICKASAW
CHOCTAW
PROCLAMATION LINE OF 1763
CHEROKEE
Savannah R
CHICKASAW
CHOCTAW
CREEK
INDIAN WESTWARD REMOVALS
Brazos R
Red R
Colorado R
BUFFALO
SEMINOLE
SEMINOLE [remnants]
Gulf of Mexico
0 Miles 500

Negroes did not attract. Compare the villainous 'Injun Joe' of *Tom Sawyer* with the delightful 'Jim' of *Huckleberry Finn.* The half-breed (though he, too, has been much ill-used in fiction, amid much muttering about 'mixed blood' being tainted) could 'pass over' much more easily than the full-blooded Indian, and some illustrious 'breeds' like Baptiste Charbonneau were made pets of by the white man, and shown the great world.[1]

The Declaration of Independence rightly accused the British monarch and his agents of using the Indians against the colonists:

> He has endeavoured to bring on the inhabitants of our frontiers the merciless Indian savages whose known rule of warfare is an undistinguished destruction of all ages, sexes and conditions.

Great Britain continued to use Indian allies against her colonists and ex-colonists right up to the end of the War of 1812. Tecumseh, the Shawnee Indian 'nationalist' leader, and his brother 'the Prophet' were on the British side.[2] This undoubtedly further hardened the hearts of the American frontiersman against the Indian, who tended to show a preference for his adversaries. By 1815 the first steps were already being taken in the policy of 'Indian removal' into remote and supposedly barren regions well beyond the Mississippi. The 'great American Desert' seemed to have been expressly created by an all-foreseeing Providence to receive these outcasts, far from 'the Garden of the World' which was the white man's heritage. The traveller and trader Breckenridge, in his *Views of Louisiana*[3] first published in 1817, asserted that the Indian nations 'will continue to wander over those plains, and the wild animals, the elk, the buffaloe, will long be found there; for until our country becomes supercharged with population,

[1] Prince Paul of Württemberg, in 1833, took Baptiste back to Germany with him, where this natural gentleman moved as easily amid the stiff etiquette of the *Schloss* as he had in the free and easy life of lodge and rendezvous. He had, of course, as a youth received an education in the ways of the white man in St Louis, as William Clark's war d, and he had the high prestige of being the son of Sacajawea the Bird Woman.

[2] See A. M. Josephy, Jr, *The Patriot Chiefs* (New York, 1961; London, Frontier Library, 1963), *passim*, for details of the career of Tecumseh, and of eight other Indian 'patriot' leaders.

[3] H. M. Breckenridge, *Views of Louisiana: Containing Geographical, Statistical and Historical Notices of that Vast and Important Portion of America* (Baltimore, 1817; reprinted in the 'Early Western Travels' series, ed. R. G. Twaites, Cleveland, 1904–7), p. 72, as quoted by Henry Nash Smith in Chapter XVI, 'The Garden and the Desert', of *Virgin Land* (Cambridge, Mass., 1950; paperbound edn in 'Vintage Books', New York, 1957, which is here used), p. 203. The whole of that chapter is devoted to the theme here briefly stated.

there is scarcely any probability of settlers venturing far into these regions'. Removal of the Eastern tribes, therefore, into what men were beginning to call 'the Indian Country' seemed at the time a permanent solution to the Indian problem.

As early as 1790 the half-Scottish, quarter-French Creek Indian chief, Alexander McGillivray, had signed away some of his tribe's lands to the United States Government in return for a perpetual guarantee of the remainder. This was only a beginning of a long process which ended with all that were left of the Five Civilized Tribes of the Carolinas and Georgia and of Florida, being pitchforked across the Mississippi. The infamous Indian Removal Act of 1830 had the effect of expelling the Creeks and Cherokees from Georgia and Alabama (which had become a state in 1819) and the Chocktaws and Chickasaws from Mississippi (a state since 1817); the removal was implemented by state laws which were much more radically anti-Indian than existing federal legislation, and President Jackson, to his lasting shame (but he was, after all, an old Indian fighter and too old a dog to change his habits and prejudices) did nothing to protect the members of the unfortunate civilized tribes. The removal caused much misery and suffering and nearly a quarter of the whole Cherokee nation died on the 'Trail of Tears' before the survivors were finally resettled west of the Mississippi in 1839. The Seminoles were brought out from Florida and resettled in the Indian Territory by 1842, but they had fiercely resisted their removal, and it cost the United States a war seven years long and of great cruelty on both sides.

The tribes of the old North-west – the great area between the Ohio and the Upper Mississippi rivers – were crushed at Fallen Timbers by Anthony Wayne in 1794, and signed away their lands to the Americans in a series of treaties, some extorted under duress, beginning with that at Greenville in 1795. Tecumseh's efforts to prevent the handing over of any more land north or west of the Ohio river by any tribe ended with his death in 1813, and in 1816 the Sauk Indians signed away part of eastern Missouri as well as additional lands in Wisconsin and Illinois. This was the beginning of the erosion of the Indian trans-Mississippi West. Second thoughts on the part of the Sauk chieftain Black Hawk, when a minor leader of his tribe, Keokuk, sought to hand over even more land, led to the forlorn Black Hawk War of 1832 and the opening-up of Iowa as well as the rest of Wisconsin to white settlement. A treaty concluded at Prairie du Chien on the Mississippi in 1825 had guaranteed certain of their ancestral lands both east of and west of that river to the Chippewa, Sauk and Foxes, Menominee, Iowa, Sioux, Winnebago, Ottowa, and Potawatomi, but within a few years the remainder of the old North-west was utterly lost by the Indians. By 1846 only about one hundred and fifty Potawatomi were left in Indiana; the rest had departed west of the Mississippi. Most of the remaining Old North-west Indians had departed sorrowfully westwards during the 1830s.

What were left of the Woodland Indians were now 'jumbled west of the Mississippi'[1] for the most part, having to share the traditional hunting grounds of the Plains Indians, who did not always take kindly to these intruders. In 1834 the High Plains had been set aside as Indian Country, to be administered by a Bureau of Indian Affairs, established in Washington in 1832. But the policy of a 'permanent Indian frontier'[2] was soon in ruins under the inexorable pressure of more and more white settlers. Many inroads were made by these on the Indian Country, and the overland parties which began to take waggons across it in the direction of the Pacific coast in the early 1840s were forced to traverse it, even if they did not stop and settle in it. The treaties which had guaranteed their trans-Mississippi lands to the Indians 'as long as the stars shall shine and rivers flow' began to be systematically abrogated in 1853, the year of Jefferson Davis's railroad surveys; and in 1854 came the Kansas–Nebraska Act, for the purpose of which Senator Stephen A. Douglas, of Illinois, secured the cancellation of the 1834 act and reduced the Indian Country to the much more restricted confines of what is now the State of Oklahoma, which was speedily to become a mere island in the ever-advancing white man's West. Kansas and Nebraska became Territories in the 1850s, and in the 1860s the Dakotas, Montana, Wyoming, Idaho, Colorado, New Mexico, and Arizona were also to be organized as such, the first step in the direction of their massive settlement by white men. The Mormons had already broken the

[1] W. Brandon, *The American Heritage Book of Indians* (New York, 1961), p. 252. The narrative portions of this book, for which Mr Brandon was responsible, have been reprinted in a paperback edition (New York, 1963), and though the original edition was magnificently illustrated, it is the Brandon narrative that is the most valuable part of the book. This constitutes a very comprehensive and sensitive treatment of the fate of the Indians of North America, to which this chapter is greatly indebted.

[2] During the 1830s the 'permanent Indian frontier' ran approximately from the south shore of Lake Superior down to Green Bay; then across northern Wisconsin to the Mississippi river; down that river nearly to Fort Crawford; through east-central Iowa to the Missouri line; and along the northern and western boundaries of Missouri and the western boundary of Arkansas to the Red river.

'Indian barrier' before the 1840s were over, to establish Zion in the Great Basin kingdom beyond the hunting grounds of the Plains Indians and the haunts of the buffalo herds. The unfortunate red man was beset on all sides. He continued to give up land by treaty, but much more was simply taken from him, while most of the treaties were no sooner made than broken by the United States Government.

No wonder was it that in 1862 the Indians of the plains abandoned their mood of fatalistic acquiescence in the depredations of the white man, and while the sons of the great White Father were engaged in slaughtering each other in the Civil War, chose to return to a more active defence of their treaty rights and their heritage. After twenty years of only intermittent and small-scale trouble on the Indian frontier – during which some tribes, such as the Winnebago, had been peaceably moved on no fewer than five times – the Sioux decided to resist, and were followed by the Cheyennes and other tribes. In 1862 the Secretary of the Interior himself had sought to justify further Indian dispossessions, as a policy which was simply 'yielding to necessity'.[1]

If the Secretary of the Interior, sitting on the right hand of the Great White Father Abraham Lincoln himself, could say in 1862 that 'the government has always demanded the removal of the Indians when their lands were required for agricultural purposes by advancing settlements' whatever their treaty rights, it was only to be expected that local and state officials in frontier regions would express themselves even more crudely on the subject. Thus in 1864 the white agent of the Osage Indians in Kansas said of the lands he was supposed to be protecting for them, 'The Indian lands are the best in the State, and justice would demand, as well as every consideration of policy and humanity, that these fertile lands should be thrown open to settlement and the abode of civilized and industrious men.'[2] The Governor of the Colorado Territory went even farther in 1870, saying, 'God gave us the earth, and the fullness thereof . . . I do not believe in donating to these indolent savages the best portion of my territory, and I do not believe in placing the Indians on an equality with the white man as landholder.'[3]

Between 1862 and 1877 the more the Indians resisted the more the

[1] Report of the Secretary of the Interior, 1862, p. 11, quoted by R. M. Robbins, *Our Landed Heritage* (Princeton, 1942; paperbound edn, Lincoln, Nebraska, 1961), p. 233.

[2] *Ibid.* (1864, p. 536), Robbins, p. 231.

[3] *Ibid.* (1870, p. 627), Robbins, p. 231.

white man hardened his heart. Whereas in the early 1860s, no one thought of limiting the extent of Indian reservations in the Plains and Rocky Mountains, except as concerned mineral lands, yet by 1871 the Secretary of the Interior had come to the conclusion that the solution of the Indian problem was simply to remove all Indians to the Indian Territory [Oklahoma].[1] Virtually no new reservations had been created in the frontier or unsettled areas of the West since 1862, and in 1871 Congress forbade the making of any more Indian treaties. President Grant's annual Message for 1872[2] accepted this policy, depicting Oklahoma as a land flowing with milk and honey where the Government could 'protect the Indians from inroads of white men for a term of years, until they become sufficiently advanced in the arts of civilization to guard their own rights'. The ominous words 'for a term of years' did not escape the notice either of redskins or of palefaces, and by 1890 even this last asylum in the Indian Territory was to be extinguished, apart from one small Osage reservation, and the description 'Cherokee Strip' became subject to a startlingly modern interpretation.

By the end of 1876 the Western tribes' resistance was broken, the humiliation of the Custer Massacre by the Sioux and the Cheyenne in June of that year only having bestirred the United States Government and Army to greater efforts to bring 'the Indian menace' to an end. The Sioux (who had been guaranteed this area by treaty only as recently as 1868) had the Black Hills – now known to be rich in gold – taken away from them after the Custer affair, and gave little more trouble. Meanwhile the Shoshones and Bannocks in Idaho (1872), and the Crows in Montana and the Utes in Colorado (1873) had been pushed and cajoled off the major part of their lands – the Utes losing 4 million acres – and the unfortunate Modocs of Oregon ejected forcibly from theirs (1873), after the incident of 'Captain Jack' and the assassination of General Canby in the larva beds.[3] The Kansas Indians were to be squeezed off their remaining lands – which the Santa Fé Railroad was already huffing and puffing to cross – in 1877.

But enough is enough, and as some of the bitterness of the Custer

[1] Robbins, p. 233.

[2] Richardson, *Messages and Papers of the Presidents*, Vol. VII, p. 200.

[3] See J. P. Dunn, *Massacres of the Mountains* (Indianapolis, 1886; photographed from the original edition, with the same illustrations, in the *Frontier Library*, London, 1963), Chapter XVIII, pp. 461–97. This old classic contains some of the best accounts ever written of 'The Indian Wars of the Far West' which is its sub-title, and is free from much of the blind prejudice against the red man of most of Dunn's contemporaries.

defeat began to die down (though not in 7th United States Cavalry circles) the glimmerings of a more humane attitude towards the Indian on the part of the Government appeared. President Hayes, a civilian, and his Secretary of the Interior, the liberal-minded German immigrant Carl Schurz (a veteran of the Revolutions of 1848 in Europe and the liberator of Professor Kinkel from the King of Prussia's jail) attempted some reforms. In his 1877 Message[1] Hayes even spoke of 'broken promises and acts of injustice on our part', and in his 1880 Message[2] urged the passing of legislation that would remedy some of these injustices. Hayes and Schurz were before their time, but humanitarian sentiment was to be aroused more strongly in the following year, 1881, by the publication of *A Century of Dishonor*, which has been called 'The Indians' *Uncle Tom's Cabin*', by Helen Hunt Jackson (best known for *Ramona*, her novel of early California). *A Century of Dishonor* was a flaming full-scale indictment of the white man's treatment of the Indians, containing long unsparing descriptions of such unsavoury episodes as the Chivington Massacre of the Cheyenne at Sand Creek in 1864. This book[3] had a wide circulation and was extensively reviewed and discussed in the Press, and quoted in Congress. Liberal journals like the *Nation*[4] were heartened in their crusade in favour of better treatment of the red man, but it was not until 1887 that Grover Cleveland, the Democratic Party's first incumbent of the White House since before the Civil War, sponsored the Dawes Act, which allowed Indians (who had hitherto been disbarred from it) to enter on the public domain of the United States, and to hold lands in severalty (instead of only collectively as members of tribes). This permitted them to benefit for the first time from the Homestead laws and to look forward to full United States citizenship, but it also meant that the remaining reservation land could now be subdivided, and, while Indians were guaranteed homesteads on it, a great deal was to fall into the hands of white settlers in the ensuing years. By 1892 over 26 million additional acres of Indian reservation land had been returned to the public domain to be a 'free for all' to which the white settler helped himself much more freely

[1] Richardson, *Messages*, Vol. VII, p. 401.

[2] *Ibid.*, p. 576.

[3] Helen Hunt Jackson, *A Century of Dishonor* (New York and London 1881; reprinted with an introduction by Andrew F. Rolle, New York, 1965).

[4] The *Nation*, on 13 July 1876, less than a month after the Custer massacre, had very courageously called the deliberate pauperization of the Indians, in the process of getting hold of their lands, 'shocking', with 'nothing in our religion, or manners, or laws, or tradition or policy, to give it any countenance or support'.

than did the Indian. On 22 April 1889 the Indian Territory itself had been effectively broken up, and the Five Civilized Tribes removed from the land guaranteed them in perpetuity after earlier removals.[1]

The Indians must have wondered exactly what, and whom, the Dawes Act had been designed to protect. While Senator Dawes and President Cleveland undoubtedly meant well by the red man, the Secretary of the Interior was able to report that 'the reservation system and the continuance of tribal relations have been broken . . . a constant effort has been made to suppress the influence of the Indian chiefs'.[2] By 1906, 'through the breaking up of the reservation system, some 75,000,000 acres, or about three-fifths of the Indian land released by the Dawes Act of 1887, had been appropriated by whites'.[3] His lands were vanishing even more rapidly than the original American himself.[4] But the Burke Act of 1906 threw a sop in his direction by granting him full title to the lands he had managed to keep, in less than the twenty-five years prescribed by the Dawes Act, if he behaved himself.

Eventually, 'Of the approximately 150 million acres owned by the Indians in 1880, most of it guaranteed by treaties made less than thirty or forty years before, over 90 million acres – an area more than twice the size of Oklahoma – was abstracted from the Indian's pocket.'[5] By the 1920s, when the Indian population, instead of obligingly vanishing altogether, had actually begun to increase again in the United States (and a quarter-Indian from Oklahoma, Charles Curtis, actually became Vice-President in 1929) there was not enough land left in their possession for them to live on. The remaining reservations tended to become overcrowded rural slums. It was not until 1934, when a new and extremely liberal head of the Bureau of Indian Affairs put through, as part of Franklin D. Roosevelt's 'New Deal' legislation, the Indian Reorganisation Act, that the 'allotment' of Indian lands under the Act of 1887 was stopped, and regeneration through the once-despised tribal organization sought. Some of the more cohesive tribes had kept their tribal systems going through the lean years, but a great many were broken beyond recall. The eloquent and energetic John Collier[6]

[1] See further, Chapter XIII, p. 327.

[2] Report of the Secretary of the Interior, 1892, p. 8, Robbins, *op. cit.*, p. 284.

[3] Robbins, *loc. cit.*

[4] By 1900 the number of Indians in the U.S.A. was down to 250,000.

[5] Brandon, *op. cit.*, p. 408.

[6] Head of the Bureau of Indian Affairs from 1933 and author of *Indians of the Americas* (Mentor Books, New American Library, New York, 1948), a warm-hearted if not over-scholarly survey and tract.

did his best, but his act of 1934 had really been bolting the stable door after the horses were stolen. The Indians regained only about 3 million out of the 90 million acres of land lost by them since 1880, and in 1950 the liberal policy of 1934 was abandoned. A new policy of streamlined and forced 'integration' of the Indian (against whom there was by now little or no remaining colour or racial prejudice in many parts of the country) with American society was tried, but soon found both wanting, and extremely objectionable, by all but the most bigoted of right-wing extremists. With the passing of McCarthyism and of Senator 'Pat' McCarran of Nevada – who disliked 'the first Americans' (the Indians) and the latest Americans (the immigrants) with equal vehemence – the so-called 'termination' programme (an unfortunate description used by an inept administration, and so redolent of the jargon of the concentration camp or, at best, of the hospital for incurables) was discontinued. Among the tribes to be 'terminated' under this programme, while it lasted, was that of the Menominee, whose small reservation near Green Bay, Wisconsin, was eliminated. They had shown the bad judgement of locating themselves on valuable timber land, now becoming scarce in the cut-over North Woods.[1]

The causes of the Indian wars of the Great Plains during the 1860s and 1870s were many and complex; it would be far too simple to explain them as the inevitable clash of the irresistible white man with the irremovable redskin. A similar large-scale resistance was not put up by the Indians of the East, or of the Old North-west, of the Pacific North-west, of California, or of the Great Basin frontier. Their stand was more sporadic, more episodic, and more despairing – apart from the Apaches, who belonged to the Great Plains as well as to the South-west.

In a way the whole problem had been created by the white man letting the horse be taken over by the Plains Indians as a primary feature of their culture and as one of their chief weapons of war, along with the rifle, which they also obtained from him. The Plains Indians had not been formidable when Coronado encountered them in 1540, nor indeed for another century and a half. Had the Great Plains been resolutely colonized by Europeans then, Indian opposition could have

[1] I spent some days camping on the Menominee Reservation in the summer of 1929 with my friends the late Felix and Marie Keesing, anthropologists from New Zealand, who found in the life and problems of the Menominee some similarities to those of the Maori. The Menominee appeared to my lay eye to be a simple friendly people, living just above the margin of subsistence and entirely incapable of facing the rough and tumble of American competitive society.

been but slight. The Plains Indians were relatively few, compared with the Pueblo Indians of the Rio Grande valley, who let themselves be dominated by a handful of Spanish soldiers and settlers in the seventeenth century, with only one revolt of major proportions in 1680. But the horse came up the Rio Grande valley with the Spaniards, spreading rapidly over New Mexico into what are now Colorado, Montana, Alberta, and Saskatchewan, into Texas, Oklahoma, Kansas, Nebraska, the Dakotas, and Manitoba, and into Iowa and Minnesota. Such Indian tribes as the Comanches, the Cheyennes, the Shoshones, the various branches of the Sioux, the Pawnees, the Crows, and finally the Blackfeet, had their whole way of life transformed before the end of the eighteenth century by the coming of the horse. 'The trudging foot people of the plains were thrown into panic by enemies transformed into centaurs nine feet tall who could dash upon their victims with the speed of the screaming wind,' writes William Brandon. 'Mounted Shoshonis were attacking the Blackfoot by 1730 . . . the horse-frontier, moving in from the south and west, and the gun frontier, advancing from the east, met on the Great Plains in a spectacular clash and created the figure that has obsessed the world ever since as the Archetype of the American Indian: the feather-streaming, buffalo-chasing, wild-running, recklessly fighting Indian of the Plains.'[1]

During the first half of the nineteenth century the Plains Indians were mainly content to fight each other, leaving the white man alone, especially when he travelled in large parties or settled *en masse*. Tribal prestige came less from scalping odd white men and driving off their horses and cattle than in 'counting coups' in the elaborately formalized internecine warfare of the plains, the rules of which in a barbaric way resembled a code of chivalry. Tribes had their hereditary enemies, but more often their battles were for some temporary advantage, like the possession of a disputed hunting ground, or of a proportion of another tribe's horses or women. The obtaining of prisoners for torture or sacrifice does not appear to have been practised on a large scale, certainly not on that of the Aztecs; even the taking of scalps was by no means widely practised until the white man began to demand them as

[1] Brandon, *op. cit.*, pp. 333–4. Immediately after his final resistance had been broken this 'fighting Indian of the Plains' could safely be depicted in all his glory and glamour by artists such as Charles Russell and Frederic Remington. Since the days of Bodmer and Catlin and Miller, half a century earlier, the Plains Indian had grown larger than life, a figure of epic proportions. Out of the water colours and the oils of Charlie Russell this noblest savage of them all stares down his long nose at lesser men and less heroic days. See, for example, plate 21.

evidence from friendly Indians engaged in mercenary warfare on his behalf with 'hostiles', before the payment of head-money or trade goods would be made. Above all, Indian warfare in the plains and the Rockies was on a very small scale; many tribal units ran into hundreds rather than thousands, and a war-party of as many as a hundred braves was unusually large. A large Indian village on the move was virtually impossible of concealment, as Dull Knife learned to his cost when Colonel Ranald S. Mackenzie, 4th U.S. Cavalry, surprised his Cheyenne village of about 1,500 Indians – only 400 to 500 of them warriors – on the Red Fork of the Powder river in Wyoming on 25 November 1876, and destroyed it.[1] Up to the end of the Civil War the United States forces engaged in convoy and garrison duty in the West and in occasional punitive or 'flag-showing' expeditions were very small.

The whole United States Army consisted of only 6,000 men in 1830, and over a quarter of these became deserters before the year was out. By 1841 the Army was only 11,000 strong. Nearly all the 'one-year volunteers' of the Mexican War interpreted their terms of enlistment very strictly, some of them even downing rifles in the midst of battles, others having to be disbanded before their time for mutinous conduct, and many more simply deserting. General Kearny's force of dragoons which rode through the West to impress the Indians in 1845 was only 600 strong, and his 'Army of the West' of the following year,[2] the largest force ever to be mustered there up to that time, contained only 1,800 men. Of these he took a mere 300 on with him beyond Santa Fé and was content to have just 100 accompany him all the way to California. Colonel Doniphan achieved prodigies in his expedition down the Rio Grande valley and to Chihuahua, with not more than 1,000 men. During the 1850s and the Civil War the Army continued to be very thin on the ground in the West. The railroad survey parties of 1853–5 were small and but lightly armed, preferring to parley with the Indians to fighting them[3] and, on the whole, managing to do so quite

[1] This was a Pyrrhic victory, for the Cheyennes left only thirty bodies behind when they retreated (though they later admitted to having had forty warriors killed); Mackenzie withdrew his force and 'elected to let General Winter administer the *coup de grâce*' and on the night after the battle, with the thermometer at 30 degrees below zero, 'eleven Cheyenne babies froze to death in the arms of their mothers' on the bare slopes of the Bighorn Mountains. Lessing G. North, Jr, 'Mackenzie against Dull Knife: Breaking the Northern Cheyennes in 1876', in *Probing the American West* (ed. K. Ross Toole, Santa Fé, 1962), pp. 90–1.

[2] See pp. 114, 143 and 167–8.

[3] Governor Stevens, when at Fort Union on the Upper Missouri, with his Pacific Railroad Survey party in 1853, recruited the services of Medicine-Snake-Woman

successfully. About 2,000 men were all the army could spare to garrison the Western forts before 1865. A command in the West was regarded as miserable exile and was one which most well-connected West Pointers managed to avoid. Only when generals became two-a-penny and brevet-colonels difficult not to step upon at the end of the war between the states did men of both integrity and ability come into positions of authority in the regular Western army, and then it was often too late to coerce the Indians peaceably. Meanwhile the Indian Bureau of the Department of the Interior and the War Department continued to fight each other when not preying on the unfortunate red man it was their duty to protect and civilize. The Indian grew to distrust them both, and this led to the first large-scale revolt of the Sioux in Minnesota in 1862. Little Crow, with 1,300 warriors, went on the rampage and killed over 700 white settlers. The state militia was able to deal with this outbreak and 400 Indian prisoners (of whom 38 were subsequently executed) were put on trial for murder and other crimes at St Paul. All the remaining Sioux lands in Minnesota were confiscated.

It was the militia, too, which 'dealt with' the Cheyennes in southern Colorado Territory in 1864, this time with far less provocation and far more savagely. The Fort Wise[1] treaty of 1861 took away the land guaranteed by Tom Fitzpatrick's treaty of 1851 to the Arapaho and Cheyennes, and since overrun by the miners of the 'Pike's Peak or Bust' gold rush, who at that time knew no law and recognized no property rights, red or white. The Indians who stood in the way of the exploitation of the Territory's mineral and agricultural potentialities were ordered on to a new reservation in the Sand Creek valley of south-eastern Colorado. In June 1864, after three uneasy years of non-compliance, Black Kettle and his band of some five hundred Cheyennes

---

the Blood Indian squaw of Alexander Culbertson, the *Bourgeois* at the Fort, to smooth the way for him through the Blackfoot and Gros Ventre country. So successful were she and her equally co-operative cousin, Little Dog, that the United States were able to conclude a treaty with the Blackfoot, for the first time, in 1855. The General and his party went through the Blackfoot country unmolested, which is more than can be said for the Union Pacific Railroad (the route of which he pioneered) a decade later, by which time the whole northern Indian frontier was aflame. There were limits to what even 'Mothers of the Mixed Bloods' could do! 'Mothers of the Mixed Bloods: the Marginal Woman in the History of the Upper Missouri' is the title of an article by John C. Ewers in *Probing the American West*, pp. 62–70, and deals most specifically with Sacajawea, with Medicine-Snake-Woman, and with Deer-Little-Woman (Mrs F. T. Denig, later Mrs Christiana Olsen) an Assinoboin chief's daughter.

[1] Fort Wise was a new military post near the site of Bent's Old Fort, on the Arkansas.

moved down to Sand Creek and encamped peaceably under a flag of truce. They had decided to resist the proclamation of the Territorial governor no longer. Here they were attacked by the paranoiac 'Colonel' J. M. Chivington (by profession a minister of religion!) and his blood-lusting Colorado militia men – who had been urged by their superior officers to spare neither man, woman, nor child – and at least half of them massacred in cold blood. About two hundred Indian women and children and seventy men were slaughtered. Casualties among Chivington's 'boys' were negligible, but the consequences for the history of Indian–White relations and for the reputation of the white man in the West were to be momentous. After more than a hundred years 'the Chivington Massacre' continues to be spoken and written about in tones of horror and incredulity. It is America's St Bartholomew.[1]

Upon the Northern Plains the Sioux had taken their grievances westward with them and a sweet revenge for the thirty-eight hangings[2] in St Paul came to them after Colonel H. B. Carrington took a detachment on to the Bozeman Trail to keep it open for the waggons and stages. He built three forts, Reno, Phil Kearny, and C. F. Smith, on the trail and it was near Fort Phil Kearny in December 1866 that Lieutenant Colonel Fetterman and his whole force of eighty-one men were exterminated by a much larger band of Sioux, led by Crazy Horse. More effective action against the hostiles was demanded in the press and in Congress, especially as the Cheyennes and Arapahoes had redoubled their depredations farther south since the Sand Creek massacre. A peace commission meeting at Fort Laramie decided to evacuate the Powder river area and thus abandon the Army's policing of the Bozeman Trail, but General William Tecumseh Sherman, a member of the commission, put in a minority report to the effect that 'all [Indians]

[1] The details of the massacre at Sand Creek and the number of Indians killed are still hotly disputed, but Chivington's responsibility for his men's excesses is not, and was even admitted by himself. The Congressional investigation into the affair disclosed much damning evidence (*U.S. Senate Reports of Committees*, 39th Congress, Second Series, Document No. 156), and this was quoted at length by Helen Hunt Jackson in *A Century of Dishonor* (1881). J. P. Dunn, in *Massacres of the Mountains* (1886), Chapter XIII, pp. 342–82, attempts a defence of Chivington, and concludes 'as a matter of retaliation and a matter of policy, whether these people were justified in killing women and children at Sand Creek is a question to which the answer does not come so glibly . . . Sand Creek is far from being the climax of American outrages on the Indian' (p. 382).

[2] Hanging was the greatest humiliation an Indian could suffer. One brave, condemned and in irons, cut off his own feet in order to be able to escape the hangman.

who cling to their old hunting grounds are hostile and will remain so until killed off . . . we must take chances and clean out Indians as we encounter them'. His former comrade-in-arms in the G.A.R., General Philip Sheridan, new commander of the Department of Missouri, had at his disposal only 2,600 men, of whom 1,200 were cavalry, to look after all the Central Plains, and General Hancock, in the Northern Plains, was even worse off, despite having such formidable Indian

fighters at their disposal as 'Buffalo Bill' Cody (who now became Sheridan's chief scout) and George Custer, another 'boy general' – like Mackenzie – of the Civil War, but now back to his substantive rank of Lieutenant-Colonel. Not much could be done with an army of this size to cover all the West. Custer's book, *My Life on the Plains*, published in the year of his death, speaks of frustration after frustration. Custer was no friend of the Indian, but at least he wanted to be allowed to fight him properly.[1]

[1] George Armstrong Custer, *My Life on the Plains* (St Louis, 1876), was reissued in a greatly expanded form – from 330 to 590 pages – as *Wild Life on the Plains* 'by a Corps of Competent Authors and Artists' in 1891. Custer's name does not appear on the title page of that new edition, though his part of the text was reprinted from the original plates.

Ten difficult years of Indian warfare which spanned the period between the Fetterman massacre and Custer's defeat at the Little Bighorn witnessed no other reverses comparable to these for the United States Army in the West. The transcontinental railroads split the buffalo herds of the plains and first the southern and then the northern herds were exterminated. The Plains Indians, deprived of the main basis of their economy – in part by the 'buffalo hunters' for the commercial value of the hides and the bones, partly as a deliberate policy of starving out the Indians – gradually let themselves be hounded into reservations, as 'wards' or pensioners of the Government, there to attempt to settle down to agriculture or cattle-ranching, if they turned their hands to anything at all. Those who continued to put up even a token resistance were only the most resolute, the most untameable and the ones possessing outstanding leaders. This was the age of the last generation of great Indian heroes.

Two of these heroes were Crazy Horse and Sitting Bull. Both were Teton Sioux (or 'Lacotas' as they called themselves), but Crazy Horse belonged to the Oglala branch of the tribe and Sitting Bull to the Hunkpapa. Both these men came to overshadow Red Cloud, the great war chief of the Sioux, who had driven the Americans from the Bozeman trail in 1868. After he made his peace with the white man and agreed to settle at the agency that was given his name, Red Cloud, the hero of eighty coups, was pushed aside by these younger men, to whom continued resistance, against whatever odds, was a holy duty inspired by their dreams. Crazy Horse was the son of a medicine-man of the same name, and Sitting Bull a medicine-man in his own right. The former was primarily a man of action, the latter a planner and schemer. In his own day Sitting Bull achieved the greater fame, which was not exactly dimmed by his participation in Buffalo Bill's Wild West Show during the 1880s, but Crazy Horse (who was killed while a prisoner in 1877) has latterly been claimed as his equal, if not his superior, as the last effective war leader of the Sioux.[1] It is clear that the Indians they led and inspired did not seek to place the one above the other, for they performed different functions in peace and in war, and were at the heads of different groups in a loose federation of tribes and sub-tribes. When the

[1] Mari Sandoz in *Crazy Horse* (New York, 1942), and Alvin M. Josephy in *The Patriot Chiefs* take this view, but William Brandon in *Indians* (p. 347) thinks that revisionism has gone too far, saying, 'There was a fashion for some years among Western historians of belittling Sitting Bull's importance: recent scholarship seems to have restored him to the place of eminence he held in his own day.'

old warrior Kicking Bear painted his celebrated pictograph[1] of the Battle of Little Bighorn, in 1898, he put Crazy Horse and Sitting Bull side by side, and the same size, in the middle of the battlefield, along with Rain-in-the-Face and himself. When Sitting Bull was interviewed by a journalist during his exile in Canada he made it clear that he himself was never in the thick of the fight and never once saw Custer alive. He was guarding the village and directing the packing-up of the lodges by the squaws[2] in case they had to move away.

Crazy Horse first achieved prominence during the Fetterman massacre of December 1866, when he was already a 'shirt wearer' at the age of twenty-four – the age at which Custer had become a brevet brigadier-general, a comparable rank. From that time on he was in nearly every important engagement of the Sioux and their allies with the American Army, until the end.[3] Black Kettle had been killed on the Washita river in Oklahoma, in an engagement with Custer which earned this dashing officer the title of 'Squaw-killer' among the Indians – Long Hair the Squaw-Killer – because they claimed that thirty-eight women and children were slaughtered along with about a hundred warriors. The heart had already gone out of Black Kettle even before Sand Creek, and those Cheyennes who continued to resist now tended to throw in their lot with Crazy Horse and the Sioux. Crazy Horse never lost a battle with the Americans and never signed a treaty with them. As a resistance leader Red Cloud was a 'used-up man' after his famous visit to Washington in 1870, where he was wined and dined by President Grant. His speech on Indian grievances at the Cooper Union Institute in New York, though, indicated that he still had great potentialities as a lobbyist, and he might have served the Indian cause better by remaining among Eastern fleshpots than by returning to play a Quisling role on the North Platte. During this return visit to Washington he made no progress in his efforts to keep for the Sioux their hunting grounds south of the Platte, and in 1873 he acquiesced in the re-

[1] Now in the Southwest Museum at Los Angeles, and reproduced here as plate 23a.

[2] *Wild Life on the Plains*, pp. 407–16. Sitting Bull was very positive about his inactive role in the battle: 'You did not personally witness the rest of the big fight? You were not engaged in it?' asked the anonymous journalist, and he replied, 'No, I have heard it from the warriors.' (*Ibid.*, p. 412.)

[3] See further, Robert Utley, *The Last Days of the Sioux Nation* (New Haven, Conn., 1963), and his *The Custer Legend* (New York, 1962). Mr Utley, Chief Historian of the National Park Service, was once an historian at the Custer Battlefield National Monument.

21. The Medicine Man, by Charlie Russell.

22. Three great Indian leaders (*a*) *top left*, Sitting Bull, medicine-man of the Hunkpapa Sioux; (*b*) *right*, Quanah Parker, head chief of the Comanches, son of a Comanche chief and a captive white woman; (*c*) Chief Joseph of the Nez Percé. The photographs of Sitting Bull and Chief Joseph are by F. Jay Haynes, that of Quanah Parker by Hutchings.

23*a*. An Indian picture of 'Custer's Last Stand' – the Battle of the Little Bighorn, 25 June 1876. The four standing figures represent (left to right) Sitting Bull, Rain-in-the-Face, Crazy Horse, and the artist Kicking Bear, whose footsteps encircle a slain enemy scout. Custer is centre left with white hat.

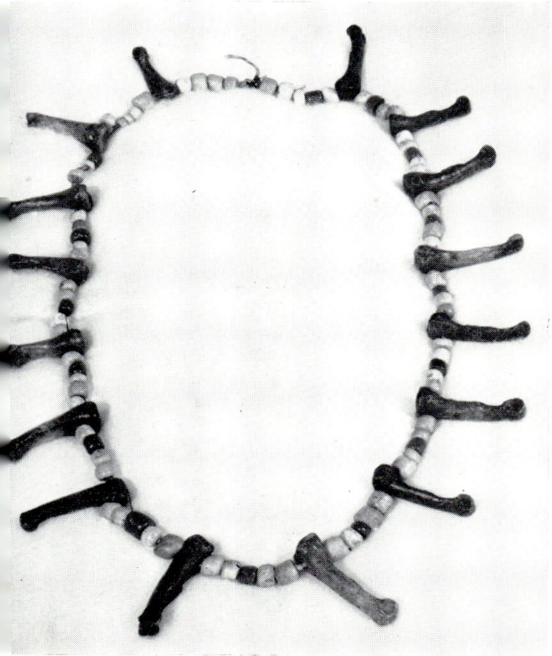

23*b*. Finger-bone necklace, made by a Sioux warrior from 16 Trigger fingers of members of 7th Cavalry killed at the Little Bighorn.

It was acquired in exchange for food by Mrs Cora Davis, a schoolteacher in the Rosebud Indian Reservation between 1896 and 1908. Months after acquiring the necklace she learned whose fingers they were and who had taken them. One of the young students from the warrior's family confided in her, 'Custer men – trigger fingers'.

24*a*. Geronimo and Nachez on horses – a posed photograph made by Fly, 1886.

24*b*. The End of the Frontier! – Geronimo (top hat) and friends in assorted peace bonnets, Oklahoma, *c*. 1905.

moval of his agency northward to the White river. This was a threat to the continued Indian possession of their 'holy land' in the Black Hills, by which Sitting Bull set such store, and drew the dissident Sioux and Cheyenne groups closer together in their 'retreat' on the Rosebud river in Montana. The Northern Pacific Railroad survey parties were probing through the Yellowstone country at that time, protected by 'Long Hair the Squaw-Killer' himself and his 7th United States Cavalry, now transferred from Oklahoma. They had several skirmishes with Crazy Horse's Indians that year, but in 1874 Custer was back with a much larger force, with which he decided to reconnoitre the Black Hills and test rumours that they were full of gold. This was probably the most provocative and questionable episode in the whole career of the 'Glory Hunter', as one of his biographers has called him, and he certainly exceeded both the letter and the spirit of General Sheridan's orders. Prospectors and other gold-hungry civilians followed him into the Black Hills, and even if the Army had tried very hard to remove them (which it did not) it probably would not have succeeded, for Custer's force only numbered 1,200, including newspaper correspondents, government scientists, and the usual Custer family hangers-on. Crazy Horse declared open season on the prospectors (for this was Indian country, still guaranteed to the red man by the treaty of 1868 and subsequent solemn promises in Washington). The prospectors on their side howled for protection, and in 1875 Red Cloud was again taken to Washington for a new round of dissipation and arm-twisting. More and more of the Reservation Sioux and Cheyennes went off to join the hostiles under Crazy Horse, sensing that a sell-out of the Black Hills was imminent. Twenty thousand Indians flocked to the Red Cloud agency to meet the United States commissioners, but the Oglala and the Hunkpapa Sioux were conspicuous by their absence. The day was saved for the moment by Red Cloud demanding the astronomical sum of $600 million for the Black Hills, to which the commissioners, perhaps mindful of the recent 'bargain basement' Alaska purchase,[1] countered with a niggardly $6 million offer, and the council dispersed. The Sioux were all ordered into the agencies and, when large numbers of them disobeyed, the Department of the Interior, in the early spring of 1876, turned their 'pacification' over to the Army. By 1 March General George Crook had opened his campaign against the hostiles. It began badly when, some days later, Colonel J. J. Reynolds attacked the camp

[1] From Russia for $7,200,000, in 1867. New Mexico and California had cost only $15 million in 1848, and the Louisiana Territory a similar sum in 1803.

of Two Moons and his Cheyennes (who were actually on their way to the agency with peaceful intent) and though destroying it, were forced to retreat. Reynolds was court-martialled and Crook deprived of a useful base for further operations on the Powder river. Crook returned to the Platte, and Two Moons, his mind changed by this unprovoked attack, joined forces with Crazy Horse. Crazy Horse was now named head of all the Oglalas, in peace and in war, and at the Sun Dance ceremonies of the Hunkpapa early in June, Sitting Bull announced the imminence of a fierce battle, based upon his visions. This was a fairly safe prediction, for Crook, as part of a three-pronged attack under himself, General Gibbon, and General Terry, who was in over-all command, was already advancing again up the Rosebud river. On 17 June a skirmish since dignified as 'the Battle of the Rosebud' occurred, in which Crook lost nine soldiers and a number of auxiliaries, and Crazy Horse, who was himself in the thick of the fight, eleven braves. Both sides withdrew, Crook considering that he needed reinforcements before advancing again. It was this decision, no doubt prudent, which left General Terry, with Custer's 7th Cavalry under his direct command, to advance alone. Custer's precipitate rush up the Rosebud ahead of the other two forces under Terry's command led him to the exposed position on the Little Bighorn river on 25 June which cost him and all the men of five companies of the 7th Cavalry their lives. Two hundred and fifty men died on the 'last stand' and about forty survivors of the three companies under Major Reno and the three under Captain Benteen, who were able to beat a retreat, were wounded. The Indians, who numbered several thousands, also retreated, without waiting for Gibbon and Terry. They had won a battle, but it soon became obvious that they had lost the war. The whole American nation, aroused and humiliated by the news of what has been called 'this moment of truth' just before the centennial celebrations of Independence were due to take place, both expected and insisted upon a massive retaliation. By September, Crook, greatly reinforced, was 'mopping up'. Sitting Bull led a handful of his tribe across the border into Alberta in February 1877 rather than surrender; Crazy Horse finally surrendered at the Red Cloud Agency (Crook had meanwhile deposed Red Cloud in favour of Spotted Tail, an even more amenable collaborator) in May 1877. In September Crook had Crazy Horse arrested and confined at Fort Robertson, where he was bayoneted to death 'trying to escape'. Red Cloud, looking on, shouted to the soldiers 'shoot to kill'. Some of the Oglala escaped, leaderless, into Canada.

In the Pacific North-west the same year (1877) started the remarkable rearguard action of Chief Joseph of the Nez Percés, who, driven by the advance of the mining frontier out of the hunting grounds that had been assigned to them in Idaho, after their earlier removal from Oregon, retreated eastwards into Montana with about six hundred of his people, only two hundred of whom were warriors. It was a forlorn trek, for there was nowhere for them to go except into the lands from which the Sioux, the Cheyennes, and the Blackfoot had just been expelled. Pursued and harried by the United States soldiers, Joseph evaded them for nearly 1,500 miles and halted only when he mistakenly thought that he had reached Canadian soil. Here he was forced to surrender with only fifty of his braves still capable of fighting, and sent with the survivors of his band into exile in the Indian Territory – instead of back to Idaho, as General Miles, to whom he surrendered, had promised. That was the end of the Nez Percés as a nation.

Apache resistance lasted a little longer. It was probably hardened by the harsh instruction of General Carleton in 1862 that 'All Indian men of that tribe are to be killed whenever and wherever you can find them.' This gave the Apache braves a desperation and intransigence they might not otherwise have maintained, under constant pressure, for another quarter-century. They were also embittered by the fact that the Americans, when they came into the South-west, continued the traditional Spanish and Mexican practice of making slaves of Apache women and children. As late as 1866 over two thousand Indian slaves were held by white people in Arizona and New Mexico.[1] The Apaches had at first sought to make friends with the Americans, possibly because the 'White Eyes' were thought to be the hereditary enemies of the hated Mexicans, but they were not trusted and their overtures were repulsed. Red Sleeves (*Mangas Coloradas*) was brutally flogged by white goldminers in New Mexico; Cochise was shot and wounded while parleying with Army representatives under a flag of truce; both these men went on the warpath against the Americans when the outbreak of the Civil War left the Arizona frontier ill guarded. By 1863 General Carleton arrived on his campaign of extermination and Red Sleeves was tricked into peace talks, at which he was murdered, before the end of the year. Even Colonel Kit Carson, no Indian-lover, found Carleton's orders too harsh, and accepted Apache surrenders as previously he had done those of the Navajos, and then let his prisoners depart in peace. The Apache survivors retreated into the mountains after the all-out campaign

[1] Brandon, *op. cit.*, p. 384.

against them in 1864. The 'war of extermination' ended with the unsavoury Camp Grant massacre at Tucson in 1876, when a civilian mob lynched eighty-five Apaches who had surrendered and were under Army protection there. The war had cost over $40 million and the Apache were still unsubdued. Conciliation was then tried, under the guidance of that very experienced Indian fighter General Crook.[1] Crook used Apache to catch Apache, his scouts being recruited from pacified sections of the tribe, which had many branches. By 1875 the Apaches who had not escaped across the border into Mexico had been herded into reservations, pacified after a fashion. Cochise, by now a moderating influence, died on the reservation in 1874, and Crook was transferred to the Black Hills to operate against the Sioux the next year. By 1876 the Apache were on the warpath again, and remained so for another decade, led by Victorio (who was killed in 1880) and Geronimo. Arbitrary treatment contrary to Crook's promises, and at times almost a return to the old extermination policy, were the chief causes of this, and Crook was brought back south in 1882 to pacify them once more. By 1886 Geronimo, having been pursued into Mexico by Crook, was talked into surrendering, but escaped while being escorted back to the reservation. General Miles, replacing Crook, received Geronimo's final surrender, saying (according to Geronimo's *Autobiography*), 'While I live you will not be arrested.' But Geronimo was almost immediately taken prisoner and sent off to exile in Florida. Miles even sent General Crook's loyal Apache scouts into exile as well, for the Army and people of the United States had by now acquired an almost pathological hatred of the Apache. (It was about this time, too, that the gangsters of the Paris 'tenderloin' districts began to be called 'Apaches' and a New-World phobia thus transferred to the Old.)

The Apache were, of course, not prepossessing either in their appearance or in their habits. No European or American could ever glamorize *them* into noble savages. They wore neither feathers nor buckskin, but loose-fitting smocks, shapeless trousers, and floppy hats, or headscarves which made them look like pirates or worse. Even General Crook – who jeopardized his career by arguing their case for better

[1] He was said to admire the Apache ('No Indian has more virtues,' claimed his adjutant, Captain J. G. Bourke), and the Apaches to trust him. Only Geronimo, old, embittered, interned, and turned pious, contributed a sour note by saying of Crook, 'I have suffered much from such unjust orders as those of Crook. Such acts have caused much distress to my people. I think that General Crook's death was sent by the Almighty as a punishment for the many evil deeds he committed' (according to S. M. Barratt, who set down Geronimo's autobiography from dictation).

treatment in Washington – never grew to like them. Geronimo lived on until 1909, having been transferred from Florida to Alabama and then to Fort Sill in Oklahoma and given his freedom. The old man made one last expedition into the white man's country in 1903, when he visited the fair at St Louis which commemorated the centennial of the Louisiana Purchase. Here he sold photographs of himself, showing him kneeling with a rifle and scowling his 'hatred', for two bits each to gawping tourists. He was, in fact, by that time a harmless-looking old patriarch, all passion spent.[1]

Chief Joseph, though a much gentler man than Geronimo, and much more handsome, and who, according to General Sherman, 'abstained from scalping, let captive women go free, and did not commit indiscriminate murder of peaceful families' during his famous retreat, was accorded very much the same treatment as the implacable Apache, and met very much the same fate. He was allowed to lead back the remnants of his people from internment in the Indian Territory to a new reservation in northern Washington in 1885, and there he died in 1904, still far from his beloved Wallowa valley.

Another resistance leader who at last made his peace with the white man fared somewhat better. Quanah Parker, who was a half-breed, son of a Comanche chief and a captive white woman named Cynthia Ann Parker, fought the intruder on his hunting grounds until 1874, but then settled down on a reservation in western Oklahoma, near Fort Sill, and collaborated with the Indian agents and army officers in every possible way to keep his fellow-Indians in order and out of trouble. On their side the whites recognized him as a chief and eventually made him a judge in the 'Court of Indian Offences' a quasi-legal tribunal which existed from 1886 to 1901. Quanah and his fellow-Indian judges dispensed 'a rough and ready type of justice'[2] and performed a valuable function on the reservation, but a new rule, prescribing that no person could be a judge in one of these courts who was a polygamist, deprived him of his seat on the bench in 1898. Meanwhile he had increased the number of his wives from five to seven and had invited the Commissioner for Indian Affairs to select the wives he should discard. It is said that the commissioner was not equal to this task.[3] Quanah Parker continued loyally to serve the cause of good

[1] See plates 24a and 24b.

[2] W. T. Hagan, 'Quanah Parker: Indian Judge' in J. Ross Toole (ed.), *Probing the American West*, p. 75.

[3] *Ibid.*, p. 77.

relations between red man and white until his death in 1911, and in 1907 he was put on the telephone by a grateful agency, at government expense. In 1905 he had ridden in Teddy Roosevelt's inaugural parade – a Western-type Roman triumph for that 'Cowboy at the White House'.

Spotted Tail, once one of the most active of the Sioux war leaders, surrendered himself at Fort Laramie as one of those responsible for the Grattan massacre in 1855 and for an attack on a stage coach a little earlier. Treated more humanely than the Minnesota Sioux in St Paul were to be in 1862, Spotted Tail never again gave serious trouble to the white men. Indeed, like Red Cloud, he was regarded by many other Indians as far too supine. He went to Washington with Red Cloud and at the 'Spotted Tail Agency' received many favours from the Army and the agents who were at last beginning to concede that a live Indian could also be a good one. It is ironical that Spotted Tail was to meet his death early in the 1880s at the hands of a really 'bad' Indian, Crow Dog, who murdered him (presumably for being a 'collaborator') and then, after conviction and being condemned to death, went scot-free, through the Supreme Court deciding that the jurisdiction of the federal courts did not extend to the reservations. The 'pacified' Indians were therefore not left in peace, even in the 1880s and 1890s. If the white man did not starve them to death by failing to give them their meagre promised rations, or by moving them on to even more barren reservations, the Indian resistance movement, though by then broken up and more or less underground, might 'get' them. While he lived Spotted Tail was only too conscious of the double jeopardy in which he had placed himself. The story is told by an old-timer in Indian country, where the 'hostiles' were still active, that he observed a group of Indians approaching. He and his companions readied their guns and waited. When the Indians were near enough it was observed that they carried a long banner stretched out in front of them by two braves. On it were inscribed the words:[1]

SPOTTED TAIL AND HIS BAND OF FRIENDLY SIOUX

A Sioux who never exactly became 'friendly', but who did eventually bury the hatchet to the extent of returning (in 1881) from his self-

[1] William M. Breackenridge, *Helldorado: Bring Law to the Mesquite* (Boston, 1928), p. 49. 'Winter of 1867 – near Sidney, Nebraska (about twenty miles east of Julesburg): The Indians had a large white canvas on which was painted in large letters, "Spotted Tail's band of friendly Sioux". In case the soldiers caught them away from their camp at North Platte, they could hold it up so that it could be read at a long distance, and they would not be fired upon.'

imposed exile in Canada, and refighting his battles (it is hoped without rancour) for the benefit of the spectators at Buffalo Bill's Wild West Show (in 1885), was Sitting Bull. His status as an Indian leader may still be debatable, but the dignity of his behaviour in his days of adversity and while he was letting himself be exhibited to the public by his former enemies is not in doubt. He did not fight again after Little Bighorn, but this failed to save him from a fate as cruel as that of Crazy Horse, or of Spotted Tail, for he was shot and killed by Indian police in the service of the Standing Rock Agency (where he had been directed to take up his abode in 1883) while being placed under preventive arrest for suspected intention of participating in the Ghost Dance demonstrations which had broken out among the Sioux in the year 1890. It is obvious that an easy excuse was taken to get rid of a man who was a possible leader or organizer of another Sioux outbreak, but there is no evidence whatsoever that he had any renewed hostile intentions.[1] 'Buffalo Bill' Cody, his old associate in war- and grease-paint, tried to meet Sitting Bull at Standing Rock once again, a short time before the latter was shot in the back by Agent McLaughlin's police, but was prevented by the agent from doing so! McLaughlin even tried to get Bill drunk and incapable in order to stop him, but had in the end to call in the Army, because the colonel had a very strong head. This frustrated meeting, think Buffalo Bill's biographers,[2] might, had it taken place, have saved Sitting Bull's life, for Bill would have protected him from victimization. But in 1891 Bill did recruit some of the ex-Ghost Dancers for his Wild West Show. He did not, nevertheless, put the Ghost Dance into the act, though he used the 'Peace Meeting at Pine Ridge' for a poster illustration.[3]

The Ghost Dance craze did not arise until Indian resistance had been broken; it was a gospel of despair. It was not a resistance movement, not even one advocating passive resistance, so much as belief in a miraculous deliverance from the white man and his depredations. Dead Indian heroes would return to life and the buffalo in their myriads come back to the plains. A golden age for the red man would exist once more. The chief prophet of this belief was Wovoka, a Paiute in Nevada who had been brought up by Christians, and who proclaimed

[1] See Utley, *Last Days of the Sioux Nation* (op. cit), and Stanley Vestal, *Sitting Bull* (Norman, Oklahoma, 1963), *passim.*

[2] V. Weybright and H. B. Sell, *Buffalo Bill and the Wild West* (New York and London, 1955), p. 190.

[3] *Ibid.*, p. 193.

the second coming of a Messiah for early in 1891, in words that oddly jumbled Indian and Christian ideas together. Some accounts call him 'Johnson Sides, the Peacemaker . . . well known to all people living along the line of the Central Pacific Railroad, in the vicinity of Reno and Winnemuca, Nevada'.[1] Whatever he is called, and however improbable that stretch of the Central Pacific between a latter-day Sodom and a new Gomorrah, as a site for the rise of a new religion, Wovoka's (or Johnson Sides') creed rapidly travelled eastwards to influence tribes as far away as Montana and the Dakotas. The Sioux, smarting under the forced purchase in 1889 by a Congressional commission headed by ex-Governor Foster of Ohio, and General George Crook, their old enemy, of vast areas of their reservation, in return for additional annuities and another million pounds of beef per year (which was not forthcoming) held a great council at Wounded Knee Creek in the spring of 1890. Here the Chief Two Lance presented the new creed to them, 'brought from the country of the Utes'. No weapons were to be used. 'We are simply to pray and trust in the Messiah and dance as he shall command.' The Ghost Dances went on all through the summer and autumn, embellishments being added, like the wearing of the ghost-shirt that was guaranteed to make an Indian impervious to the white man's bullets, until the agency whites became thoroughly, though unjustifiably, alarmed, and began to fear another Indian outbreak. That was why they moved in on potential trouble-makers like Sitting Bull, long before any overt acts on their part. Sitting Bull's arrest and murder (for such it was) was an act of panic on the part of the white agent, McLaughlin, who even admitted that, in conversation with him, Sitting Bull had expressed some scepticism concerning the Messiah-cult and a willingness to test its validity.[2]

The news of the death of Sitting Bull threw the Sioux in South Dakota into a frenzy such as the Ghost Dance craze could not of itself have caused and led to the tragic events at Wounded Knee at the end of December 1890. At first hundreds of warriors made off for the inaccessible Badlands, there to attempt to establish an impregnable fortress. After a Ghost Dance lasting thirty hours, during which 'people went into trances by the dozen . . . several remained in trances as long as twelve hours . . . People were so excited they trembled all over, their eyes rolled and the muscles of their faces twitched',[3] a Council

[1] *Wild Life on the Plains*, p. 533. [2] *Ibid.*, p. 567.

[3] According to Louis Shargraux, a half-breed interpreter participating in the peace parleys. *Ibid.*, pp. 576–7.

was held and General Brooke's peace commission listened to. Then the Ghost Dance went on for another two full days. Two Strike and Crow Dog (the slayer of Spotted Tail) then accepted the offer that 'the Agent will forgive you if you will return now, give you more rations, but not permit you to dance', but the band under Short Bull, after reluctantly following them for some distance, decided to return to the Badlands. The 7th Cavalry, under Colonel Forsythe, were ordered after them by General Miles, from his headquarters in Chicago. Many more Indians subsequently came in peaceably to the Red Cloud Agency, but a group led by Big Foot did not, and were caught up with on 27 December at Wounded Knee. Here Big Foot came forward alone and formally surrendered to Major Whiteside. There were about 150 warriors, 250 squaws, and a large number of children with him. The white troops numbered about 2,500. The next morning, while the Indians were being disarmed, some braves were alleged to have fired on the soldiers with weapons they had concealed, but a great deal of contrary evidence exists as to exactly where the provocation came from. Still it was enough for the trigger-happy 7th Cavalry, whose motto was 'Remember Custer', and they turned the Hotchkiss quick-firing machine-guns they were now armed with on to the unfortunate Sioux. Some thirty soldiers were killed, but nearly all the Indians were mown down, women and children as well as men. 'It was the saddest, apparently the most senseless of all the tragedies connected with the dealings of this nation with its "wards",' concluded the by no means pro-Indian account in *Wild Life on the Plains*,[1] published the following year. It was also the last, for Wounded Knee and an Indian attack on a supply train (which was repulsed by the teamsters) at about the same time were 'all the real fighting in that which has passed into history as the great Sioux outbreak'.[2] It can hardly now be maintained, as was thought at the time, that 'it promised to involve all the tribes of the northwest, and extend its devastating terrors from the Missouri to the Pacific' or that 'the master mind of Sitting Bull had thought out the chance for the red man in such a cult conflict'.[3]

The Ghost Dance cult was fundamentally harmless, perhaps indeed a good way of working off the frustrations of the by then almost helpless Indian tribes, if only the white man had not remembered

[1] P. 585. [2] *Ibid.*, p. 588.

[3] Compare the attitude expressed in *Wild Life on the Plains* from which these last two quotations are taken, with the recent scholarly reappraisal by Robert Utley, in *The Last Days of the Sioux Nation.*

Custer too vividly and discerned a scalp hunter inside every ghost shirt. Two Lance in his harangue had counselled peace and called for prayer; it was not so much another Little Bighorn that the Ghost Dancers longed for, but for the Big Rock Candy Mountain. Said Little Wound, 'When I fell in the trance a great and grand eagle came and carried me over a great hill where there was a village such as we used to have before the Whites came into the country. The tepees were all of buffalo hides and we made use of the bow and arrow, there being nothing of White Man's manufacture in the beautiful land. Nor were any White permitted to live there. The broad and fertile lands stretched in every direction and were most pleasing to my eye,' while Kicking Horse, a Sioux who claimed to have just returned from heaven, told the following curious story:[1]

> He entered heaven through a hole in the sky, and saw the Great Spirit, who told him that the Indians had suffered long enough, and that the time had come for their deliverance. They were to occupy the earth once more, which had been taken from them by the Whites, but they were not to kill or molest them. The Great Spirit told him that the earth was getting full of holes, and many places were rotten. He would gradually send a wave of earth 20 feet or more over the country, and that it would move slowly. The Indian must keep dancing so as to be on top, and when the wave passed all the pale-faces would be buried underneath and the Indians would be on top. All the dead Indians would be restored to life again, and the buffaloes, horses, game, and their old hunting grounds would be as they were hundreds of years ago, and the Indians would for all time in the future own and occupy the earth. All Indians who would not listen to the words of the prophet and keep dancing would be turned into fishes and dwell in the rivers and streams.
>
> He said that whilst talking to the Great Spirit the devil came to them. He describes the devil as being very tall, with immense knee-joints, a monster mouth and long teeth. He was covered all over with coarse hair. He asked for half of the people, meaning the Indians, but the Great Spirit replied: 'You can have none of my chosen Indian children, but you can have all the Whites.'

Revenge is sweet, if only in words!

[1] *Wild Life on the Plains*, pp. 536–7.

CHAPTER XI

The Cowman's Frontier

The Great Plains have been called the 'great obstacle',[1] and it is true that until the days of the cattle drives of the 1860s the American people did not seem to know what to do with them. The Spaniards had been equally nonplussed by these vast areas of 'cows and sky' – and deficient rainfall. Both peoples just treated the plains as a nasty experience to be got over as soon as possible so that they could press on to Quivira or El Dorado or to gather the golden apples of the Willamette valley. 'They were in reality seeking the familiar and shunning the necessity of working out new ways in the Plains.'[2]

The 'great obstacle' was not easily overcome – Coronado, Castañeda, Pike, and Long had not so grossly exaggerated its uselessness to civilized man at the state of technological advance of their time – but when rangy herds of mean-looking Mexican longhorns began to be propelled up into Texas by even meaner-looking Mexican *vaqueros* and Texas 'cowboys', a useful two-pronged weapon for dealing with its intransigence had at last appeared. The Nueces valley began to fill up with such lean kine, which, finding there one blade of grass growing where none (in the deserts of Coahuila and other points south) had grown where they had been before, waxed fatter (but not yet fat), increased and multiplied, and began to low for a market. At about the same time or a little earlier the cattle-ranching era had also begun for California. Here, too, came the Mexican cattle with their lariat-twirling and seraped *vaqueros*, about whose equestrian skills the Boston merchants and young Mr Dana serving before the mast wrote home with bated breath. The age of hides and tallow in California, rather than an age of iron or silver, preceded the age of gold. Hides became the local currency, slightly more awkward to carry around shopping than gold-dust, but just as widely used as that commodity was later to become in those same valleys. The easy-going Spanish-Californians bought at high prices shoes made in Massachusetts from those very hides they had sold one to two dollars apiece, delivered at the cliff edge, in creak-

[1] Walter Prescott Webb, *The Great Plains*, p. 149.
[2] *Ibid.*, p. 149.

ing bullock-waggons. When the British fleet under Admiral Sir George Seymour came cruising up from Mexico to watch what Commodore Sloat was doing in July 1846 in Californian waters, the enterprising Abel Stearns (out of Lunenburg, Massachusetts, by way of Valparaiso) wrote to an employee from the *pueblo* of Los Angeles (his hide-shed was then one of the two buildings at the San Pedro anchorage down on the coast): 'I received yours of the first inst. in which you observe there is a prospect of some English men-of-war arriving. I hope it may be the Case and that they may want a plenty of beef . . . If you have a chance, try and make something out of it. John Bull is a lusty old fellow and has a stiff purse.'[1] Nearly every other American in California at the time thought that Seymour had come to establish a British colony in, or a British protectorate over, California, but Abel Stearns, faced with a surplus of *novillos*, thought only about supplying him with beef. Yet California's surplus cattle, unlike those of Texas, did not long remain in search of a market. Some had been driven up into Oregon for the American settlers there (of whom there were many more until the late 1840s than there were in California) and Ewing Young, it will be remembered,[2] had turned from fur trapping to ranching to engage in this trade as early as the 1830s – but even as long a drive as that soon became unnecessary, as beef-hungry miners and would-be miners poured into the now golden state in 1848 and 1949. Not for the last time did California thus solve a pressing economic problem in a unique way, and Abel Stearns' 'Cattle on a Thousand Hills'[3] soon made him one of the richest men in the state, without benefit of gold mines.

It was a much longer trek from hoof to mouth for the Texas longhorns. The cattle trails they blazed had to go from south to north, against the grain of the Westward movement, because while there was a surplus of cattle in the South there were shortages in the East as well as in the new settlements of the West and North-west. If the miners may be said to have pock-marked the map of the undeveloped West, then the Texas cattlemen can be claimed to have cross-hatched it. It was the second major assault by man on the Great American Desert and one which it did not survive. While the cattle kingdom, depending on the existence of the vast 'open range' of government land for grazing

[1] Abel Stearns to James Johnson, 3 July 1846. Printed from the Stearns Collection in the Huntington Library, San Marino, California, in J. A. Hawgood (ed.), *First and Last Consul* (San Marino, 1962), p. 82.

[2] See supra, p. 127.

[3] R. G. Cleland, *Cattle on a Thousand Hills* (San Marino, California, 1947), is the best account of the ranch cattle industry in California, and of Stearns' part in it.

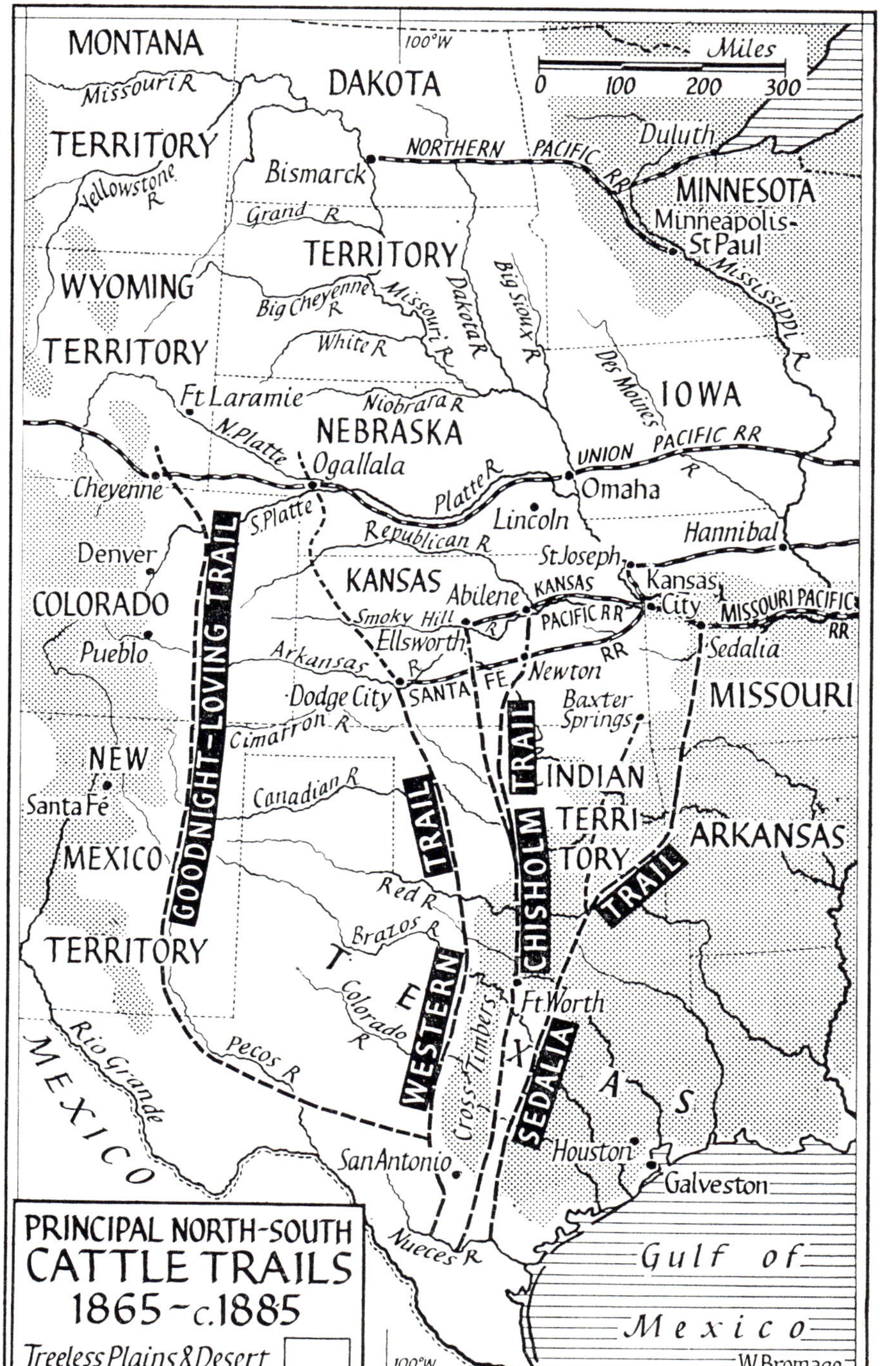
PRINCIPAL NORTH-SOUTH CATTLE TRAILS 1865–c.1885
Treeless Plains & Desert
Miles
0 100 200 300
100°W
MONTANA
TERRITORY
DAKOTA
TERRITORY
WYOMING
TERRITORY
MINNESOTA
IOWA
NEBRASKA
KANSAS
COLORADO
NEW MEXICO TERRITORY
INDIAN TERRITORY
MISSOURI
ARKANSAS
TEXAS
MEXICO
Missouri R
Yellowstone R
Grand R
Big Cheyenne R
Missouri R
White R
Dakota R
Big Sioux R
Des Moines R
Mississippi R
Niobrara R
N. Platte
Platte R
S. Platte
Republican R
Smoky Hill R
Arkansas R
Cimarron R
Canadian R
Red R
Brazos R
Colorado R
Pecos R
Rio Grande
Nueces R
Cross Timbers
Bismarck
Duluth
Minneapolis-St Paul
Ft Laramie
Ogallala
Cheyenne
Omaha
Lincoln
Hannibal
St Joseph
Kansas City
Denver
Pueblo
Abilene
Ellsworth
Newton
Sedalia
Dodge City
Baxter Springs
Santa Fé
Ft Worth
San Antonio
Houston
Galveston
NORTHERN PACIFIC RR
UNION PACIFIC RR
KANSAS PACIFIC RR
MISSOURI PACIFIC RR
SANTA FE RR
GOODNIGHT-LOVING TRAIL
WESTERN TRAIL
CHISHOLM TRAIL
SEDALIA TRAIL
Gulf of Mexico
W. Bromage

the herds as they found their way north, was developing, 'the frontier line was held practically stationary along the vicinity of the ninety-eighth meridian. During this period (which lasted, roughly, from 1840 to 1885) the agricultural frontier first jumped across the plains, established itself on the Pacific slope, and then began to work backwards.'[1] All this, while mighty convenient to the cattlemen (Webb might have added), badly knocked askew the as yet unformulated 'Turner hypothesis'[2] of the orderly advance *westward* of civilization and settlement behind a 'cutting edge' of frontiersmen.[3] One thing this grain-crossing did was to inject a way of life, hitherto Southern, indeed quasi-Mexican (especially in its vocabulary), on to the northern plains of Kansas and Nebraska, Colorado, Wyoming, and Montana and even on to Canada's prairie provinces. The 'cowboy culture' of the cattle kingdom was to penetrate far beyond the Missouri and Kansas railheads which were the first objectives of the trail herds. Soon the 'Texas Cowboy' was all over the Great Plains, sometimes appreciated, often resented; free-spending, painting the town red – and widely imitated. In the decades after the Civil War the spread of the 'cow culture' up out of Texas helped to knit the divided country together again and keep the West 'one society' – as it had always tended to be, even during the war. Men who had driven a herd of cattle all the way from the Rio Grande on to the Blackfoot reservation in Northern Montana – as did Andy Adams' outfit in his famous *Log of a Cowboy*[4] – could not but acquire a wide knowledge of their enormous country and an easy tolerance of sectional and local differences and idiosyncrasies. These differences sometimes caused trouble, for many of the cowhands were Confederate veterans, but the long drive tended to be a melting-pot rather than a tinder-box.[5] The railhead cow towns contained (like the mining camps)

[1] Webb, *The Great Plains*, p. 205.

[2] See further, Chapter XII.

[3] Though, even in 1893 F. J. Turner, in his famous essay, played relatively little attention to the significance of the cattle kingdom, he did say (*Frontier in American History*, p. 16), 'The ranges of the Great Plains, with ranch and cowboy and nomadic life, are things of yesterday and today . . . the effect of these great ranches on the subsequent agrarian history of the localities in which they existed should be studied', but he was obviously much more interested in the farmers' frontier.

[4] Boston and New York, 1903 and 1931. Cast in fictional form, but based upon actual experience, this is one of the best accounts ever written of life on the old cattle trails of the West.

[5] Lovell, the owner of the herd, 'had carried a musket in the ranks of the Union army', but young Tom 'couldn't help feeling friendly toward him, Yankee that he was' (Adams, *Log of a Cowboy*, pp. 12 and 23).

elements from all over the country, some good, some bad, but very few of them indifferent to the fact that here – as on the long trails, and the new ranches that were being established all over the Great Plains – a new type of frontier history was being made and a new type of American being forged. Owen Wister's 'ideal' cowboy was not a Texan in Texas, but a Virginian in Wyoming;[1] yet he and his fellow Virginians, New Yorkers, Vermonters, Kentuckians, and assorted mid-Westerners and North-westerners had to learn their craft (if not their manners) from the Texas cowboys up from the Rio Grande, the Nueces, and the Pecos. They might not readily acknowledge this debt, but it existed nevertheless.[2]

The word 'cowboy' seems at first to have been almost synonymous with cattle rustler. The Tory 'cowboys' of Westchester country, New York, in the American Revolution, plundered the cattle of the patriot 'skinners' and vice versa[3] and in the Texas revolution a 'cowboy' was one who ran Mexican-owned cattle across the Rio Grande in the general direction of Louisiana's markets. 'The name "cowboy" was even then – and still more emphatically later – one name for many crimes, since those engaged in it [*sic*] were mostly outlaws confessedly.'[4] The name had to travel far and have many rough edges rubbed off it before it could sit becomingly on the lithe and graceful shoulders of that perfect gentle knight, *sans peur* and *sans reproche*, Owen Wister's *Virginian*!

The first cattle king was of course a Texan, one Taylor White, who drove longhorn cattle to Louisiana long before the 1840s. When he moved to Texas in 1823

[1] *The Virginian* was published in 1902.

[2] Frantz and Choate, *The American Cowboy*, p. 35. 'It was the Texas cowboy who taught his northern cousin the techniques of handling cattle in the vastnesses of the open range . . . The Montana cowboy was a legitimate copy of the Texas cowboy, but he was just that, a copy of the original . . . the cattleman frontier was a Texas story from beginning to end.'

[3] See *A Dictionary of American English* (eds Craigie and Hurlbert), Vol. II, p. 658.

[4] C. W. Webber, *Tales of the Southern Border* (Philadelphia, 1853), p. 124, quoted by Franz and Choate, *op. cit.*, p. 74.

'his whole fortune was three cows and calves two small poneys a wife and three children, he now [1842] owns about 40,000 acres of land upwards of 90 negroes about thirty thousand head of cattle, has sixty thousand dollars in specie deposited in new orleans, marked and branded thirty seven hundred calves last spring and sold last fall in new orleans 11 hundred steers weighing about 1000 lbs each which he says cost him no more than 75 cents a head to drive them to market at orleans and what is extraordinary he cannot read or write and has made his fortune raising stock alone'.[1] Similar fortunes continued to be made by Texas cowmen, both lettered and unlettered, up to the outbreak of the Civil War in 1861. After the Mexican War had ended any possibility that their former Mexican owners would recover any of the herds marooned north of the Rio Grande, the unbranded longhorns – and some branded ones – became public property and increased exceedingly, especially in the Nueces valley. Various attempts were made to get these animals, almost valueless in Texas, to profitable markets. In addition to the drives to New Orleans some were shipped out by sea from Galveston and other Texas ports and roadsteads; others were driven up to Missouri, St Louis, Chicago, and even New York. This last operation took two whole seasons (despite a ride by train on the last leg, from Muncie, Indiana, to New York) in 1854. During the gold rush some were even driven to California and a steer worth less than $5 in Texas at that time could fetch $160 on the booming Pacific coast where the inrush of population had even overtaxed the supplies of 'cattle on a thousand hills'. But the way to California was long and hazardous and the Middle-Western farmers feared the Texas cattle fever, and so placed increasing obstacles in the way of the Texas drovers. In addition, Indian cattle thieves were a nuisance everywhere. From 1861 to 1865 the long-distance cattle drives were made impossible by war conditions, especially in border states like Kansas and Missouri. Most of the pre-war demand had been from the more populous North. An attempt to reopen the trade in 1866 proved disastrous; though over 250,000 Texas cattle were sent north and east that year, very few were ever sold at a profit;[2] Texas cattlemen – and their longhorns – were still not welcome there.

It required a stroke of genius to bring these Texas cattle into the packing stations, sleek, fat, and profitable, and this was provided by

[1] 'A Letter Book of Joseph Eve' in *Southwestern Historical Quarterly*, Vol. XLIII, No. 4 (April 1940), p. 488, quoted by Hogan, *Texas Republic*, p. 21.

[2] E. E. Dale, *The Range Cattle Industry* (Norman, Oklahoma, 1930), p. 50.

25*a*. A buffalo hunters' camp in the Texas Panhandle, 1874.

25*b*. California Cattle Drive, (1876–7), by James Walker.

26*a*. Harrows on the Grandin Farm, Red River Valley, and

26*b*. A Marsh self-binder drawn by oxen. Two photographs by F. Jay Haynes.

one Joseph McCoy – the authentic 'Real McCoy' – out of Illinois. After an unsuccessful attempt to interest the Missouri Pacific Railroad in his project he made a deal with the Hannibal and St Joseph and the Kansas Pacific for the transportation of cattle at preferential rates eastwards to Chicago, and he then set up his cattle barn, corrals, and scales at the end of the earth, or so it looked that summer of 1867, 'a small dead place . . . of about one dozen log huts', called Abilene.[1] Abilene's only merit, besides good grass and plentiful water, was that it was about to be reached by the railroad from the East. Despite assiduous advertising, both in Texas and along the trails, McCoy only attracted some twenty-five thousand cattle to Abilene in 1867; but it was the start of a movement, which, lasting until 1872, was to bring hundreds of thousands of Texas longhorns into Abilene each year, and to see both the birth of a new industry and the crystallization of a new frontier-type. 'Abilene, more than four hundred miles north of the Red River and nearly a thousand miles from the Nueces country, was to become the commercial capital of Texas . . . to know in prosperity a lustiness and a greed which would make it legend wherever cattlemen stopped to talk. It would be superseded by other and better towns . . . but Abilene would be the first and most fondly remembered . . . In Abilene the Texas cowboy was discovered and first became a distinct type, and here he first displayed for a national audience those extremes of temperament that make a hero.'[2]

By 1872 Abilene had grown more or less respectable (in 1871 Wild Bill Hickok, its trigger-happy marshal, proved too tough for it, and his commission was allowed to lapse), and, besides, the railroad had pushed out beyond it. Other cow towns arose as the railroad moved west, Ellsworth, Newton, Julesburg, Wichita, Hays City, Ogallala, Cheyenne, Laramie, and others. Dodge City, a little west of where the Santa Fé Railroad reached the Great Bend of the Arkansas river and near

[1] J. G. McCoy, *Historic Sketches of the Cattle Trade of the West and South West* (1940 edn, ed. R. P. Bieber, Glendale, California), p. 116 ff. McCoy's book, first published in 1874 when the cattle trails were still warm, has become a classic. Ralph Bieber has annotated his occasional inaccuracies and overstatements.

[2] Franz and Choate, p. 32.

Coronado's Quivira, was the last, the wildest and the most notorious of them all. Dodge City received and trans-shipped more than 250,000 head of Texas cattle a year during the boom of the late 1870s and early 1880s. 'In its moment of glory Dodge City was better known than Denver or St Paul or Kansas City.'[1] Andy Adams' *Log of a Cowboy* describes visits to both 'Dodge' and Ogallala. Adams gives Dodge rather a good name, thanks to its formidable peace officers:[2]

> 'I've been in Dodge every summer since '77,' said the old cowman, 'and I can give you boys some points. Dodge is one town where the average bad man of the West not only finds his equal, but finds himself badly handicapped. The buffalo hunters and range men have protested against the iron rule of Dodge's peace officers, and nearly every protest has cost human life. Don't ever get the impression that you can ride your horses into a saloon, or shoot out the lights in Dodge; it may go somewhere else, but it don't go there. So I want to warn you to behave yourselves. You can wear your six-shooters into town, but you'd better leave them at the first place you stop, hotel, livery, or business house. And when you leave town, call for your pistols, but don't ride out shooting; omit that. Most cowboys think it's an infringement on their rights to give up shooting in town, and if it is, it stands, for your six-shooters are no match for Winchesters and buckshot; and Dodge's officers are as game a set of men as ever faced danger.'
>
> Nearly a generation has passed since McNulta, the Texan cattle drover, gave our outfit this advice one June morning on the Mulberry, and in setting down this record, I have only to scan the roster of the peace officials of Dodge City to admit its correctness. Among the names that graced the official roster, during the brief span of the trail days, were the brothers Ed, Jim, and 'Bat' Masterson, Wyatt Earp, Jack Bridges, 'Doc' Holliday, Charles Bassett, William Tilman [Tilghman], 'Shotgun' Collins, Joshua Webb, Mayor A. B. Webster, and 'Mysterious' Dave Mather. The puppets of no romance ever written can compare with these officers in fearlessness. And let it be understood, there were plenty to protest against their rule; almost daily during the range season some equally fearless individual defied them.

To him it is Ogallala that is Gomorrah:[3]

> Below us in the valley of the South Platte, nestled Ogallala, the Gomorrah of the cattle trail. From amongst its half hundred build-

[1] Riegel, *America Moves West*, p. 521.
[2] Adams, *Log of a Cowboy* (1931 edn), pp. 191–2.
[3] *Ibid.*, pp. 259–61.

ings, no church spire pointed upward, but instead three fourths of its business houses were dance halls, gambling houses, and saloons. We all knew the town by reputation, while the larger part of our outfit had been in it before. It was there that Joel Collins and his outfit rendezvoused when they robbed the Union Pacific train in October, '77. Collins had driven a herd of cattle for his father and brother, and after selling them in the Black Hills, gambled away the proceeds. Some five or six of his outfit returned to Ogallala with him, and being money-less, concluded to recoup their losses at the expense of the railway company. Going eighteen miles up the river to Big Springs, seven of them robbed the express and passengers, the former yielding sixty thousand dollars in gold. The next morning they were in Ogallala, paying debts, and getting their horses shod. In Collins's outfit was Sam Bass, and under his leadership, until he met his death the following spring at the hands of Texas Rangers, the course of the outfit southward was marked by a series of daring bank and train robberies.

We reached the river late that evening, and after watering, grazed until dark and camped for the night. But it was not to be a night of rest and sleep, for the lights were twinkling across the river in town; and cook, horse, wrangler, and all, with the exception of the first guard, rode across the river after the herd had been bedded. Flood had quit us while we were watering the herd and gone in ahead to get a draft cashed, for he was as money-less as the rest of us. But his letter of credit was good anywhere on the trail where money was to be had, and on reaching town, he took us into a general outfitting store and paid us twenty-five dollars apiece. After warning us to be on hand at the wagon to stand our watches, he left us, and we scattered like lost sheep. Officer and I paid our loans to The Rebel, and the three of us wandered around for several hours in company with Nat Straw. When we were in Dodge, my bunkie had shown no inclination to gamble, but now he was the first one to suggest that we make up a 'cow', and let him try his luck at monte. Straw and Officer were both willing, and though in rags, I willingly consented and contributed my five to the general fund.

Every gambling house ran from two to three monte layouts, as it was a favorite game of cowmen, especially when they were from the far southern country. Priest soon found a game to his liking, and after watching his play through several deals, Officer and I left him with the understanding that he would start for camp promptly at midnight. There was much to be seen, though it was a small place, for the ends of the earth's iniquity had gathered in Ogallala. We wandered through the various gambling houses, drinking moderately,

> meeting an occasional acquaintance from Texas, and in the course of our rounds landed in the Dew-Drop-In dance hall. Here might be seen the frailty of women in every grade and condition. From girls in their teens, launching out on a life of shame, to the adventuress who had once had youth and beauty in her favor, but was now discarded and ready for the final dose of opium and the coroner's verdict – all were there in tinsel and paint, practicing a careless exposure of their charms. In a town which has no night, the hours pass rapidly, and before we were aware, midnight was upon us. Returning to the gambling house where we had left Priest, we found him over a hundred dollars winner, and, calling his attention to the hour, persuaded him to cash in and join us. We felt positively rich, as he counted out to each partner his share of the winnings! Straw was missing to receive his, but we knew he could be found on the morrow, and after a round of drinks, we forded the river.

Nevertheless, his outfit was better behaved in Ogallala than in Dodge City. In Dodge they had to paint the town red on the twenty-five dollars in gold advanced to each of them by the trail boss, but made such nuisances of themselves that they were shot up by peace officers (without material damage to man, but one of their horses was killed) on the way out. In Ogallala, on a second visit after getting the balance of their pay, 'Tom' and his two bunkies won fourteen hundred dollars playing monte at 'The Black Elephant', and departed quietly after buying new outfits, including 'cheap new suits the colour of which we never knew until the next day'.

> As we scaled the bluffs we halted for our last glimpse of the lights of Ogallala, The Rebel remarked, 'Boys I've traveled some in my life, but that little hole back there could give Natchez-under-the-hill cards and spades and then outhold her as a tough town.'[1]

Not every outfit was five months on the way as was that of foreman Jim Flood, which took Andy Adams' *alter ego* young 'Tom' along as a trail hand in the early spring of 1882, and after receiving the herd from across the Rio Grande river in Old Mexico, delivered it intact on the Blackfoot Indian reservation in the north-west corner of Montana at the end of August. When all was over Don Lovell, the owner of the herd, took his cowboys to the railhead of the Northern Pacific at Silver

[1] Adams, *op. cit.*, p. 274. 'I stayed the night in Ogallala in 1952, seventy years after this, but the glory had departed. The little town was so dull that I went up to a motel in the Kingsley Dam resort area and spent the evening writing. I left at dawn without hearing even one shot!'

Bow, Montana, and stood drinks all round while they waited for the train. 'Turn to and help wait on these thirsty Texans,' he said, 'and remember that there is nothing too rich for our blood today. This outfit has made one of the longest cattle drives on record, and the best is none too good for them.'[1]

The cattle drives to the northern railheads followed many trails, but the principal ones were the Sedalia Trail, opened up in 1866, but veering too far east into the wooded Ozarks to be followed in later years; the Chisholm Trail to Abilene via Fort Worth and the Indian Territory, resulting from McCoy's enterprising idea; the Goodnight-Loving Trail to the Pecos river and then north through New Mexico and Colorado and beyond; and the Western Trail (which Andy Adams' heroes followed in 1882) up through the later notorious cow towns of Dodge City, Kansas, and Ogallala, Nebraska, and thence into Montana across north-eastern Wyoming, or south-western Dakota. The Goodnight-Loving Trail was named after two well-known cattlemen who used it, and it belied its cosy name, for it went through Comanche country and was perhaps the most hazardous of all. Every one of these trails had to cross a number of eastward-flowing rivers, very few of them 'two miles wide and half an inch deep', like the Platte was

[1] Adams, *op. cit.*, p. 274.

claimed to be, for many were swift-flowing, deep and treacherous. In Andy Adams' book the trail-boss or foreman of one herd loses his life at one such crossing, and, at another, a full day is spent in improvising a bridge of brushwood and logs and cajoling the unwilling longhorns across this makeshift causeway, using, as a last resort, a bellowing calf as a decoy, lugged on the end of a rope and followed by its anxious mother. The inquisitive steers found it impossible to resist investigating this intriguing situation, and crowded across in her wake.

Only in the earliest years after the Civil War were the Texas cattle driven north principally for shipment east by rail, though this remained an important trade well after 1880. They were also used to stock the northern plains, there to be cross-bred with beef cattle of higher quality but lower stamina from the East; the expensive stud-bulls worth importing all this way went by rail. As the population of the northern Great Plains increased, Texas cattle were also used for local consumption there, after a period of fattening at the end of their long drives. This would have been the fate of most of the herd driven up by Andy Adams' outfit in 1882 from the Mexican border to the Blackfoot reservation in Montana. The Federal Government had undertaken to deliver beef cattle on to the Indian reservations regularly, and in most cases it fulfilled its obligations. The Indians, deprived of the now almost extinct buffalo herds and not yet acclimatized to subsistence agriculture or cattle ranching, might have starved without this 'subsidy'. Sometimes they did.

The total of the railhead shipments eastwards of Texas cattle up to 1880 were given by the Tenth Census Report[1] of the United States as nearly 4¼ million head. Of these nearly 1½ million passed through Abilene between 1867 and 1871, over a million through Wichita and Ellsworth between 1872 and 1875, and over a million through Dodge City and Ellis between 1876 and 1879. The record year was 1871 when over 700,000 Texas cattle reached Kansas. There had still been over 4 million longhorns in Texas in 1870, about as many as in 1860, despite the size and number of the long drives of the second half of that decade.

The cattle boom in the Great Plains continued until the mid-1880s and in its later years attracted large amounts of foreign capital. In the peak-price year of 1882 range cattle, worth only $7 or $8 a head in 1878, were fetching $30 to $35. As a result the drives increased and the northern range became overstocked. The Chicago packers slashed the prices they offered, in view of this glut, and cattle were back to $8 a

[1] Vol. III (1883), 'Statistics of Agriculture', p. 975.

head by 1885. The severe winter of 1885–6 brought disaster to many cattlemen and bankrupted even some of the large stockmen's corporations – like the Swan Company of Wyoming and the Niobra Company of Nebraska. Millions of cattle died that winter on the ranges and ranches.[1] 'The winter of 1885–1886 was the sort of sharp punch calculated to puncture permanently an overblown speculative bubble,'[2] and by 1887 prime beef cattle were down to under $2.00 per 100 lbs on the Chicago market. A 1200-lb steer, claims Walter Prescott Webb,[3] could net the owner as little as $5, after all shipping and other expenses had been met. The wheel had thus come full circle to the 'almost valueless' cattle which had roamed the Nueces valley a quarter-century earlier, threatening to become a pest.[4] An era in the history of the American frontier and in the development of the Great West was over, and within a generation! 'To sum it all up,' says Webb,[5] 'the collapse of 1885 converted ranching from an adventure into a business, which is today carried on with as much system as farming and manufacturing.' But this transition and the necessary readjustments took time. 'By 1892 the story of the frontier ranch and its cowboys had already been lived, and many cowboys were getting ready to reminisce in print and at cowboy reunions.'[6] It was not until after 1900 that the Western 'cattle business' began to take on its soulless modern form; not until around 1950 that the cowboy began to foresake his horse for a jeep and learn his songs from the radio, and the cattle barons to ride the range in air-conditioned Cadillac ranch waggons, with built-in bars and telephones, or to 'mend their fences' on stock-markets of a different kind via their own executive aircraft. 'Waiting for a Chinook'[7] took a long time, but when the warm winds began to blow again on the cattle industry it was, in the twentieth century, to become bigger than ever before. By then the romance had gone from it – or had it?

There never was very much romance about the cattlemen, the owners, the tycoons, 'the cattle kings',[8] any more than there was about

[1] See E. S. Osgood, *Day of the Cattleman* (Minneapolis, 1929), pp. 220–1.
[2] Franz and Choate, *op. cit.*, p. 66.
[3] Webb, *Great Plains*, p. 237.
[4] *Ibid.*, p. 212. [5] *Ibid.*, p. 240.
[6] Franz and Choate, *op. cit.*, p. 67.
[7] The title of Charles Russell's famous miniature water-colour picture of an emaciated steer 'drifting' before a snowstorm on the northern plains. The original is in the Gallery of The Historical Society of Montana. Enlarged copies, by the original artist, can be found in several other collections.
[8] As Lewis Atherton, their latest and best chronicler calls them, *The Cattle Kings* (Chicago, 1961), *passim*.

the mine-owners and the entrepreneurs who waxed rich out of the mining boom. Even the gifted turn-of-the-century novelist Frank Norris failed to make an exciting character out of Collis P. Huntington. John Mackay was almost ostentatiously unglamorous; Joseph McCoy was about as featureless as the Illinois prairies from which he hailed, and he obviously disapproved of the picturesque Texas cowboys out of whom he made his fortune;[1] the most romantic thing about Charlie Goodnight was his name.[2] It is the hired hands, from the trail boss or foreman down to the wrangler (and even including the cook, usually an ex-cowboy grown too old or too heavy for the saddle, and nearly always an 'ornery' character)[3] who have become the heroes of high romance, as imperishable as the knights of the Round Table and the paladins of Roncesvalles. The noble cowboy has followed the noble savage into literature, and has stayed in much more successfully. Eighty years after the frontier cowboy passed his apogee, three-quarters of a century after the open range disappeared from the West, more is written, sung, 'shot' or projected every year about the cowboy than about any other 'hero' of the American frontier, old or new – perhaps about all of them together. Acres of this effluvia are sheer pulp, following well-worn grooves and repeating stereotypes, but every now and then the cowboy frontier still produces a classic, or the old-time cowboy evokes a bit of descriptive writing, a piece of sculpture, a painting or drawing, a poem, a song, a film-script, a piece of acting, or a realistic reappraisal that has true inspiration. Nearly all these (and we all have our favourites) – except perhaps the last category – tend to paint the cowboy larger than life and twice as handsome. But who cares! Owen Wister's *Virginian* at his bright dawn, Gary Cooper at *High Noon*, or Ramon Adams[4] in the camp-fire's evening glow have all depicted him as we would like him to have been, even if he was not quite like that.

[1] J. G. McCoy, *op. cit.*, p. 131 ff.

[2] Though Charlie knew the rigours of the long drive at first hand he forsook them as soon as he could for married bliss and the comforts of his 'JA' Ranch, 'a two-storey plank-and-log structure with water piped in . . . and a separate mess-house for the men'. See Frantz and Choate, *op. cit.*, p. 55, and J. E. Haley, *Charles Goodnight, Cowman and Plainsman* (Boston, 1936; reprinted Norman, Oklahoma, 1949), *passim.* Andy Adams attempted, in *Reed Anthony, Cowman* (Boston, 1907), to make a hero out of Charlie Goodnight, but only suceeded in making him a worthy. His hired hands in *The Log of a Cowboy* are much more alive.

[3] 'As techy as a cook' the saying went.

[4] See p. 299. See also Ramon Adams' anthology, *The Best of the American Cowboy* (Norman, Oklahoma, 1957), for a ripe selection of twenty-seven items beginning with the classic and anonymous 'A Man suited to his Times' (pp. 3–26).

Painting the Town Red (above) and *Making a Tenderfoot Dance* (below), two drawings from Theodore Roosevelt's *Ranch Life and the Hunting-Trail* by Frederic Remington. On the next page appears *Riding a Bucking Bronco.*

When Frederic Remington, illustrating young Theodore Roosevelt's *Ranch Life and the Hunting Trail* in 1888 with cowboys drawn from life, shows the cowboy (on page 72) as he really is *most* of the time, riding the range and mending barbed-wire fences in winter, blue with cold, muffled up to the eyebrows, sagging on an equally sorry-looking pony, sombrero-less, scarfless, chapless and bored, we turn eagerly to page 92, where he and his bunkies are painting the town red, or to page 40,

where he rides a bucking bronco, or to page 91, where he scares the daylights out of a city slicker. This is the cowboy as we *want* to remember him, but as he very rarely, and only for brief moments, was.[1] Ramon Adams, no cowboy himself and no kin to Andy, except under the skin, but a skilled chronicler and bibliographer of the cowboy era came up to Denver in 1962 and told members of the newly formed Western History Association what 'The Old-Time Cowhand' was really like. Though Paul Horgan has produced a highly literary[2] and greatly respected

[1] Remington drawings from Roosevelt, *Ranch Life and the Hunting Trail* (London and New York, 1888), are reproduced on this and the previous page, and also on pp. 287 and 293.

[2] Franz and Choate call it 'belletristic'.

evaluation of the cowboy,[1] the present writer prefers the saltier and more down-to-earth treatment (which really requires to be intoned aloud in a slow, Texas drawl), given by Ramon Adams:[2]

I have been interested in the cowboy and his lingo for more than sixty years – way back, as the cowboy would say, since I was 'fryin' size'. My real interest probably started when Jim Houston, a typical Texas cowboy, told a group of other cowmen, into which I had poked my young ears, of the time he had a narrow escape from a cow on the prod while he was afoot in a branding pen:

'There's no love-light in that cow's eyes as she makes for me,' said Jim. 'I fogs it across that corral like I'm going to a dance, an' she's a-scratchin' the grease off my pants at ever' jump. Seein' I can't make the fence in time, Brazos Gowdy jumps down off the fence an' throws his hat in the old gal's face. Seein' a cowboy come apart in pieces like that makes her hesitate till I climb the fence without losin' anything more'n some confidence, a lot o' wind, and a little dignity. You can take it from me, a cow with a fresh-branded calf might be a mother, but she shore ain't no *lady*. . . .'

The real cowhand's typical day was anything but romantic. There was no romance in getting up at four o'clock in the morning, eating dust behind a trail herd, swimming muddy and turbulent rivers, nor in doctoring screw worms, pulling stupid cows from bog holes, sweating in the heat of summer, and freezing in the cold of winter.

If, when he got to town, after long months out in the brush, on the lone prairie, or on the long, long trail, the cowboy 'cut his wolf loose' and had a little fun, he could hardly be blamed. He was a robust animal, full of vinegar and pride, and generally came from venturesome ancestors.

The old-time cowhand lived in the saddle. He was strictly a riding man, and detested walking, even for short distances A self-respecting cowhand would never be going far on foot. This is why he was mighty particular about a straight riding job. When he was out of work and rode to a new range seeking a job, he was careful to inquire about the outfit before he arrived. He didn't want to sign up with some little 'three-up' outfit that didn't own enough beef to hold a barbecue. On such an outfit there would be chores to do that were beneath his dignity, such as feeding, digging post-holes, or cutting

[1] Paul Horgan, *Great River* (New York, 2 vols, 1956), Vol. II, pp. 874–86.

[2] Ramon Adams, 'The Old-Time Cowhand' in *The American West: An appraisal. Papers from the Denver Conference on the History of Western America* (ed. R. G. Ferris), pp. 15–24. This is adopted from an 'impression' under the same title that Mr Adams himself contributed to *The Best of the American Cowboy* (see *supra*).

stove wood, and the only place a cowhand could cut wood and not hurt his pride was at a line camp where it was chop wood or 'no eat'.

When he 'hit' a fenced ranch for a job, he hoped that all the fencing and cross fencing had been done and no more post-holes needed to be dug. He didn't want to be caught on the blister end of no damned shovel. High-heeled boots weren't made for foot work, and he wouldn't be caught in a low-heeled shoes. But he didn't shirk any duty as long as it could be done from horseback. He worked without complaint long hours through flood and drought, heat and cold, and dust and blizzard, never once thinking of his own discomfort if the cattle and the welfare of his hoss demanded his attention.

Fighting prairie fires, the dangers of stampedes, the loneliness of range riding, the discomforts of standing guard in the rain or sleet – none of these things seemed unusual if he could do them from the back of a horse. On the other hand, he didn't even want to open a gate unless he could lean over and do it from the saddle. His profession was born of necessity, and with it was born a tradition that he followed jealously until he became the most colorful and picturesque hired man ever known. About the only footwork he considered honorable was roping in the corral, or doing the branding.

A lot of sunshine put that squint in the old-timer's eyes, and a lot of prairie wind tanned his face. That ten-gallon hat and those fancy boots were not what made him look like a cowman. It was the elements, the corral dust, the horse smell, and the cow-camp chuck that branded him. He could go away from the cow country and dress in fancy society togs, and another cowman would still know him to be a cowman.

After the fences came, most of these old-timers were always belly-aching with a yearning to go somewhere where they could spread a loop without getting it caught on a fence post. Most of the real old-timers have now saddled a cloud and ridden into the Great Beyond, and their like will never be seen again.

Ramon Adams' cowhand is a 'character', but he is hardly a glamorous figure. If his is the cowboy as he really was, then the cowboy of Western mythology is a man transformed – and made larger than life. The old-time cowhand was no hero, not even to his horse (and quite a number of cow horses were reputed to be a sight more intelligent than their riders), yet look what has happened to his latter-day image! Clifford Westermeier asks,[1]

[1] Ferris, *op. cit.*, p. 34, in 'The Modern Cowboy – An Image'.

> What is there about him that makes a halo of his stetson and a dragon-slaying sword of his six-shooter? The West had other heroes with traits just as admirable – the explorer, the trapper, the prospector, the homesteader. . . .

Westermeier thinks that the *mystique* is connected with the cowboy's horse – *pas de cheval, pas de cowboy*, as that Westernized Frenchman, Paul Coze, has aphorized – but then other frontiersmen have ridden horses. The Freudians have, as usual, pushed their way into the argument, not to propound a centaur-complex but to suggest, less originally, that 'the cowboy hero is the eternal son, repetitively and compulsively acting out an archetypal fantasy . . . The villain represents the "bad" father, who deprives the narcissistic "king of the nursery" of his heart's desire, the good mother. In overwhelming the villain, the hero is simultaneously re-enacting the oedipal crime against the father, making restitution for it, and avenging both his father and himself . . . The saloon and the "hang-out" are allusions to the primal scene . . . the gun-battles are threats and counter-threats of castration . . . The Western story may be considered as a heroic myth in which are concealed themes of oedipal and other conflicts'[1] – and so on. It is all so simple. If he could read Dr Barker's psychoanalysis of the hired man on horseback, it is to be feared that the bones of Eugene Manlove Rhodes would buck in his grave at the summit of Rhodes Pass in his beloved San Andrés Mountains of New Mexico.[2]

[1] Warren J. Barker, M.D. (Pittsburgh), 'The Stereotyped Western Story', in *The Psychoanalytic Quarterly*, Vol. XXIV, No. 2 (1955), pp. 270–80.

[2] Eugene Manlove Rhodes (1869–1934) was a real cowboy who made his living – off and on – by writing about the cowboy as he really was, but weaving a web of romance around him by telescoping his real-life adventures and moving the scenic wonders around him in a little closer. In many ways the life of this *Hired Man on Horseback* – the title of his wife's happy and entirely uncloying biography of him (May D. Rhodes, *The Hired Man on Horseback*, Boston, 1938) – was more interesting than any of his stories, in which he drew copiously on his own memories of the old West of the last open range. 'I came to Mexico the year that Billy the Kid was killed, 1881,' he proudly proclaimed, and although he never met Billy, he knew Pat Garratt, the Kid's slayer, well, and once (at least) hid a couple of 'wanted' men from this redoubtable sheriff, smuggling them into another county to secure them less summary justice. Gene Rhodes, who was forced by circumstances to live for many years *en famille* with his wife's parents, once confessed, 'I have been friendly with a number of outlaws . . . Outlaws are more interesting than in-laws.' W. H. Hutchinson, in *A Bar Cross Man. The Life and Personal Writings of Eugene Manlove Rhodes* (Norman, Oklahoma, 1956), has written a compelling tribute to a most attractive personality. For Freud and the Freudians Rhodes had no more use than for what he called 'Menckens and Supermenckens', and he spoke once of 'the sticky doctrine of Siegmund Freud'. In pursuing his vendetta against 'The Euramericans of New York and Chi-

Whether we define the American cowboy in the words of Andy and Ramon Adams, of Eugene Manlove Rhodes and Emerson Hough, of Charles Siringo and Philip Rollins,[1] or in those of Dr Barker and Dr Freud, he is still with us a hundred years after he first came up from Texas to Baxter Springs and Sedalia. The myth and the reality (as Frantz and Choate have demonstrated) have become inextricably intermingled. What he was like in the great drives between 1865 and 1885 we can now fairly clearly discern; but what he has since become is beyond history and is the stuff that dreams are made of. The Rodeo 'cowboy' of today, always 'on the road', is essentially a showman and more than a bit of an actor. He possesses great skill, takes great risks and wins (if he is lucky) big prizes. His long drives are in three-hundred-horsepower ranch-waggons. He shuttles from Dallas to Cheyenne; to Pendleton; to Albuquerque; to Madison Square Gardens, New York; to Calgary; to Denver. In 1955 there were 421 rodeos approved by the national Rodeo Cowboys' Association, and in 1961 there were 542, offering over $3 million in prize money. Cheyenne's 'Frontier Days' Rodeo, called by its proud sponsors 'the Daddy of them All', is worth $2 million to that city in business annually. One rodeo cowboy, Jim Shoulders, won over $43,000 in prize money in a year.[2]

The 'cowboy' who 'learned his songs on the rad-io' and makes his living playing in horse-operas and the like, may never have been on

cago' he said, 'They are devotees of Old Doctor Freud's Dream Book and they are propagandists of Phallicism . . .', which he then went on to describe (Hutchinson, *op. cit.*, p. 204) in somewhat more Anglo-Saxon terms. Few people now read Gene Rhodes' books, such as *Good Men and True* (1910), *The Desire of the Moth* (1916), *Stepsons of Light* (1921), and *The Trusty Knaves* (1934), but they are better than their glossy titles and do not deserve to die. In Armed Services editions, published during World War II, five of his novels totalled at least 250,000 distributed copies. He could have done with some of those royalties in his lifetime, for he was almost always acutely hard up, subsisting on publishers' advances on books as yet unwritten. See also J. Frank Dobie, *My Salute to Gene Rhodes* ('A Christmas Remembrance from Bertha and Frank Dobie', El Paso, Texas, 1947), 12 pp.

[1] See Bibliographical Note p. 388.

[2] Westermeier, *op. cit.*, p. 300.

the range at all. William S. Hart, Tom Mix, and Will Rogers were ranch-fed all right, but some of their singing, guitar-strumming successors have been less authentic, though most of them can at least ride a horse. The 'Western' movie has had a long innings, with its cowboy hero, ever since Bronco Billy Anderson played in *The Great Train Robbery* in 1903, and television has given it (the old as well as the new, especially the early talking 'Western'), a new lease of life. Japan now makes her own 'Westerns' and, by way of retaliation, *The Seven Samurai* was remade in the 'Western' idiom – as *The Magnificent Seven*.

Westerners' societies, or 'corrals' have been founded in many countries beside the United States and Canada, and have flourished, particularly in Great Britain and in Germany. The President of the German 'Westerners' is himself a prolific writer of Western paperbacks like *Stolz der Vergessenen*,[1] the story of a 'Grubline Rider', and the cult of the works of Karl May, 'the German Fenimore Cooper', has produced an annual festival attended by thousands to watch the cowboy hero 'Old Shatterhand' worst his Apache foe.[2] The cowboy craze has even penetrated the iron curtain, though Westerner 'corrals' do not as yet apparently exist in Moscow or Pekin.

As for rodeos, since the celebrated one at the British Empire Exhibition in London in 1924 (of which this writer has vivid adolescent memories) they have been organized as far afield as China, the South Pacific, Honolulu, Guam, and North Africa, and, of course, 'Down Under'.[3]

Though the big ranchers never acquired the literary glamour of the cowboys they hired in the summer and (too often) turned loose in the winter to forage for themselves, they were, of course, much more important factors in the cattle industry that grew up on the open ranges of the Great Plains after the Civil War than were their hired hands. To begin (and to end) with, the hired hands on horseback rarely grew rich. Even as recently as 1962 David Brinkley[4] found that a twenty-three-year-old cowboy in Wyoming 'who began work at a salary of $90 a month, plus room and board, is now earning $150. He spends fourteen hours a day in the saddle, riding approximately forty miles;

[1] Robert Ullman, *Stolz der Vergessenen. Western* (Rastatt, Baden, 1964).

[2] And to be reported by *Time* magazine as '*Schnell* on the Draw'.

[3] Westermeier, *op. cit.*, p. 228.

[4] David Brinkley's Hour, N.B.C. colour television programme put out in July 1962, and depicting in fifteen exciting but sobering minutes the life of the typical present-day cowboy on a Wyoming cattle ranch.

his excursions to town include drinking beer, watching television and eating chicken.' The typical cowboy works, according to Brinkley, a seven-day hundred-hour week for wages 'that would make a union agent cry like a baby' and leaves the world as devoid of personal wealth as when he enters it.[1] Walter Prescott Webb expressed the fear[2] in 1931 that

> cowboys at work, eighteen hours a day, for the herd left the bed ground by daybreak and kept it until dark; cowboys at work, riding, singing, nursing the cattle; yet it is difficult for those who now read of their hardships to realise that they worked at all . . .

but programmes like 'Brinkley's Hour' serve to keep the record straight and realistic and help to dispel the illusion that all the modern cowboy does is to strum a guitar in an air-conditioned bunkhouse. Very few

American teenagers today, in all probability, want to run off and become cowboys – at $90 a month for a hundred-hour week – although Andy Adams' hero had, in 1880, taken 'to the range as a preacher's son takes to vice'.[3]

But even in 1880 nobody wanted to become a sheep-man. These despised rivals of the cowboys were nobody's ideal. Following their flocks alone and usually on foot they were as much a prey to predatory and resentful humans, both white and red, as were their charges to the wolves and coyotes. 'A cowboy might marry a squaw, but associate with a shepherd – never!'[4] The feuds of cattle- and sheep-men sometimes almost reached the scale of pitched battles. On the Green river in Wyoming eight thousand sheep were clubbed to death in one night;

[1] 'Brinkley's Hour,' N.B.C., 4 July 1962.
[2] Webb, *The Great Plains*, p. 268.
[3] *Log of a Cowboy*, p. 7.
[4] Frantz and Choate, *op. cit.*, p. 112.

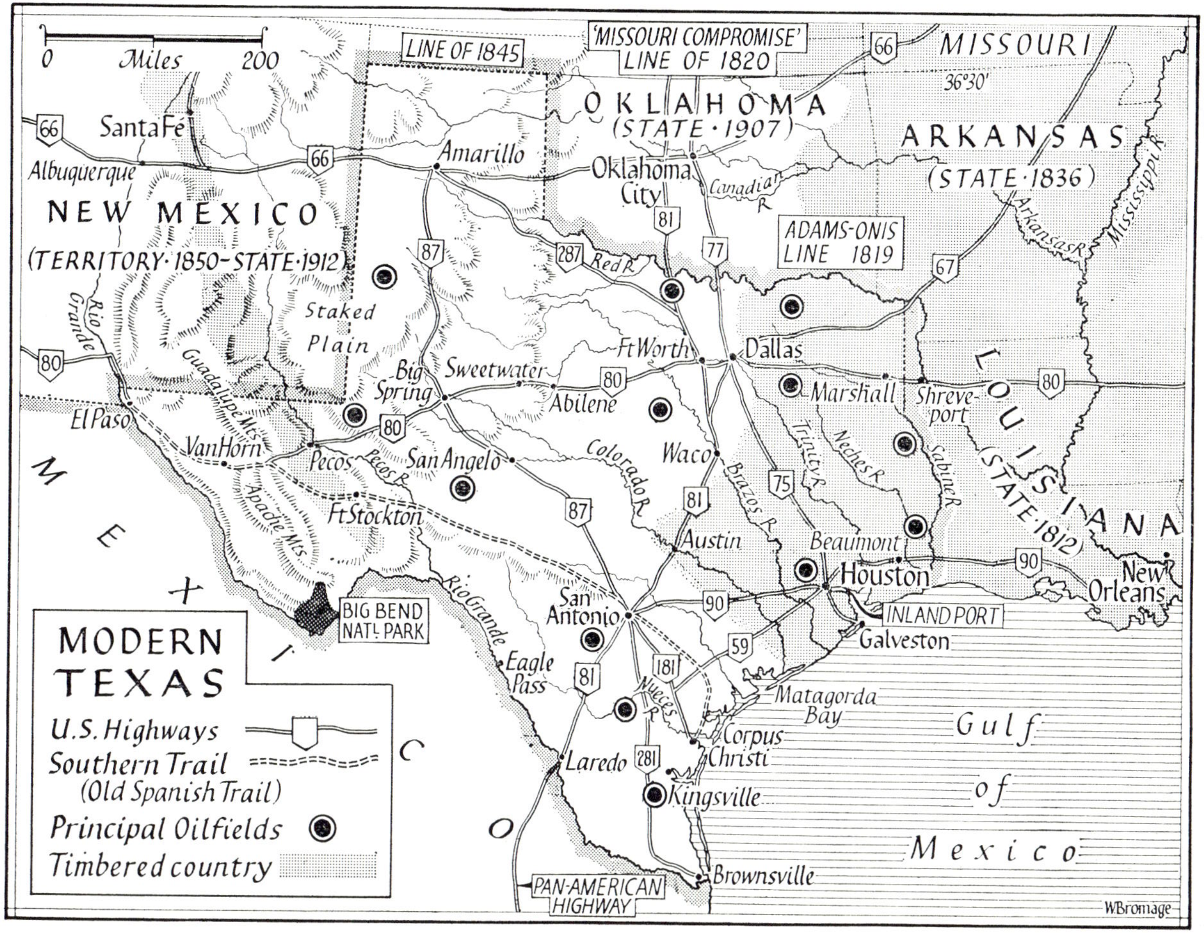
MODERN
TEXAS
U.S. Highways
Southern Trail
(Old Spanish Trail)
Principal Oilfields
Timbered country
0 Miles 200
LINE OF 1845
'MISSOURI COMPROMISE' LINE OF 1820
ADAMS-ONIS LINE 1819
MISSOURI
36°30'
OKLAHOMA
(STATE·1907)
ARKANSAS
(STATE·1836)
LOUISIANA
(STATE·1812)
NEW MEXICO
(TERRITORY·1850-STATE·1912)
MEXICO
Gulf of Mexico
Santa Fé
Albuquerque
Amarillo
Oklahoma City
Canadian R
Red R
Arkansas R
Mississippi R
Staked Plain
Rio Grande
Guadalupe Mts
Apache Mts
El Paso
Van Horn
Pecos
Pecos R
Ft Stockton
Big Spring
Sweetwater
Abilene
San Angelo
Ft Worth
Dallas
Marshall
Shreve-port
Waco
Colorado R
Brazos R
Trinity R
Neches R
Sabine R
Austin
Beaumont
Houston
New Orleans
INLAND PORT
Galveston
San Antonio
Eagle Pass
Nueces R
Matagorda Bay
Corpus Christi
Laredo
Kingsville
Brownsville
BIG BEND NATL. PARK
PAN-AMERICAN HIGHWAY
66
87
287
81
77
67
80
75
90
59
181
281
W Bromage

in the Tonto Basin of Central Arizona twenty-six cattlemen and six sheep-men were killed in the Tewkesbury–Graham feud in five years.[1] There was only one thing that the open range cattleman hated more than sheep and that was barbed wire.[2] But he had to learn to live with it. This he found as hard at first as he had the existence of the sheep-men and their herds. During a few days in 1881 'fence-cutters' destroyed five hundred miles of barbed wire in Coleman County, Texas, alone. But it was a losing battle and W. S. James[3] conceded in 1893 that 'between barbed wire and the railroads the cowboys' days were numbered'. Yet 'though barbed wire revolutionized ranching it did not destroy it, and would not have threatened it seriously, had it not been for its effects on the farmer's frontier . . . It was barbed wire and not the railroads or the homestead law that made it possible for the farmers to resume, or at least to accelerate, their march across the prairies and on to the Plains'.[4]

[1] Frantz and Choate, p. 114. See further, C. W. Towne and E. R. Wentworth, *Shepherds' Empire* (Norman, Oklahoma, 1945), *passim.*

[2] J. F. Glidden's U.S. Patent No. 157,124, of 24 November 1874, and that of Jacob Haish a little earlier (17 June 1874), revolutionized the appearance and changed the economy of the prairies and the Great Plains. W. P. Webb has sung the prosaic but penetrating saga of Barbed Wire (*Great Plains*, pp. 295–318), making use of the Washburn Company's archives.

[3] W. S. James, *Cowboy Life in Texas* (Chicago, 1893), p. 116.

[4] Webb, *The Great Plains*, pp. 316–17.

CHAPTER XII

Land for the Farmer

If the myth (and in some places the reality) of the Great American Desert held up the orderly westward advance of the farming frontier of the United States and Canada for a whole generation after the first tier of trans-Mississippi states filled up, the advance was also delayed until further technological advances in agriculture, in fencing, and in the provision of water, had occurred, and the Indian menace had been removed from the plains. There was, nevertheless, a tremendous amount of agricultural 'in-filling' in those parts of the Far West which (like the Willamette and San Joaquin valleys) were well watered or easily irrigated, or which were reached earliest by railroads.

It has already been seen how easily certain areas (as in Colorado east of the Continental Divide and central Montana) turned to farming after their mining booms had first opened them up and then passed them by. The Far West[1] was patched and striped with agricultural in-filling long before the middle 1880s saw the break-up of the open range and the end of the great cattle drives up from Texas. The farmer – or 'nester' – was breathing down the neck of the stockman even in the High Plains, by the early 1870s. By the late 1870s he had been recognized as yet another of his enemies, like cattle-fever, sheep-men, rustlers, and barbed wire. But the farmer had powerful allies. These included the transcontinental railroad promoters and the Federal Government itself. Such a combination was to prove irresistible!

The public lands policy of the Federal Government – which also comprehended the railroad land grants not made by separate states – played a dominating part in shaping the settlement of the United States west of the Alleghenies. The greatest landmarks in this policy were the Ordinance of 1785 (passed by the Continental Congress) for the surveying, division and sale of public domain land; the Pre-emption Act of 1841, – which provided further sale of land on favourable terms to those who had settled on it; the Homestead Act of 1862, which gave settlers free land on the public domain, and the ending of all private purchase of public land in 1935. Up to 1841 the national

[1] See map on next page.

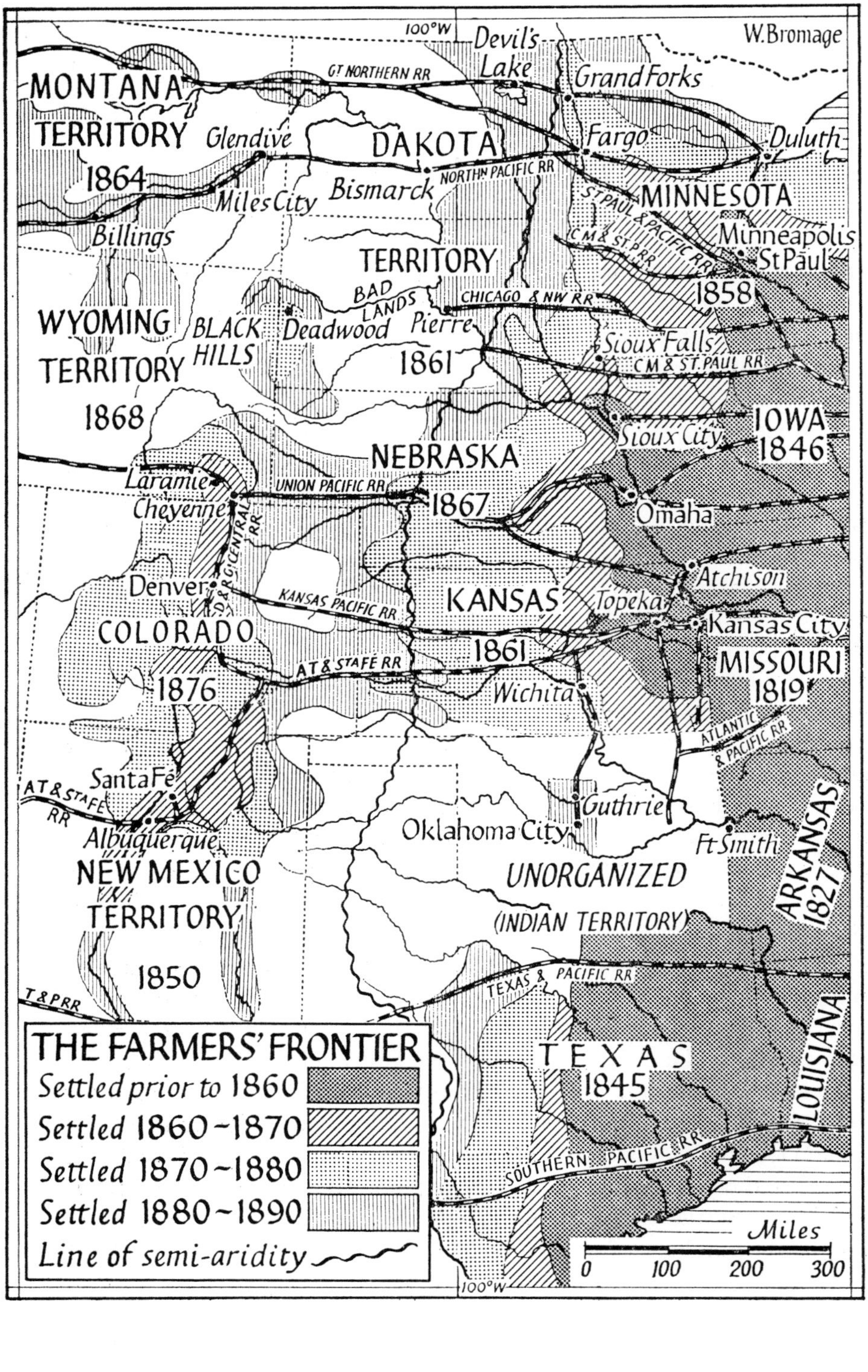

W. Bromage
100°W
MONTANA TERRITORY 1864
DAKOTA TERRITORY
WYOMING TERRITORY 1868
NEBRASKA 1867
KANSAS 1861
COLORADO 1876
NEW MEXICO TERRITORY 1850
MINNESOTA 1858
IOWA 1846
MISSOURI 1819
ARKANSAS 1827
LOUISIANA
TEXAS 1845
UNORGANIZED (INDIAN TERRITORY)
BLACK HILLS
BAD LANDS
Devil's Lake
Grand Forks
Fargo
Duluth
Glendive
Bismarck
Miles City
Billings
Minneapolis
St Paul
Deadwood
Pierre 1861
Sioux Falls
Sioux City
Omaha
Laramie
Cheyenne
Denver
Atchison
Topeka
Kansas City
Wichita
Santa Fé
Albuquerque
Guthrie
Oklahoma City
Ft Smith
GT NORTHERN RR
NORTH'N PACIFIC RR
ST PAUL & PACIFIC RR
CM & ST P RR
CHICAGO & NW RR
CM & ST PAUL RR
UNION PACIFIC RR
D & R G CENTRAL RR
KANSAS PACIFIC RR
AT & STA FÉ RR
ATLANTIC & PACIFIC RR
TEXAS & PACIFIC RR
T & P RR
SOUTHERN PACIFIC RR
THE FARMERS' FRONTIER
Settled prior to 1860
Settled 1860–1870
Settled 1870–1880
Settled 1880–1890
Line of semi-aridity
Miles
0 100 200 300

land policy was conservative, favouring Eastern and monied interests; after 1841 it tended to be radical, favouring the Western settlers and farmers; but at no period did it fully or even adequately fulfil its ostensible objectives. When it did not openly favour the land speculator (as did the Act of 1820, which ended the purchase of land on credit) the speculator found a way round its provisions. This applied particularly to the famous Homestead Act of 1862, passed by Lincoln's administration in the midst of the Civil War,'[1] which, after nearly a century of agitation, at last provided, on paper, free land for the poor and land-hungry settler, but, in fact, poured many more millions of acres – and of dollars – into the hands and the pockets of capitalists, speculators, railroad magnates, and other strictly non-agrarian interests. Congress did not mean to make its legislation ineffective, or the administration its policy inefficient, but even in the agrarian West opinions were often sharply divided as to how best, and most equitably, to distribute the public domain. Nor did the small farmer himself refrain from speculating. Some farming families moved on to new land seven or eight times in one lifetime, not through failure, but in order to benefit financially from either the improvements they had made or from the unearned increment that had accrued from the increased demand for land in the areas where they had settled.[2] When every small farmer was a land speculator or a would-be land speculator, and individual gain was the guiding star, it was hard for a land system devised for the greatest good of the greatest number to remain valid.

The somewhat conservative Ordinance of 20 May 1785 applied to the Western lands handed over by seven of the original states to the

[1] The public interest and enthusiasm aroused by this purely domestic measure, in the midst of great national peril and crisis, can only be compared with the reaction of the British public to the announcement of the Beveridge Social Security plan in 1942 and to its adoption as government policy in the White Paper of 1944. Lincoln, as a Westerner, was in favour of the Homestead Bill, whereas Churchill, concentrating on winning the war to the exclusion of all else, barely tolerated the Beveridge Report and obviously resented the attention it attracted.

[2] Sometimes, it has to be admitted, a farming family moved on out of sheer restlessness, and did not necessarily improve its lot by doing so. The Garlands and the McClintocks, their kinsmen, were a case in point. Hamlin Garland, in his vivid autobiography, *A Son of the Middle Border* (New York, 1925), tells how they moved in the 1840s from Maine to Ohio, then on to Wisconsin (where he was born in 1860), to Iowa and to the Dakota Territory, where (in 1889) 'after eight years of cultivation, father's farm possesses neither tree nor vine . . . Doesn't the whole migration of the Garlands and the McClintocks seem a madness? After nearly a third of a century the Garlands were about to double on their trail.'

Continental Congress and which now constituted the public domain of the United States. This land was to be surveyed, divided up into six-mile squares (*townships*) and every alternate township divided into 36 *sections*, each a mile square (640 acres). Apart from the five sections in each township reserved by Congress for special purposes (the sixteenth was to provide common schools), each section could then be offered by public auction to the highest bidder at a minimum price of $1 per acre. Surveying fees, payable by the purchasers of the land, were fixed at $1 per section. This was a workman-like system and had many merits, which were enhanced by the more comprehensive Northwestern Land Ordnance of 1787. The new Federal Government accepted these land ordinances of the Continental Congress and continued to apply them; unfortunately, the ordinary settler possessing little or no capital could not afford even the minimum possible cost of $640 for a section, plus the cost of transporting himself and his family to it. At first he could instead pick up land, with ample credit facilities, at 20 cents per acre in western New York, for instance, and for some years the separate states possessing unsettled public domains could sell easily below the federal minimum. It was the monied interests that moved into the national domain. By the year 1800 only about 50,000 acres of land had been sold to settlers under the terms of the Ordinance of 1785, and an Act of 10 May 1800 attempted to make the acquisition of land easier for them. It provided liberal credit and reduced the minimum amount of land to be offered for sale, but the minimum, at $2 an acre for 320 acres, and the down payment of one-fourth of the purchase price of the land at auction were still too high. An effort to introduce the principle of *Pre-emption* – or sale of land on specially favourable terms to the actual squatters who had settled on it and improved it, while it was still unsurveyed – was unsuccessful, and pre-emption had to wait for adoption until 1841.

With the Louisiana and Florida purchases a liberal land policy became all the more urgent for the United States, and many settlers went into Mexican Texas in the 1820s and early 1830s on account of the more liberal system obtaining there, especially in the Austin colonies. In fact, a fresh outburst of land speculation accompanied these great national land purchases, and the speculators were also to get hold of most of the land made available by Indian removals in these years. The economic depression in the West which produced the panic of 1819 was attributed by many (including Andrew Jackson) to the deficiencies of the national land system, although the pro-government

National Intelligencer declared in 1819 that 'so wise, beautiful and perfect a system was never before adopted by any government or nation on earth'.[1] An Act passed in 1820 made matters even worse by eliminating credit facilities in the purchase of the public domain altogether. A minimum of 80 acres could now be purchased for as little as $1.25 per acre – but only for cash. This played straight into the ever-ready hands of the speculator. 'The land act of 1820 brought the whole population of the frontier to the brink of ruin.'[2]

A half-way Pre-emption Act of 1830 gave the squatter some privilege in the purchase of 160 acres of the land he actually occupied; Senator Benton's plea for a 'graduated price' for Western land, to accord with its fertility and accessibility, was met by the Eastern campaign (with which Henry Clay was associated, although a Westerner) for 'distribution' of the Public Domain among the several states. Clay's Distribution Bill passed Congress, but President Jackson subjected it to a 'pocket veto'. The limited pre-emption system of 1830 was continued in 1838 and again in 1840 on a temporary basis, with some modifications, but it was not until 1841 that the frontier interests at last triumphed in the shape of full-blooded pre-emption for squatters. The panic of 1837 had served to bring this nearer as a measure of relief for the poor or impoverished farmer, driven by foreclosure from his farm farther east, although some of these foreclosures had been prevented by the action of 'claim clubs' or settlers' associations. In 1838 the Territory of Wisconsin protected 'sitting' settlers by law against the speculative buying-up of land occupied and improved by them.

The 'Battle between the Log Cabins and the Palaces' of 1840–50 produced Benton's 'Log Cabin Bill', which Clay fiercely opposed. Clay then produced his own bill which the Democrats proceeded to emasculate. Both distribution and pre-emption remained features of the bill, but distribution was not to take effect if the tariff were raised above a 20 per cent level. Thus Clay was ultimately defeated and Benton was partially triumphant. Occupation prior to purchase by a 'squatter' was no longer legally a trespass, and the pre-emption of 160 acres at $1.25 per acre was now open to heads of families and single men over twenty-one years of age who were citizens or who had taken out first papers. Lands reserved by the Government for special purposes or granted to railroads, or for public improvements, were not subject to pre-emption. The frontier had triumphed – but at a price – though free homesteads for all were still a long way off.

[1] Quoted by Robbins, *Landed Heritage*, p. 33. [2] *Ibid.*, p. 38.

The enormous accessions of land to the United States resulting from the Texas and Oregon settlements of 1846, and the cessions by Mexico in 1848 greatly increased the public domain (though it did not extend to Texas, which itself kept control over its own unsettled land) and also greatly complicated the situation. In California, in particular, the old Spanish and Mexican land grants were challenged in the courts, and many of them were subjected to the depredations of squatters who, knowing that the titles might be questioned, took a chance and settled upon land they knew to be claimed by others. This was a rather different and much more aggressive procedure than simply moving out ahead of the official United States land surveyors and hoping to retain land by the process of pre-emption or priority right to purchase when it was put up for sale. The gold rush greatly increased the pressure on land in California. Not only did persons holding Mexican land grants, like John Augustus Sutter, suffer greatly from 'squatter trouble' but John C. Frémont and others who bought land after the American occupation had commenced, and who had always been American citizens, were harassed in the same way. Many Mexican grants had been obtained for less than value received and a few by outright fraud, but most were genuine and the lands held had often been considerably improved. Most of these were overrun by squatters in the early 1850s, and the large landowners like General M. J. Vallejo, and Sutter (with his 33 square leagues) suffered most. Even the 11 square leagues to which Sutter was given full title by the United States courts after the 22 square leagues granted to him by Governor Micheltorena had been taken away, were the happy hunting ground of squatters who not only took his land but destroyed his crops, slaughtered his cattle, and attacked his servants and field hands. This was the man who had shown so many kindnesses to the overland settlers from the United States in their time of need in the early and middle 1840s. Landowners who were 'just Mexicans' suffered even greater indignities at the hands of the land-hungry and gold-greedy squatters, not all of whom, by any means, were from the United States.

Lawyers argued the cause of the California squatters with great ingenuity and skill through many courts, and much eloquence and special pleading was poured out on their behalf in the state legislature and in Congress. More lately, historians[1] have sought to explain, and in some cases to justify, the actions of the squatters, on account of their

[1] For example, Paul W. Gates in 'California's Embattled Settlers', *California Historical Quarterly*, Vol. XLI, No. 2, June 1962, pp. 99–130.

need for land and the wide extent, lack of development, and shaky titles of some of the Mexican land grants. But it remains a sordid story, one of the most disreputable in the history of the American frontier (as Josiah Royce long ago pointed out), and it left a legacy of bitterness which lasted for a whole generation between the Spanish-Mexican and American peoples in California.

While the advance of the American frontier of settlement (except in the gold and silver regions) tended to mark time between 1842 and 1862 under the blighting influence of sectional rivalries and of an inadequate land-disposal system, reformers, both Northern and Southern, continued to be active. In 1843 Robert J. Walker of Mississippi initiated a new drive for Benton's old 'graduation' of the price of public land. Horace Greeley, still a distributionist at this time, claimed in the *New York Tribune* that 'demagogues . . . are incessantly trying to squander the public lands by reducing their price'.[1]

Walker, as President Polk's Secretary of the Treasury, continued to work for 'graduation' and persuaded Polk to advocate it with respect to swampy or sterile land at least, in his annual Message of December 1845. The Whigs' opposition (and Henry Clay's in particular) to 'graduation' brought them much unpopularity. Clay's opposition to pre-emption, said an opponent,[2] and his 'unjust and impolitic aspersions' upon 'honest squatters', his advocacy of distribution which led him into opposition to graduation, induced the people of the Western states to turn away from him 'with odium and disgust'. The advocates of completely free land for 'homesteaders' on the public domain now began to press their case, led by such men as G. H. Evans. His philosophy was a sort of advanced Fourierism applied specifically to the American public domain. Land reform was to effect a social revolution and finally to defeat the speculator. Even Horace Greeley who, as late as 1843 had claimed 'Pre-emption is trespassing', was won over to this crusade, and by 1845 was being accused openly of being 'a Fourierist, an Agrarian, and an Infidel'. A national party was advocated, with the slogan 'Vote Yourself a Farm' and with the objective of a free grant of a quarter section (160 acres) from the public domain to every landless man. Greeley went on even to propose something akin to the French National Workshops, set in the midst of rural areas – a crude foreshadowing of Henry Ford's celebrated idea of 'Industrial Barns' nearly a century later. He urged the urban unemployed to migrate to

[1] *New York Weekly Tribune*, 3 February, 1844.

[2] Jacob Thompson, in the House of Representatives, 9 July 1846.

rural areas, only to be told by his opponents that 'We should soon have the whole contents of European poorhouses emptied down upon our fertile West'. He replied by asking, 'Whoever heard of a farmer starving *on his* land,' and proposed that the starving Irish should be welcomed to 'the untilled lands of the great West' to help create 'a mighty empire resting upon the Great Lakes and the Northern Mississippi'. He then went West himself on a trip which reinforced his new stand on land reform.

The first true homestead bill was introduced into Congress by Representative McConnell of Alabama on 9 March 1846. Andrew Johnson of Tennessee produced another three days later. But homestead legislation was an early casualty of the Mexican War, which broke out that same spring, and none of the three parties – even the Free Soil Party of Martin Van Buren – which fought the 1848 election could be persuaded to adopt land reform and homestead legislation as planks of their official platforms. Greeley thought that 'land reform' could have elected Van Buren, and when the latter would not advocate it, the mercurial editor threw in his lot with General Taylor and the Whigs. Greeley, when an interim member of Congress in 1848, introduced a homestead bill of his own, but could get only twenty members to support it. By 1849 both Sam Houston and Stephen A. Douglas were advocating homestead legislation. William H. Seward and Daniel Webster were also supporting land reform. A homestead bill which passed the House on 12 May 1852 by 107 votes to 56, failed even to get debated in the Senate. This bill, reintroduced in 1854, again failed to pass, and further homestead legislation was now to be smothered by the great Kansas–Nebraska debate, which absorbed everybody's attention. 'Suddenly in 1853 and 1854,' says Paul Gates, 'the Kansas–Nebraska country beyond the Mississippi loomed up as a tremendously attractive area, and there erupted in Congress, the press and the pulpit an ominous war of words . . . For the next forty years Kansas was the focus of greater public attention than any other western community,'[1] and for that reason the fight for free homesteads and the fate of the homesteads on the sod-house frontier can be no better studied than on the wide expanses of the Sunflower State where 'In God We Trusted – in Kansas We Busted'.

Kansas was in many ways an ideal testing ground for the system the

[1] P. W. Gates, *Fifty Million Acres: Conflicts over Kansas Land Policy, 1854–1890* (Ithaca, 1954), pp. v–vi. He calls 'The Kansas Story a grotesque composite of all the errors involved in the growth of the American West'.

United States had so laboriously worked out by the middle of the 1850s for the disposal of her public lands. If the system would work there it would probably work anywhere. Kansas Territory was on the borders of the North and the South, lying as it did between 37° and 40° N, and while two-thirds of it lay in the reasonably well-watered prairies east of the 100th meridian, the other third stretched westwards in the treeless and water-deficient High Plains, as far as the 102nd meridian; an almost unbroken Indian barrier of tribal lands stretched from the southern to the northern border of eastern Kansas.[1] This meant that when the Kansas Territory was officially opened to settlers on 30 May 1854, 'not an acre of land was available for pre-emption or purchase'.[2] Much Indian land was very soon afterwards made available to settlers by the ratification of Indian treaties, but this easement was to be more than cancelled out by the enormous extent of the land grants to railroad companies (all of which land had to be withdrawn from public sale) in the later 1850s and the 1860s. These grants, in some cases, cut wide swathes right across the state.[3] Federal land grants to railroads in Kansas amounted to 8,346,603 acres, while nearly another 2 million acres were given by the State of Kansas to these railroads or purchased by them for nominal sums per acre from the Indians or the Government. Only a very small proportion of these grants were subsequently voided or forfeited through non-compliance of the railroads with the conditions on which they had accepted them, though in many cases these conditions were either not met at all, or only after delays running sometimes into decades. While they were in some places very enterprising in advertising and selling their lands (at considerably 'improved' prices in most cases) to settlers, the railroads in others were most dilatory, especially as they did not have to pay taxes on any land they had not yet patented for sale. The Kansas and Pacific Railroad, which stretched right across the state from east to west was a special offender in this respect. The 'K.P.' began land sales in 1869, completed its line in 1870, and finished surveying the adjacent land in 1875, but patented no land in Kansas before 1873 or in Colorado before 1875. As late as 1882 the Kansas Pacific had taken title to little more than one-sixth of its land, and therefore paid no tax on the other five-sixths. The record of the Santa Fé railroad was very much better.

Thus, before the Homestead Act of 1862 gave settlers free land in

[1] See Gates, *Fifty Million Acres*, map on p. 23. [2] *Ibid.*, p. 22.

[3] *Ibid.* Alternate sections of these strips were granted to the railroads, and others reserved.

Kansas and elsewhere on the public domain – if only they could locate themselves legally on it – such land was very hard to reach and find, and even after 1862, in Kansas at least, it still tended to be inaccessible and of poor quality, for the speculators and the railroads were there first and wanted money for their 'improvements'. Things also became worse before they became even theoretically better; for the extremely illiberal land policies of the Pierce and Buchanan administrations in the latter part of the 1850s played – it would almost seem deliberately – into the hands of the speculators once again, just as had the legislation of the 1820s. Eighteen Indian reserves in Kansas were barred from becoming part of the public land of the United States (including the Osage reserve of nearly 9 million acres) or subject to homestead or pre-emption laws. Instead they 'became the booty of speculators, land companies and railroads, with substantial benefits accruing to helpful politicians.'[1] In addition, the period of grace for pre-emption was cut back sharply to one year. This greatly contributed to the depression of 1857, for squatters who had expected up to four years to finish paying for their lands under the pre-emption acts, now had to find the balance right away or forfeit. This illiberal land policy contributed largely to the decisive defeat of the Democratic Party in 1860. Kansas moved almost bodily into the Republican camp, as became even more evident in the presidential election of 1864, the first in which voters from that state participated.

A bill passed the House of Representatives in May 1860 to restore the right of squatters, in frontier areas not yet surveyed, to purchase their claims over a period of four (even in some cases extended to eight) years, but again failed to be debated in the Senate. Then an even more radical House bill, providing free homesteads, was amended by the Senate to give squatters on public land two years' more grace, and reducing the cost of land occupied for at least five years to 25 cents an acre. The Southern opponents of land reform let it pass thus 'eviscerated', though Greeley called it 'a miserable makeshift', but President Buchanan, with incredible stupidity, vetoed it, giving as one of his reasons that 'It is a boon exclusively conferred upon the cultivators of the soil.'[2] It was only natural that the Republicans should now make full political capital out of the land reform issue, which the Democrats had so woefully fumbled during the last two administrations, and their

[1] Gates, *Fifty Million Acres*, p. 6.

[2] *Congressional Globe*, 36th Congress, 1st Session, IV, 3263–4. This is a strong competitor for the title of the crassest state paper in American history.

presidential election platform of 1860 contained a strong plank favouring free homesteads. Most Western Democrats wanted this also and many left the party when neither of its wings came out in that election unequivocally in favour of the policy.

The bill vetoed by Buchanan in 1860 was reintroduced with some emendations in 1862 after Abraham Lincoln had become president, and with its Southern opponents – who had been its strongest critics – now absent, passed both houses of Congress without undue difficulty. It was signed by Lincoln, who had long been in favour of free homesteads, on 20 May 1862, almost exactly ten years after the House of Representatives had first accepted a homestead bill.[1]

Both by personal inclination and by his election pledges Abraham Lincoln was bound to approve the passing of a free homesteads bill. 'I am in favour,' he said on 1 February 1861,[2] 'of settling the wild lands into small parcels so that every poor man may have a home.' It is doubtful whether he or anyone else living at the time was able to judge what would be the effect upon Western settlement of the bill which was at last to become law in 1862. Certainly Horace Greeley was not, for he called the bill 'one of the most beneficient and vital reforms ever attempted in any age or clime'[3] and it was in that year of great decisions regarded as far more important than the Morrill bill for land-grant colleges or the first Pacific Railroad Act, and as equal in significance to the Emancipation Proclamation itself.[4] That the Homestead Act was to have far less beneficient results than its promoters and well-wishers hoped for was, to a large extent, due to circumstances beyond both their control and their ken; it has indeed only gradually dawned upon economic and agricultural historians that the Homestead Act turned out to be a fiasco; some popular histories still speak of it in superlatives. That it was a landmark is undoubtedly true, but even as

[1] Horace Greeley in the *New York Weekly Tribune* of 30 June 1860, in criticizing Buchanan's veto of the earlier homestead bill as typical of a man who 'has no sympathy for the poor, and who regards only the interests of the speculators' had rightly prophesied that Abraham Lincoln would never veto such a bill. Greeley was probably the author of the homestead plank of the Republican Party platform of 1860.

[2] Nicolay and Hay, *Works of Lincoln*, Vol. I, p. 637.

[3] *New York Semi-Weekly Tribune*, 9 May 1862.

[4] A contemporary Canadian view of the Homestead Act of 1862 declared it to be 'the complement of the prohibition of slavery' and commented 'the civil transactions of the last few months at Washington will make their impression upon ages to come, when the battles on the Potomac and Tennessee will be regarded as mere incidents in history'. *Montreal Herald* quoted in the *New York Daily Tribune* of 27 May 1862. Robbins, *op. cit.*, p. 209.

recently as 1931 Walter Prescott Webb exaggerated somewhat when he claimed, 'There is no question but that the Homestead Act gave a great impetus to the advancing frontier while it remained in the fertile prairie region',[1] though he did go on to point out that 'The Homestead Act had not solved the problem in the region where it had to do most of its work' – the arid regions of the United States beyond the 100th meridian. The judgements of later critics, such as Robbins (1942), Shannon (1945), and Gates (1953) grew increasingly severe,[2] until the Homestead Act, instead of being one of the two 'most important land acts in the history of the world',[3] has almost been demoted into a costly mistake.

What did the Homestead Act of 1862 really seek to do, and to what extent and for what reasons did it fail? Under the act any American citizen or alien immigrant who had filed his first papers of intention to become a citizen, provided that he was over twenty-one years of age or the head of a family or had served for fourteen days in the armed services of the United States, could claim 160 acres of surveyed and unappropriated public land on paying $10, and after occupying this land for five years received full title to it upon paying a further small fee. No charge per acre was payable unless the homesteader wished to accelerate the grant of the title, when he could secure the freehold after only six months residence by paying $1.25 per acre. These and other simple conditions appeared straightforward and easy to administer, but in fact the act turned out to be full of holes. 'In its operation,' claims Shannon, 'the Homestead Act could hardly have defeated the hopes of the enthusiasts of 1840–1860 more completely if the makers had actually drafted it with that purpose uppermost in mind.'[4] Poor farm tenants or labourers, or city-dwellers in the East could neither afford the cost of travel to the trans-Mississippi West where nearly all the remaining public domain was situated, nor even the modest claim and registration fees amounting to from $22 to $34 in all; they could not maintain themselves until their first year's crops were harvested and sold; they had no money wherewith to build houses or to fence their land. Such people were simply non-starters in the race for free homesteads. Most of the actual homesteaders were, in 1862, already farming in the Middle West, in states like Wisconsin and Illinois – like the Garland

[1] Webb, *The Great Plains*, p. 411. [2] See Bibliographical Note, p. 389.

[3] A. E. Sheldon, *Land Systems and Land Policies in Nebraska* (Lincoln, Nebraska, 1936), p. 75.

[4] Shannon, *The Farmer's Last Frontier*, p. 54.

family – and even at that, about two-thirds of all homestead claimants up to 1890 failed to make successes of their farms. Not more than two million people settled on free government land up to the year 1900, although between 1860 and that year the population of the United States increased by forty-five million. In the same period, by contrast, over seven million additional people settled on farms which they had either to buy or rent or where the breadwinner was a hired labourer.

Beside bringing far too few of the people who most needed free land on to the homesteads the act gave inadequate protection against the speculator. The commutation clauses of the act, and of amending legislation, permitted speculators and capitalists to secure large numbers of homesteads through nominees and then to obtain title after six months for $1.25 an acre. The title could then be transferred to the large landowners. These and the speculators could also purchase foreclosed or forfeited homesteaders' claims at public auction. After 1900 a speculator could double his money, for anybody who had already commuted one homestead was thenceforward permitted to claim and commute a second. This meant 320 acres, at $1.25 an acre, in his own name, plus all that he could arrange to secure in addition through nominees, plus all he managed to buy cheaply at public auction ou of the two-thirds of all homesteads that had to be forfeited by their original claimants.

Finally, the size of the free homestead under the act of 1862 was far too small to be economically viable in the arid lands beyond the 100th meridian where, after 1865, vast numbers of would-be homesteaders sought their fortunes and ended up, like the Lane County Bachelor, starving to death on their government claims.[1] Whereas even 80 acres were as much as a farmer needed, or could manage, to start with, on the untilled lands of the well-watered and abundantly

[1] How happy am I on my government claim,
Where I've nothing to lose and nothing to gain,
Nothing to eat and nothing to wear,
Nothing from nothing is honest and square.
But here I am stuck, and here I must stay,
My money's all gone and I can't get away;
There's nothing will make a man hard and profane
Like starving to death on a government claim.

runs one verse of this famous folk-ballad, and the chorus runs:

But, hurrah for Lane County, the land of the free,
The land of the grasshopper, bedbug and flea,
I'll sing loud her praises and boast of her fame,
While starving to death on my government claim.

timbered East and Middle West, he required much more even than 160 acres to make a living for himself and his family on the high plains of Western Kansas, where 'Lane County' was situated, even if they used dry farming techniques. From 10,000 to 25,000 acres of grazing rights was the best economic unit in many parts of the farther West,[1] of which (before 1890) 1,280 acres at most could be secured free by any one individual directly from the Government by the use of every legal resource available. Larger holdings cost money (which most settlers did not have) and often involved the use of extra-legal devices as well.

The plight of a homesteading family which had failed to make good in Kansas and then had moved back farther east as tenants of a run-down farm owned by a speculator (and when they sought to purchase the holding they found they were being charged for the improvements they had themselves put into it), is poignantly told by Hamlin Garland in his story *Under the Lion's Paw*:[2]

> 'Sarah, this is Mr Haskins, from Kansas. He's been eat up 'n drove out by grasshoppers . . .'
>
> 'I didn't like the looks of the country, anyhow,' Haskins said . . . 'I was ust t' Northern Ingyannie, where we have lots a timber 'n lots o' rain, 'n I didn't like the looks o' that dry praire. What galled me the worst was goin' s' far away acrosst so much fine land layin' all through here vacant.'
>
> 'And the 'hoppers eat ye four years hard running, did they?'
>
> 'Eat. They wiped us out. They chawed everything that was green. They jest set around waiting f'r us to die t'eat us too.'
>
> 'Waal, why didn't you stop and settle here?'
>
> 'Fer the simple reason that you fellers wanted ten 'r fifteen dollars an acre, fer the bare land, and I hadn't no money for that kind o' thing . . .'

The results of the Homestead Act were by no means all bad, even though it failed utterly in the primary object of its promoters. Its magic promise of 'free land' for the land-hungry did draw people from all over the United States, and also many hundreds of thousands from Europe[3] into the under-populated second tier of states – Kansas, Nebraska, and the Dakotas – of the trans-Mississippi West, and on into the arid regions of the Great Plains which had so recently been desig-

[1] Shannon, *The Farmer's Last Frontier*, p. 58.

[2] Hamlin Garland, *Main-Travelled Roads*. A collection of short stories (New York, 1891; illustrated 2nd edn, 1899; revised and enlarged 3rd edn, 1922). Paperback edition (text of 1922) published in 'Signet Classics', 1962. The quotation is taken from the last named, pp. 144–5.

[3] For the story of 'the Great Immigration', see Chapter XIV, p. 354ff.

EARLY DAYS IN OKLAHOMA

27*a*. Two armed men holding down their town lot claim in Guthrie, Oklahoma, 22 April 1889 (see page 328).

27*b*. Three men at their claim shack in Guthrie shortly after the 'Run'.

27*c*. At Guthrie the sign painter was the busiest man in town!

28*a*. General view of the centre of Guthrie in its first week.

28*b*. The opening of the Cherokee Strip, 16 September 1893 – H. Worrall's impression of the Grand Rush at noon.

29*a*. A family group outside their sod house in the Cherokee Strip, *c.* 1894. Left, three Cherokee girls in Sunday best.

29*b*. An Oklahoma homesteader, his family and possessions – including a McCormick reaper and a wind pump – outside their sod house.

30. An early Oklahoma oil well, with wooden derrick and steam engine.

nated the Great American Desert. It took the American farmer a whole generation to subdue these plains and make them agriculturally profitable, but though this was done at a colossal expenditure and much waste of human effort, man could not have subdued the plains had he not been brought to them first. The Homestead Act may have been something of a will o' the wisp but westward it made the land look bright. Its propaganda value was enormous.

Added, of course, to the shimmer and gleam (even if it sometimes turned out to be a mirage) of 'free land for the settler' was the enormous promotional activity of railroads, land companies, and private speculators with land to sell, and of State and Territorial governments with the desire for taxable population and (in many cases) with considerable amounts of public lands to dispose of themselves. All these combined to draw farmers and would-be farmers westward almost as compellingly as the gold and silver of the mining areas had worked on the previous generation of Americans and immigrants – but the population of the United States was now much larger and the immigrant tide had resumed after 1862 to become greater than ever before. There was enormous hunger for the land – any land – and if this land was marginal or sub-marginal for purposes of agriculture, perhaps blood and sweat and tears – and science – could make it productive. There were plenty who were ready to try.

There are two ways of judging how the undeveloped lands of the United States came into the hands of settlers. One is to emphasize the enterprise and initiative of the explorers, the railroad promoters, the speculators, the financiers, and the politicians who made them known, accessible, and purchasable. Another is to concentrate upon the hard life of the frontier farmer, the sacrifices made by his wife, the cultural deprivations of his family, the ways in which he was exploited and cheated by promoters, middlemen, and bankers, and the failure of the Government to give him a square deal. It is hard to strike a balance between these two extremes, but it is at least clear that the agrarian ideal of such men as Greeley and Evans was not attained during the nineteenth century, even though the subsidized and featherbedded American farmer of the second half of the twentieth century may indeed have attained that Nirvana.

Many attempts were subsequently made to put teeth into the ineffective Homestead Act of 1862 and to reduce the opportunities for speculation provided by its commutation clauses. The Timber Culture Act of 1873 was perhaps the most fruitful of these. A further 160 acres was made available to a homesteader, provided that he planted a quarter of it with trees within ten years.[1] This act really did benefit homesteaders possessing too little land to make a living off it but, for various reasons, far too few of them.[2] By contrast the Desert Land Act of 1877 was lobbied through by the big cattle companies and was the monopolist's bonanza. In exchange for a first payment of 25 cents an acre (and a subsequent and final payment of another $1 per acre) and a completely un-watertight promise to irrigate the land within three years,[3] each claimant could secure title to 640 acres within designated Western states (extending as far east as the Dakota Territories) of land which would not grow crops without irrigation. Much of this was, in fact, good grazing land and the cattle kings managed to get hold of most of it. It is estimated that some 95 per cent of the patents granted under the Desert Land Act were obtained by fraud. The genuine homesteader benefited hardly at all. In 1891 the act was extended to Colorado, very little of which state can be claimed to be 'desert land' by any stretch of imagination.[4] The Timber and Stone Act of 1878 also benefited the monopolist rather than the homesteader: a quarter section of land 'unfit for cultivation' in four of the most westerly states (extended in 1892 to all states with public lands) could be bought by any individual for $2.50 per acre. This was made by the great timber companies to include most of the unexploited timber-covered land of the United States, so that by 1901 'immense tracts of the most valuable timber-land . . . have become the property of a few individuals and corporations', and in the year 1903 alone 'nearly half as much timber land was monopolised as in the whole period from 1878 to 1900'.[5] Some of this was achieved by frauds which led to prosecutions in the courts, but much of it was completely legal under the laxly drawn Timber and Stone Act and even more outrageous legislation subsequently passed.[6]

[1] This was changed to one-sixteenth within eight years by a law passed in 1878.

[2] By 1904, when the Timber Culture legislation was finally repealed, only 65,292 grants had been made under it, involving under 10 million acres in all. Shannon, *op. cit.*, p. 59.

[3] Placing one bucket of water on it appeared to be accepted as qualifying in some cases.

[4] The maximum amount of land obtainable by one entrant under the Desert Land Act was reduced in 1890 to 320 acres, but this provision could be easily evaded.

[5] Public Lands Commission of the U.S.A. *Report* for 1905, p. 186. Shannon, *op. cit.*, p. 62.

[6] See S. A. D. Puter and H. Stevens, *Looters of the Public Domain* (Portland, Oregon, 1908), and J. Ise, *The United States Forest Policy* (New Haven, 1920), for details of some of these transactions.

A new land reform movement was bound to arise to attempt to deal with the most glaring abuses and inadequacies of the policies initiated in 1862. By the early 1870s this was in full swing. It found its apostle in Henry George, a San Francisco printer,[1] who gave early warning that the United States was rapidly becoming a land of tenant farmers and after that could easily deteriorate into a land of agricultural labourers working for big landlords. 'Under present conditions the small American freeholder is doomed,' he prophesied.[2] In Congress the most active land reformer was now Representative George Julian, of Indiana, who spearheaded the attack on railroad land grants which led to their discontinuance in 1871, and a less successful demand for the forfeiture of existing ones when the conditions of the grants had been met. The Democratic Party made forfeiture a plank of its platform in 1874, claiming that the Republicans had 'squandered 200 million acres on railroads'. It was not until 1890 that all grants not utilized by railroads up to that date were declared forfeited, but probably only about 2 million acres were actually returned to the public domain under this legislation, so resourceful were the railroads in taking court action to avoid forfeiture,[3] and in some cases even, belatedly, to meet the terms of their grants. Though the railroads had by their practices made themselves vulnerable to attack by the land reformers, their exploitation of their grants had not always operated against the interests of the homesteader, or of the would-be farmer possessing but little capital. Quite apart from the way in which they opened up otherwise inaccessible tracts of country to settlement and to markets, they were sometimes generous in the way in which they were prepared to sell land. It is true that they were never known actually to give it away in any quantity, but the price at which railroad land in the West was disposed of did not average above $5 an acre between 1862 and 1890,[4] and when a colony of German Mennonites from Russia came to Kansas in 1874, the Santa Fé Railroad sold them 60,000 acres for the $250,000 in gold that these 1,900 immigrants brought with them. This averaged about $4 an acre, but the railroad also built them

[1] See *Dictionary of American Biography*, Vol. VII, pp. 211–5.

[2] These ideas, first presented in newspaper articles, were developed further in Henry George, *Our Land and Land Policy, National and State* (San Francisco, 1871).

[3] See B. H. Hibbard, *History of Public Land Policies* (New York 1924), p. 250.

[4] The Northern Pacific, for instance, only charged from $2.50 to $8.00 an acre, depending on the distance of the land from the line, and gave credit for seven years at 7 per cent. See J. B. Hedges, *Henry Villard and the Railways of the Northwest* (New Haven, 1930).

temporary barracks and gave them a number of sections of land free to help them establish a poor fund. This was all very profitable to the railroad, but it was not in any sense exploitation of the unfortunate, as is testified by the wording of the historical monument set up beside U.S. Highway 56 by the Mennonites near the site of the first church to be built on their Kansas land. Here, we are told, the Mennonite community established itself 'by the Graces of God and with the Aid and Assistance of the Atchison, Topeka, and Santa Fé Railroad . . .' Never did an American Western railroad approach nearer to a state of bliss! The Southern Pacific Railroad of California did not emerge from the notorious Mussell Slough affair of 1880 with any similar halo. Here it attempted to sell railroad land to settlers it had invited on to this land in Tulare County as leaseholders before it had been patented, at from $25 to $40 an acre instead of the basic $2.50 (the government price, which they had expected to pay). The railroad sought to benefit from all the improvements that its tenants had put into the land. Before the suit brought by the local Settlers' League in the Federal Courts could be appealed, a fracas occurred between the local U.S. marshal and two Southern Pacific 'strong-arm men' on the one side, and a group of militant tenants on the other, which led to several deaths. The S.P. was subsequently to win its suit in the State Supreme Court, but this and similar incidents caused it to become unpopular in the 1880s and 1890s: the three leading newspapers of San Francisco were at one time all attacking it at once. All this inspired the title *The Octopus* which Frank Norris gave to his powerful novel published in 1901, and which he based in part on the Mussell Slough incident. An interview with Collis P. Huntington, President of the S.P., while the novel was in progress – which Norris wrote into the book as the encounter between the poet-hero Presley and the tycoon Shelgrim, head of the 'Pacific and South-Western Railroad' – softened Norris' attitude somewhat towards 'the octopus', but it and its minions (especially the malevolent 'S. Behrman', who, like Presley himself, is never given a Christian name throughout the novel) remain the villains of the piece, the despoilers and exploiters of honest farmers and mechanics, the bringers of misery and degradation to their families; and though 'occupying the position of Greek gods, Huntington and his pals were immune, like the gods, to punishment'.[1]

[1] According to Oscar Cargill, editor of the 'Mentor Classics' paperback edition of *The Octopus* (New York, 1964), who has convincingly advanced the argument that Norris was actually intimidated by Huntington much more than was Presley by

Despite the legislation of 1890, land reformers continued their attacks on the railroad grantees and the speculators. Senator William A. Peffer, of Kansas, speaking for the Populist Party, said in 1891: 'The farmer has been the victim of a gigantic scheme of spoliation. Never before was such a vast aggregation of brains and money brought to bear to force men into labour for the benefit of the few.'[1]

As early as 1880 a specially appointed Public Land Commission had proposed a comprehensive new land code, but this failed to pass, and the reforms advocated by A. J. Sparks, President Cleveland's General Land Commissioner, in 1886 were also not adopted; but between 1889 and 1891 most forms of cash sale of land were terminated, the amount of land one individual could secure was limited to 320 acres and the Pre-emption and Timber Culture Acts were repealed, while the Desert Land Act was restricted in its application. This, says Fred Shannon sardonically, 'locked other stables after the horses were stolen',[2] but as late as the year 1902 Theodore Roosevelt's Secretary of the Interior was still asking for the final repeal of the Desert Land Act, the Commutation Clause, and other measures which had favoured the speculator, so that the government could 'preserve' the remaining public lands as homes for actual settlers.

Thus, even by the beginning of the new century many of the demonstrable inadequacies of the homestead legislation had not been remedied though some of the holes had been plugged. One sweeping criticism of the land laws of the United States as they existed in the year 1901 stated:

> There is not a land law in effect which applies intelligently to the public agricultural domain as it is now to be found, and each and every law which is in force is used daily as a means for the fraudulent segregation of land from the public domain by those whom the law does not contemplate as possible beneficiaries.[3]

Shelgrim in the novel. 'Was he obsessed by his own metaphor and afraid that if he attacked the octopus a punishing tentacle would reach for him?' Collis P. Huntington had a reputation for neglecting nothing – not even literature. It was he who put up anonymously $750 for the best answer to Markham's 'socialistic' poem, 'The Man with the Hoe', 'the influence of which he feared in California', points out Cargill ('Afterword' to *The Octopus*, Mentor Edition), pp. 464–9.

[1] W. A. Peffer, *The Farmer's Side, his Troubles and his Remedies* (New York, 1891) p. 73.

[2] Shannon, *op. cit.*, pp. 73–4.

[3] J. D. Whelpley, 'The Nation as a Landowner', *Harper's Weekly*, 30 November, 7 and 14 December 1901, quoted by Shannon, *op. cit.*, p. 75.

CHAPTER XIII

Frontiers with a Difference: Oklahoma, Utah, and Canada

In 1860 the line of agricultural settlement had barely advanced beyond the Missouri river, and places like Atchison and Topeka, Lawrence and Omaha, St Joseph and Kansas City were still frontier towns. Aided by the building of east–west railroads (which were also to play so big a part in the development of the cattle kingdom) Kansas and Nebraska filled up with farmers to approximately the 100th meridian by 1880, in which year the former had over 850,000 inhabitants and the latter over 450,000. Immigration into the Dakota Territory farther north did not get into its stride before the middle 1870s (aided by the driving out of the Sioux from the Black Hills and the discovery of gold there), but by 1885 the Dakotas had a population of 550,000 – three out of every four of whom had arrived within the last five years. Two transcontinental railroads, the Northern Pacific and the Great Northern, were advancing across these territories, bringing settlers, many of them freshly arrived from Europe, in their hundreds of thousands. No wonder the city of Bismarck could consider itself to be a world metropolis of the future during these years.[1] By contrast, Wyoming and Montana, both in the arid belt well beyond the 100th meridian and still given over mainly to ranching (whereas wheat bonanza farming had come to Minnesota and North Dakota farther east) still had only 62,000 and 132,000 inhabitants respectively by 1890. Nevertheless, Wyoming (along with Idaho) was made into a State of the Union that year, following the admission of the two Dakotas, Montana, and Washington in 1889. Nebraska had achieved statehood in 1867, and Colorado in 1876, so now (in 1890) only the Arizona and New Mexico Territories in the old Spanish South-west, the 'outlawed' territory of Utah with its peculiar (Mormon) institutions, and the former Indian Territory, now called Oklahoma, had still to achieve statehood out of all the lands which had constituted the United States at the end of the Civil War.

[1] See *supra*, Chapter IX, pp. 233–4.

As the availability of fertile, accessible, free or at least cheap agricultural land became less; and as the terrible series of droughts in the late 1880s made many 'marginal' farms elsewhere unprofitable or unworkable, the pressure upon the Government of the United States to open to the settler the one remaining extensive area of good farm land east of the 100th meridian became irresistible. This area was the 'Indian Territory', all that remained of the great Indian reserve which had stretched from the Texan to the Canadian border half a century earlier. Despite the fact that much of it had been handed over to the already-once-displaced Five Civilized Tribes, and subsequently to many other tribes, in perpetuity, the floodgates were opened in 1889 and the 'Oklahoma Territory' was organized in 1890. Exploited by the white man with incredible rapidity, Oklahoma became a state in 1907 even without benefit of the great 'oil boom' that it was later to experience. The opening up of Oklahoma presents a case-study of the operation of the force of land-hunger, and of the opening up of new frontiers, comparable in some ways to the California Gold Rush itself. At the beginning of 1889 the Indian Territory had not a single white man legally settled on it; by 1905 its population was already at the half-million mark; by 1920 it was to contain over two million inhabitants, having outstripped both Kansas and Nebraska, and was rapidly approaching Minnesota and Iowa. Even by 1900 it had far outstripped the Dakotas, and every one of the Mountain and Pacific states except, of course, California.

The opening up of Oklahoma followed a decade of ceaseless agitation on the part of interested railroads, and of ceaseless illegal activity by the 'Boomers' – illegal immigrants – who burst into 'the Oklahoma District' prematurely. David Payne, the first leader of the 'Boomers', died in 1883, but they remained as active as ever and in 1885 Congress agreed to negotiate with the Indian tribes for the opening of the Oklahoma District and the Cherokee Outlet, two as yet unsettled areas of the Indian Territory. Early in 1889 the tribes surrendered their rights to the Oklahoma District and it was declared open to homesteaders. On 22 April 1889 occurred the remarkable 'land rush' into the District which not only brought over sixty thousand[1] pioneers into the District in one day, but conjured brand-new cities into existence in an afternoon.[2] Similar scenes were witnessed as fresh areas of Oklahoma

[1] Billington, *Westward Expansion*, p. 721, says 100,000.

[2] 'In some respects the recent settlement of Oklahoma was the most remarkable thing of the present century. Unlike Rome the city of Guthrie was built in a day. To be strictly accurate in the matter it might be said that it was built in an afternoon

were added to the public domain between 1889 and 1893, thus providing 'eloquent testimony to the preference of farmers for land where there was sufficient rainfall to ensure crops'.[1] In addition to many 'busted' Kansans and Nebraskans, people also came down out of the Dakotas, driven by drought and hard winters, into the lush Indian Territory, which was unimaginable at that time as the future centre of the dust-bowl of the 1930s.[2] By contrast with Oklahoma, Kansas and Nebraska hardly increased in population at all during the 1890s.[3]

Oklahoma richly deserved its statehood in 1907; indeed, by then it had over sixteen times the population with which California had come into the Union in 1850 and over twenty times the population that the prematurely born state of Nevada still possessed after nearly half a century in the Union. Other farming frontiers have opened up since then, but nearly all of these have been man-made – by dams, as in eastern Oregon and Washington, and by the flooding of former deserts as in southern California, for instance – and on a much smaller scale. Oklahoma was the last big agricultural bonanza, worthy (even without benefit of oil) of the way in which it has since been celebrated in song and story by such writers as Rogers and Hammerstein, Edna Ferber, and Marquis James.[4]

All of Oklahoma but the western half of its panhandle, which forms

---

. . . making a total population for the first day of about ten thousand.' W. W. Howard, 'The Rush to Oklahoma', *Harper's Weekly*, 18 May 1889, pp. 391–2.

[1] Shannon, *The Farmer's Last Frontier*, p. 219.

[2] Oklahoma's decennial population figures over fifty years are instructive:

1890 –	258,657
1900 –	790,391
1910 –	1,657,155
1920 –	2,028,283
1930 –	2,396,040
1940 –	2,336,434

[3] Kansas increased from 1,428,108 (1890) to 1,470,495 (1900), and Nebraska from 1,062,656 (1890) to 1,066,300 (1900). Kansas had grown from 107,206 in 1860 to 996,096 in 1880!

[4] *Oklahoma*, the fabulously successful Rogers and Hammerstein musical play, and *Cimarron*, Edna Ferber's best-selling novel, are very widely known. Marquis James' *Cherokee Strip* (New York and London, 1947) tells of a boyhood spent in the Oklahoma Territory and indicates that it possessed as many of the romantic attributes of frontierland as had the Upper Mississippi valley half a century earlier, in the days of *Tom Sawyer* and *Huckleberry Finn*. Marquis once proudly found himself introduced by his father to Temple Houston, son of the great Sam, as 'The Strip's own Huck Finn' (*Cherokee Strip*, London edition, p. 29). But it was Dick Yeager (who died in Garfield County jail on 7 September, 1895) who was Marquis's real hero, and 'any Cherokee Strip youngster's ideal of what an outlaw should be and do'. (*Ibid.*, p. 30.)

part of the Cimarron desert, has a rainfall of twenty inches or more in a normal year, so that part of the state which was not naturally forested was (with the exception of the small area mentioned, forming not one-twentieth of its area) natural tall or prairie grassland, where grain also would grow 'as high as an elephant's eye' once it was cleared.

Utah, or, as the Mormons first called it, the State of Deseret, was by contrast not only wholly west of the 100th meridian with only a very small proportion of it having as much as twenty inches of rainfall, but nearly half of the state had under ten inches of rain and was by nature sage-brush desert. From the beginning, therefore, the practice of farming in Utah taxed human ingenuity to the limit, and could only have been started at all by a disciplined and dedicated body of settlers convinced not only that 'this is the place', despite its obvious disadvantages, but that no other place would do. The advance of the farming frontier into Utah, jumping a whole tier of territories farther east at the end of the 1840s, was a remarkable phenomenon, comparable in modern history only with the Great Trek of the Boer farmers in South Africa a decade earlier. Because the frontier history of Utah was so different from that of every other part of the American West in the nineteenth century, it deserves special attention. The Great Salt Lake valley was most unpromising land and yet was made to blossom like the rose. Brigham Young spoke of 'these barren valleys, these sterile mountains, this desolate waste, where none but Saints can or would live'.[1]

The population of Utah did not grow spectacularly fast, like California's between 1850 and 1860 or that of Kansas between 1860 and 1880 or Oklahoma's between 1890 and 1910. Uninhabited in 1846 the Territory contained 11,380 people in 1850, 40,273 in 1860, 86,786 in 1870, and 143,963 in 1880. By 1890 it had reached 210,779, though Utah was still denied statehood on account of its peculiar institutions. But to sustain even 11,000 people in 1850, let alone well over 325,000 by 1900, meant not only back-breaking toil but masterly planning and execution. Mormon methods of colonization (already worked out in other communities in the course of the migration of the 'Saints' westward), plus extensive irrigation – the first time it had been attempted on a really large scale in North America – provided the answer.

Indians had dug irrigation ditches in the pre-Columbian Southwest, the mission Fathers and the Spanish soldiers had supervised the building of dams in the vicinity of their settlements, but the Anglo-

[1] Brigham Young, *Journal of Discourses*, Vol. IV, p. 344, quoted by P. A. M. Taylor, *Expectations Westward* (Edinburgh and London, 1965).

American settlers had nowhere encountered a pressing need for irrigation, before crops of any kind would grow, until the first advance party of Mormons reached the Salt Lake valley on 22 July 1847. Even before Brigham Young had caught up with them two days later they had dammed a stream and irrigated a field for planting potatoes.[1] From this small beginning the Mormons spread a wide network of irrigation works over every part of Utah where sources of water could be tapped at all, and even into adjoining territories. 'To the pioneer water was not only the basis of wealth, but of human existence; the irrigation canal was the first and highest of public utilities . . . A destitute people having no resources save the genius of their leader and the labour of their own hands, resolved to associate and organize their efforts to bring the water on as the people of Holland were compelled to keep the water out.'[2] The way in which the Mormons' faith and their organization contributed towards the establishment of their communities in an inhospitable environment which most men at that time believed to be uncultivable desert, is relevant to the theme of this chapter, and of this book.[3]

'Making the waste place blossom as the rose, and the earth to yield abundantly of its diverse fruits, was more than an economic necessity; it was a form of religious worship. As one early writer later wrote, the construction of water ditches was as much a part of the Mormon religion as water baptism,' says Leonard Arrington,[4] and, indeed, the earliest irrigation dam built in the valley served a dual purpose, for many of the first arrivals in 1847 were rebaptized 'in the dam' as a sign of dedication to their new life in Utah,[5] just before Brigham Young returned east to lead the 1848 migration. On 2 December 1847 Young was nominated as First President of the Church of Jesus Christ of Latter-day Saints (this nomination was confirmed or 'sustained' the following year) and was to rule with an iron authority, assisted by his two counsellors, twelve apostles, and a growing bureaucracy. These controlled not only the detailed settlement and exploitation of Utah,

[1] Orson Pratt, 'Extracts from the Private Journal of Orson Pratt' in *Utah Genealogical and Historical Magazine*, Vol. XV (Salt Lake City, 1924), pp. xvii, 119, 209–12, quoted by Taylor, *op. cit.*, p. 51.

[2] C. H. Brough, *Irrigation in Utah* (Baltimore, 1898), p. 12.

[3] See Bibliographical Note, pp. 390–1, for general works upon the Mormon Church, its leaders and its history.

[4] L. J. Arrington, *Great Basin Kingdom. An Economic History of the Latter-day Saints, 1830–1900* (Cambridge, Mass., 1958), p. 26.

[5] P. A. M. Taylor, *op. cit.*, p. 52.

but the migration of converts from overseas and their conveyance to the Promised Land. All this was big business and was run in a thoroughly business-like way. Yet they followed a well-tried, indeed (Arrington[1] claims convincingly) an 'Early American' pattern.

It should be obvious that in establishing their institutions and in meeting their first problems in the Great Basin the Mormons relied primarily on their own early ideals and experiences. The careful planning which preceded the development of their great city, the patriarchal husbanding of resources and sharing of burdens, the pooling of productive efforts, the nature of their property institutions – all these might have been predicted long before the Mormons reached the Great Basin. The pattern had been foreshadowed in Jackson County, Kirtland, Far West, and Winter Quarters, and it had been formally incorporated in Mormon theology. Moreover, in acknowledging, as the first colonists in the Salt Lake Valley acknowledged, the social responsibility of government (in this case a theocracy) to arrange and supervise their economic life, the Mormons were recalling the policies and practices of early Americans in Massachusetts, where many of their ancestors were born; in Pennsylvania, where their first prophet was baptized and given the priesthood; and in Missouri, where their first economic experiments were tried. Far from being unique, the spirit and technique of Mormon colonization and organized activity were common, if not typical, in the age which produced Mormonism.

Yet, Mormon economic institutions *were* unique in the contemporary American West. To be sure, there was the same hunger, the same improvisation, the same struggle for success, as in all Western settlements. But the unity, homogeneity, joint action, and group planning all stamped the Mormon frontier as unique – as a contrast with the scattered, specialized, exploitative, 'wide open' mining, cattle, lumber, and homestead frontiers with which historians have familiarized us. . . .

The character of Mormon economic organization, as early as 1847–1849, and more certainly in the succeeding half-century, suggests the feasibility of regarding Mormon institutions as the more typically early American, and the individualistic institutions of other Westerners as the more divergent. The Mormon response to the problems imposed by the settlement of the Great Basin – a response which becomes ever clearer in succeeding decades – suggests that Mormon economic policies bore a greater resemblance to those of the ante-bellum northeast than did the economic policies of the

[1] Arrington, *Great Basin Kingdom*, pp. 62–3.

West during the years when the West was won. Isolated as they were from American thought-currents after 1847, and under the necessity of continued group action to solve the many problems which plagued them, the Mormons were not affected by the growing accommodation to the private corporation, rugged individualism, Social Darwinism, and other concepts which account for the rise of laissez-faire after 1850. It may yet be conceded that the well-publicized conflicts and differences between the Mormons and other Westerners and Americans were not so much a matter of plural marriage and other reprehensible peculiarities and superstitions as of the conflicting economic patterns of two generations of Americans, one of which was fashioned after the communitarian concepts of the age of Jackson, and the other of which was shaped by the dream of bonanza and the individualistic sentiments of the age of laissez-faire.

Less 'Early American' was the decision that water for irrigation should remain under public management and control even after the land through which it flowed had been parcelled out as individually owned lots. The old doctrine of riparian rights adhered to in the better watered East was unworkable in the arid regions of the West, and the Mormons in 1847–9 developed a new doctrine which was to be widely followed in other States and Territories as well.[1]

As expressed by Brigham Young, this policy was as follows: 'There shall be no private ownership of the streams that come out of the canyons, nor the timber that grows on the hills. These belong to the people: all the people.' The same principle was applied to mineral resources.

The decision with respect to water was particularly crucial. Although water was first turned on the land on July 23, 1847, it took the Mormons at least three years to learn the importance and effective use of irrigation. In this they had little precedent to guide them. Anglo-Saxon law, as adopted generally in the East, provided that water must not be taken from the streams unless it could be returned undiminished in volume. Known as the doctrine of riparian rights, this principle of law protected streams for use as sources of power and as channels of transportation. It also tended to restrict the establishment of homes on the banks of streams and gave privileged protection to the few who could profitably utilize the water.

The public ownership and management of water in the Great Basin prevented the application of this principle in curtailing irrigation, for obviously every use of water for irrigation robbed a stream of part of its water supply. Under the arrangement worked out by

[1] Arrington, *Great Basin Kingdom*, pp. 52–3.

the Mormons in 1847–1849, dams and ditches were constructed on a community basis, rights to use the water were associated with the utilization of land, and a public authority was appointed to supervise the appropriation of water for culinary, industrial, and agricultural purposes. The avowed goal of this supervision was equitable division and maximum use of available water supplies. In 1847–1848, for example, a community ditch furnished water primarily for culinary purposes, and its distribution was under the control of a 'watermaster' appointed by the high council.

It was during the next two years, however, when water matters were in the hands of the bishops of the various wards, that the Mormons developed the well-known principles by which canals and ditches were to be constructed and the water divided. When a group of families found themselves in need of water (or additional water) to irrigate their farms and gardens, the bishop arranged for a survey and organized the men into a construction crew. Each man was required to furnish labor in proportion to the amount of land he had to water. Upon completion of the project the water would be distributed by a ward watermaster in proportion to this labor. The labor necessary to keep the canal in good repair was handled in the same way, in accordance with assignments made in regular Sunday services or priesthood meetings.

On this cooperative nonpecuniary basis, then, water was diverted from a natural source into a general canal, and from that into 'laterals' and ditches which carried the water to the individual plots of ground needing it. 'Corrugates' were dug next to each row to carry water to the crops. 'Waste ditches' carried the water from one watered field to the next one below it.

When Utah became a territory this system of public ownership was confirmed by the legislature and placed under the legal supervision of the county courts. The territorial government gave additional recognition to this system of cooperative construction and ownership in 1865 by providing for the creation of irrigation districts, resembling Western mining districts, with a large degree of local autonomy. Even today, farmer-owned 'mutual' companies control virtually all the irrigation canals in Mormon communities in the West.

As another authority expresses it, the majority of Utah's canals 'were built by farmers, owned by farmers, and operated by the farmers. In fact they constitute one of the greatest and most successful community or co-operative undertakings in the history of America.'[1]

[1] G. Thomas, *Development of Institutions under Irrigation, with Special Reference to Early Utah Conditions* (New York, 1920), p. 27. Quoted by Arrington, p. 53.

An even grander project of the Saints, to utilize systematically the water flowing from Utah Lake into Salt Lake via the Jordan valley through a 'Deseret Irrigation and Navigation Canal Company' – almost a Jordan Valley Authority, though it was, of course, before the days of hydro-electric power – was checkmated by the veto of a gentile governor in the middle 1860s. In words almost worthy of a 'barefoot boy from Wall Street', championing private power and irrigation interests in the 1930s, Governor Charles Durkee explained that, while the project 'awakens my admiration by its magnitude and boldness, it would exclude competition . . .'[1] No possible competition, in fact, existed.

Irrigation agriculture was expensive, both in labour and in maintenance cost, but while the Great Salt valley remained isolated, competition within the Territory (with its produce raised in this way) could not come from more cheaply produced crops from the prairie states farther east. With the completion of the transcontinental railroad through Utah in 1869 this competition became a reality, but Mormon enterprise and initiative, and the injunction 'grow your own or do without it', helped to prevent serious damage to the economy through produce and manufactured goods being imported from outside the Territory. Joseph Smith's 'Word of Wisdom' (a revelation dating back to 1833) was now strictly enforced with regard to the consumption of tea and coffee, liquor and tobacco, in a campaign launched by Brigham Young in 1867, and pursued by such organizations as the male School of the Prophets and the Women's Relief Society. A boycott of gentile business establishments was also organized and the School voted in 1868 that 'those who dealt with outsiders should be cut off from the Church'. The Zion Co-operative Mercantile Institution was founded and co-operative retail stores opened in many communities.[2] The School of the Prophets also constituted itself the guardian of the interests of Mormons who had settled on land which might be claimed by the Pacific railroads under their Federal grants and appears to have helped to resolve any such disputes with a minimum of friction.

The Women's Relief Society took the battle into the homes of the Saints. Household manufactures were encouraged and enjoined; imported fashions were to be spurned. Brigham Young himself took a hand in this campaign by pouring scorn on the 'Grecian bend', which he said made a woman look like a camel, and on leg-of-mutton sleeves which were sinfully wasteful, taking 'seven yards for the sleeves, and

[1] Arrington, *Great Basin Kingdom*, pp. 224–6. [2] *Ibid.*, pp. 298–322.

three for the dress'. He called the female members of his by then not inconsiderable family together in the parlour of his multiplex office-cum-residence *The Lion House* in November 1869 and urged them to set an example and to 'retrench from their extravagance in dress, in eating, and even in speech'.[1] As a result Young Ladies' Retrenchment Societies were set up all over the Territory, and a senior department was later added to deal with the possible extravagances of older women. 'Let the Sisters think of what they can wear that is Zion made' they were told, but the Relief Society tempered the wind to the shorn lamb (or mutton) by setting up a 'Deseret Silk Association'. By 1877 there were five million silkworms in Zion.[2]

In addition to the silk industry a number of others were established to meet the economic threat presented by the railroad. These included the making of waggons, carriages, and agricultural machinery, furniture, woollen and cotton goods, ink, and matches. In July 1869 the First Presidency even decided to go on the offensive and initiate an export drive, now that the railroad had actually arrived at Ogden, only thirty-seven miles from Salt Lake City. The first step was an attempt to reduce local wages 'in order that Utah might be able to compete with the manufactures of the States', and the second was to build the Utah Central Railroad, linking Salt Lake City with Ogden and the Union Pacific depot there. Wages were not brought down by anything like the one-third to one-half demanded, but the railroad was completed as a Mormon public enterprise, with Brigham Young as

[1] Arrington, *Great Basin Kingdom*, p. 253. Brigham Young can hardly be said to have obeyed the last part of this injunction himself. His language remained flowery and, at times violent, to the end. He was, after all, a prophet in the Old Testament tradition. In a speech uttered in 1853 he had shouted, 'I will unsheath my bowie knife and conquer or die,' according to John D. Lee (*A Mormon Chronicle*, Vol. I, p. 83; eds R. G. Cleland and Juanita Brooks, 2 vols, San Marino, California, 1955). On another occasion Young warned food-hoarders that their heads might be 'found wallowing in the snow', and on yet another said, 'If you are not heartily on the Lord's side, you will be hewn down.'

[2] The spearhead and the battle-axe of these Women's Retrenchment Societies were wielded by the redoubtable Eliza Snow, once a wife of Joseph Smith and later an inmate of *The Lion House*. Sister Snow, as much renowned for her poetry as for her piety, ran a number of campaigns both for the Prophet and for the First President. She managed at one and the same time to be a plural wife and an ardent feminist. It was perhaps too much to expect her also to be a good poet. See further (*passim*), Fawn M. Brodie, *No Man knows My History* (New York, 1945, and London, Frontier Library, 1963), the best life of Joseph Smith, by no means hostile to him, though highly critical of the divinity of his relevations; and Kimball Young (a descendant of Brigham) *Isn't One Wife Enough?* (New York, 1954), a careful sociological analysis of Mormon polygamy, despite its catchpenny title.

president of the line, by 10 January 1870. At its dedication Brigham Young indulged in a little very justifiable boasting:[1]

> Since the day that we first trod the soil of these valleys, have we received any assistance from our neighbors? No, we have not. We have built our homes, our cities, have made our farms, have dug our canals and water ditches, have subdued this barren country, have fed the stranger, have clothed the naked, have immigrated the poor from foreign lands, have placed them in a condition to make all comfortable and have made some rich. We have fed the Indians to the amount of thousands of dollars yearly, have clothed them in part, and have sustained several Indian wars, and now we have built thirty-seven miles of railroad.
>
> All this having been done, are not our cities, our counties and the Territory in debt? No, not the first dollar. But the question may be asked, is not the Utah Central Railroad in debt? Yes, but to none but our own people. . . .
>
> We have felt somewhat to complain of the Union Pacific railroad company for not paying us for the work we did, in grading so many miles of their road. But let me say, if they had paid us according to agreement, this road would not have been graded, and this track would not have been laid today. It is all right. . . .
>
> I also thank the brethren who have aided to build this, our first railroad. They have acted as Elders of Israel, and what higher praise can I accord to them, for they have worked on the road, they have graded the track, they have laid the rails, they have finished the line, and have done it cheerfully 'without purse or scrip'.

An official of the Union Pacific attending the celebration followed the same theme. He said:

> The Utah Central Railroad, although thirty-seven or thirty-eight miles long, is perhaps the only railroad west of the Missouri River that has been built entirely without Government subsidies; it has been built slowly with money wrung from the soil which, a few years ago, we used to consider a desert, by the strong arms of men and women who stand before me.

These and other speeches delivered on the occasion of the completion of the road manifested the pride felt by the Mormon people in building the road 'without outside help'.

The City and Territory of the Saints was now well and truly part of the great world from which they had fled barely more than two decades

[1] Arrington, *Great Basin Kingdom*, pp. 272–3, quoting from *Deseret News*, 11 January 1870.

earlier. After the setbacks of the 1850s due to the quarrel with the Federal Government and the abandonment of outlying settlements such as San Bernardino and the idea of a Mormon outlet to the Pacific, the Territory had been reduced in 1861 to little more than the present boundaries of Utah; a new self-sufficiency on more modest lines was sought in the 1860s, so that Zion would be impregnable and unassailable economically when the transcontinental railroad finally came. Political isolation was now known to be impossible, but economic isolation might still be maintained, it was thought. 'Even the approach of the transcontinental railroad in the late 1860s brought no relaxation in the drive for independence from the economy of Babylon.'[1] The

result was a drawn battle. The Mormons continued to trade with the gentile world, and to benefit from this trade, but they did so to a large extent on their own terms. Sir Richard Burton had somewhat distorted the situation in 1860 when he wrote,[2] 'The Mormons having lost all hopes of safety by isolation, now seek it in the reverse: mail communication with the Eastern and Western states is their present hobby: they look forward to markets for their produce and to a greater facility and economy of importing.' Agricultural progress in Utah had rather over-impressed him, though he admitted that 'Utah Territory is pronounced by Immigrants from the old country to be a "mean land" hard, dry and fit only for the steady, sober and hard-working Mormon.

[1] Arrington, *Great Basin Kingdom*, p. 195.
[2] Burton, *The City of the Saints*, p. 319.

Scarcely one fiftieth part is fit for tillage.'[1] During the 1860s 'the group struggle for self-sufficiency manifested itself in immigration, public works, communications, colonization, industry, transportation, and in the church's investment policy generally. In each case one sees an attempt to develop an economy with few entangling alliances, and yet with a capacity for growth and expansion through superior organization. If group achievement was somewhat less than expected, it was due to the failure of Great Basin agriculture to produce bounteous harvests.'[2] Yet the population of Utah doubled (rising from 40,000 to 80,000) between 1858 and 1869. The 90 Mormon settlements in the Territory of 1857 rose to 200 by the end of 1867 and to 300 or more by 1877.[3] Long before 1877 (the year Brigham Young died) the easily irrigable areas of Utah were nearly all under cultivation and, to increase the productive acreage further, resort had to be made to dry farming. As with large-scale irrigation, 'it was in Utah that the first considerable success was achieved in dry farming'.[4] After several failures in the 1850s it appears that a Scandinavian settlement at Bear River City was the site of the first successful experiment in Utah, about 1863.[5]

Dry farming or 'dry land farming', the use of the stored capillary water in the soil just under the growing crops, which without proper and constant cultivation (especially after rain has fallen) would be lost, was known and practised even in antiquity, but it was not widely resorted to in the United States outside northern Utah before the end of the nineteenth century. By 1909 more land was being tilled in Utah by dry-farming methods than by irrigation, though in 1900 there had already been about 6 million acres under irrigation. Dry farming was not practicable where the rainfall was less than ten inches a year on the average,[6] so much of Utah could still not benefit from it, but it was very suitable for Kansas and Nebraska west of the 100th meridian and for many other areas with between ten and thirty inches a year. The practice pioneered in Utah (and on a very local scale in parts of California, under the stimulus of the ideas of the soil scientist

[1] Burton, *op. cit.*, p. 312. [2] Arrington, *op. cit.*, p. 205.

[3] M. R. Hunter, *Brigham Young the Colonizer* (Salt Lake City, 1940) whose figures are critically appraised by P. A. M. Taylor, *op. cit.*, pp. 95–6.

[4] Webb, *Great Plains*, p. 368.

[5] Webb quotes J. A. Widsoe, *Dry Farming* (New York, 1913) as his authority for this and also used W. Macdonald, *Dry Farming: Its Principles and Practice* (New York, 1911).

[6] According to Webb. Shannon (*Farmer's Last Frontier*) says fifteen.

F. W. Hilgard) nevertheless spread only slowly into other states and Territories. There was some dry farming in Edward County, Kansas, in the 1880s, but it required the evangelical zeal of Hardy W. Campbell to bring dry farming into Nebraska at the turn of the century[1] and Colorado was equally slow in making use of the technique to which, it has been estimated, fully 300 million acres of the United States were suited, compared with 350 millions cultivable without special techniques and only 80,000 irrigated or irrigable.[2]

By the year 1900 irrigation as the result of federal or state action (against which the formidable Major Powell[3] had set his face so resolutely in 1878) was still in its infancy in the United States. The 'bungling'[4] Carey Act had only been passed in 1894, a timid first step into the shallow end of the problem; barely 4 million acres had been irrigated by the turn of the century, and under 9 millions by 1902. Shannon estimates that only about 250,000 acres of this irrigation was due to the Carey Act, instead of the 17 million allowed for!

If the year 1890 saw the end of an era for American agriculture through the break-up into 'islands' of the hitherto unbroken belt of free uncultivated land westwards of the settlements, a new era had hardly commenced by 1900, and the 380 million acres of the United States capable of cultivation by means of irrigation and dry farming (more than the total area cultivable or under cultivation without such aids) remained to a large extent unexploited. The new techniques had been pioneered by the Saints in Utah and American agriculture owes a great debt to them for this pioneering, but they were being only very slowly learned and adopted elsewhere. So 'the end of the century came with the farmer on his last frontier, always hopeful that the next year would reverse his luck but never sure that he could "keep his belt buckle from chafing his backbone" till the next crop was raised'.[5]

[1] Macdonald, *Dry Farming*, pp. 18–19. Webb, *op. cit.*, p. 369.

[2] Webb, p. 366.

[3] J. W. Powell, *Report on the Lands of the Arid Region of the United States* (Washington, D.C., 1878), and W. Stegner, *Beyond the Hundredth Meridian* (1950), which contains the best appraisal of Powell's importance.

[4] So called by Shannon in *The Farmer's Last Frontier*, p. 216.

[5] *Ibid.*, p. 220. Fred Shannon, in his commendable effort not to appear a Pollyanna, has painted a somewhat too sombre picture of the plight of the American farmer during the last third of the nineteenth century. Reading his volume on the Agricultural History of the United States it is sometimes hard to remember that not all farmers were ruined and that some of them even made fortunes. Shannon, a professional iconoclast, was an academic curmudgeon who, while infinitely kind and helpful to younger scholars, much enjoyed quarrelling with his contemporaries. When he took on men of the calibre of Frederick Jackson Turner, Walter Prescott

No attempt has been made in this book to separate the frontier experiences of Canadian history from that of the United States, for they are inseparable. The 49th parallel, from the Lake of the Woods to Puget Sound, though politically and psychologically of great significance, has no physical or climatic or zoological or anthropological existence. The Indian and the buffalo did not recognize that border, neither did the maize plant or the salmon, the elk, the moose, or the bear. The scenery does not change as you journey up from the Great Falls to Calgary, or from Bellingham to Vancouver, any more than it does farther east between Bismarck and Regina, Duluth and Port Arthur, Detroit and London, Buffalo and Hamilton, Montpelier and Montreal. Glacier and Waterton, split by the border, constitute one great mountain National Park area.

But although they are inseparable they have, paradoxically, tended to grow apart as time has gone on. In the era of exploration and in the Mountain Man era they cannot be disentangled: Mackenzie and Ogden have been given equal billing in this book with Lewis and Clark and Jedediah Smith. While the Condominium lasted the Oregon country was both no-man's-land and Everyman's. Smith was up at Fort Vancouver, and Ogden down on the Colorado and the San Joaquin. Dr McLaughlin succoured Americans (even when he suspected their motives) on the Columbia and the Hudson's Bay Company opened up a trading post on San Francisco Bay. The Reverend Samuel Parker (a Yankee Methodist) was far better received by the Roman Catholic Canadian Dr McLaughlin than was the Rev. Thomas Beaver (a British Anglican); Thomas Oliver Larkin loathed his fellow-Yankee, Hall Jackson Kelley, and gave him short shrift at Monterey in 1834, but he did all he could for his Canadian trading rival, the unfortunate John McRae, representative of the Hudson's Bay Company at Yerba Buena, and McLaughlin's son-in-law. McLaughlin and George Simpson were also, themselves, well received at Yerba Buena and Monterey when they visited the California coast in 1841. Camaraderie on those remote frontiers seemed not only to go with but to extend far beyond joint-occupancy.

After 1846 lines were drawn more tightly and the new Canadian colony of British Columbia blossomed, in and after the Fraser river

Webb, and Avery Craven (see Bibliographical Note, pp. 390–1), the battle tended to be royal and sparks, fur and dirt to fly. He gave no quarter and to him no holds (even with the teeth) were barred. But there was no malice in him.

gold rush of 1858, into a bulwark and outpost of Canadian nationalism in the Far West. The organization of the Oregon and Washington Territories, and Oregon's statehood, served to crystallize American sentiment on the other side of the border. The Canadian Federal Act of 1867 made it clear that the northern nation would not fall like a ripe pear before a new onward march of Manifest Destiny. Indian troubles in the border regions in the 1860s and 1870s, especially after the Canadian opening-up of the Red river valley area and the American penetration of the Sioux hunting grounds in the Black Hills, found the two countries pursuing rather different policies towards the tribes which bestrode or tried to cross the 49th parallel. The Great White Queen at Windsor appeared more tolerant at times towards the cause of the red man than did the Great White Father in Washington. Both Sitting Bull and Chief Joseph sought refuge in Canada. The 'Mounties' sometimes fed and protected the very same Indians that the Seventh United States Cavalry had hoped to starve and exterminate. No events quite so ugly as the Chivington massacre or Wounded Knee occurred north of the border,[1] but on the Indian side there was nothing comparable either to the Whitman or the Fetterman massacres, no Lava Beds affair, no crushing and embittering defeat of the white man comparable to Little Bighorn.

Canada's Indian policy may be said to have learned as well as profited from some of the mistakes made by the Americans. On the whole it was more humane and more even-handed; no jurisdictional conflict comparable to that between the Department of the Interior and the Department of the Army of the United States bedevilled Indian relations in Ottawa or in the provincial capitals. The Indians were exploited and had their lands taken away on the Canadian side all right, but rather less crudely. As a result, perhaps, Canada's Indians produced no last-ditchers like Chief Joseph and Geronimo.

Canada's mining frontiers were also less lawless than those of the United States. The system of licensing on the Fraser river, though greatly resented by the miners, made the rush there more orderly – and also more directly profitable to the Government. When the great rush into the Yukon came at the end of the century the Canadians had in front of them the lessons learned on many more American mining frontiers, as well as on several of their own, and the Mounties were there almost from the beginning. The rush over the high pass to Dawson

[1] There were, of course, the two Red River rebellions of dissident half-breeds, the leaders of which were savagely punished.

City was not exactly a Sunday-school outing, but it was more orderly and safer for all concerned than the early days in, say, western Nevada, Colorado, Montana, and South Dakota. It was also far less picturesque.

Canadian and American frontier experience, then, was linked at the 49th parallel, but not inflexibly so. A. L. Burt had convincingly and wittingly applied the Turner[1] touchstone to Canada. 'If Turner had looked at Canada . . .'[2] he had said, he would have found, even in colonial New France 'a surprising confirmation of the thesis he was propounding' that frontier conditions produce and nurture Democracy.[3] 'If Turner had looked north,' Burt continued,[4] 'he could not have failed to see that the frontier movement crossed and recrossed the international border.' Before the Revolution, New Englanders had for two decades been migrating into Nova Scotia; after Independence this migration was resumed, but now it consisted of refugees – the dispossessed Loyalists! A smaller number of United Empire Loyalists founded Upper Canada, farther west. 'The Upper Canada Loyalists put the American frontier north into British territory,' where there were no Indian troubles, the land was fertile, and 200 acres were to be had free (or almost free) for the asking. This exodus went on until the outbreak of the War of 1812. After the war Upper Canada's population came to be reinforced by a new immigration from the Old Country, and there Disraeli's 'two nations' fought it out until a more democratic

[1] See *infra*, p. 345.

[2] A. L. Burt, 'If Turner had looked at Canada, Australia, and New Zealand when he wrote about the West' in Wyman and Kroeber (eds) *The Frontier in Perspective* (Madison, Wisconsin, 1957, pp. 59–77). This illuminating little essay is one of the best in an excellent collection, based upon lectures delivered in the summer session of 1954 at the University of Wisconsin in honour of the memory of Lyman Copeland Draper, father of the State Historical Society. Coming there as unpaid corresponding secretary in 1854, he parlayed a collection of fifty books into the magnificent library it had become by the time of his death in 1891, since when it has become far more magnificent. It was Draper who provided men like Turner with the tools of their trade, ready to hand. See further, W. B. Hesseltine, *Pioneer's Mission* (a biography of Draper, Madison, 1954).

[3] Burt takes B. J. Wright to task for his remarks on New France in 'American Democracy and the Frontier' (*Yale Review*, XX (1931), p. 350), one of the earliest and least effective attacks upon Turner and his school. Different conditions in the New World made it impossible to transplant French feudalism to Canada and also impossible for the Roman Catholic Church to collect tithes there, except to a token extent. *Lods et ventes*, *banalités* and all the other burdens imposed upon the peasant in France were shrugged off by the *habitant*, who always had the safety valve of becoming even more free as a *coureur de bois*. The *habitant*, according to the Jesuit Charlevoix, 'breathed from his birth the air of liberty'.

[4] *Ibid.*, p. 68.

governmental system and a broader franchise were achieved by the reforms of the 1840s.

Meanwhile, westward advance north of the border had been checked by the barren 'Laurentian Shield' of virtually unusable pre-Cambrian rock-strewn soil, and back the frontier of settlement went across the border into the United States. Canada suffered a severe drain on her still meagre population, amounting perhaps to one-third of its total, during the middle years of the nineteenth century in the direction of the free (or believed to be free) lands of the new Middle Western and Prairie territories of the United States. Gold discoveries in the extreme west of Canada in 1858, and the stimulus to national development by the formation of the Dominion out of a group of separate colonies in 1867, began the reversal of this southward tide (which the California gold rush had of course only served to stimulate), but not until it was – however prematurely – noised abroad in the 1890s that 'free land' was no longer available in the United States, did Canada's own prairie provinces beyond the infertile Laurentian Shield begin to fill up. The building of railroads across this barrier had to precede this. The first transcontinental line, the Canadian Pacific, was (after innumerable political and financial hitches) completed in 1885, but the Canadian Trunk, which was the second, not until 1911. Canada's total population was still only 4,300,000 in 1881 (barely more than that of the U.S.A. in 1790) and it had only increased by one million in 1901. Spectacular increases had to wait until the twentieth century. By 1911 it was over 7 million (twice the 1871 figure) and by 1931 over 10 million. Immigration had been very small (compared with that into the United States) before the turn of the century, having reached only 21,716 in the year 1897, but by 1904 it was 146,000 in that one year, and in 1912 it was over 400,000, a figure which still stands as the record influx for any single year. Only 2,000 people emigrated from the United States to Canada in 1897, but over 43,000 did so in 1904 and nearly 140,000 in 1912. This last total represented almost as many people as reached Canada from the United Kingdom that year (150,000) and more than the 112,000 who came from all other countries combined. Over 860,000 people emigrated from the United States to Canada in the ten years 1904–13 inclusive. Canada's frontier certainly had not 'gone', for a good proportion of these went to her western provinces, and two new ones, Saskatchewan and Alberta, were created in 1905. Immigration did not recover to its pre-war size after 1918, despite the fact that restrictions similar to those obtaining in the United

States were not imposed by Canada. The highest post-war figure was 167,000 in 1929, but by 1932 it was down to 25,000 and by 1937 to 15,000. By then Canada, also, had temporarily ceased to be a 'land of opportunity' and, like the United States, was re-exporting to Europe more people than she received each year. Not until 1931 did Canada have a larger urban than rural population and even in 1941 only eight of her cities contained more than 100,000 inhabitants each. She was still predominantly a farming country and a producer of basic raw materials, such as wood-pulp, rather than a manufacturing one, even by the middle of the twentieth century. This made her very different from the United States. Her untapped mineral resources still remained enormous, though by 1945 she was already the world's greatest producer of nickel, radium, platinum, and asbestos, and its second greatest of gold, aluminium, uranium, molybdenum, and wood-pulp. As each new mining area was opened up, frontier conditions continued to break out all over Canada, and will continue to do so. The Great Bear Lake area, just below the Arctic Circle in the North-west Territories, has been a true 'frontier' in the classic tradition during the last thirty years, since large deposits of pitchblende were found there in 1936. The vastly increased strategic importance of uranium since that date has made these deposits of primary importance in the nuclear age.

When Frederick Paxson claimed in 1930 that 'the West is Gone'[1] 'he wore a blinker on his north eye', says Burt[2] and failed to notice that it was still in full flower in Canada, especially in and beyond the 'Whoop-Up Country' about which Paul Sharp has written[3] so vividly. Since then the Great Bear Lake mines have opened up and enormous hydro-electric projects like the Kootenay in British Columbia have been initiated. In 1958 Vancouver celebrated its centennial with every manifestation of 'Western' enthusiasm, even if Victoria may have rattled its teacups in mild disapproval. In the Canadian Far North the climate, the remoteness, the sparse population, and the barrenness of the soil have retarded development, but surely the fuller exploitation of this great area will open up yet another set of frontiers. The building of the 'Alcan Highway' as a war measure in the 1940s, and the coming of the air age, have brought this nearer to realization.

[1] F. L. Paxson, *When the West Is Gone* (New York, 1930).

[2] *Op. cit.*, p. 72.

[3] Paul Sharp, *The Agrarian Revolt in Western Canada* (Minneapolis, 1948), 'When our West Moved North' (*Am. Hist. Review*, Vol. LV, 1950), and *Whoop-Up Country* (New York, 1955).

CHAPTER XIV

The End of the West? Twentieth Century Frontiers

'In the remoter West, the restless rushing wave of settlement has broken with a shock against the arid plains. The free lands are gone, the continent is crossed, and all this push and energy is turning into channels of agitation. Failures in one area can no longer be made good by taking up land on a new frontier; the conditions of a settled society are being reached with suddenness and with confusion.' Thus wrote Frederick Jackson Turner, the Wisconsin historian, in the *Atlantic Monthly* magazine for September 1896[1] in an attempt to popularize a conclusion which had first been stated in the report of the Superintendent of the United States census in 1890, and which he himself had presented to a scholarly audience in his famous essay on 'The Significance of the Frontier in American History' in 1893.

This unpalatable truth, if truth it was, was that the free lands of the United States were running out. It was soon also to be trumpeted abroad by the politicians and the leaders of business. From Theodore Roosevelt's fear that the nation's population would soon outstrip its food supply (though the population of the United States was still under 100 million) and James J. Hill's warning of a nationwide famine, to Franklin D. Roosevelt's famous remark thirty years later (when the population had risen above 125 million, with still no famine, and indeed a vast over-production of foodstuffs) that 'we can no longer escape into virgin territory, we must master our environment', the note of alarm continued to be sounded. Only after the legislation of the New Deal had been applied to this problem and the coming of the Second World War had ushered in another era of farm prosperity did scholars and economists begin to express a different sort of alarm. Then, in the 1950s, the United States was told that it contained a 'people of plenty' whose high standard of living and tendency to over-produce was a danger to the well-being of the nation, and whose 'affluent society' was arousing the envy and the hatred of the whole outside world, no

[1] Vol. LXXVIII, p. 289.

matter how high a proportion of their superabundance the Americans were prepared to give away. Such public philosophies could only create as much confusion in the mind of the citizen as when he had been told some sixty years earlier that the great safety-valve of 'free land' was now closed and that the consequences were bound to be dire.

Whatever economic ups and downs the future may hold in store for this 'people of plenty' and this 'affluent society', the prophecies of doom uttered by those who viewed with alarm the census figures of 1890 turned out to be oddly at sixes and sevens with reality. The early 1890s (like the late 1880s) were indeed a period of falling prices and rural distress. The Populist Party, dedicated to raising 'less corn and more hell', sought by various panaceas – including bimetallism which found its apostle in William Jennings Bryan in 1896 – to deal with the problem. But ironically, from 1897 onwards, after the electoral defeat of Bryan and the Populist cause and in an era of continued Republican ascendancy, prosperity suddenly and somewhat unaccountably reappeared. The price of farm land skyrocketed and on an average it had risen over 100 per cent by 1910 – in the Dakotas (from which there had been a serious rural exodus in the early 1890s) by over 300 per cent – and the general price index for produce rose between the 1899 baseline of 100 to nearly 190 in 1910. This boom was achieved without bimetallism, without Bryan at the helm of affairs and without the safety-valve of free land. To Professor Turner and the Superintendent of the Census, and even to Theodore Roosevelt, it must all have appeared very mysterious. It was not until 1920 that a new agricultural depression began to set in, and once again the pundits were taken by surprise.

It was when the agricultural depression of the 1920s was deepened by the stock-market crash of 1929 and the industrial depression of the 1930s, that critics began to turn really savagely on the 'safety-valve theory' which Turner had espoused. They claimed that not only was there no longer a safety-valve in free or cheap farmland farther west for the economic and social ills of settled American communities in the East and Middle West but that there never had been one. It was pointed out that during depression years – after the panic of 1837 and those of 1857, 1873, and 1893 – migration westwards as well as immigration from overseas had slowed down rather than accelerated. It was in years of relative prosperity or of boom that the westward movement was greatest as also was immigration. The 'peak years' of the German

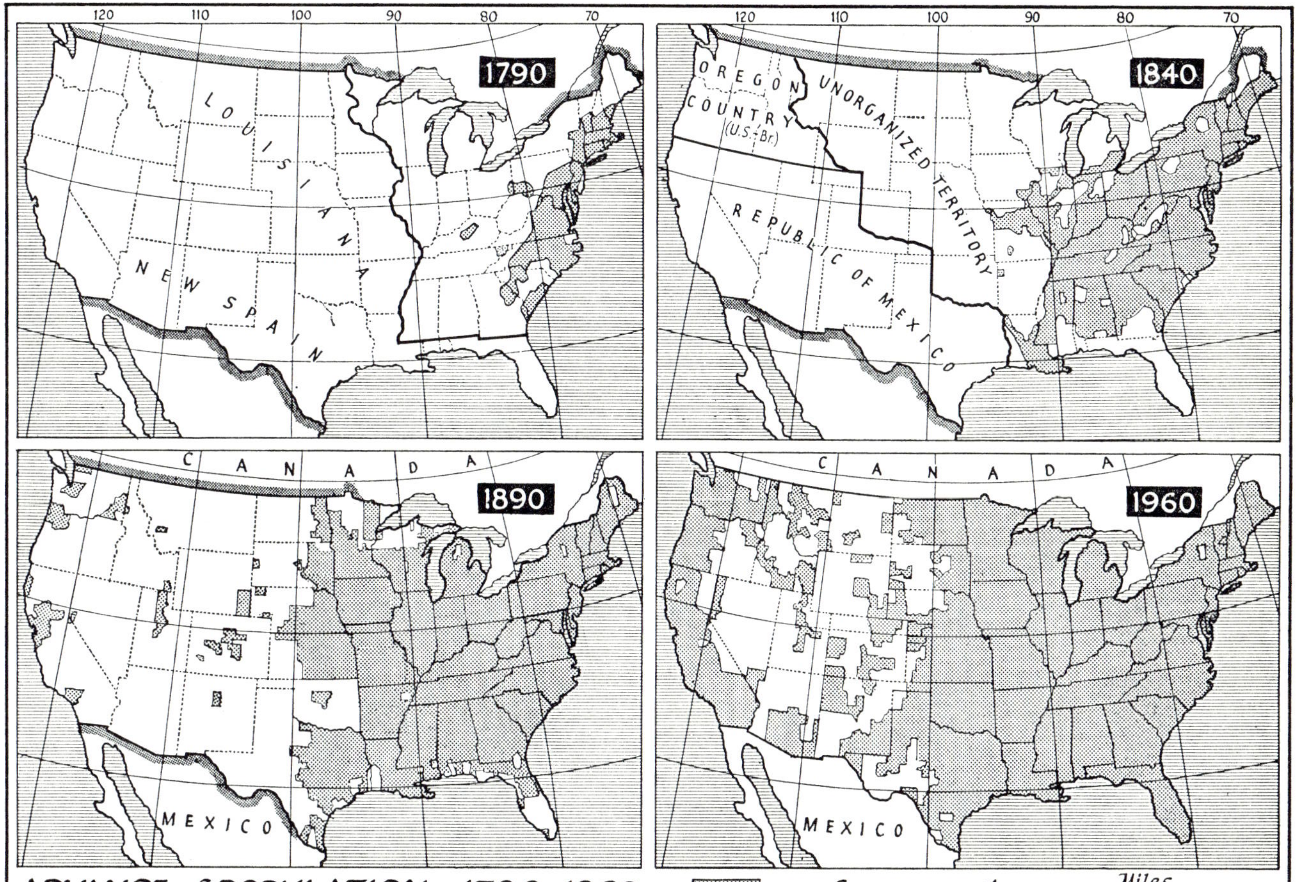

ADVANCE of POPULATION • 1790–1960

immigration were 1854 and 1882, and the all-time record year for immigration from all sources was 1907. In the year 1931 a severe shock was administered to the American ego by a reversal of the tide of immigration for the first time since records had been accurately kept in 1820, for three times as many emigrants departed from the United States that year as immigrants reached its shores. Fred Shannon's mordant 'Post-mortem on the Safety Valve'[1] came only at the end of a decade of attacks on the theory which left it pretty effectively shredded to pieces.

The discrediting of the safety-valve theory did not, of course, automatically invalidate the remainder of the Turner hypothesis, although it did bring out the jackals and the buzzards in considerable numbers. Every aspect of the hypothesis now came under close scrutiny and budding historians (as well as others well past the budding stage, like Charles A. Beard) seemed to consider it their professional duty to get themselves blooded in the attack on it. Not every attack was as clinical as that of Shannon, as vicious as that of Beard or as doctrinaire as that of Hacker. The most effective criticisms, such as those of George Pierson, Carlton Hayes, and David Potter, tended to be those which conceded much validity to the Turner hypothesis, yet pin-pointed its shortcomings; the most successful defenders of Turner tended to be those, like Avery Craven, or Frederick Paxson, or Ray Billington, who did not demand a one-hundred-per-cent adherence to every opinion that Turner had expressed. An all-out apologia, such as Joseph Schafer's attempt to justify the safety-valve theory, tended to play into the hands of the enemy.

It began to be realized that Turner, in 1893, had been generalizing about an American agrarian society that had already passed its apogee; that he had not given sufficient weight to the effect of the technical advances of the industrial revolution; and that 'by failing to recognise that the frontier was only one form in which America offered abundance, he cut himself off from an insight into the fact that other forms of abundance had superseded the frontier even before the supply of free land had been exhausted, with the result that it was not really the end of free land but rather the substitution of new forms of economic activity which terminated the frontier phase in our history'.[2] This still

[1] Fred A. Shannon, 'A Post-Mortem on the Labor-Safety-Valve Theory,' *Agricultural History*, Vol. XIX (Jan., 1945), pp. 31–7; adapted for, and incorporated in, his *The Farmer's Last Frontier*, already quoted.

[2] D. Potter, *People of Plenty* (Chicago, 1954), p. 156.

left the Turner hypothesis as a very valuable asset to the historian, as was demonstrated most strikingly in 1952 by one of his leading disciples, Walter Prescott Webb, who sought, not without success, to expand the Turner hypothesis from America to the whole world. In *The Great Frontier* Webb may at times, with characteristic Texan verve, have overstated his case, but he did 'bring Turner up to date' by giving adequate weight to the exploitation of the mineral wealth of the soil (whereas Turner had concentrated too exclusively on the products of its tillage) in the modern world (and thereby 'clarifying a vital factor which remained obscure in Turner');[1] but he also stressed the importance of commerce in 'that form of wealth classed as Things or commodities' – and of the piling-up of surplus wealth in other forms than that of the abundance of the soil; his simplified version of a Keynesian *obiter dictum* that the loot of the *Golden Hind* had been parlayed into the wealth of Britain – the Britain of Joint Stock Banks and the National Debt – within little more than a century – has at least pointed to the fact that there were alternative ways for men and nations to become rich (even prior to the eighteenth century) to pursuing the agrarian ideal. Turner, it is true, recognized the existence of 'the trader's frontier, the rancher's frontier and the miner's frontier'[2] as well as the farmer's frontier; but the frontier speculator, the frontier town-builder and the frontier technologist and inventor get short shrift from him. Webb, in *The Great Frontier* (as he had, on a narrower stage, in earlier works, such as *The Great Plains* and *The Texas Rangers*) filled in the gaps. Colt and his revolver, Glidden and his barbed wire, Halladay and his self-regulating wind-pump, play no part in the Turner story, but they are major characters and properties in Webb's. It is true that Webb, like Turner, concluded on a note of gloom: four hundred years of abundance on *The Great Frontier* of the New World and the Old had ended, just as free land even to the westward no longer existed for North America, and man faced an uncertain and more restricted future. 'Science can do much but it is not likely to find a new world or make the one we have much better than it is,' wrote Webb in 1952. Even two years later David Potter was questioning this assertion,[3] and today, with Mars and Venus probes in the news and a landing by man on the moon quite likely in the near future, it already seems to have been a very dangerous one.

[1] D. Potter, *op. cit.*, p. 160.
[2] Turner, *The Frontier in American History* (1920), 1962 edn., p. 12.
[3] Potter, *People of Plenty*, p. 164.

Webb may be said not so much to have exposed the inadequacies of the Turner hypothesis as to have disclosed its wider possibilities.[1] Turner was anything but a prolific writer and managed during over forty years of historical teaching and research to produce twenty-six short, seminal essays and just one book.[2] Had he published more he might have produced a more rounded and less assailable philosophy of history and the famous hypothesis might not have been left so full of holes. His posthumous publications display an interest in many themes he did not fully develop, such as the significance of the Section (a major geographical area comprising a number of states or territories) in American history and the influence of increasing urbanization upon American life.[3] Billington's mature judgement is that[4]

> Most modern scholars, then, would agree with Turner that the frontiersman did develop certain traits and that these have been perpetuated to form the principal distinguishing characteristics of the American people today. Americans display a restless energy, a versatility, a practical ingenuity, an earthy practicality to a degree unknown among Englishmen and other Europeans. They do squander their natural resources with an abandon unknown elsewhere; they have developed a mobility both socially and physically that marks them as a people apart. In few other lands is democracy worshipped so intensely, or nationalism carried to such extremes of isolationism or international arrogance. Rarely do other peoples display such indifference toward intellectualism or aesthetic values; seldom in comparable cultural areas do they cling so tenaciously to the shibboleth of rugged individualism. Nor do residents of non-frontier lands experience the same degree of heady optimism, the blind faith in the future, the belief in the inevitability of progress,

[1] See also Bibliographical Note, p. 391.

[2] See R. A. Billington's instructive and highly entertaining article in the *Mississippi Valley Historical Review* (Vol. L, No. 1, June 1963, pp. 3–27), entitled 'Why Some Historians Rarely Write History: A Case Study of Frederick Jackson Turner'. The one book was *The Rise of the New West, 1819–1829* in the 'American Nation' series, ed. A. B. Hart, New York, 1906 (paperbound edn, ed. R. A. Billington, New York, 1962). 'It ought to be carved on my tombstone,' wrote A. B. Hart, 'that I was the only man in the world that secured what might be called an adequate volume from Turner.'

[3] Other scholars have, since Turner's death, begun to pursue these topics further: for instance, Roy F. Nichols, 'The Territories: Seedbeds of Democracy' (*Nebraska History*, Vol. XXXV, September 1954, pp. 159–72), and Richard C. Wade, *The Urban Frontier* (Cambridge, Mass., 1959).

[4] Billington, *The American Frontier* (American Historical Association pamphlet, Washington, D.C., 1958), p. 22.

that is part of the American creed. These were pioneer traits, and they have become part of the national heritage.

These traits, so frankly stated by an American historian, have been noticed with varying degrees of sympathy and understanding by foreign observers from Crèvecoeur to the Chinese 'Silent Traveller',[1] by Tocqueville, by Dickens, by Frederika Bremer, by James Bryce, by Rudyard Kipling, by André Siegfried, by Halvdan Koht, by Louis Adamič, by Karel Čapec, by Sir Denis Brogan, and by Nikita Khrushchev. Khrushchev was happiest during his visit to the United States when on an Iowa farm, unhappiest when, in California, he was taken to a Hollywood studio, but prevented from going to Walt Disney's 'Frontierland'. Bryce praised the exuberance of the 'Western Parts of America', already living in the future, with today only half-finished and yesterday already forgotten. Brogan noted (as early as 1935) 'The Rise and Decline of the American Agricultural Interest' which had bulked so large in the United States from Jefferson to Turner, and had remained important, though on the defensive, in the shape of the 'Farm Bloc' even thereafter. Not all these commentators could agree on what exactly constituted the American creed and why it was different from the national heritage of the peoples of Europe, but they all admitted that it *was* different.

Turner, in one of his most celebrated and poetic passages wrote 'American democracy was born of no theorist's dream, it was not carried in the *Susan Constant* to Virginia nor in the *Mayflower* to Plymouth. It came stark and strong and full of life out of the American forest, and it gained strength each time it touched a new frontier.'[2] In this resounding and often-quoted passage Turner issued a challenge not only to the 'germ theory' of G. B. Adams[3] but also to those who think that free institutions, hard-won in seventeenth- and eighteenth-century political struggles in England may possibly have been brought to America by the emigrants in their little ships, and that the thirst for

[1] Even the Far East has paid its tribute to the pioneering spirit of the American West. See Chiang Lee, *The Silent Traveller in San Francisco* (London and New York, 1964), p. 365.

[2] F. J. Turner, 'The West and American Ideals' (*Washington Historical Quarterly*, Vol. V, October 1914), p. 245 and – slightly modified – reprinted in *The Frontier in American History* (1920 and 1931), p. 293.

[3] The 'germ theory' postulated that the 'germs' of democratic principles originated among the primitive Anglo-Saxon tribes and were carried by them both to Britain and to America. G. B. Adams, Europe-trained, taught it at Johns Hopkins University, where Turner was a graduate student.

liberty, even if unslaked (but intensified on countless barricades) in France, in Spain, in Italy, in Germany, in the Habsburg realms, and even in Russia, may have been carried across the Atlantic in cabin and steerage alike, all through the Great Immigration of the nineteenth century. Tom Paine and Robert Owen, Carl Schurz and Lajos Kossuth, Wilhelm Weitling and Karl Heinzen needed no refresher course in the American backwoods on the meaning of freedom or the pursuit of democracy, according to their lights. Had Tocqueville ever met Davy Crockett (and how one wishes that this could have happened!) he would have found him a very crude practitioner indeed of 'Democracy in America', though he might have discovered how to buy a man's vote with a swig of brandy and a quid of tobacco. The Americanization of Edward Bok (from the Netherlands), of Felix Frankfurter (from Austria), of Andrew Carnegie (from Scotland), and of Louis Adamič (from Slovenia) proceeded without any visible benefit from the American Forest. Even indigenous American apostles of democracy could do without the inspiration of trees. George Norris came from the treeless plains of Nebraska; if William Alan White wanted a tree to grow in Emporia, Kansas, he had to plant it himself and keep it watered; Fiorello La Guardia took his inspiration from the asphalt jungle of New York;[1] the men who owned most of the Big Trees in California were not the biggest democrats in that state, or in any other: their beliefs (if they had any) ran to feudalism rather than radicalism: even the radicals who established their temporary 'Utopian Colonies' among the Giant Sequoias administered the unkindest cut of all to the 'Democracy-comes-out-of-the-American-Forest' theory by naming the largest of them all (now reconsecrated and christened 'The General Sherman') 'The Karl Marx Tree'.[2]

It is perhaps too easy to make fun of one of Frederick Jackson Turner's very rare naïveties and to forget his many words of wisdom, and the inspiration he gave to others. Though he himself may not have fully acknowledged the ideological value of what the European immigrants brought over with them to plant in the American Forest, he

[1] The 'Little Flower' was born in New York all right, but he also went to school in Arizona, served for three years (1907–10) as an interpreter on Ellis Island and commanded a United States Army Air Corps base in north Italy in the First World War. This all happened before he went into Congress and to even greater glory (and national fame) as Mayor of New York. It may with confidence be said that New York has never been the same since.

[2] Robert V. Hine, *California's Utopian Colonies* (San Marino, California, 1953), p. 90.

31*a*. Colonel Cody ('Buffalo Bill') at his own oil field in Wyoming, 1909.

31*b*. Immigrants awaiting admission at Ellis Island, about 1907.

32. 'Standing Up Country' – the Court House Towers Section, Arches National Monument, near Moab, Utah. Part of the undeveloped West.

did nurture the genius of Marcus Lee Hansen, whose pioneering and, unhappily, incompleted studies of *The Atlantic Migration 1607–1860* (1940) and of *The Immigrant in American History*,[1] gave due weight, perhaps for the first time, to a number of factors that Turner had failed to stress. 'Unlike most historians of Immigration,' Arthur M. Schlesinger, Sr, has written,[2] Hansen 'takes his stand in Europe rather than in America'.

> As the story grows under the author's pen, no reader can fail to perceive its epic character. Less familiar than the advance of the pioneers into the American West, the long continuous migration across the ocean forms the necessary background for that movement. To the courage and determination of these humble folks from Europe historians ascribe some of the finest traits of the national character.

The author of *New Viewpoints in American History*[3] had already, in that seminal book, pointed out the importance of immigration in the making of America and the opening up of the West. By presenting the fruits of Hansen's researches to the world he underlined this importance.

[1] M. L. Hansen (1892–1938) was, according to Oscar Handlin, 'the first serious student of the history of American immigration'. Though that judgement ignores the by-no-means valueless works (even today) of John R. Commons, *Races and Immigrants in America* (New York and London, 1907), and of N. W. Stephenson, *A History of American Immigration* (Boston, 1926), it has a good deal of truth in it. The native-born son of Scandinavian immigrants, Hansen went from the University of Iowa to Harvard in 1917 to work under the Master. There 'Turner directed the young man's attention to the opportunities for creative scholarship on the history of immigration' (Handlin). Twenty years of arduous research were overtaken by his premature death in 1938 before he had published any of his main conclusions, but Professor H. Hale Bellot had persuaded him to give a course of public lectures on *The Immigrant in American History* at University College, London, in 1935 (which the present writer attended, to his very great profit), and these were published as the posthumous book, *The Immigrant in American History* (New York and London, 1941). Hansen in his turn had influenced a whole new generation of writers on immigration problems, including Oscar Handlin, Charlotte Ericson, Maldwyn Jones, Theodore Saloutas, and myself, for in 1935 he read through my *Tragedy of German-America* in typescript (it was to be published by Putnam, New York, in 1940) and made many valuable suggestions, though we agreed to differ on a number of points regarding the hyphen in German-Americanism. *The Atlantic Migration 1607–1860*, which was prepared for publication from Hansen's manuscripts and notes by Henry M. Schlesinger, Sr, deservedly won the Pulitzer Prize for History in 1941. It has since been reissued as a paperback in 'Harper Torchbooks' (New York, 1961) with Schlesinger's original Foreword and an extra Introduction by Handlin.

[2] *Atlantic Migration*, p. xix.

[3] Arthur M. Schlesinger, Sr, *New Viewpoints In American History* (Harvard, Mass., 1921).

Hansen had intended to write two more volumes, taking the story of *The Atlantic Migration* up to 1914, but his published volume (edited by Schlesinger) though it breaks off in 1860 before the really 'great' immigration (statistically considered) had really commenced, contains enough signposts to how the rest should be written to have enabled other scholars to complete the story, not perhaps quite as he would have done it, but adequately enough.

Much of the story of the Great Atlantic Migration from Europe to the United States – and, in a lesser degree, to Canada – is irrelevant

to a history of the American West and will not be considered here, but it is not without significance that the really huge immigration did not commence until easily available free land in the West was no longer to be had. The record of 790,000 immigrants in 1882 stood for over twenty years and during the depression of the 1890s the annual figures dropped to 216,000 in 1897. They then rapidly climbed to a million a year and stayed above the million mark (with no fewer than 1,285,000 in 1907 alone) until the middle of 1914. The impact of these new millions, most of them crowding into the cities, not only alarmed politicians, publicists, trade-union leaders, women's clubs and all red-blooded two-hundred-per-cent Americans – however recent their own arrival – but even scared Frederick Jackson Turner.

> Where Braddock and his men [at the Battle on the Monongahela, 1755], 'carving a cross on the wilderness rim' were struck by the painted savages in the primeval woods, huge furnaces belch forth perpetual fires and Huns and Bulgars, Poles and Sicilians struggle for

> a chance to earn their daily bread, and live a brutal and degraded life.[1]

How unlike the home life of our own dear Daniel Boone! But Marcus Lee Hansen and his school have discovered why these Huns and Bulgars, Poles and Sicilians chose to emigrate to America and how they succeeded in doing so, often against incredible odds. The young girl from off a Galician (or Bessarabian or Calabrian) farm who walked barefoot[2] down the gang-plank on to Ellis Island around the year 1907 may never have gone back on to the land, but she could well have become, by 1965, another Helena Rubenstein.[3]

It is Hansen's contention that the statistically 'greatest' migration into the United States (1898–1914) was less 'great' in its effects upon American life than that between 1850 and 1860,[4] when

> Something like 2,600,000 aliens poured into the country and the foreign-born inhabitants increased from 2,244,600 to well over 4,000,000 . . . This migration was great in comparison with the native American population, great in the trails of settlement it broke, great in the cultural foundations it laid. Subsequent decades were to see a larger volume of arrivals, but no later migration paid richer dividends to American civilization.

This view is perhaps open to argument and what Hansen does not point out (as he might have done had he completed a sequel to this volume) is that the later migrations may well have paid richer dividends in happiness and well-being to the migrants than this earlier one. While the earlier did bring relief from the consequences of the potato famine in Ireland and help to assuage land-hunger among Germans and Scandinavians, a relatively small proportion of the middle-nineteenth-century emigrants from Europe were seeking to escape religious and political persecution in addition to adverse economic conditions. A much higher proportion of the emigrants from 1881 onwards had these additional incentives. This applied less to the Italians, whose motives remained mainly economic, but after 1881 the active and systematic persecution of the Jews in European Russia commenced. This began

[1] 'The West and American Ideals' (1914) as reprinted in *Frontier and Section* (ed. R. A. Billington, Spectrum Books, New York, 1961), pp. 105–6.

[2] See Illustration, plate 31b, taken from J. R. Commons, *Races and Immigrants*, p. 230. She also appears in the photograph facing p. 78 of that book.

[3] Helena Rubenstein, the famous manufacturer of cosmetics, was born near Cracow, in Austrian Poland, around 1875. She died an American citizen, and a multi-millionairess, in 1965.

[4] Hansen, *Atlantic Migration* (Torchbook edn, 1961), p. 281.

a great exodus to America, hastened by occasional pogroms and rumours of more to come. The Great and White Russian peasant did not emigrate, and 98 per cent of the emigration from the Russian Empire to the United States came from its 'subject' peoples or races. Of these, in the year 1906, 125,000 were Jews, 46,000 Poles, 14,000 Lithuanians, 13,000 Finns, and 10,000 Germans. Five-sixths of all the Jewish emigration from Europe to the United States in that year came from Russia, and the remaining one-sixth almost entirely from Austria-Hungary and Rumania.[1] Most, of course, of the Russian Jews were German-speaking, and classifiable by the United States Census Bureau (which ceased after 1900 to record the religion of an immigrant) as 'Russian-Germans'. Their *lingua franca* was the hybrid Yiddish tongue, though a proportion of the Orthodox Jews also understood Hebrew. While many of these persecuted people came from rural areas in Russia (though there they were not permitted to farm the land), Austria-Hungary, and Rumania, they almost invariably stayed in the larger cities in America where the skills they possessed were in more demand and where their abject poverty on arrival was less of a bar to getting a new start in life. As it was, many of them had to be supported by relatives and by relief organizations at first. While they helped to relieve the urban labour shortage in the 'boom' years after 1897, they aroused resentment among the native-born and the earlier immigrant groups for being willing to accept low wages and inferior living conditions, just as had the Irish peasants who had fled the famine half a century earlier. A half a century later it was to be the Puerto Ricans' turn!

Even more people (265,000) emigrated from Austria-Hungary to the United States in 1906 than from Russia. As opposed to the 1880s and 1890s, when most emigration was from the more northerly parts of the Empire, the Southern Slavs – Croats and Slovenes – now led the emigration with 43,000 in that one year. There were also 16,000 Ruthenians – a large number from so small an area – and 11,000 Rumanians. German-speaking subjects of the Habsburgs emigrating numbered 35,000. There were fewer Magyars than before on account of measures taken by the Hungarian government to discourage their emigration. As J. R. Commons wrote in 1907:[2]

> Practically the entire migration of the Slavic element at the present time is that of peasants. In Croatia the forests have been

[1] Commons, *Races and Immigrants*, p. 88.

[2] *Ibid.*, p. 84.

> depleted, and thousands of immigrant wood-choppers have sought the forests of our South and the railway construction of the West . . . So it is with the Slovak peasants of the Northern mountains and foot-hills. With agricultural wages only eighteen cents a day, they find employment in the American mines, rolling mills, stockyards and railroad construction at $1.50 a day.

Before very long some of them would be receiving Henry Ford's $2.00 a day minimum. Many of those who worked on the early Model-T assembly lines were Middle Europeans.

Italy sent 273,000, or more than a quarter of all immigrants received by the United States, in 1906. In 1876 she had only sent 3,000! Italian emigration, principally from the south and Sicily, was mainly to relieve economic distress, for there was little political oppression (though also little good or efficient government) in the easy-going kingdom of those days, though a large number of young men emigrated to escape conscription. Many Italians were only 'temporary emigrants', aiming to make a little money and then return home. Fully 150,000 did so in 1906 from various countries abroad. A goodly number of these were Italians who had emigrated to the United States, and many of those who did not return sent back remittances to their families or remembered to send for their wives and sweethearts. 'It is said that already there are several small country towns in Southern Italy which have risen from squalor to something of prosperity through the money and influence of those who have come home,' wrote Commons again in 1907.[1] They swaggered through the dusty little piazzas, criticizing everything; unmortgaged or purchased the family farm, extending its miserably small holding to a decent size; built a garish villa complete with victrola and running water; loaned money at high interest to the hard-up local squire and sometimes even married his daughter as an alternative to foreclosure. They introduced machinery and know-how and the *Saturday Evening Post*; they told incredible tales (all of them believed – some of them true) of the sinful and salubrious city of Columbus, Ohio, or of Wilkes Barre, Pennsylvania, or of Fresno, California. They were the *Americani*, back from El Dorado, their pockets full of gold and 'You bechas' on their lips. Up and down the Dalmatian coast and in the broad uplands of Croatia and Slovenia, on Greek islands and mainland valleys these *Amerikanči* – or whatever they were called locally – also appeared. They tended to be the ones who had succeeded only moderately well in the United States, for those who failed in the New World

[1] Commons, *op. cit.*, p. 77.

rarely returned home (even if they had the passage money) to explain their shame, and those who became really well-heeled usually stayed in America resolved to make even more money and bring up their children as real Americans, which they knew they could not themselves ever quite become. The successful tended to get themselves Americanized with almost indecent haste. The movie magnate Carl Laemmle, reminiscing in 1934 on the fiftieth anniversary of his emigration to America from Germany (a signed photograph of Franklin D. Roosevelt on the wall behind his desk), confessed that he had turned his back on Germany from the beginning, had allowed only English-language newspapers into his home and had forbidden the use of the German language in his family circle.[1] This may be an extreme example, but if a Jewish emigrant from Germany (where anti-Semitism was in its infancy in 1884, and pogroms unknown) felt this way, how much greater was the incentive to the refugee from the ghettos of Warsaw and Lodź and Lublin – who could have no hope of or incentive for returning, even on a visit, and whose remittances might well never reach their destination – to forget Old World ties completely amid the stresses and excitements of the New.

What have the recent immigrant 'hordes' contributed to the development of the trans-Mississippi West? By the very nature of things they appear superficially to have contributed less than the Germans and the Irish in the Old and the New North-west between the Ohio and the Mississippi. Although the Scandinavians have set an unmistakable stamp on Minnesota and Iowa, western Kansas and Nebraska, and the Dakotas, there has never been any city there so 'Scandinavian' as (in their turn) Cincinnati, St Louis, and Milwaukee were once German – concentration points of German settlement and social, cultural, and business centres for a German-born population spread through the small towns and villages and farms of Ohio, Illinois, Missouri, and Wisconsin. The central, the eastern, and the southern Europeans, arriving even later than the Scandinavians, have never succeeded in 'taking over' any large city, or state, or section of the country, even for a short period. The Poles in the Connecticut valley have not de-Yankeefied it; the Italians in the Napa valley and the Valley of the Moon of California have trodden and pressed (and now presumably atomize) its grapes without eradicating its old-time Spanish atmosphere; the

[1] In an interview granted to the author at Universal City, California, in 1934. Mr Laemmle's life story had been told by John Drinkwater, *Carl Laemmle* (New York and London, 1931), in a book written between scenario assignments at Universal City.

French-Canadians have rescued neither Massachusetts' politics from the Irish nor its culture from the Puritans. Nevertheless, the Poles and the French-Canadians have put back into cultivation derelict fields and farms deserted by their earlier, more improvident, more foot-loose Yankee exploiters, and the Italians, assisted by smaller numbers of other European immigrants, have provided the inherited skill, the patience, and the acceptance of rural standards of living (such as could not be found in sufficient quantity among Americans, either of Anglo-Saxon or of Spanish descent) that the specialized agriculture of the Napa and other Californian valleys needed. These peoples were not the first to break the soil in such areas, and they did not even (except here and there) come to own it outright; the place-names were not of their coinage, but they have contributed mightily to its prosperity. No incorporated place in Minnesota has a recognizably Welsh or Cornish name, despite the Welsh and Cornish contribution to the exploiting of the iron mines of that state; the same state even has only two names that are unquestionably Scandinavian. While Wisconsin has a 'Cambria', its largest city still bears an Indian name, instead of being called something like 'Schlitzburg'.[1] 'Kohler of Kohler' (the German-American bath-tub king) had to create and incorporate a company town to get out from under the wing of nearby Sheboygan, named after another forgotten Indian worthy; neither Anheuser nor Busch – nor even Jefferson – has been able to push a saintly king of France off his pedestal down at St Louis; Pittsburgh, the birthplace of Czechoslovakia,[2] despite this association and the very large number of Bohemians and Slovaks and Ruthenians who settled there in the age of steel, is still named after an English eighteenth-century statesman who never crossed the Atlantic; New York, the world's largest Jewish community still bears the name of a seventeenth-century English king who was certainly, among his other unpleasant traits, anti-Semitic.[3] The en-

[1] A famous advertising slogan of the Schlitz Brewery of Milwaukee is 'The Beer that made Milwaukee Famous'.

[2] The Pittsburgh Proclamation of 1918 is recognized as Czechoslovakia's 'Declaration of Independence'.

[3] James Stuart, Duke of York, afterwards James II. New York also, in 1900, near the peak of the Great Immigration, had two and a half times the number of Jews as Warsaw, nearly as many Germans as Hamburg, twice as many Irishmen as Dublin, and half as many Italians as Naples, Bohemians as Prague, and Swedes as Stockholm. 'New York excels Babel,' wrote Commons in 1907 (*op. cit.*, p. 165), with 'Sixty-six languages spoken, forty-nine newspapers published in foreign languages, and one school . . . with children of twenty-nine nationalities.' The Negroes, the Mexicans, and the Puerto Ricans had not yet arrived in any numbers.

gaging habit of changing all the place-names when you take over a region or a settlement has not yet spread from the Polish People's Republic and other European 'succession states', or from the new nations of Africa and Asia, to the United States, where 'first come, longest preserved' seems to be the rule.

It is impossible to say what proportion of the post-1890 immigrants became and remained city-dwellers in the United States. That this proportion was far higher than that of those who arrived before 1890, and, particularly before 1860, only follows from the whole population trend of the United States into the cities. With the end of free or cheap land, with increasing farm mechanization – meaning fewer farm jobs even on larger acreages – with a larger demand for workers in steel mills, coal mines, automobile factories, and industry generally, the trend was an inevitable one. Only the most resolute and the most fortunate of the millions of European peasants who crowded into the United States after the 1880s managed to become farmers there; a very small proportion were able to contemplate ever owning their farms – unless they were prepared to accept abandoned or marginal land that the native-born stock and earlier immigrants had scorned or given up. They had to go into the towns as ordinary unskilled workers, or acquire some skill or craft by hard work and unusual enterprise. This was in most cases neither their fault nor their inclination. It was the terms on which American society in the machine age was prepared to absorb them.

Thus an ingrowing urban frontier had replaced an ever-advancing rural frontier before the turn of the century. No more Oklahomas existed, and reclamation on a large scale was in its infancy. Between 1900 and 1914 the big cities grew great and many small cities grew big. All of them, by the outbreak of the First World War, had a polyglot population, often concentrated in 'Little Italys', 'Little Polands', Lithuanian belts, Greek quarters, Jewish ghettos, and the like. This would have astounded Benjamin Franklin, who even resented a few thousand 'Palatine Boors' in Pennsylvania, or Jefferson, who envisaged the population of the United States doubling itself every twenty-six years without the aid of immigration – for in 1790 only 3 per cent of the population of the United States lived in cities, whereas by 1900 the percentage was over 33 per cent in places of 8,000 inhabitants and more, and was soon to rise to 50 per cent and more.[1] In 1900 two-fifths

[1] Taking the U.S. census criterion of places with 2,500 or more inhabitants being classed as 'urban', the urban percentage of the population rose from 5.1 in 1790 to 58.7 in 1950. By this computation the urban percentage in 1900 was 39.7.

of the foreign-born population lived in cities of 100,000 inhabitants or more. The average for the whole population was one-fifth.[1] This great transformation in a hundred years completely changed the face of America. It had now an urban civilization, in which the 'American farmer' of Crèvecoeur and Dickenson was rapidly becoming a minor figure, and in the big cities every other person was now an immigrant or the son or daughter of an immigrant. It was the opportunities for jobs in the cities which now dominated the relative rate of growth of the different states and sections and not the availability of free or cheap land. The frontier, in the Jeffersonian or Turnerian sense, had indeed gone.

Immigration as a stimulus to phenomenal urban growth in the United States was not to be a continuing phenomenon. By 1930 the 'Great Immigration' was over, and the increase in the percentage of urban population in the United States between 1930 and 1940 was only three-tenths of 1 per cent.[2] As one expert[3] sums it up:

> Immigration has largely ceased, except for a relatively few refugees and some displaced persons, who are being afforded a haven in America; so the immediate past and probabilities in the future make this source practically insignificant. There have been some periods in the past, however, when this source has been a large factor. The twentieth-century immigration tended to settle disproportionately in the cities. The first decade was an all-time peak of immigration to the United States – in four of these years the number exceeded one million. The total for ten years was a little over 8,750,000, the equivalent of more than half the total increase of population during that decade and three-quarters as much as the increase in urban population. From 1911 to 1920, with only two years over one million and a big decrease with the coming of World War I, the total dropped to just under 5,750,000 but still represented 42 per cent of total population growth and 47 per cent of urban increase. In the decade 1921–30 the total was a little more than 4,000,000 and the percentages 24 and 28 respectively. In the 1931–40 decade there were just over half a million immigrants, which represented 6 per cent of the total population increase, and a little less than 10 per cent of the urban population growth. Since 1940 even smaller numbers have entered America.

[1] Commons, *op. cit.*, p. 160–1.

[2] By contrast, it was 5 per cent between 1920 and 1930, 5.5 per cent between 1910 and 1920, and 6 per cent between 1900 and 1910.

[3] W. C. Hallenbeck, *American Urban Communities* (New York, 1951), pp. 64–5.

If this were a history of American immigrations rather than of the American West, much further attention would need to be paid to this change in the rural–urban balance of population and to the opening up of 'new frontiers' in the streets, suburbs, and metropolitan and 'ex-urban' areas of cities. As it is, all we need to ask is to what extent this was a Western phenomenon rather than a national one. Up to the year 1930 it was not. The great immigration flooded into the Eastern cities because it reached them first and then favoured the more easily accessible of the Middle-Western ones to those across the Missouri and in the Far West. Direct immigration by sea into California and the Pacific North-west was no longer a common practice after the 1860s, when the transcontinental railroad was opened. Even as inveterate a seafarer as Robert Louis Stevenson went *Across The Plains*[1] in an immigrant train to California in the year 1879. Between 1910 and 1930 the cities growing fastest in the United States were scattered all over the country, but in 1930–40 they were nearly all in three states – California, Texas, and Florida – two of which are in the West. This tendency continued during the 1940s, when half of the cities in the country increasing in size by 50 per cent or more were in these same three states. Florida's growth was, of course, a special phenomenon connected with the real-estate booms there, the increasing popularity of the state for retirement and the growth of the winter resorts there, with the increase in the amount of leisure among the American people and the vogue for 'two holidays a year'. The wartime decade of the 1940s was atypical in many ways, but it sent vast numbers of people into certain Far Western cities from other parts of the United States to work in the industries such as aircraft manufacturing and shipbuilding. The San Francisco–Oakland area gained a phenomenal 39 per cent in population between 1940 and 1947, the Los Angeles metropolitan area increased by 35 per cent, Seattle by 33 per cent, and Portland, Oregon, by 31 per cent.[2] This urban increase in population was not lost at the end of the war, and continued, in the California cities especially, to increase hugely all through the 1950s and into the 1960s. Seventy per cent of the immigrants from outside California between 1950 and 1960 settled in the southern part of the state, and the state's population as a

[1] R. L. Stevenson, *Across The Plains* (New York and London, 1892).

[2] *U.S. Bureau of the Census, Current Population Reports series P-21*, No. 35 (Washington, D.C., 1947), *passim*. These west coast cities were only matched by Washington, D.C., with 33 per cent and San Antonio, Texas, with 31 per cent, due mainly to increases in Civil Service personnel and armed forces establishments respectively.

whole increased by 48·5 per cent to 15,717,204, and was estimated as probably reaching over 25,000,000 by 1975. The metropolitan area of Los Angeles alone is expected to contain fully 11 million people in that year. In 1890 Los Angeles had barely 50,000 inhabitants. The City area already had just on 2 millions by 1950, and during the next three years alone[1] increased by 6·8 per cent or 134,305, of whom nearly a quarter were Negroes. It was said at this time that an average of over 600 persons *a day* were arriving by train at the Union Station in Los Angeles from other states with the intention of taking up permanent residence in southern California. This is larger than the whole population of the *pueblo* of Los Angeles in 1846 (when American rule commenced) and vast areas of farmland and even of citrus groves disappeared in Los Angeles and the adjoining counties during the 1950s and 1960s under the subdivider's hand, enormous stretches of 'tract' housing appearing on the old Spanish and Mexican *ranchos*. To get these people to and from their work, and the beaches and mountains nearby a colossal network of super-highways, or 'freeways' had to be built.[2] One presumably sober prophet[3] has discerned in his crystal ball that

> One day a solid city will stretch northward from San Diego to Los Angeles, then to Santa Barbara and perhaps even to San Luis Obispo. Its east–west line will probably run from the Sierra Madre Mountains to the ocean. In northern California a second decentralized, sprawling urban complex is being formed. This may become a continuous metropolis around San Francisco Bay – with offshoots into the valleys northward, southward and inland from the bay.

The population of the San Francisco 'Bay Area' in 1950 was 2¼ million and by 1975 was confidently expected to be 5½ million.

In case it should be thought that the foreign-born have continued to cling to the Eastern and Middle-Western states and cities since 1930, leaving the subsequent great domestic migration entirely to the native-born, it should be noted that in 1950 California had nearly a million

[1] Up to the special Census of 23 September 1953.

[2] The California freeways really are 'free' and no tolls are payable on public highways (though there are many bridge tolls) because by state law the entire revenue of the state's gasoline tax has to be devoted to highway improvement. This tax amounts to 7 cents a gallon and California has over 9 million automobiles currently in use.

[3] Andrew F. Rolle, *California: A History* (New York, 1963; revised edn, 1964), p. 612.

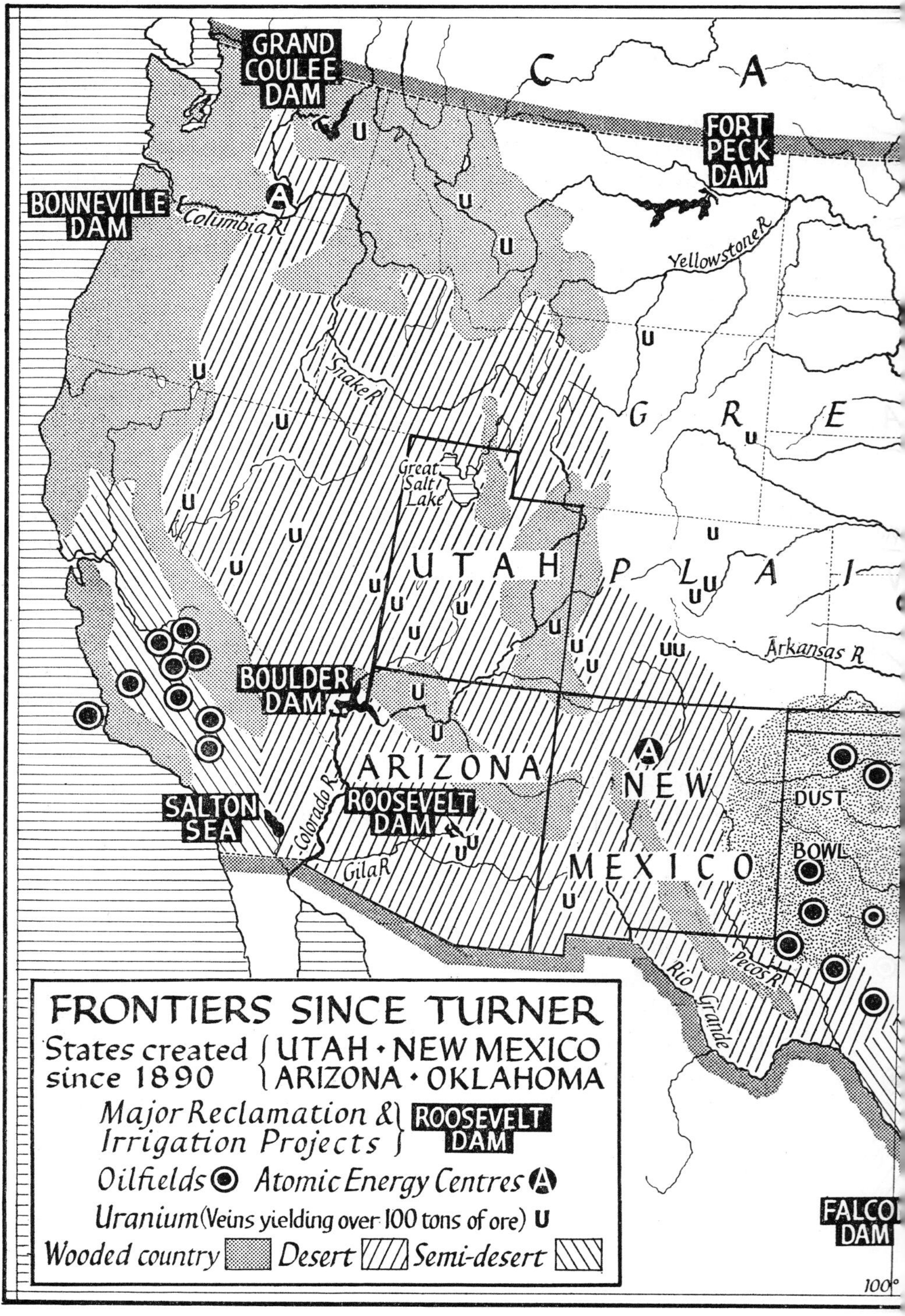

GRAND COULEE DAM
FORT PECK DAM
BONNEVILLE DAM
Columbia R.
Yellowstone R.
Snake R.
C A
G R E
P L A I
Great Salt Lake
UTAH
Arkansas R.
BOULDER DAM
ARIZONA
NEW MEXICO
Colorado R.
SALTON SEA
ROOSEVELT DAM
Gila R.
DUST BOWL
Rio Grande
Pecos R.
FALCO DAM
100°
FRONTIERS SINCE TURNER
States created since 1890 UTAH • NEW MEXICO ARIZONA • OKLAHOMA
Major Reclamation & Irrigation Projects ROOSEVELT DAM
Oilfields Atomic Energy Centres A
Uranium (Veins yielding over 100 tons of ore) U
Wooded country Desert Semi-desert

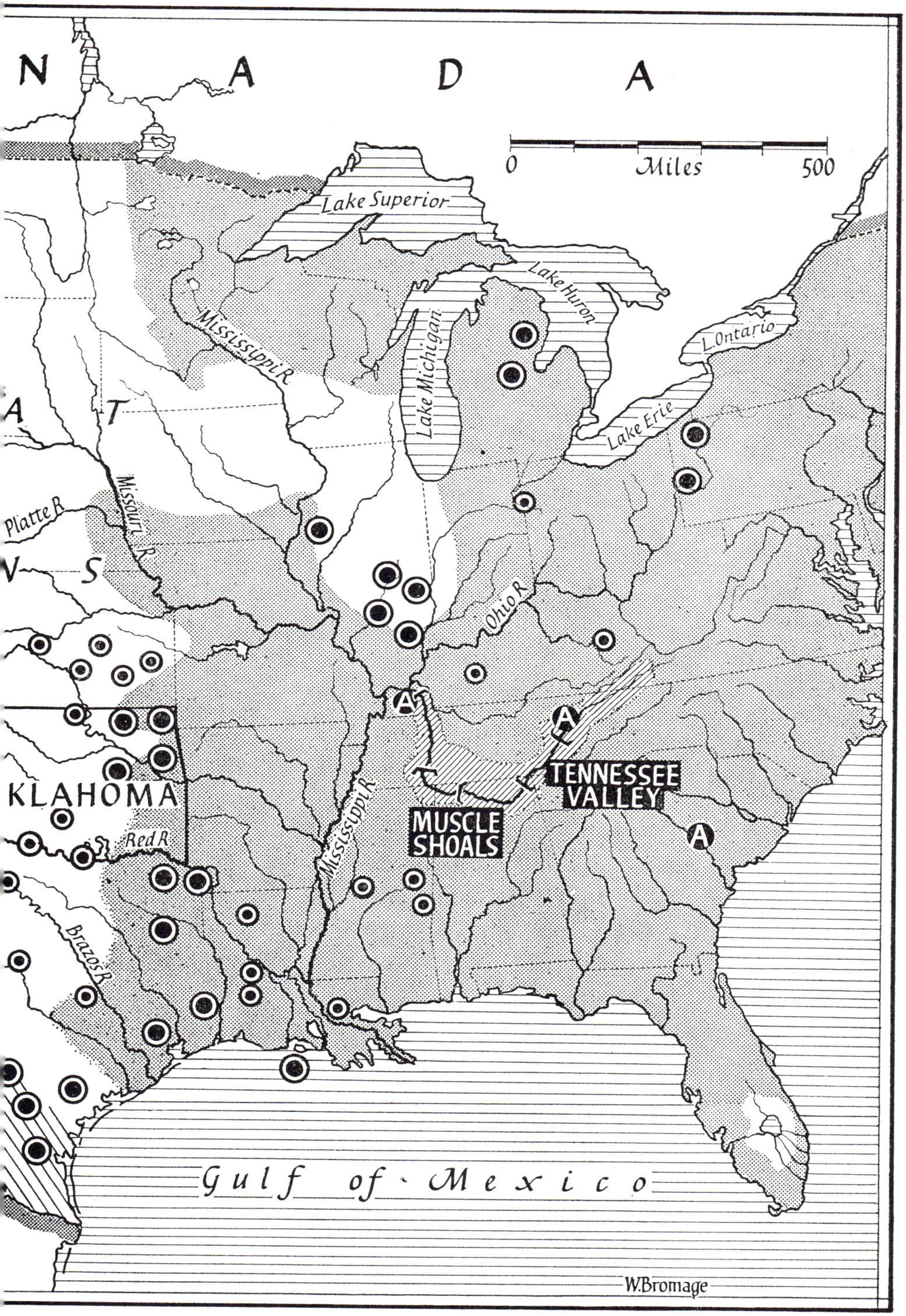
N A D A
0 Miles 500
Lake Superior
Lake Huron
Lake Michigan
L. Ontario
Lake Erie
Mississippi R
Missouri R
Platte R
Ohio R
A T
V S
KLAHOMA
Red R
Brazos R
Mississippi R
A
A
A
TENNESSEE VALLEY
MUSCLE SHOALS
Gulf of Mexico
W. Bromage

foreign-born citizens,[1] second only to New York (with 2½ million)[2] while the State of Washington had 191,000 and Oregon 83,000. Colorado had 58,000 and Montana 43,000; Texas had 276,000 – of whom 196,000 came from Mexico. Of the European-born immigrants more Danes and Swiss were living in California than in any other state in 1950, more Belgians, Dutch, and Finns in Michigan, more Lithuanians and Swedes in Illinois, more Norwegians in Minnesota, more Czechs in Pennsylvania, more Yugoslavs in Ohio, and more Portuguese in Massachusetts. New York State had the largest numbers of the remaining European-born groups. Thus, although the foreign-born Europeans have continued to participate in the twentieth-century movement into the Far West, the native-born have dominated it, just as they dominated the nineteenth-century migrations westward across the United States.

In the early and middle 1930s a new rural migration westward out of the 'dust-bowl' states[3] of the plains occurred. This stream of destitute or near-destitute farming families – so vividly described by John Steinbeck in *The Grapes of Wrath* – sought to resettle mainly in California, where they were most unwelcome, and many of them ended up there living in shanty-towns, as migrant workers, with little hope of ever becoming landowners or tenant farmers or even share-croppers again. The huge demand for labour in California during the war emergency years from 1939 onwards absorbed most of these people in other than farming occupations and solved for California's relief and employment agencies a problem which might otherwise have continued to exist for a generation. The 'Arkies' and 'Okies' continued to migrate westward through the 1940s, but by this time they were no longer unwelcome, and nor were the Negroes from the Old South,[4] who were beginning to rival them in numbers.

The industrialization of the Far West, and of California in particular,

[1] 104,000 from Great Britain, 104,000 from Italy, 70,000 from Germany, and 28,000 from the Republic of Ireland, though 110,000 came from Canada and no fewer than 162,000 from Mexico.

[2] Illinois came third with 783,000.

[3] See map on previous pages for the approximate location of the 'dust bowl'.

[4] The states which declined in population between 1930 and 1940 were Kansas, Nebraska, Oklahoma, and North and South Dakota. In the 1940s Arkansas also had a net loss in population, and so did Mississippi. North Dakota and Oklahoma continued to decline, but there was a slight net increase in Kansas, Nebraska, and South Dakota. All other states increased in population during both decades, except for little Vermont, which remained static during the thirties. During these two decades California increased in population from 5,677,000 to 10,586,000. There were nearly half a million Negroes in California by 1950.

during the twentieth century, has made further large-scale westward migration across the United States possible and has continued to encourage it. This is a story in itself of which only the principal landmarks can be noticed. Before the end of the nineteenth century the mining boom had long since been succeeded by the farming and lumbering boom in the Rocky Mountain and Pacific coast states. The canning and food-processing industries arose naturally out of the former. Citrus-fruit growing in southern California, in particular, was put on an industrial basis, and the famous 'Sunkist' trade-mark and guarantee of quality established. The motion-picture industry was another one, which, though it originated in the East, had firmly established its centre in southern California, with all its climatic advantages, by the beginning of the 1920s. A cultural exodus from the New York stage and literary scene was to follow and to include all three of the famous Barrymores, writers of the calibre of F. Scott Fitzgerald, and producers, musicians, and stage designers without number. Europe sent such 'names' as Lang, Lubitsch, Hitchcock, Garbo, Dietrich and Laughton. Improvised studios on vacant lots out among the oil-rigs near Santa Monica, or up Cahuenga Pass, suddenly blossomed into 'Cities' – such as Culver City and Universal City – and became big business. The new movie tycoons came from the ends of the earth – Louis B. Mayer from Minsk, Russia (by way of New Brunswick, Canada), Carl Laemmle from Laupheim, Germany (by way of Oshkosh, Wisconsin), and Sam Goldwyn (*né* Goldfisch) from Warsaw, Poland. But Jesse L. Lasky (by way of exception) was a native son, born in San Francisco, who had been in the Alaska gold rush, and in show business in Hawaii, before taking up an option on the foot of the rainbow.

Oil was another new industry of the West, for not only was it found there but its refining required a complicated industrial process before it could pass into the thirsty tanks of America's automobiles and trucks, which increased in numbers from 8,000 in 1900 to 10 million in 1921, to nearly 20 million by 1925 and to over 40 million by 1948.[1] Oil was found in Pennsylvania in the 1850s, in Kansas as early as 1860, in Texas in 1866 (though the first boom there was not until the 1880s) and the famous Spindletop gusher, at Beaumont on the Gulf Coast did not come in until 1901. The enormous East Texas oilfield became a big producer only in the 1920s and the West Texas field beyond the Pecos

[1] In 1963 there were over 82 millions of them; 9 million in California alone; over 3 million of these were registered in Los Angeles County! *Automobile Facts and Figures*, 1964 edn (Automobile Manufacturers' Association, Detroit, 1964), pp. 18–19.

later still. Wyoming and Montana oilfield exploitation dates from 1908. California oil was late on the scene, but soon made up for that. Santa Maria and Coalinga were early developments, around 1910, and then came Long Beach and the forest of derricks on Signal Hill, one of the greatest oilfields in the world. Offshore oil discoveries have latterly become important along the California as well as along the Texas and Louisiana coasts, and when the Eisenhower government, in the 1950s, handed over offshore oil to the separate states, its exploitation was stimulated, though much revenue was lost to the Federal Government. Oil was also found in many inland areas of California, the Bakersfield region proving one of the richest. In Oklahoma oil was discovered in the 1890s, and by 1907, the year of statehood, Oklahoma produced over $43\frac{1}{2}$ million barrels of crude. Gushers on the Osage Indian reservation made rich men of some of the hitherto indigent Braves, and they squandered their new-found wealth right royally. Arkansas also saw important oil discoveries, and more was found in Kansas.

Every one of the major oilfields opened up in the twentieth century was in the trans-Mississippi West, and half of them were beyond the 100th meridian. Texas and California became, and have remained, the greatest producers. The opening of each new oilfield tended to produce 'frontier conditions' once again, with lawlessness, honky-tonks, wide-open towns, and hangers-on of every kind, in addition to the solid oil engineers and the wide-eyed oil lessors, some of whom found oil-rigs in their backyards and among their flower-beds and had to learn to live with a sickly smell than which only the smell of the lessee's money was stronger – and sweeter. Texas benefited even more than California from the oil boom. Houston, a city and inland port of 44,000 inhabitants in 1900, had reached nearly 600,000 by 1950, and was pushing 1 million by 1965. Dallas grew with almost equal rapidity from 42,000 in 1900 to 434,000 in 1950; it and its twin and rival city, Fort Worth, together now come above the million mark. San Antonio, without benefit of a nearby oilfield, grew more slowly until 1940, but then jumped up by 30 per cent in one decade to 408,000 and, with defence establishments all around and a splendid climate for the oil-rich to retire to or recuperate in, is now well over the half-million. Rural Texas did not increase in population so spectacularly[1] as its well-oiled cities in the twentieth century, for with twice California's population in

[1] But could rest on its laurels after producing two Presidents of the United States (Dwight D. Eisenhower, born in Denison, Texas, in 1890, and Lyndon Baines Johnson, born in Johnson City, Texas, in 1908).

1900 it only had three-quarters as many people as the Golden State in 1950.

Oil continued to be of great importance, but new sources of industrial energy and employment arose to challenge it, and once again it was mainly in the West that these were developed. The great atomic plants started up during the Second World War had to be near to abundant water and hydro-electric power. The Columbia river valley was one of the greatest available sources of both. The atomic proving grounds needed to be in uninhabited areas, and the deserts of the West provided these. Defence projects like Hanford in Washington and Los Alamos in New Mexico had to be created out of nothing, and the thousands of scientists, technicians, craftsmen, and others needed to start up new communities in the wilderness were drawn to them from all parts of the United States and also from abroad. Once again new frontiers were opened up, this time sophisticated frontiers, orderly balanced societies unlike the old unruly frontiers of the past, but in the early days of Hanford, Los Alamos, and the like, the excitement of living on a frontier certainly existed even if some of its traditional discomforts were never experienced. The Coca-Cola bottling plant was usually in production before the reactor, the supermarket opened up before the saloon and the schoolmarm arrived even before the stripper.

The atomic frontier also created the need for new raw materials, such as uranium ores, which caused some of the remotest wildernesses of the United States to be re-explored, re-prospected, and sometimes even settled. Such new developments occurred in south-eastern Utah where only hunters and Indians had penetrated before, and on the Navajo Reservation of northern Arizona. The Navajo, from being one of the poorest of the tribes of the South-west, subsisting miserably from their herds of sheep and from sporadic craftsmanship in silver, pottery, and rug-making for the tourist trade, suddenly found themselves, when they leased their uranium-bearing soil, one of the richest. The Tribal Council, profiting from the knowledge of how the Osage had squandered their oil-lease money, has used these funds for social services and education, and to start up profitable community enterprises. The high school and hospital at Window Rock, the tribal capital, have become showplaces, and the tourist may stay at a Navajo-owned and run luxury motel there. Since Kit Carson 'pacified' the Navajoand corralled them on their desolate and barren reservation just a century ago the wheel has truly come full circle; well-armed Navajo mobile police now keep over-inquisitive *Anglos* off restricted areas of their reservation! New frontiers can open up for the first Americans as well as for the newest ones, even in the second half of the twentieth century.

From Columbus' *Santa Maria* to the jet-propulsion laboratories of Pasadena, from Coronado to the proving grounds of Los Alamos and the slaughter houses of Wichita, from Jedediah Smith to that air-conditioned nightmare which is Las Vegas, Nevada, from Marcus Whitman to the Grand Coulee Dam in eastern Washington, from the cliff houses of Mesa Verde to the City of the Saints, from Cabeza de Vaca to Lyndon Baines Johnson, from Drake to Disney, is a long haul, but all are part of the never-ending story that is the history of the American West. 'What the Mediterranean Sea was to the Greeks, breaking the bond of custom, offering new experiences, calling out new institutions and activities, that, and more, the ever-retreating frontier has been to the United States directly and to the nations of Europe more remotely.'

BIBLIOGRAPHICAL NOTE AND INDEX

Bibliographical Note

This is in no sense to be regarded as a comprehensive bibliography. It does not include many of the specialist accounts and monographs referred to or cited in the footnotes to this book. It is intended as a guide to further reading on the subject matter of each succeeding chapter, and is highly selective. Where the same field is covered in a number of different books, as is often the case with different aspects of the history of the American West, only one or two of such books are listed; the author of this work is aware that other books at least as good are omitted. For these a comprehensive scholarly bibliography of the history of the Westward Movement, such as is Ray Allen Billington's in *Westward Expansion* (New York, third edition, 1966), should be used. His bibliography extends to over a hundred closely printed two-column pages, and includes articles, as well as monographs, and books printing contemporary accounts and other source material. A number of regional or topical bibliographies also exist, which, in their more limited fields, are even more comprehensive than is Billington's. That very learned bibliographer Henry R. Wagner was responsible for a number of these, including *A Bibliography of Printed Works in Spanish relating to those parts of the United States which formerly belonged to Mexico* (Santiago de Chile, 1917. *Supplement*, Berkeley, California, n.d.), *The Spanish Southwest. A Bibliography* (Berkeley, 1924; revised, Albuquerque, 1937), and *The Plains and the Rockies, 1800–1865: A Contribution to the Bibliography of original Narratives of Travel and Adventure* (San Francisco, 1921; revised and extended by C. L. Camp, San Francisco, 1937; third edition, Columbus, Ohio, 1953). Most students will find Billington's Bibliographical Note more than adequate and it possesses the great advantage of being thoroughly up-to-date. In smaller compass Nelson Close, *A Concise Study Guide to the American Frontier* (Bison Books, Lincoln, Nebraska, 1964, paperbound), lists over 600 titles in his 'Bibliography of Frontier History', topically arranged. For periodicals O. O. Winther, *A Classified list of the Periodical Literature of the Trans-Mississippi West, 1811–1957* (Bloomington, Indiana, 1961), is indispensable. This lists over 9,000 articles, no fewer of them than 5,500 published since 1938.

THE PRE-COLUMBIAN WEST

While Frederick W. Hodge (ed.), *Handbook of American Indians North of Mexico* (2 vols, Washington, D.C., 1912), and Clark Wissler, *The American Indian* (New York, 1922) and his *Indians of the United States* (New York, 1940) remain standard treatments, they have now been supplemented by more recent treatments. These include Harold E. Driver, *Indians of North America* (Chicago, 1961), and William Brandon's eloquent and lavishly illustrated *The American Heritage Book of Indians* (New York, 1961; text only in Dell 'Laurel' paperbound edition, 1964). Helen M. Wormington's *Prehistoric Indians of North America* (Denver, fourth printing, 1959) is a valuable short handbook by a leading authority in her field. George E. Hyde is equally authoritative on the Plains Indians in *The Indians of the High Plains* (Norman, 1959) and other works dealing with specific tribes, both in the Pre-Columbian period and since. The terrain of the Pre-Columbian West is discussed by Eugene W. Hollon, *The Great American Desert: Then and Now* (New York, 1966), as well as in the older, classic treatment of Walter P. Webb, *The Great Plains* (Boston, 1931). An even older work, Ellen C. Semple, *American History in its Geographic Conditions* (Boston, 1903 and 1933) still has value. For the geographical background the standard work is Nevin M. Fenneman, *Physiography of Western United States* (New York, 1931); for historical geography (including reproductions in facsimile of many early maps), both Pre- and Post-Columbian, see *The Atlas of the Historical Geography of the United States* (ed. C. O. Paullin and J. K. Wright, Washington, D.C., 1932). The introductory sections to Brandon (*op. cit.*) and to the companion volume by David Lavender, *The American Heritage History of the Great West* (New York, 1965), deal with the Pre-Columbian period, and both contain excellent simplified maps. By no means to be despised, even by adults, is *Indians of the Plains*, by Eugene Rachlis in consultation with John C. Ewers (New York, 1960), in the American Heritage Junior Library. It, like the other volumes in the same series, is superbly illustrated.

OVERLAND EXPLORATION OF NORTH AMERICA (TO 1800)

Two reasonably short and still valuable general surveys are John B. Brebner, *The Explorers of North America, 1492–1806* (New York and London, 1933; reprinted, 1955), and Herbert E. Bolton, *The Spanish Borderlands* (Chronicles of America Series, New Haven, 1921). Bolton's important paper on 'The Mission as a Frontier Institution in the Spanish–American Colonies' (*American Historical Review*, October 1917, Vol. XXIII) has been reprinted together with fifteen other of his essays by John F. Bannon, S.J. (ed.) as *Bolton and the Spanish Borderlands* (Norman, 1964). Bolton's *The Rim of Christendom* (Cleveland, 1936), on Father Kino and the Spanish colonization of Sonora and southern Arizona, and his short biography of Kino, *The Padre on Horseback* (San Francisco, 1932; reprinted, Chicago, 1963), as well as his *Coronado, Knight of Pueblos and Plains* (New York, 1950), are standard monographs. A popular and detailed account of the colonization of New Mexico, and much besides, is Paul Horgan's *Great River* (New York, 2 vols, 1954). Less 'literary' in their approach are Eugene W. Hollon, *The Southwest: Old and New* (New York, 1961), Stephen Clissold, *The Seven Cities of Cíbola* (London and New York, 1961), and Warren A. Beck, *New Mexico: A History of Four Centuries* (Norman, 1962). For specific periods in the history of Spanish Texas there are Herbert E. Bolton's essay, 'The Spanish Occupation of Texas, 1519–1690' (*Southwestern Historical Quarterly*, Vol. XVI, July 1912; reprinted by Bannon, *op. cit.*), Henry Folmer, *Franco-Spanish Rivalry in North America, 1542–1763* (Glendale, 1953), comprehending Florida and the Mississippi River valley as well, and Odie B. Faulk, *The Last Years of Spanish Texas, 1778–1821* (The Hague, 1964). Robert S. Weddle's *The San Saba Mission: Spanish Pivot in Texas* (Austin, 1964) is a new specialist survey in the best Bolton tradition, which some scholars had thought and a few had hoped was dead.

IMPERIALISM ON THE PACIFIC

There is a vast and growing literature on Spanish California. Henry R. Wagner, *Sir Francis Drake's Voyage around the World. Its Aims and Achievements* (San Francisco, 1926), is dogmatic but massively documented on the subject of Nova Albion. The earlier portions of Robert Glass Cleland's *From Wilderness to Empire*, a general history of California (New York, 1933; reprinted 1959) contain one of the most readable accounts, and the inevitable Herbert E. Bolton's *Outpost of Empire* (New York, 1921) tells the story of the founding of the mission and presidio of San Francisco. A recent scholarly history of one of the most important of the Franciscan missions in Alta California is Maynard Geiger, O.F.M., *Mission Santa Barbara* (Santa Barbara, 1965); an exhaustive treatment of the histories of all the missions being Zephyrin Engelhardt, *The*

Missions and Missionaries of California (4 vols, San Francisco, 1908–15). The best biography of Father Serra is Maynard Geiger, *The Life and Times of Fray Junipero Serra, O.F.M.* (2 vols, Washington, 1959). The editions by Herbert E. Bolton of the various accounts and diaries of secular and missionary explorers in Spanish California are detailed in the footnotes to Chapter III (*supra*) and need not therefore be listed again in this bibliography: the results of some of these are summarized in Herbert I. Priestley, *Franciscan Explorations in California* (Glendale, 1947). Charles E. Chapman, *A History of California: The Spanish Period* (New York, 1921), is still one of the most useful and readable surveys available, but for further general histories of California, during as well as after that period, see also the Bibliographical Note, 'By Land and Sea to Eldorado', which follows. Foreign visits to Spanish California are narrated by George Vancouver, *A Voyage of Discovery in the North Pacific Ocean*, Vol. II (London, 1798); Jean François Gallup de la Pérouse, *Voyage autour due Monde*, in Vol. I (Paris, 1797, English translation, London, 1798); T. C. Russell (ed.), *The Rezanov Voyage to Nueva California in 1806* (San Francisco, 1926), and his *Langsdorff's Narrative of the Rezanov Voyage* (San Francisco, 1927); *A Voyage of Discovery in the South Sea* by Otto von Kotzebue (English translation from the German, London, 1821); and *Voyage pittoresque autour du monde* by L. Choris, (Paris, 1822), with interesting illustrations by the author, who was Kotzebue's artist.

EXPLORING THE LOUISIANA PURCHASE

Walter P. Webb, *The Great Plains*, is again useful for background. Richard Van Alstyne, *The Rising American Empire* (Oxford and New York, 1960), presents an unorthodox and anti-nativist viewpoint and does not hesitate to call Thomas Jefferson an imperialist. The documentation of the Louisiana purchase was usefully collected in a government publication for the purposes of its centennial by Binder Hermann, *The Louisiana Purchase* (Washington, 1898), of which the documents and maps are more useful than the commentary. The Lewis and Clark expedition is put into its historical perspective by E. W. Gilbert, *Exploration of Western America, 1800–1850* (London, 1933), and this book also usefully summarizes other explorations of the period it covers. Lewis' and Clark's own account of their expedition was not printed until 1814 (written up by Nicholas Biddle, ed. P. Allen); it was reprinted, and edited, by Elliott Coues as *The History of the Expedition of*

Lewis and Clark, in four volumes (New York, 1893) – with notes and additional material – and is now available paperbound in three volumes (New York, 1965); but they were anticipated by their own Sergeant, Patrick Gass, whose *Journal* (for full title, see Chapter IV, page 98) came out first in 1807 in Pittsburgh, and in a French translation in Paris in 1809, and is quaint but not very reliable. The recent discovery of the actual field-notes from which Clark wrote up his story is leading to a new series of publications, of which *The Field Notes of Captain Thomas Clark, 1803–05* (ed. Ernest S. Osgood, New Haven, 1964) lavishly illustrated by documents in facsimile, was the first. We can now look over the shoulders, as it were, of the two explorers, as they wrote their day-by-day accounts. Most students not engaged on fundamental research will prefer to use one of the several excellent abridged versions of the Lewis and Clark journals, such as Bernard de Voto, *The Journals of Lewis and Clark* (Boston, 1953 and London, 1954), or John Bakeless, *The Journals of Lewis and Clark* (New York, 1964, paperbound), each in one volume. Both of these have excellent introductions and notes giving continuity to the journals. The best scholar's edition remains that of Reuben G. Thwaites, *The Original Journals of the Lewis and Clark Expedition . . . printed from the original manuscripts in the American Philosophical Society*, to which the texts of the journals of Floyd and Whitehouse and facsimiles of many of Clarks own maps are added (8 vols, New York, 1904–5), but for more recently discovered material, now see Osgood (*op. cit.*) and *The William Clark Papers. A Description of the Notes of Captain William Clark in the Papers of General John H. Hammond* (Alderman Library, Charlottesville, 1953). A handy joint biography of the two explorers is John Bakeless, *Lewis and Clark, Partners in Discovery* (New York, 1947); and Donald Jackson (ed.) *Letters of the Lewis and Clark Expedition, 1783–1854* (Urbana, 1962) is useful, but authoritative biographies of each, using the new material, remain to be written. The best edition of Washington Irving, *The Astorians* (first published in 1846), is that of Edgeley Todd (Norman, 1963). Zebulon Montgomery Pike's own published *Journal . . .* (New York, 1810 and London, 1811) should be supplemented by Elliott Coues (ed.), *The Expeditions of Z. M. Pike . . .* (3 vols, New York, 1895), while a useful biography is Eugene. W. Hollon's *The Lost Pathfinder* (Norman, 1949). Donald Jackson has now definitively edited *The Journals of Z. M. Pike, with Letters and Related Documents* (2 vols, Norman, 1966). R. G. Thwaites edited *Edwin James's Account of an Expedition from Pittsburgh to the Rocky Mountains . . .* in his invaluable 'Early Western Travel' series (Vol.

XVII). Any library which possesses this magnificent and now rare *Early Western Travels, 1748–1846 . . . A series of annotated reprints* (32 vols, Cleveland, 1904–6) is indeed fortunate. For the history of the West it is invaluable. It has now been reprinted.

FUR TRADERS AND TRAPPERS OF THE FAR WEST

[*This chapter is extensively annotated and much bibliographical information concerning individual traders and Mountain Men will be found in its footnotes. With a few exceptions, only works of a more general and comprehensive nature will be listed here.*] The first serious attempt to write a complete history of the fur trade, Hiram M. Chittenden's *The American Fur Trade of the Far West* (3 vols, New York, 1902; reprinted New York, 1935), remains valuable. It needs to be complemented by Harold D. Innis, *The Fur Trade in Canada* (New Haven, 1930; revised 1962). Robert Glass Cleland's *This Reckless Breed of Men, The Trappers and Fur Traders of the Southwest* (New York, 1950), both scholarly and absorbingly readable, deals more specifically with the trappers than with the traders, as does also Ray Allen Billington's *The American Frontiersman . . . An inaugural lecture . . .* (Oxford, 1954), although the chapter based on this in his *Far Western Frontier, 1830–50* (New York, 1956, in the 'New American Nation' series) is more comprehensive and has a good bibliography. Grant Foreman, *Pioneer Days in the Old Southwest* (Cleveland, 1926), is a general survey of the trade between 1800 and 1840; William H. Goetzmann, *Army Explorers in the American West, 1803–63* (New Haven, 1960), deals with Mountain Men's trails as well, and reproduces one of the few Mountain Man maps (that of Jim Baker) to have survived, for many of these men were illiterate. He also reproduces the important central section of Preuss's Second Frémont Expedition map. Carl L. Wheat's *Mapping the American West, 1540–1857* (in *Proceedings of the American Antiquarian Society*, Vol. 64, Philadelphia, 1954, pp. 19–194), is a useful guide; more specialized are Dale L. Morgan and Carl L. Wheat, *Jedediah Smith and his Maps of the American West* (San Francisco, 1954). Dale Morgan's model biography of the most important of the Mountain Men, *Jedediah Smith and the Opening of the West* (Indianapolis, 1953; paperbound, Lincoln, 1962) with full bibliography, is also an account of the fur trade in wider perspective up to 1831, while his *The West of William H. Ashley. The International Struggle for the Fur Trade of the Missouri, the Rocky Mountains and the Columbia, 1822–1838* (Denver, 1964), is as broad in scope as its title is long. Earlier works of Dale Morgan,

The Great Salt Lake (Indianapolis, 1947), and *The Humbolt, Highroad of the West* (New York, 1943), gave the historical geography of the Great Basin area. The activities of the Hudson's Bay Company in this period are best summarized by Frederick Merk in his introduction to *Fur Trade and Empire, George Simpson's Journal, 1824–25* (Cambridge, Mass., 1931), and by E. E. Rich in his edition of *The Letters of John McLaughlin . . . First Series, 1825–38* (Toronto and London, 1941). Rich has acted as General Editor of the important series of Records of the Hudson's Bay Company, including the absorbing *Peter Skene Ogden's Snake Country Journals, 1824–25 and 1825–26* (London, 1950), an epic story comparable to Harrison Dale's *The Ashley Smith Explorations and the Discovery of the Central Route to the Pacific, 1822–29* (Cleveland, 1918), which included the diary of Smith's ebullient but unfortunate clerk, Harrison Rogers. Life in two important bases for the fur trade is described in Leroy R. Hafen and Francis M. Young, *Fort Laramie and the Pageant of the West, 1834–1890* (Glendale, 1938) and in David Lavender's somewhat more popularly presented *Bent's Fort* (Garden City, New York, 1954), both of which are also relevant to the following chapter. New editions of J. Cecil Alter's *Jim Bridger* (Norman, 1962) and J. T. Kelly's *Old Greenwood* (with the collaboration of Dale L. Morgan, Georgetown, California, 1965) are vast improvements on earlier editions, which should no longer be used, while Leroy R. Hafen's monumental *The Mountain Men and the Fur Trade of the West. Biographical Sketches by Scholars of the Subject with introductions by the Editor* (in progress; 3 vols so far published, Glendale, 1963–) bids fair to tell us, when completed, all that we need and perhaps more than we ought to know about these rugged and picturesque characters; but a broadly based, scholarly and up-to-date history of the Fur Trade of the Far West, within reasonable compass and with a critical bibliography, is still required and impatiently awaited.

BREAKING THE WAGGON TRAILS WEST

Goetzmann's *Army Explorers* (*op. cit.*) continues valuable for this topic, to be supplemented by his *Exploration and Empire* (New York, 1966) and W. Turrentine Jackson, *Wagon Roads West. A Study of Federal Road Survey and Construction in the Trans-Mississippi, West, 1846–1869* (Berkeley, 1953; new edition, New Haven, 1965), for the later phases of establishing the waggon trails. While awaiting William Brandon's new book on the Santa Fé Trail one can still use Henry

Inman, *The Santa Fé Trail: The Story of a Great Highway* (New York, 1898), and R. L. Duffus, *The Santa Fé Trail* (New York, 1930), but the classic contemporary account is Josiah Gregg, *Commerce of the Prairies* (2 vols, New York, 1844; many times reprinted; the Dallas, 1933, and Norman, 1954, editions are among the best; also available paperbound). This should be supplemented by James J. Webb, *Adventures on the Santa Fé Trail, 1844–47* (Glendale, 1931), and Philip St George Cooke, *Scenes and Adventures in the Army* (New York, 1857), Cooke having been on the Trail both in 1829 and in 1843. Eugene C. Barker, the biographer of *Stephen F. Austin, Founder of Texas* (Nashville, 1925), also wrote *Mexico and Texas, 1821–36* (Dallas, 1928), and William Hogan's is the best general history of *The Texas Republic* (Norman, 1946). W. M. Binckley's *Expansionist Movement in Texas, 1836–50* (Berkeley, 1935) portrays the Lone Star State's overweening ambitions. Marquis James's *The Raven* (Indianapolis, 1929) is a satisfactory life of Sam Houston. For the opening up of the Oregon country, O. O. Winther's *The Great Northwest: A History* (New York, 1947) is a good scholarly account. More popular accounts are W. J. Ghent, *The Road to Oregon* (New York, 1929), which is very readable, Jay Monaghan, *The Overland Trail* (Indianapolis, 1937), dealing with other trails as well, and David Lavender, *Westward Vision* (New York, 1962; London, 1965). More detailed treatments are to be found in Leroy R. and Anne Hafen, *To the Rockies and Oregon, 1832–1842* (Glendale, 1955), and Clifford Drury, *Marcus Whitman, M.D., Prophet and Martyr* (Caldwell, Idaho, 1937), *H. H. Spaulding* (Caldwell, 1936), *Elkanah and Mary Walker* (Caldwell, 1940), and *First White Women over the Rockies* (3 vols, Glendale, 1963 and 1966). The Hafen and Drury books contain skilfully edited diaries and letters of major importance, some never previously published. The diary of Narcissa Prentiss Whitman has literary as well as historical value. William N. Bischoff, S.J., has written a survey of the activities of *The Jesuits in Old Oregon* (Caldwell, 1945); a definitive biography of Pierre-Jean De Smet is eagerly awaited from the pen of Father W. L. Davis. James C. Bell, *Opening of a Highway to the Pacific, 1838–46* (New York, 1921), dealt with both the Oregon and the California trails, but George R. Stewart, *The California Trail* (New York, 1962 and London, 1964), treats the latter in much greater detail, while his *Opening of the California Trail* (Berkeley, 1953) and his *Ordeal by Hunger* (New York, 1936; revised edition, Berkeley and London, 1961) print original diaries and letters of the Stevens–Murphy and the Donner parties, respectively, as well as telling their stories. Norman A. Graebner, *Empire on the Pacific* (New York, 1955), and Frederick Merk, *Manifest Destiny and Mission* (New York, 1960), present interesting if not entirely convincing new interpretations of the Americanization of the Pacific slopes. The Mormon trek to Utah is discussed by Nels Anderson, *Desert Saints: The Mormon Frontier in Utah* (Chicago, 1942), by Andrew L. Neff, *History of Utah, 1847–60* (Salt Lake City, 1949), and by Leonard Arrington in *Great Basin Kingdom* (Cambridge, Mass., 1958). Says Wallace Stegner in his skilfully written and carefully researched *The Gathering of Zion: The Story of the Mormon Trail* (New York, 1964, and London, 1966), 'The literature on the Mormons is enormous, repetitious, contradictory and embattled', and his 'Word of Bibliography' (*op. cit.*, pp. 313–19) offers the handiest guide, to date, to that battlefield. He points out that a comprehensive Mormon Trail Bibliography yet remains to be compiled, not by himself but, preferably, by 'someone who is in the confidence of the Church Historian' (*op. cit.*, p. 315).

BY LAND AND SEA TO ELDORADO

The American 'take-over' of Mexican Alta California, before and after the conquest, is discussed in R. G. Cleland, *The Early Sentiment for the Annexation of California . . . 1835–1846* (Austin, Texas, 1915), in the introduction by John A. Hawgood to *First and Last Consul: Thomas Oliver Larkin and the Americanization of California – A Selection of Letters* (San Marino, California, 1962), by Josiah Royce, in *California . . . 1846–1856* (first published in The American Commonwealth Series, New York, 1885; reprinted with a valuable introduction by R. G. Cleland, New York, 1948), in Cleland's *From Wilderness to Empire*, in Rolle's *California: A History*, and in Graebner's *Empire on the Pacific* (all already cited). An excellent contemporary account is Walter Colton's *Three Years in California* (New York, 1850), covering the period 1846–9, and thus including the American occupation, the early stages of the Gold Rush and the framing of California's first constitution (which is reproduced in an appendix) as well. The *Memoirs* of William Tecumseh Sherman (Vol. I, New York, 1890) cover the occupation and the Gold Rush, while he was Adjutant to the Military Governor, Colonel Mason, but those of John Charles Frémont do not, only the first volume (New York, 1887), which breaks off in 1845, ever having been published. His *Geographical Memoir on California* (Washington, D.C., 1849; reprinted with an introduction by Allan Nevins, San Francisco, 1965) was a compilation of material from a number of sources, rushed out to meet public demand. Mrs Jessie B. Frémont's *A Year of American Travel* (New York, 1878; reprinted, San Francisco, 1960) contains a vivid account of the journey to California via the Isthmus of Panama and up the Pacific coast in 1849, and of the riches of the 'Mariposa Grant'. Women, despite their scarcity in California at the time, have written some of the best first-hand descriptions of the early mining camps, among them Louise Clappe ('Dame Shirley') in *The Shirley Letters from the California Mines* (best edition with notes by Carl Wheat, New York, 1949), and Sarah Royce (mother of Josiah Royce) whose letters were edited by Ralph H. Gabriel as *A Frontier Lady* (New Haven, 1932). Mrs Clappe includes a good account of mining methods, and so does the Swiss traveller Carl Meyer in *Nach dem Sacramento* (Aarau, 1856; translated by Ruth Axe, edited by Henry Wagner, Claremont, 1938, under title *Bound for Sacramento*). Rodman W. Paul's *California Gold: The Beginning of Mining in the Far West* (Cambridge, Mass., 1947) is a useful modern summary of mining developments, and he has edited (San Francisco, 1949: originally published San Francisco, 1858) *The Miner's Own Book: Containing correct Illustrations and Descriptions of the Various Modes of California Mining*. Published memoirs and diaries of participants in the California Gold Rush are legion, and grow more numerous yearly. Carl Wheat, in *Books of the California Gold Rush* (San Francisco, 1949), critically appraises many of these. A handy anthology, containing long extracts from a number of the best first-hand accounts is *Pictures of Gold Rush California* (illustrated by contemporary drawings; Chicago, 1949), edited by M. M. Quaife. Perhaps the most renowned book to come out of the California Gold Rush was Bayard Taylor's *Eldorado* . . . (2 vols, New York, 1850; best modern edition, R. G. Cleland (ed.), in one volume, New York, 1949). Less polished but more spontaneous are *The Journals, Drawings and other Papers of J. Goldsborough Bruff*, with his own delightful if crude illustrations (eds. Georgia W. Read and Ruth Gaines, 2 vols, New York, 1944). San Francisco's remarkable history up to the end of 1855 was chronicled in detail by Frank Soulé, John H. Gihon, and James Nisbet, *Annals of San Francisco* (copiously illustrated, New York, 1855). Less detailed but more comprehensive is John S. Hittell, *History of the City of San Francisco and Incidentally of the State of California* – a revealing title (San Francisco, 1878). His *Resources of California* (San Francisco, 1863) is valuable for statistics of early growth, to be compared with the more impressionistic word-picture of San Francisco and California in 1859 written by Dana for the revised edition of his *Two Years before the Mast* (see *supra*, pp. 182–4).

THE MINING BOOM MOVES INLAND

The 'Essay on Bibliography' (pp. 217–30) to Rodman W. Paul's *Mining Frontiers of the Far West, 1848–1880* (New York, 1963) is most valuable. The book itself is a useful introductory guide to the various mining frontiers, and especially to the evolution of mining techniques. W. P. Morrell, *The Gold Rushes* (London, 1940. New York, 1941), broadens the canvas and sets the American gold strikes in their world perspective. Mark Twain's *Roughing It* (first edition, Hartford, 1872; many subsequent editions) is important both for the literature and for the history of the Nevada silver frontier, but factually 'Dan de Quille' (William Wright), *History of the Big Bonanza* (Hartford, 1876; reprint with original illustrations, New York, 1947), and Grant H. Smith, *History of the Comstock Lode, 1850–1920* (Reno, 1943), are more dependable. Eliot Lord, *Comstock Mining and Miners* (U.S. Geological Survey Monograph, Washington, D.C., 1883), should be used in the modern edition of David F. Myrick (Berkeley, 1959). Samuel Bowles, *Our New West* (Hartford, 1869), describes the Nevada and Colorado mining districts as he saw them in the course of two official trips (in the entourage of Vice-President Schuyler Carfax), one by stage coach and one by train. Other well-known journalists who took and wrote up this grand tour of the diggings were Horace Greeley (*An Overland Journey*, New York, 1860), A. D. Richardson (*Beyond the Mississippi*, Hartford, 1867), and Henry Villard (*Past and Present of the Pike's Peak Gold Region*, St Louis, 1860). Specialist and technical material on the Colorado mines is listed by Rodman Paul in his Bibliography (*op. cit.*), pp. 223–5. A selection of contemporary Colorado material was presented by Leroy R. Hafen in *Colorado Gold Rush. Contemporary Letters and Reports, 1858–1859* (Glendale, 1941). M. G. Burlingame and K. Ross Toole, *A History of Montana* (3 vols, New York, 1957) give the not-always sober truth about the Montana Gold Rush, and T. J. Dimsdale, *The Vigilantes in Montana* (Virginia City, 1866; reprinted, Norman, Oklahoma, 1953), and N. P. Langford, *Vigilante Days and Ways* (2 vols, Boston, 1890), mix truth with a certain amount of fiction. Two of the best accounts by participants are Granville Stuart, *Journals and Reminiscences* (2 vols, Cleveland, 1925), and James K. P. Miller ('J. Sidney Osborn'), whose diary was edited by Andrew F. Rolle as *The Road to Virginia City* (Norman, Oklahoma, 1960). William J. Trimble's *The Mining Advance into the Inland Empire: A Comparative Study of the Beginnings of the Mining Industry in Idaho and Montana, Eastern Washington and Oregon, and the*

Southern Interior of British Columbia . . . (Madison, Wisconsin, 1914) is as useful and comprehensive as its portmanteau title indicates, and is still not 'dated'. Richard B. Hills's *Pioneer Years in the Black Hills* was edited by Agnes Wright Spring (Glendale, 1957). Mrs Spring's own *The Cheyenne and Black Hills Stage and Express Routes* (Glendale, 1949; paper-bound reprint, Lincoln, Nebraska, 1964), while even more relevant for the succeeding chapter, is also useful here, as is *Custer's Gold* by Donald Jackson (New Haven, 1966). A good scholarly history of mining in the Black Hills is still needed, though the amount of trash written about bad men and bad women in Deadwood Gulch has been voluminous. Estelline Bennett's reminiscences, *Old Deadwood Days* (New York, 1928), are, by way of exception, authentic as well as colourful. The publication of Moses Manuel's 'Forty Eight Years in the West' (an incomplete typescript copy of which is in the possession of the Home-stake Mining Company of South Dakota) would seem to be overdue, judging by the samples of it quoted by Dr Rodman Paul. The Southern Arizona mining region has also suffered badly from the pulp merchants, from whom the eagerly expected book by John Gilchriese, of Tucson, on the Earps at Tombstone (and points north, east and west), may rescue it. Meanwhile, one has to be content with the semi-scholarly works of Stuart Lake on *Wyatt Earp* (Boston, 1931), of Walter Noble Burns on *Tombstone* (Garden City, 1927), but now see *It Happened in Tombstone* ed. J. Gilchriese (Flagstaff, 1965). Some useful articles on the Arizona and other mining frontiers are listed in Winther's *Classified List of Periodical Literature* (*op. cit.*). John M. Myers's *The Last Chance. Tombstone's Early Years* (New York, 1950) breaks off in the middle of a good story, but is useful as far as it goes. Historians of the Copper frontier in Montana have met with certain frustrations, but Joseph Kinsey Howard's charmingly written *Montana: High, Wide and Handsome* (New Haven, 1943 and 1966), and K. Ross Toole's *Montana: An Uncommon Land* (Norman, 1959), both took courageous bites at that cherry. The true *History* of the Anaconda Company (a useless 'Company History' already exists) is anticipated from the pen of Dr Toole.

THE REVOLUTION IN WESTERN TRANSPORTATION

Another Winther bibliography, that to his *The Transportation Frontier: Trans-Mississippi West, 1865–1890* (New York, 1964), pp. 198–210, is valuable here, and the book itself is indispensable. We are also indebted to Oscar Osburn Winther for *Express and Stagecoach Days in California*

(Stanford, 1936), while Chapter 18 of his *Old Oregon Country: A History of Trade, Transportation and Travel* (Stanford, 1950) performs a similar service for the Pacific North-west. The works, all already cited, of W. Turrentine Jackson, William Goetzmann (his *Exploration and Empire* New York, 1966, should now be added to his *Army Exploration*), Agnes Wright Spring, James K. P. Miller (edited by Andrew Rolle), continue relevant here, as do the contemporary descriptions of western stage-coach travel by Samuel Bowles, Horace Greeley and – of course – Mark Twain. Sir Richard Burton, in his celebrated *The City of the Saints* (London, 1861; reprinted, New York and London, 1963, with an introduction by Fawn M. Brodie), gives a detailed itinerary of his stage-coach travel to Salt Lake and California, making illuminating comparison with the rigours of Old World travel. Lyle H. Wright and Josephine M. Bynum have edited W. L. Ormsby's sprightly diary of the first westward run of *The Butterfield Overland Mail* (San Marino, 1942; reprinted 1955) over the southern route in 1858, and Roscoe P. and Mary B. Conkling have written its history exhaustively in three volumes, *The Butterfield Overland Mail, 1857–1860* (Glendale, 1947). Leroy R. Hafen's *The Overland Mail, 1849–1869* (Cleveland, 1926) is a comprehensive account, while the Russell, Majors and Waddell enterprises are covered in *Empire on Wheels* by Ramond W. and Mary L. Settle (Stanford, 1949; revised 1965), and those of Holladay in J. V. Frederick, *Ben Holladay: The Stagecoach King* (Glendale, 1940). O. O. Winther's *Via Western Express and Stagecoach* (Stanford, 1945) is a useful and readable introduction to a vast subject. Railroad history can also only be dealt with here most selectively. Robert E. Riegel's *The Story of the Western Railroads* (New York, 1926) is a still-useful general account, but Ira G. Clark's *Then Came the Railroad: The Century from Steam to Diesel in the Southwest* (Norman, 1958) is more up to date, though geographically more restricted in its scope. John F. Stover's *American Railroads* (Chicago, 1961) covers the whole country, including the West. Professional engineers' accounts of trans-continental railroad building include Grenville M. Dodge, *Romantic Realities: The Story of the Pacific Roads* (Omaha, 1889), and John D. Galloway, *The First Trans-Continental Railroad* (New York, 1950). Robert L. Fulton's stop-gap *Epic of the Overland* (San Francisco, 1924) still leaves the saga of the Central Pacific only partially recited. Later scholarly histories of individual western railroads include Leslie L. Waters, *Steel Trails to Santa Fé* (Lawrence, Kansas, 1950), and Robert Athearn *Rebel of the Rockies* (New Haven, 1962) – the story of the Denver and Rio Grande Western Railroad – and Richard C. Overton, *Burlington West* (Cambridge, Mass., 1941), while James B. Hedges in *Henry Villard and the Railways of the Northwest* (New Haven, 1930) has perhaps produced the best book on the career of one of the great railroad building and promoting tycoons. George T. Clark's *Leland Stanford* (Palo Alto, 1931) deals in detail with Stanford's connection with the Central Pacific; Oscar Lewis's *The Big Four: The Story of Huntington, Stanford, Hopkins and Crocker, and of the Building of the Central Pacific* (New York, 1938) is a more readable but somewhat popular account – and a good introduction to the subject – but adequate biographies of Collis P. and Henry E. Huntington remain to be written when pious descendants and trustees come to realise that there is really nothing left that is worth hiding, and that the truth is the best way of scotching ugly rumours. They should recollect how Collis himself dealt with Frank Norris (see *supra*, p. 324). James J. Hill and E. H. Harriman also await definitive and all-revealing biographies. It will probably be just as difficult to produce scholarly biographies of the airline tycoons of America when the time comes to sum up men like Howard Hughes, Juan Trippe, Cyrus Smith, Eddie Rickenbaker and 'Bud' Maytag.

THE INDIAN PROBLEM AND ITS SOLUTION

William Brandon's *The American Heritage Book of Indians* (illustrated edition, 1961; paperbound edition containing all of Brandon's excellent text, New York, 1964) is by far the best general account of a non-technical nature. It is better than either Oliver La Farge's *A Pictorial History of the American Indian* (New York, 1956), which nevertheless possesses many virtues, or the National Geographic Society's publication *Indians of the Americas – a Color-illustrated Record* (edited by Matthew W. Stirling, Washington, D.C., 1955), which is most uneven in the quality of its contributions and illustrations, though some are very good indeed. Both these books remain useful, but Brandon's is outstanding, though it does not, unfortunately, contain a bibliography. For this one must use Harold E. Driver's *Indians of North America* (Chicago, 1961), the approach of which is mainly anthropological, and other and older works of a similar nature already cited in the first section of this *Bibliographical Note*. Books, varying in quality, on almost every important Indian tribal group, exist, and many of these have been published by the enterprising University of Oklahoma Press, whose list itself constitutes a valuable bibliography. A more general work, also published by that Press, is Edward E. Dale, *The Indians of the Southwest: A Century of Development under the United States* (Norman, 1949), while Carl C. Rister, *The Southwestern Frontier, 1865–1881* (Cleveland, 1928), dealing more specifically with Indian warfare, is still useful. A classic treatment of the Indian wars is J. P. Dunn, Jr, *Massacres of the Mountains* (New York, 1886; reprint with original illustrations, introduced by John A. Hawgood, London, 1962). Less satisfactory is Alvin M. Josephy, *The Patriot Chiefs* (New Haven, 1961; London, 1963), comprising nine biographical sketches of Indian resistance leaders, from the semi-mythical Hiawatha to Chief Joseph, but the same author's *The Nez Percé Indians and the Opening of the West* (New Haven, 1965) is better. A bibliography of Indian battles, army frontier reminiscences and of biographies of army generals in the West would fill a volume in itself, and one of Custer and his Last Stand would alone occupy many pages. Robert Utley's *The Custer Legend* (New Haven, 1962) contains a critical appraisal of much Custer literature. George Custer's own reminiscences, *My Life on the Plains* (St. Louis, 1876), still remains more readable – and revealing – than most other books about him, while its anonymous continuation in *Wild Life on the Plains* (Minneapolis, 1891) is an interesting period-piece displaying White Man attitudes at about the time of the Ghost Dance crisis. Official Indian policy is discussed more systematically and dispassionately in Loring B. Priest, *Uncle Sam's Stepchildren: The Reformation of United States Indian Policy, 1865–1887* (New Brunswick, 1942), and in Flora W. Seymour, *Indian Agents of the Old Frontier* (New York, 1941), while Roy L. Robbins, *Our Landed Heritage* remains invaluable. Helen Hunt Jackson's *A Century of Dishonor* (New York, 1881), has recently been twice reprinted. Richard H. Pratt's *Battlefield and Classroom: Four Decades with the American Indians* has been re-edited by Robert M. Utley (New Haven, 1964).

THE COWMAN'S FRONTIER

The Ranching Frontier has perhaps inspired more good writing, and it has certainly spawned more bad writing than any other. The following works stand in the first class: Ernest S. Osgood, *The Day of the Cattlemen* (Minneapolis, 1929), Edward E. Dale, *The Range Cattle Industry* (Norman, 1930), Louis Pelzer, *The Cattlemen's Frontier* (Glendale, 1936), and Lewis Atherton *The Cattle Kings* (Chicago, 1961), to mention only general surveys. More specialized studies of high quality are Wayne Gard, *The Chisholm Trail* (Norman, 1954), and Robert Glass Cleland,

Cattle on a Thousand Hills (San Marino, 1947), and *The Irvine Ranch* (San Marino, 1952; revised and up-dated by Robert V. Hine, San Marino, 1962) – the two last dealing with the cattle industry in Southern California. Out of the vast array of cowman and cowboy reminiscences a few only can be mentioned, but every short list should include Joseph G. McCoy, *Historic Sketches of the Cattle Trade of the West and Southwest* (first published 1874; reprinted, Washington, D.C., 1932, and Glendale, 1940), Charles A. Siringo, *A Texas Cowboy, or Fifteen Years on the Hurricane Deck of a Spanish Pony* (New York, 1885; reprinted, New York, 1950), W. S. James, *Cow-Boy Life in Texas* (Chicago, 1893), and – best of all, though recounted in fictional form – Andy Adams, *The Log of a Cowboy* (Boston, 1903, and New York, 1931; paper-bound, New York and London, 1963). Andy Adams also attempted, with far less success, to write a fictionized life of Charlie Goodnight (*Reed Anthony, Cowman*, Boston, 1907), but the biography by J. Evetts Haley, *Charles Goodnight: Cowman and Plainsman* (Boston, 1936; reprinted Norman, 1949) is more dependable. W. H. Hutchinson, *A Bar Cross Man: The Life and Personal Writings of Eugene Manlove Rhodes* (Norman, 1956), tells the engaging story of another literary cowboy, while May D. Rhodes' tribute to her husband, *The Hired Man on Horseback* (Boston, 1938), is altogether delightful. The best critical analysis of the cowboy cult is Joe B. Frantz and Julian E. Choate, *The American Cowboy: The Myth and the Reality* (Norman, 1955), and it has an excellent bibliography, which now could do with a little judicious updating. Another useful bibliography is Ramon Adams, *Six Guns and Saddle Leather: A Bibliography of Books and Pamphlets on Western Outlaws and Gunmen* (Norman, 1954), for those who find bad men and outlaws more interesting than 'good men and true'. J. Frank Dobie's salty *Guide to Life and Literature of the Southwest* (Dallas, 1943; revised edition, Dallas, 1952) is literature in itself and disposes of *My Reminiscences as a Cowboy* (by that arch-phoney Frank Harris) in one well-barbed line, as 'A blatant farrago of lies, included in this list because of its supreme worthlessness' (p. 64). Frantz and Choate have runners-up as analysts of the ethos of the cowboy in Douglas Branch, *The Cowboy and his Interpreters* (New York, 1926), Paul Horgan (in Vol. II of *Great River*, New York, 1954; see *supra*, p. 299), and Ramon Adams' *The Best of the American Cowboy* and *The Old-Time Cowhand* (Norman, 1957, and New York, 1961, respectively), the last two being part analysis and part anthology. [*For a ripe piece of Ramon Adams, see supra, pp.* 299–300.] Walter Prescott Webb, once again, in *The Great Plains* (*op. cit.*) and

The Texas Rangers (Boston, 1935), has much to say, and all of it worth reading and re-reading, on the Cowman's frontier. His somewhat dated references to the barbed-wire frontier can now be supplemented from F. T. and H. D. McCallum, *The Wire that Fenced the Plains* (Norman, 1965). Clifford P. Westermeier's *Trailing the Cowboy: His Life and Lore as told by Frontier Journalists* (Caldwell, Idaho, 1955) is another valuable anthology. Westermeier is also one of the best interpreters of the contemporary cowhand, as in his paper, 'The Modern Cowboy – An Image', in *The American West* (ed. R. G. Ferris, Santa Fé, 1963), p. 34 ff. The despised Sheepman has been dealt with by Charles W. Towne and Edward N. Wentworth in *Shepherd's Empire* (Norman, 1945).

LAND FOR THE FARMER

Webb's *Great Plains* and Robbins' *Landed Heritage* remain most useful, while Fred A. Shannon, *The Farmer's Last Frontier: Agriculture, 1860–1897* (New York, 1945), one of the best volumes so far published in the series 'The Economic History of the United States', is not only the standard work on the subject but also devotes a whole chapter (pp. 379–414) to its 'Literature'. For works published before 1945 this is comprehensive, and titles of books it mentions need not be repeated here. Since 1945, Paul W. Gates has given further dimension to the study of the American agricultural frontier in books like *Fifty Million Acres: Conflicts over Kansas Land Policy, 1854–90* (Ithaca, New York, 1954), and *The Impact of the Civil War on Agriculture* (New York, 1965), to supplement his articles in periodicals and his earlier book on *The Illinois Central Railroad and its Colonization Work* (Cambridge, Mass., 1934). His volume on American agriculture between 1815 and 1860 in the 'Economic History of the United States' series (New York, 1962) is also valuable, and an essential background to much of Shannon's story. Shannon was a feuding historian, tilting not only at the windbags but also at some of the National Monuments of the profession. He even took on Webb in 'An Appraisal of Walter Prescott Webb's *The Great Plains:* A Study in Institutions and Environment' (*Critiques of Research in the Social Science,* New York, 1940), and Turner in 'A Post-Mortem on the Labor-Safety-Valve Theory' (*Agricultural History,* Vol. XIX, January 1945, pp. 31–7 – see *supra*, p. 339). The crusade against inadequate land policies was blasted off by Henry George in *Our Land and Land Policy, National and Federal* (San Francisco, 1871); Hamlin

Garland's *Main Traveled Roads* appeared in 1891, and so did W. A. Peffer's *The Farmer's Side, His Troubles and his Remedies;* Frank Norris's *The Octopus* (see *supra*, p. 324) was first published in 1901. All these constitute landmarks in the literary expression of agrarian unrest. The life and writings of Hamlin Garland provide revealing commentary on two generations of American agrarian history, and his autobiographical novel, *A Son of the Middle Border* (New York, 1917), sketches many of its ecstasies and agonies. One of the best recent accounts of the whole process of agrarian political protest since the Civil War is Russell B. Nye, *Midwestern Progressive Politics. A Historical Study of its Origins and Development, 1870–1950* (Lansing, Michigan, 1951). This fills in details which the inevitably more impressionistic literary contributions to the subject tend to omit.

The dramatic opening up of Oklahoma to agricultural settlement in and after 1889 is recounted in Edward E. Dale's and Morris L. Wardell's *History of Oklahoma* (New York, 1948), and in Grant Forman, *A History of Oklahoma* (Norman, 1942). The birth of cities overnight is told in *Guthrie: Oklahoma's First Capital* (Norman, 1938) by Gerald Forbes, and in *The First Eight Months of Oklahoma City* (Norman, 1939) by Irving Geffs. Marquis James, in *Cherokee Strip* (New York and London, 1947), retails with delightful touches his boyhood and adolescence in the Oklahoma Territory and the new State before taking off (in 1911) for Kansas City and the great world. The best brief account of the farming frontier in Utah is to be found in Leonard J. Arrington's *Great Basin Kingdom. An Economic History of the Latter Day Saints, 1830–1890* (Cambridge, Mass., 1958), and an early but still useful account of *Irrigation in Utah* (Baltimore, 1898) was written by C. H. Brough. Mormon colonization policy and techniques in Utah are described by M. R. Hunter, *Brigham Young the Colonizer* (Salt Lake City, 1940), and by P. A. M. Taylor, *Expectations Westward. The Mormons and the Emigration of their British Converts in the Nineteenth Century* (Edinburgh and London, 1965). This has an excellent classified bibliography, comprehending far more than the emigration of British converts to Utah. Dry-farming techniques, with special reference to Utah, are discussed by W. MacDonald, *Dry Farming: its Principles and Practice* (New York, 1911), and by John A. Widtsoe, *Dry Farming* (New York, 1914), as well as by W. P. Webb in *The Great Plains.* J. Wesley Powell's highly influential *Report on the Lands of the Arid Region of the United States* (Washington, D.C., 1878) has been discussed and appraised by Wallace Stegner in *Beyond the Hundredth Meridian: John Wesley Powell and the Second*

Opening of the West (New York, 1954; also available paperbound) – a brilliant study. Brigham Young's most important pronouncements have been edited by John A. Widtsoe, *Discourses of Brigham Young* (Salt Lake City, 1946). The farming frontier as it was in 1876 is well displayed in *Rand McNally's Pioneer Atlas of the American West*, and in *The Business Atlas of the Great Mississippi Valley and the Pacific Slope* (first edition, Chicago, 1876, reissued, and edited by Dale L. Morgan, Chicago, 1956). Gilbert Fite, *The Farmer's Frontier 1865–1900* (New York, 1966), has now appeared to supplement Shannon and update his bibliography.

THE END OF THE WEST? TWENTIETH CENTURY FRONTIERS

The latest appraisal of Frederick Jackson Turner and his influence is Ray A. Billington, *The Frontier Heritage* (New York, 1966), with comprehensive Bibliographical Notes. Dr Billington's biography of Turner is eagerly awaited by the whole Western Americanist fraternity, bouquets and long knives poised. Wilbur R. Jacobs has already edited *Frederick Jackson Turner's Legacy* (San Marino, 1965), containing the Master's unpublished writings in American History. Lone wolf Fred A. Shannon's attack upon Turner in 'A Post-Mortem on the Labor-Safety-Valve Theory' (*op. cit.* – also reprinted, with other attacks upon and defences of Turner, in *The Turner Thesis*, George R. Taylor, ed., 'Problems in American Civilization' Series, Boston, 1949, and by R. A. Billington, *The Frontier Thesis: Valid Interpretation of American History?* in 'American Problem Studies', New York, 1966) attracted a number of jackals in his wake, but the controversy surrounding the validity of the Turner Frontier Hypothesis has also helped to produce such excellent and thoughtful books as Henry Nash Smith, *Virgin Land* (New York, 1949), David Potter, *People of Plenty* (Chicago, 1954), and Carl F. Kraenzel, *The Great Plains in Transition* (Norman, 1955). The counter-attack on the anti-Turner reaction has now commenced, as in Ellen von Nardroff, 'The American Frontier as a Safety Valve – The Life, Death, Reincarnation and Justification of a Theory' (*Agricultural History*, Vol. XXXVI, 1962, pp. 123–42). Some effects of the ending of the frontier phase in American history are discussed by John C. Parish, *The Persistence of the Westward Movement and other Essays* (Berkeley, 1943), and in the series of papers contributed to a University of Wisconsin symposium in 1954 and edited by Walker D. Wyman and Clifton B. Kroeber as *The Frontier in Perspective* (Madison, 1957). On Immigration a useful general survey is Maldwyn Jones, *American Immigration* (Chicago,

1960). The standard treatments include John R. Commons, *Races and Immigrants in America* (New York and London, 1907), N. W. Stephenson, *A History of American Immigration* (Boston, 1926), Marcus W. Hansen, *The Immigrant in American History* (New York and London, 1941), and *The Atlantic Migration, 1607–1860* (Cambridge, Mass., 1940; reprinted paperbound in Harper Torchbooks, New York, 1961), and Oscar Handlin, *The Uprooted* (New York, 1951). Handlin's main thesis is about to be challenged in *The Upraised*, by Andrew F. Rolle (with an introduction by Ray A. Billington). Rolle's *California: A History* (*op. cit.*) contains useful statistics and forecasts concerning the population explosion in the Golden State during the twentieth century. Earl S. Pomeroy, in his history of *The Pacific Slope* (New York, 1964), broadens the survey to the whole West coast region, while his *In Search of the Golden West. The Tourist in Western America* (New York, 1957), and Glenn S. Dumke's *The Boom of the Eighties in Southern California* (San Marino, 1944), discuss earlier periods of prosperity and promotion in the Far West. What may be called the ultimate oddball frontier is beautifully dissected in Robert V. Hine, *California's Utopian Colonies 1850–1950* (San Marino, 1953, and New Haven, 1966). The urbanization of western America is discussed by Richard C. Wade, *The Urban Frontier* (Cambridge, Mass., 1959), and by Wilbur C. Hallenbeck, *American Urban Communities* (New York, 1951). For the early oil frontier, see Harold F. Williamson and Arnold Daum, *The American Petroleum Industry – The Age of Illumination, 1859–1899* (Evanston, Illinois, 1959). See also J. S. Clark, *The Oil Century* (Norman, 1958).

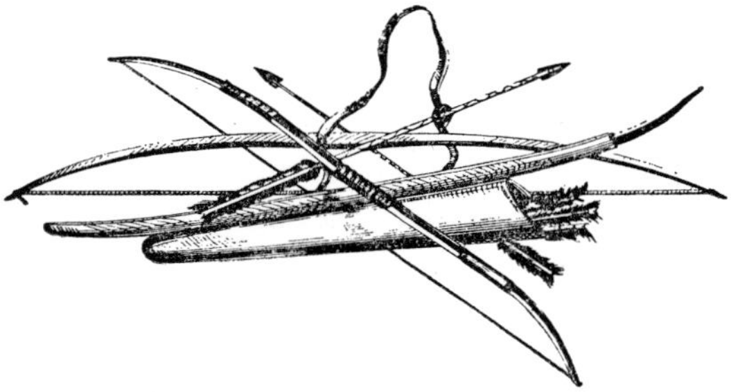

A Note on Novels

The English reader, aware of the vast output of 'Westerns', might appreciate a word of guidance on fiction. The list that follows is not exhaustive, but does include novels of literary merit which reveal, through their different settings and subjects, something of the authentic history and atmosphere of the American West.

Andy Adams	*The Log of a Cowboy*
Elliott Arnold	*Blood Brother*
Thomas Berger	*Little Big Man*
Benjamin Capps	*A Woman of the People*
Willa Cather	*Death Comes to the Archbishop; O Pioneers!*
Walter van Tilburg Clark	*The Ox-Bow Incident*
James Fenimore Cooper	*The Last of the Mohicans; The Prairie*
Howard Fast	*The Last Frontier*
Edna Ferber	*Cimarron; Show Boat*
Hamlin Garland	*Main Traveled Roads*
A. B. Guthrie, jr.	*The Big Sky; The Way West*
Bret Harte	*Tales of the Argonauts, etc.*
Paul Horgan	*A Distant Trumpet; Mountain Standard Time*
Dorothy M. Johnson	*Indian Country; The Hanging Tree*
Sinclair Lewis	*Main Street*
Charles O. Locke	*Road to Socorro*
Milton Lott	*The Last Hunt*
Alan le May	*The Searchers*
Eugene Manlove Rhodes	*The Trusty Knaves; Pasó Por Aquí*
Conrad Richter	*The Sea of Grass; The Light in the Forest; The Awakening Land—The Trees, The Fields, The Town*
O. E. Rölvaag	*Giants in the Earth; Peder Victorious*
Jack Schaefer	*Shane; First Blood*
Wallace Stegner	*The Big Rock Candy Mountain; A Shooting Star*
Michael Straight	*Carrington; A Very Small Remnant*
Stewart Edward White	*The Long Rifle*
Owen Wister	*The Virginian*

Index

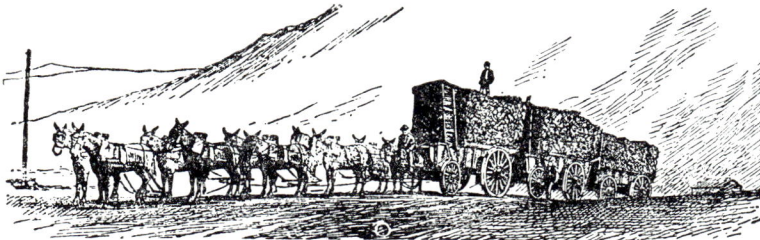

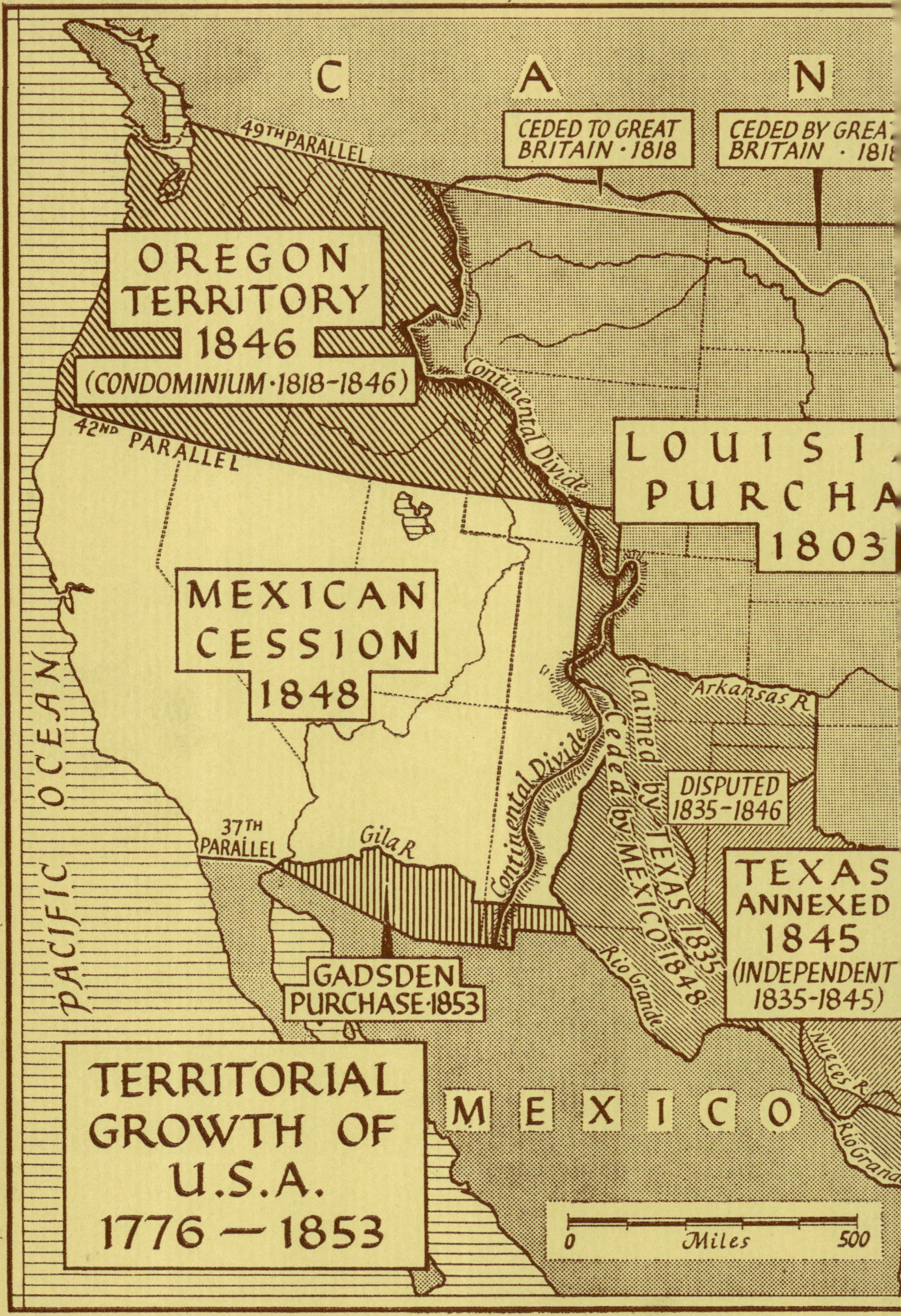
C A N
CEDED TO GREAT BRITAIN · 1818
CEDED BY GREA BRITAIN · 181
49TH PARALLEL
OREGON TERRITORY 1846
(CONDOMINIUM · 1818-1846)
Continental Divide
42ND PARALLEL
LOUISI PURCHA 1803
MEXICAN CESSION 1848
Arkansas R.
Claimed by TEXAS 1835
Ceded by MEXICO 1848
DISPUTED 1835-1846
Continental Divide
37TH PARALLEL
Gila R.
TEXAS ANNEXED 1845
(INDEPENDENT 1835-1845)
PACIFIC OCEAN
Rio Grande
GADSDEN PURCHASE · 1853
Nueces R.
TERRITORIAL GROWTH OF U.S.A. 1776 — 1853
M E X I C O
Rio Grande
0 Miles 500